CONTEMPORARY SOUTH AFRICAN DEBATES

CONTEMPORARY SOUTH AFRICAN DEBATES

Other titles available in this series:

People and violence in South Africa

edited by
Brian McKendrick and Wilma Hoffmann

CONTEMPORARY SOUTH AFRICAN DEBATES

1990
Oxford University Press
Cape Town

Oxford University Press
Walton Street, Oxford OX2 6DP, United Kingdom

Oxford New York Toronto
Delhi Bombay Calcutta Madras Karachi
Petaling Jaya Singapore Hong Kong Tokyo
Nairobi Dar es Salaam Cape Town
Melbourne Auckland

and associated companies in
Berlin Ibadan

ISBN 0 19 570 581 5

Cover: *The shadow boxers* (front) and *Fortune beating virtue* (back)
by Graeme Germond, a postgraduate student at the Michaelis School
of Fine Art, University of Cape Town.
Cover design by New Leaf Design, Cape Town.

Published by Oxford University Press Southern Africa
Harrington House, Barrack Street, Cape Town, 8001, South Africa

DTP conversion by CAPS of Cape Town in 10 on 12 pt Garamond
Printed and bound by Clyson Press, Maitland, Cape

Contents

This book is dedicated to the memory of

Dr David Webster

Born 19 December 1945.
Murdered 1 May 1989.

Preface

All societies are violent to a greater or lesser degree, and the level of violence within any of them will wax or wane with war or peace, civil disturbance or national unity, political oppression or democratic freedoms. When, for whatever reasons, a nation becomes severely polluted by violence, the corrosive effects perforate all layers of society, damaging national institutions, community life, and family living, so that no individual within the society remains untouched by its insidious presence. A high level of societal violence is thus not an abstract concept: it is a concrete circumstance that defiles the quality of life of every person in society.

South Africa is a country that is currently ravaged and despoiled by widespread violence. Yet, at the same time, it is a country poised on the brink of a national transition to a new social order, hopefully one that will be characterized by justice and egalitarianism. Whether or not the transition will be achieved and violence will abate, only history will show; for the present all that South Africans can do is to use their every effort to promote the realization of the hoped-for transformation. This book is intended as a contribution towards the evolution of a renewed South Africa. Its focus is on the nature, extent, and dynamics of violence in the country, and the resultant contamination of the quality of human life; its aim is to promote an awareness and analysis of the consequences of a high level of violence in society; and its ultimate purpose is to attempt to provide the beginnings of an understanding upon which the means to reduce violence may be founded.

In terms of this focus, aim, and purpose, the book is divided into five parts. The first provides a broad overview of violence, an interpretation of it as a social phenomenon, and a survey of some of its causes, manifestations, and consequences. The second, third, and fourth parts are the heart of the book, and contain detailed explorations of aspects of violence in South Africa — in society, in domestic settings, and in institutions. The fifth and final part draws extensively on the preceding detailed discussions to distil from them the key characteristics of violence most relevant to its reduction, and to suggest possible targets and strategies in this respect.

South Africa in 1990 is epitomized by a rapidly altering social order, swiftly unfolding political developments, and an unprecedented fluidity in thinking about future options. It is therefore inevitable that some of the contemporary circumstances and situations recounted in this book will have been overtaken by events subsequent to the book being written. Nevertheless, the editors are confident that the book's main themes and conclusions will continue to have relevance not only for the immediate future, but for decades to come. This confidence is grounded in the belief that as South Africans strive towards the creation of a more just and democratic nation, they will recognize non-violent means of conflict resolution and stress reduction as an increasingly important component of any new society.

B. W. McKendrick
W. Hoffmann
Johannesburg, May 1990

Contributors

ADELE THOMAS is Director of the Johannesburg Child Welfare Society, which was the first welfare organization in South Africa to offer formal helping services to child detainees and their families.

BILL WINSHIP is Principal Paediatrician at Addington Hospital, Durban, and Chairman of the Durban and District Child Protection Co-ordinating Committee.

BRIAN MCKENDRICK is Professor and Head of the School of Social Work at the University of the Witwatersrand, Johannesburg.

CHRIS GILES is a consulting clinical and community psychologist, attached to a non-racial welfare organization in Cape Town.

DANA LABE is a Johannesburg social worker who has worked in the area of women abuse.

GILLIAN STRAKER is Professor of Applied Psychology at the University of the Witwatersrand, Johannesburg.

HELESE SANDLER was formerly Co-ordinator of Childline, Johannesburg, and social worker at the Johannesburg Child Abuse Clinic, which she was instrumental in establishing.

JACKLYN COCK is Associate Professor of Sociology at the University of the Witwatersrand, Johannesburg, and co-editor of the recent book *War and Society: The Militarization of South African Society.*

JULIA SLOTH-NIELSEN is a lawyer who lectures in Criminal and Procedural Law at the University of Cape Town.

LEN HOLDSTOCK is Professor of Psychology at the Free University, Amsterdam. He was previously attached to the University of the Witwatersrand, Johannesburg.

LLOYD VOGELMAN is a lecturer in Psychology at the University of the Witwatersrand, Johannesburg. He is also Director of the University's Project for the Study of Violence, and author of the recent book *The Sexual Face of Violence — Rapists on Rape.*

MEL SIFF is Senior Lecturer in Communication Studies at the University of the Witwatersrand, Johannesburg, where he was previously Head of Sports Administration. He is a national weight-lifting coach.

NICOLA SEPEL is a social worker who has worked in the Johannesburg Child Abuse Clinic, and who has been a supervisor for Childline, Johannesburg.

S. I. DU TOIT is Professor of Psychology at the University of Pretoria.

SIDNEY ECKLEY is Director of the South African National Council for the Aged.

THE HUMAN RIGHTS COMMISSION monitors and investigates human rights violations in South Africa, and disseminates information in this regard.

TRACY SEGEL is a social worker and Co-ordinator of People Against Women Abuse (POWA) in Johannesburg.

WILMA HOFFMANN is Associate Professor and Deputy Head of the School of Social Work, University of the Witwatersrand, Johannesburg.

Part 1

Introduction

1 The nature of violence

W. Hoffmann and B. W. McKendrick

INTRODUCTION

Human violence, in contrast to natural violence, is as old as humanity, being rooted in its earliest myths and history. Being a purely human phenomenon, its existence is deeply enmeshed in human interaction, on both an interpersonal and intergroup level. As acknowledged by social scientists and, more particularly, proponents of alternate dispute resolution approaches, there are alternatives to violence, such as mediation and negotiation, and the process of problem-solving itself (Lauer, 1989; Van der Merwe, 1989; Bartol & Bartol, 1986; Folberg & Taylor, 1984; Deutsch, 1973). The examination of the many faces of violence which follows in this chapter presents a perspective on why people choose violent rather than non-violent forms of behaviour. The exploratory framework comprises an interpretation of the phenomenon of violence; a description of the forms in which violence manifests itself; a list of interrelated factors leading to violence; a discussion of selected common features of violence; a review of its impact as a social problem on interpersonal, intergroup, and international relations, and its impact on other social arrangements. The explication concludes with comments on means of addressing violence in society.

Lystad (1986) emphasizes that violence is not a unique product of our time and place. This insight on its universality and historical roots does not, however, preclude the notion that an escalation in violence may manifest itself in certain times and places, nor that an increase in certain forms of violence may be assumed, purely because of its exposure in the media.

That South Africa is currently a particularly violent society has been emphasized not only by writers in this book, but also by others (Van der

Merwe, 1989; SAIRR, 1989; Van Zyl Slabbert, 1989; Burman & Reynolds, 1986). It therefore seems appropriate to highlight the South African condition in the examination of the universal features of human violence.

WHAT IS VIOLENCE?

Violence ordinarily implies the use of force to harm, injure, or abuse others (Lauer, 1989). Violence can also feature in constraining a person. It occurs on an interpersonal and on an intergroup level. Lauer (1989: 204) distinguishes intergroup violence from interpersonal violence in the following way:

> In inter-group situations the violence ultimately means confrontation between individuals, but the individuals behave violently because of their group affiliation rather than because of some interpersonal difficulty.

A further distinction is that much of the violence occurring interpersonally is between people known to each other, while intergroup violence is more likely to involve people who were strangers to each other before the confrontation.

Contemporary sociology, and in particular contemporary criminology, has alerted students of violence to be wary of definitions, because what constitutes 'violence' is always a social construction. Acts of violence deemed as legitimate in one society or in one cultural group in society may be considered illegitimate or culturally unacceptable in another. These considerations, therefore, call for a broad definition of violence, yet a definition specific enough to facilitate the protection of persons in a particular society against violence, irrespective of race, culture, or creed.

Walter (1969: 8), cited in Freeman (1971: 1), has defined violence as 'destructive harm ... including not only physical assaults that damage the body, but also ... the many techniques of inflicting harm by mental or emotional means'. 'It is generally understood,' to quote Walter (1969: 12), 'as measured or exaggerated harm to individuals either not socially prescribed at all, or else beyond established limits,' and is often 'socially defined to include processes that *originate* as authorised, measured force, but that go beyond the prescribed conditions and limits'. This interpretation affirms that the line between socially acceptable force and illegitimate violence is a thin one — a debate frequently pursued in present-day South Africa which is racked with political violence. Violence of this kind is a manifestation of a struggle around the socio-political system, apartheid. The system of apartheid prescribes behaviours and sanctions which violate the dignity and integrity of groups within South African society, applying:

> ... force, action, motive or thought in such a way (overt, covert, direct or indirect) that a person or group is injured, controlled, or destroyed in a physical, psychological or spiritual sense (Van der Merwe, 1989: 16).

Thus, the system in itself commits violence through the legal machinery and institutions of its social system by creating inequalities of opportunity and treatment. Structural or institutional violence of this nature elicits counter-violence. The actions of the state, whereby counter-violence is met, are usually described as legitimate 'force', or 'control' which is sanctioned by law. The improper use of 'force' to meet the counter-violence in itself constitutes violence, and thereby perpetuates an intensifying spiral of violence. Whether the action contained within this spiral is interpreted as legitimate force or as destructive violence depends on the allegiances of the persons in conflict.

Walter's description of violence includes not only abuse but also neglect (Walter, 1969). Negligence has been defined as:

> ... the failure to exercise ordinary care. It is the doing of some act which a person of reasonable prudence would not do, or the failure to do that which a person of reasonable prudence would do, if he were actuated by those considerations which ordinarily influence everyday conduct (Bar Association of the District of Columbia, 1968).

Abuse and neglect, whenever they occur, infer two dimensions of violence, namely acts of commission, and acts of omission (Hart *et al.*, 1987).

THE CATEGORIZATION OF VIOLENCE AND ITS LEGAL, SOCIAL, AND INDIVIDUAL DETERMINANTS

Manifestations of violence fall into two main categories, those occurring in nature and those made by people.

Aspects of the physical environment can erupt in episodes of violence. Extremes in weather conditions such as tornadoes can be experienced as violence by people, as can be geophysical events, such as earthquakes and volcanic eruptions.

Human violence, on the other hand, is perpetuated by persons, singly or in groups, or by people collectively. This category of violence can be subdivided into 'wilful acts of violence' and 'accidental violence'.

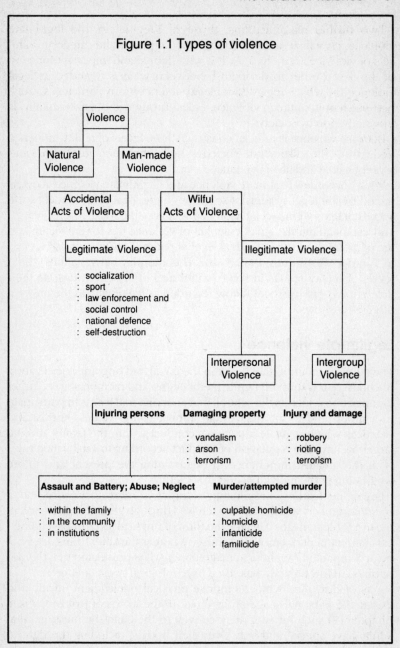

Figure 1.1 Types of violence

Two further classifications, those of illegitimate and legitimate violence, crystallize out of a further subdivision of the category 'wilful acts of violence' (see Fig. 1.1). It is a traditional and important function of the social order to distinguish between what is regarded as legal violence and what is regarded as illegal violence in any particular society, because harmful human violence, unless brought about accidentally, is frowned upon by society.

Because violence is a social construct, three levels of reality influence and guide the distinction societies make between justifiable, and reprehensible and illegal violence.

What constitutes legitimate violence and illegitimate violence is determined by the legal systems of societies — the legal level of reality; the social contexts within which violence occurs — the social level of reality; and the meaning that a particular act of violence has for the victim and the perpetrator — the individual level of reality (McClintock, 1974, cited in Van der Westhuizen, 1982: 9–10). The interplay between these three levels of reality results in some 'wilful acts of violence', despite their deleterious consequences, being regarded as legitimate, as the ensuing discussion shows.

Legitimate violence

The family is an important factor in the initial and ongoing socialization of children. It is through family membership and membership of larger organizations, such as the school, that an individual learns to participate in a group and to internalize and adhere to the values, norms, and practices which regulate a person's conduct within the family and the larger society. The regulation of conduct according to established rules is of the greatest importance in determining the present and future well-being of the individual and of society.

Discipline features prominently as a *child-rearing practice* and a *socialization act* which can be exercised through violent or non-violent means. Violent means can take the form of physical force or psychological maltreatment or emotional abuse. Whereas the latter forms need not be accompanied by physical maltreatment, it is postulated that the use of physical force always has some psychological consequence.

Acts of discipline which comprise physical punishment invade and violate the personal space of the child. In the words of Holdstock (see Chapter 12) such invasion may convey to the child the message 'that adults have special authority over their bodies, including the right to inflict pain', which may lay the ground for sexual abuse or spouse abuse. Apart from the physical damage suffered, it disempowers and humiliates the child, depriving him/her of dignity. Aggressive discipline brings the person into disrepute and disfavour, which corresponds to the 'degradation of a person', an act of maltreatment included in the definition of psychological maltreatment compiled by the International Conference on Psychological Abuse of Children and Youth, in association with the Office for the Study of the Psychological Rights of the Child (Hart *et al.*, 1987). It stands as an indictment that physical punishment is condoned by society at all. Moreover, it is argued that physical punishment administered in school, which is in some instances controlled by law, constitutes legalized child abuse.

Acts of discipline which constitute psychological maltreatment are not uncommon. Hart *et al.* (1987) list the following as abusive forms of discipline: rejection, degradation, terrorization, isolation, and denial of emotional responsiveness. These forms of punishment not only feature in the repertoires of disciplinary acts of families, but also in the repertoires of institutions which cater for delinquents and offenders, including persons in detention, as seen in Chapters 14 and 15 of this book.

A legitimized socialization act depicted as emotional abuse by Straker in Chapter 6 is that of teaching the child acts that debase and degrade people who are racially or ethnically different and reinforcing that teaching. Corruption, whereby children and youth are taught criminal behaviour, also constitutes psychological and emotional abuse, as does the portrayal in the public media of antisocial and unrealistic models as normal, usual, or appropriate (Hart *et al.*, 1987: 7).

All societies subscribe to certain ritual practices, or *rites de passage*, which mark transition points in the life cycle of an individual, according to the person's cultural heritage. Some acts, such as circumcision and other features of initiation ceremonies, which mark the transition from puberty into adulthood, resort under the category of legitimate violence.

The induction and socialization of individuals into certain 'open' organizations in society can also include acts of violence. School and university 'initiation' rites fall into this category of legitimate violence, as does entry into closed, or 'total' institutions such as prisons. Institutions of the latter type may develop intra-organizational subcultures, which refer to patterns of thought and customary action, which accommodate violent features (Roux 1982: 172–81; Lauer, 1989: 190).

Violent manifestations in *sport* are woven into the fabric of society. The very nature of sports like boxing and wrestling is one of violent physical contact. In Siff's examination of this phenomenon in Chapter 5, it is pointed out that the nature and degree of permissible or legitimized violent acts are defined by the rules of the game, the laws of society, and the acceptable standards of interpersonal behaviour as tacitly laid down by society and the participants in each sport. Yet the perpetrators of aggressive physical acts intended to injure, damage, or destroy, which may be punishable in terms of these three controls, are not necessarily stigmatized by other sports people or by sport spectators. Nor do the victims of such aggressive displays generally lay charges of assault against opponents who transgress the laws of the game, the laws of the land, and the standards of acceptable interpersonal behaviour. This may contribute to the paucity of statistics on wilful destructively harmful acts in different types of sport. It also contributes to the lack of knowledge of the epidemiology of sports injuries, a lack acknowledged in the Human Sciences Research Council (HSRC) Sports Investigation (1982).

It is common knowledge that traffic accidents, even the more serious ones which are often the direct result of wilful or wanton acts of violence, are not regarded as seriously as other acts of violence by the average member of the public. Indeed, traffic accidents are not necessarily perceived as violence.

For this reason, the stance taken in this chapter is to classify certain violent manifestations on the road as human violence, rather than to regard them as being accidental in nature. Moreover, although traffic law enforcement does criminalize acts of violence on the road, thereby regarding them as illegal, much of *violent and reckless driving* behaviour rests with socialization and modelled behaviour.

South African statistics on road-traffic collisions and casualties, especially over holiday periods, make alarming reading and support the notion that violence in South Africa may also have spread to this arena. A total of 418 485 collisions occurred during 1988, in which 9 017 people died, and 20 411 suffered serious injury (Central Statistical Services, 1989: 13–31). In a newspaper article entitled 'Minibus-Taxi Carnage is an Everyday Horror', it was reported that every day there are 130 minibus accidents resulting in a high number of fatalities. For example, for every 100 minibus accidents in May 1989, 120 people died. The total number of minibus accidents in South Africa during 1989 was 47 953 (*The Star*, 26 March 1990). Road traffic prosecutions totalled 41 623 for the period July 1987 to June 1988, of which 22 908 were for 'driving under the influence of liquor' (Central Statistical Services, 1988: 8).

Bothuis (1982: 118–20) classifies acts of violence occurring on the road in the following way:

1.   An act of violence *per se*, where the behaviour of the driver in itself constitutes violence and where the results may be more or less violent, for example, wilful collision with another vehicle or driving

into someone's property with the intent to do damage and/or bodily harm.

2. An act of recklessness or negligence, where the driver of a vehicle drives recklessly or negligently or in wilful or wanton disregard for the rights and safety of persons and other road users or property.

3. A malicious act, such as throwing articles out of a moving vehicle, with the intent to damage a passing or following vehicle and/or harm its occupants; or shooting at road traffic signs or other roadside effects as an act of vandalism; or dropping objects from overhead structures onto vehicles, or throwing objects at moving vehicles.

Mob violence directed at motorists may be added to the above descriptions in the light of recent violent events in South Africa, such as the killing of a white motorist near Sebokeng by a mob acting to counter an anticipated violent invasion by another ethnic grouping.

The legal system features prominently alongside other socialization systems in society as the one of ultimate social control. As pointed out by Sloth-Nielsen in Chapter 3 of this book, *law enforcement* and practices authorized by its penal structures have for centuries been characterized by the use of brutal and inhuman practices, authorized as legitimate violence. Two brutal physical punishments which constitute wilful acts of violence, and which are still retained in South Africa, are whipping and the death penalty. A further brutal punishment which has deleterious physical and psychological consequences, as illustrated in Chapters 14 and 15, is detention without trial, during which solitary confinement can feature — a penal procedure evolving out of the Emergency Regulations and laws of repression.

Laws of repression are in themselves legitimized violent responses to social forces perceived to be acting against the interest of the state in order to control such forces. According to Van der Merwe (1989: 29), and as illustrated in Chapter 14, security legislation in itself constitutes a source of conflict and violence. Security legislation and another form of repressive law, emergency legislation, are forms of institutional violence whereby political opposition is criminalized, with far-reaching consequences. Of note is that legislation of this kind overrides all other existing legislation.

In documenting the extent and scope of these forms of legal violence, the authors of Chapter 14 have estimated that at least 22 677 detentions occurred during the fifteen-year period from 1963 to the first six months of 1989. Detentions under the Emergency Regulations during the six states of emergency since 1960 are estimated to have been in the region of 50 000 detentions.

The last form of legitimized violence selected for discussion is war. All nations recognize the validity of violence used by agents of the state, such as police and troops. Van der Merwe (1989: 71) points out that:

> ... while violence is usually abhorred in public rhetoric, all politicians and virtually the entire Christian church believe that violence in its most destructive form, warfare, can be justified under certain conditions.

Lauer (1989: 475–85) emphasizes that *war*, like aggression and violence, is linked with cultural values and patterns, and is influenced by social structural factors related to economics and militarism. Indeed, harmful and destructive acts, perceived as legal violence, are formally taught by the military.

Cock, in an examination of political violence in South Africa in Chapter 2, estimates that 3 500 people have died in incidents of political violence between 1984 and early 1989. It is debated whether the manifestations causing these casualties can be seen as terrorism or criminality, or acts of warfare in a war of liberation. The African National Congress presents its strategy of the 'armed struggle' as a form of guerrilla warfare, a 'people's war', legitimizing it as a last-resort response to state oppression. The state has responded over the years by increased militarization.

Since the lifting of the ban on black political groups in February 1990, and the release and unbanning of political leaders, the roots of the violence sweeping the country are not that clearly visible. In the opinion of Laurence (*The Star*, 5 April 1990), the roots are only partly political, and the violence is also fed in large measure by underlying demographic and socio-economic forces. He classifies the current wave of violence into three broad categories: police action against protesting crowds; fighting between rival ideological factions in the black community; and clashes between competing interest groups in townships — the latter two root causes are epitomized by the civil war presently raging in Natal.

Illegitimate violence

Wilful acts of violence regarded by society as illegal are punishable under criminal law or are regulated by civil law.

Illegal acts of violence can be directed at persons or at property. Those directed at the person include acts, known as violent crimes, which inflict injury on others. These include murder, assault and battery, and acts of abuse and negligence.

Felonies like murder and non-negligent manslaughter, aggressive assault, forcible rape, robbery, burglary, and larceny-theft are classified by Glaser (1969, cited in Lauer, 1989: 169) as predatory crimes.

Illegal acts of violence directed at property, known as property crime, comprise burglary, larceny-theft, and motor-vehicle theft.

For purposes of detailed discussion, acts of violence directed at persons will be grouped into those directed against a person (interpersonal); those directed against certain groups of persons (intergroup); and wilful acts of violence against a nation or a national leader, other than formal warfare (international), and which may be directed from within a country or from without.

Interpersonal violence

Acts of violence wilfully directed at a person invade the personal space of an individual, and as such his or her rights.

Predatory crimes, described by Lauer (1989: 169), include:

☐ *Murder and non-negligent manslaughter:* which denote the wilful killing of a person, and exclude deaths by negligence, suicide, or accident.

☐ *Aggravated assault:* which implies an unlawful attack by one person upon another for the purpose of inflicting severe bodily injury, and usually involves a weapon.

☐ *Forcible rape:* which is defined as actual or attempted sexual intercourse through the use of force or the threat of force.

☐ *Robbery:* which is the use of force or threat of force to take something of value from a person.

☐ *Burglary:* which denotes the unlawful entry into a structure by a person to commit a felony or theft.

☐ *Larceny-theft:* which involves the unlawful taking or stealing of property or articles, without the use of force, violence, or fraud, and includes crimes such as bag-snatching or pickpocketing. Although physical violence may not always feature, emotional anguish is caused.

☐ *Motor-vehicle theft:* which is not generally associated with interpersonal violence. However, in South Africa the hijacking of motor vehicles is becoming a common phenomenon, during which the driver/owner may be physically threatened, assaulted, or murdered.

Moreover, the predatory crimes of robbery and burglary are frequently accompanied by another crime of the same type — rape, in cases where the victim is a woman.

Statistics compiled for the period July 1987 to June 1988 show that the number of prosecutions dealt with by the South African courts in respect of burglaries and related matters totalled 50 055; theft from the person, or gaining advantage by means of force or threats numbered 19 201; while other thefts, such as shoplifting, theft by employees from employers, theft of fire-arms, explosives, bicycles, motor cycles, and vehicles, and thefts from out of a motor vehicle, led to 125 614 prosecutions (Central Statistical Services, 1988: 6–7).

Whereas *assault and battery and abuse* of one person by another can occur within or outside of the family, wife battery or abuse always occurs within the domestic context. The physical abuse and neglect of children and dependent elderly persons can occur either within the home or within the community, in institutions of care.

Wife abuse may involve emotional assault as well as physical attack (Freeman, 1971). Segel and Labe in Chapter 9 of this book confirm the taking of a broad perspective on this phenomenon, and describe it as involving physical, sexual and/or psychological force, coercion, emotional humiliation, degradation or torment, verbal assault, and economic deprivation or exploitation. These authors extend spousal abuse to violence occurring between intimate partners regardless of whether the couple is legally married or not, an approach borne out by Lauer (1989). He contends that abusive behaviour in dating relationships, such as pushing, slapping, kicking, hurting, and hitting with the fist lays the basis for spousal abuse.

Child physical abuse is defined by Gil (1970: 6) as:
> … the intentional, non-accidental use of physical force, or intentional non-accidental acts of omission, on the part of a parent or other caretaker interacting with a child in his care, aimed at hurting, injuring or destroying that child.

Child sexual abuse, which is emerging as one of the most common forms of child abuse, is defined comprehensively in Chapter 8 of this book by Sandler and Sepel as constituting:
> … any sexual activity, whether it be ongoing or a single occurrence ranging from sexual overtones to sexual intercourse, between a sexually maturing or mature person and an unconsenting or consenting child who is cognitively and developmentally immature. This pertains whether or not the perpetrator has himself/herself

committed the sexual act or has permitted or encouraged the child to indulge in any sexual activity, for example child prostitution.

In South Africa the prescriptions of its child care legislation, the Child Care Act 74 of 1983, guide the procedures to be followed in cases of child physical and sexual abuse and neglect. One prescribed procedure is the admission of an abused/neglected child to an institution, by an order of court where the child will be cared for in a group other than his/her close family. However, as described by Giles in Chapter 13, children and youths in protective group care are not necessarily protected from these forms of abuse. This phenomenon can be regarded as an indictment on society when the rights of children in group care are violated through acts of violence against them, especially as they are isolated from sources of redress. This comment also applies to elderly persons receiving group care.

The *abuse, ill-treatment, neglect, and victimization of older persons* is a growing violent phenomenon. A comprehensive definition of elder abuse must include neglect, and must acknowledge that it includes not only the wilful infliction of physical pain, injury, or debilitating mental anguish (which can include unreasonable confinement of an elderly person), but also the deprivation of services to maintain mental and physical health. Such acts can be perpetrated against an old person in his/her home or in an institution where the person is receiving group care.

It is noteworthy that to date no reliable, comprehensive, nation-wide statistics are available in South Africa which describe the incidence of the above forms of family violence, including rape. At best, the authors examining these violent manifestations in this book can only provide estimates of incidence, or figures pertaining to a particular treatment organization.

However, available figures on *criminal acts against aged persons* make alarming reading. Attacks on the elderly in white residential areas increased by 100 per cent between February 1987 and February 1990. In the months July to December, 1989, 225 senior citizens, during 207 incidents in white residential areas, were murdered, raped, robbed, or seriously assaulted by strangers in their own homes (*The Star*, March 1990).

A form of family violence currently subjected to intensive empirical research by a multi-disciplinary team at the Human Sciences Research Council is the phenomenon of *family killings*, which hitherto has mostly been perpetrated by members of the white Afrikaans-speaking community in South Africa. The perpetrators are commonly fathers, and the victims comprise all the other members of the family. The research project referred to above aims to arrive at the aetiology of the phenomenon, referred to as 'familicide'. Du Toit examines this phenomenon in Chapter 10 of this book. According to Steyn (1989) 40 family killings occurred during 1988. Of these families, 29 were white; 9 African; 3 'coloured'; and 1 Asian.

Intergroup violence

Acts of violence directed at certain groups of persons denote intergroup violence. The groups may be racially or ethnically defined or may be groups constituted around a common goal or purpose, such as a political group. Violence erupts when the attitudes, beliefs, and values of persons in different groups become incompatible. Force is then used illegitimately to attain divergent objectives (Van der Westhuizen, 1982). Violent manifestations of such conflicts are community disturbances, rioting, and group/faction confrontations, which can kill or inflict injury, as well as cause the wilful destruction of property through vandalism and arson. Strikes and organized labour disturbances can erupt into violence, punishable under criminal law. 'Groups and group cleavages, be they economic or cultural, do not exist in a vacuum; they are politically manipulated' (Van der Merwe, 1989: 12).

Intergroup, politically-motivated violent acts, prevalent in South African society over decades, have now reached endemic proportions. Political violence refers to 'acts of destruction that impact on power relations in society' (Cock, Chapter 2). Terrorism, a strategy of political violence, is described as involving systematic acts of destruction aimed at altering or maintaining power relations through the spreading of extreme fear. Political violence, according to Van der Merwe (1989: 17) extends beyond a divergence of attitudes, beliefs, and values to also include structural conditions. In addition to the violence founded in the opposition to the policy of apartheid, conflict over the norms and methods between adherents of the same ideology has erupted in violence. Van der Merwe (1989: 48) points out that extremely vehement disagreement can often arise between different factions of liberation groups.

Manifestations of political violence in South Africa other than those already mentioned have taken the form of violent acts perpetrated by members of resistance parties, such as the assassination of agents; arson and bomb attacks against security and civilian targets; the 'necklacing' method of murder; and the formation of vigilante groups.

Violent acts countering the 'resistance' have taken the form of repressive security emergency legislation, the implementation of which has often resulted in detention without trial and the torture of detainees; the execution of persons found guilty of political crimes; the use of 'death squads' — officially sanctioned or unofficial; 'legal' police killings in the control and dispersion of riotous and potentially riotous crowds; and arson and armed attacks against anti-apartheid organizations and their premises.

The current violent political milieu of South Africa may be summed up in the words of Van Zyl Slabbert (1989: 80) who writes:

> South Africa is not caught up in a revolution in any classical sense of the word. Nor is it even in a (declared) state of civil war, which by definition means that the opposing parties rely on violence to achieve their objects and goals. But what we are caught up in, unfortunately is … a state of siege. In other words, a period of … violence during which problems of stability and order outweigh … political, social and economic considerations.

International violence (other than war)

At times political groups opposing a particular government have been banned from operating within the country concerned, as was the case in South Africa until recently. Such action has led to the establishment of external wings of political groups which continue to implement violent resistance in the countries from which they have been excluded, either through an internal wing, through insurgents, or through mustering moral and/or financial resources from other governments. In this way intergroup violence spans international boundaries. Depending on the political side taken, such acts are described as 'terrorism' or treason, or resistance or 'freedom fighting'.

INTERRELATED CAUSATIVE FACTORS

Violence in all its manifestations at family, community, national, and international levels is currently a major problem. Because human violence is a social problem, theorizing about its origins is commonplace, as is the ensuing controversy concerning divergent premises about human nature and violence.

Controversy has raged over the question of whether an innate aggressive drive would account for people's endemic violent behaviour, or whether aggressive behaviour is environmentally grounded and essentially learned behaviour (Freeman, 1971: 2).

To more fully explain the causes of violence, it is necessary to consider psychological, social, and environmental factors that contribute to violence in society. In pursuit of this, the multifaceted causation of violence will be examined in terms of psychological needs or motives (psychological factors); psychological factors coupled with societal needs and social structures, statuses, and roles (socio-psychological factors); and, lastly, societal aspects coupled with cultural values, which legitimize violence (socio-cultural factors).

Psychological factors

Some theorists have attributed the cause of violence to instinct conceptions of aggression (Freud, 1948; Hartman, 1949; Storr, 1970). Violence is thus linked to a human need to be aggressive. According to Storr (1970):

> ... in man, as in other animals, there exists a physiological mechanism, which, when stimulated, gives rise to both subjective feelings of anger and also to physical changes which prepare the body for fighting. This mechanism is easily set off, and like other emotional responses, it is stereotyped, and, in this sense, 'instinctive'.

While discrediting instinct theories, more recent psychologists have postulated that aggression is linked to frustration.

The first major change of the original frustration-aggression hypothesis extended the one side of the 'equation', resulting in the hypothesis that although aggression is always the result of frustration, frustration can be expressed in other forms of behaviour (Dollard & Miller, 1950 and Meyer, 1972, both cited in Bartol & Bartol, 1986; Lauer, 1989). This hypothesis acknowledged that people are able to exercise cognitive control over their behaviour — that they have self-regulatory capabilities (Bartol & Bartol, 1986: 190–1). Under certain conditions, however, actions are directed more by external stimuli than by cognitive, self-regulatory mechanisms.

A further modification in the frustration-aggression hypothesis was the acknowledgment that aggression can be caused by other factors besides frustration, for example, environmental stimuli associated with aggressive behaviour, which could create a situation in which aggressive behaviour is more likely to occur than in other situations. Powerful environmental stimuli can cause people to 'fall into' a rage, impulsively striking out in response to unpleasant feelings brought on by aversive or noxious stimuli. Nevertheless, the individual is not likely to strike out unless he or she has been in rage in past situations. Impulsive behaviour, then, is not necessarily unusual; it reflects habitual responses that might be rejected by the individual under low arousal or normal conditions. 'The environment and the relevant external stimuli take control over the internal mediation processes that have been weakened by extremely high levels of arousal' (Bartol & Bartol, 1986: 188).

Bandura and Walters (1963) further extended learning theory by demonstrating how people acquire behaviour not only through trial and error learning and the process of the reinforcement of successful behaviour (instrumental conditioning), but also through the process of modelling. Within these hypotheses, violence can be viewed as learned aggressive behaviour that is continually reinforced, a postulation supported by the research of others (Steele & Pollack, 1968; Steinmetz, 1977).

Toch (1969) theorizes that most violent episodes can be traced to well-learned systematic strategies of violence which some people have found effective in dealing with conflictful interpersonal relationships.

Social learning theory further hypothesizes that under certain circumstances self-regulatory processes become disengaged from conduct, and at times people appear to be swept away by their emotions, or by a crowd (Bartol & Bartol, 1986: 192).

In the opinion of Bartol and Bartol (1986) human beings, with their intricate cognitive equipment, have an uncanny knack for neutralizing, disregarding, minimizing, rationalizing, and misjudging their deeds. This involves disengaging beliefs and internal standards from actions, resulting in desensitization. According to Bandura (1983) certain common practices can be called upon in this respect. These involve:

☐ *Cognitive restructuring:* making reprehensible acts honourable, such as the act of a father who murders his family; or trivializing a violent act, such as atrocities committed in war, or in rape, when the rapist convinces himself that rape is not really serious.

☐ *Using euphemisms to neutralize anti-social acts:* for example, to 'terminate' or 'neutralize' instead of 'kill'.

☐ *Diffusing responsibility:* for example, 'just following orders', 'just following the crowd'.

☐ *Detaching oneself from the consequences of violent actions:* not allowing oneself to think about the consequences.

☐ *Dehumanizing the victim:* removing in thought all the human, dignifying qualities from the victim or intended victim.

Disengagement is particularly evident in mob violence. In a crowd, the threshold of normally restrained behaviour is lowered. People feel anonymous, less responsible for their behaviour, and less inhibited, resulting in a process of de-individuation. Zimbardo (1970) and Diener (1980) (both cited in Bartol & Bartol, 1986: 197) believe that a person's normal self-regulatory behaviour is reduced by the unusual and exciting activity of the crowd, and that this reduced self-awareness creates an internal state of de-individuation.

In addition to theories formulated around social learning, other major psychological theories have developed around specific types of violence, such as child, wife, and elderly abuse.

For example, in wife abuse early psychological theories of wife abuse presented women as masochistic, and as provocative of their own abuse. Attribution theories analyse people's beliefs in the causes of what happens to them, whereby battered women would be more likely to attribute the cause of their abuse to powerful others and uncontrollable forces. Another theory, that of cognitive dissonance, postulates that women begin to doubt their own reality, and then substitute their men's world view in an attempt to reduce the conflict between the two opposing views. Aggression theorists have examined whether the interaction between victims and perpetrators can stimulate further aggressive behaviour. In the opinion of Lystad (1986) and Walker (1986) most theories require further testing.

Socio-psychological factors

Personal and group standards dictate much of behaviour, which confirms the assumption that acts and episodes of violence are located in the interactions between persons and other people in their human environment, based on the values and attitudes generated by them. The family, as the primary human environment of the individual, can help to perpetuate forms of violence, both within and outside of the family. Similarly, attitudes held by some people in the wider environment can influence those of other individuals.

The socio-psychological perspective, developed into a theory, has been used world-wide in attempts to explain and to understand the causes and consequences of abuse in the family. In such a model the causes of abuse are located within the interactions between family members, and within other features of the family system.

Values and attitudes can legitimate violence, either to perpetuate a myth, such as 'spare the rod and spoil the child', or as a means of social control. In this way personal standards about human nature can become a built-in justification for violent acts. If a held value translated into an attitude might be that 'life is cheap' and if insensitive conduct is the norm, violence can become a way of life. Violence can therefore be manifested because it reflects a person's or a group's implicit theory of human nature.

Others believe that violence is the only way to achieve social change. A pertinent local example of the latter example was that adopted by black South African youth in the struggle: 'liberation before education'.

Lauer (1989: 216) cites research undertaken by Blumenthal *et al.* in 1972 to ascertain the attitudes of men in the United States on the justification of violence at the intergroup level to maintain social control, and to achieve social change. Out of a national sample, one-half to two-thirds justified shooting, in the situation described, as a legitimate means of social control. The proportion of men who believed violence was justifiable to bring about social change was far less.

The notion of relative deprivation, which means that people have a sense of deprivation in relation to some standards, further explains violence. Lauer (1989: 216) points out that the attitude people have towards their deprivation is more important than any objective assessment of that deprivation. Revolutionary situations can be created out of the perceived discrepancy, whether real or imagined.

Values, which guide and reinforce attitudes held about violence, in themselves also perpetuate violent acts. For example, retribution and self-defence are both values which support violence for social control (Lauer, 1989: 217). The latter stance may lead to vigilante behaviour. Values which support violence under certain circumstances become internalized and in turn result in the legitimization of certain violent acts, such as corporal punishment and capital punishment; whereas macho values appear to be a factor in rape, introducing tolerance of the violent act of rape.

Socio-cultural factors

Socio-cultural factors presumed to contribute to the manifestation of violence locate the causes of violence within the broader society: social-cultural factors such as norms, based on beliefs and values; social structures; and institutional arrangements.

The significance of norms as determinants of violence cannot be underestimated. 'Norms are shared expectations about behaviour. Normative behaviour is therefore prescribed behaviour that is expected by each of us by the rest of us' (Lauer, 1989: 11). People learn to abide by norms in accord with the groups of which they are part. In this way interpersonal and intergroup violent behaviour becomes a legitimated or legally sanctioned norm which can advocate violence — a feature present in nearly every society. Thus, in the name of social control children may be taught the norms of using violence in defending themselves; of the use of power and force in instilling discipline; or of the use of power or force to control group action against the state or officialdom. From a feminist perspective adherence to rigid gender roles and the belief that women are less powerful than men in the home may lead to violent acts such as wife abuse and rape.

Certain socio-political arrangements may promote violence, such as structural inequalities based on economic, cultural, or racial factors. Gil (1986) sees violence in human relations as rooted in institutionalized inequalities of statuses, rights, and power between the sexes, and among individuals, ages, classes, races, and peoples. These inequalities in themselves isolate the individual development of persons and bring forth violent reactions from oppressed individuals and groups. The inequalities of human relations and social institutions are not the result of freedom of choice by the individuals and groups who are victimized, but rather are the consequences of the more powerful social group's use of coercion, which has become institutionalized into legal systems, and justified through mythology, religion, philosophy, ideology, and history.

The coercive processes induce violent responses from the individuals and groups which are exploited, which in turn is met by violence from the dominant groups, creating vicious spirals of ever-escalating violence and repression.

Conflict and violence in South Africa can be well understood in terms of Gil's theoretical construct. The total population of South Africa and the TBVC countries (Transkei, Bophuthatswana, Venda, and Ciskei) countries amounts to 33,67 million, of which 14,7 per cent are whites and 74,3 per cent Africans (Eberstadt, 1988: 22, cited in Van der Merwe, 1989). While Africans predominate, they are deprived of property rights in 86,3 per cent of the country, and are also effectively prevented from owning and controlling the means of production in the country. Racial inequality is also conspicuous in the comparison of income of the racial groups. Further inequalities exist in educational opportunities. The infant mortality rate among Africans is estimated to be between nine and ten times higher than that of whites, a further indicator of inequalities in the provision of basic human needs and health facilities. 'The objective conditions of inequality make it clear that South Africa is a highly stratified society, characterized by intense structural and institutional injustice and violence' (Van der Merwe, 1989: 18).

Lauer (1989) includes the politics of gun control as a social structural factor which contributes to violence. The availability of weapons, such as guns, is essential in certain premeditated crimes such as robbery. The availability of a gun may also lead to more severe consequences in unpremeditated violent actions or responses. In some instances a victim may not have been wounded or killed were a gun not available (Bartol & Bartol, 1986: 187).

Registered firearms in South Africa total 2,8 million and more than half have been licensed in the last decade. Police statistics show that gun owners have been registering new weapons at an average of at least 150 000 a year (*The Star*, 27 March 1990).

Other contributory factors

Further factors may contribute to acts of violence. Some of these factors resort under the medical, intra-individual theoretical model of manifestations of violence such as abuse. These factors include pathological behaviour, mental retardation, and alcohol or drug abuse.

Bartol and Bartol (1986: 160–4) recount research done on the effects of environmental factors on violent behaviour. Included are such factors as overcrowded conditions, extreme heat, noise, air-pollution, and erotica, the latter especially in relation to sexual violence.

Acts of omission rather than commission are also factors which may result in violent acts. A lack of knowledge and understanding of the needs of children and elderly persons, coupled with a lack of necessary skills, could result in unintended abuse and neglect.

Research on the effects of the mass media on human violence points to the fact that mass-media violence increases the level of violent behaviour in society (Baker & Ball, 1969, cited by Lauer, 1989; Bandura, 1965, cited in Bartol & Bartol, 1986). The research of Baker and Ball showed that as a short-term effect the individuals exposed to mass-media violence learn how to perform violent acts and are likely to emulate these if confronted with similar situations as those portrayed in the media. The long-term effect is the socialization of people into the norms, attitudes, and values for violence. Moreover, repeated exposure to violence in the mass media may 'habituate' heavy viewers to violence and may also distort their perceptions of the world. On the other hand, Chaffee and McLeod (1971, cited in Bartol & Bartol, 1986: 165), and Goldstein (1975) have found that positive parental models are likely to override the violent models portrayed on television programmes which children watch.

COMMON FEATURES OF HUMAN VIOLENCE

Examination of the manifestations of human violence, on an interpersonal level or an intergroup level, reveals common features. These features are prevalent irrespective of the context in which violence occurs, the persons involved, and whether the violence is manifested physically or structurally. Recognition and study of such features deepens the understanding of violence as a phenomenon and provides valuable directions for intervention.

1. It is postulated that all forms of violence share one characteristic, namely, conflict. Van der Merwe (1989: 14) affirms that conflict is neutral, pointing out that people are conditioned into regarding conflict as negative or destructive. Inner conflict reflects difficulties experienced by individuals in reconciling differing stimuli, whereas outwardly, conflict is a manifestation of differences in thought and behaviour, according to people's individual social and personal histories. Conflict generates energy, and if such energy is constructively channelled, violent action is improbable. However, if conflict is destructively managed, violence results.

2. Force is a feature of violence, whether the force denotes the use of strength, or physical or mental power, or whether force is used to constrain a person in a way which constitutes violence, or whether a person is forcefully compelled to act in a certain way, to succumb to an action, or to refrain from acting.

3. Whether repressed or not, fear is evident in episodes of violence and fear can evoke further or retaliatory violence, or may suppress retaliation.

4. A victim and a perpetrator feature in all acts of violence. In some episodes of violence it may be unclear and even arguable as to who constitutes the victim and who the perpetrator, particularly in the eruption of a spiral of violence and counter-violence. In such situations the designation reflects the particular bias of the person doing the labelling.

5. Violence is a communication. As such, its message may be conveyed directly to the person or persons concerned — the perceived adversary — or the message contained in the violent communication may be directed at a person or a group via an innocent victim. Van der Merwe (1989: 61) argues that 'violence, as coercion, is best interpreted as a way of communicating with the adversary'.

6. A violent act may be dispassionately planned and executed, or may occur spontaneously, as an impulsive outburst. In the case of the latter type of occurrence self-regulatory processes fail, or in other instances they may be consciously adapted in pursuit of survival or in the face of a threat to one's safety, or own perceived interest.

7. Any act of violence violates the dignity and rights of an individual, whether adult or child, whether the violation takes the form of physical, emotional, or spiritual injury or damage, or whether it is an act of commission or omission.

8. Generally acts of violence invade the personal and the physical space of persons.

9. The settings for violent manifestations can be public or private. Intergroup violence tends to occur or overflow into public places, whereas the private environment of the home constitutes the stage for forms of domestic violence, like child and wife abuse. Reluctance to violate the sanctity of the family prevents a private matter — abuse — from being made a public issue. Moreover, the privacy of a home lends itself to secrecy about abusive interactions.

10. In similar vein, violence committed by the state in the name of national security is also veiled in secrecy.

11. Violence is mostly a learned response. It may be inculcated by precept, as is the case in rituals; by personal experience as a victim; or through observation. Moreover, substantial evidence gleaned from research supports the cycle of violence theory which postulates that abused children grow up to be abusing adults (Roy, 1977; Straus *et al.*, 1980; Steinmetz, 1986).

12. Desensitization to violence can occur as a process of social learning or as a process of cognitive restructuring.

13. Violence may be perpetuated inter-generationally. Children who have been victims of violence, who have become desensitized to violence through prolonged exposure, are likely to repeat violent patterns of behaviour when they are adult.

14. Whereas illegitimate family violence is always abhorred in public rhetoric, illegitimate structural violence may be advocated, and all nations validate and, indeed, enforce violence 'in pursuit or protection of national interests' (Van der Merwe, 1989: 17).

15. Violence is generally countered by violence, and reactive violence features as a consequence of repressive violence.

16. Ideologizing conflict usually leads to its intensification (Van der Merwe, 1989: 16). It follows then that should violence be advocated as a means of conflict resolution, violence would escalate.

IMPACT OF VIOLENCE

Violence has an overwhelming and decisive influence on individuals and society. It pervades all aspects of the environment, and no person remains untouched by violence. If not directly involved in violent manifestations, people are indirectly drawn in by the mass media, and are affected by the fallout resulting from violence. People either indirectly carry its financial cost, or experience the social and emotional stress of living in a violent environment, or both.

It is obvious that people respond differently to participation in or indirect exposure to violence. Some individuals who have been subjected to violent acts have been able to overcome and interpret the abuse constructively. The human organism is capable of tremendous strength, determination, and resilience in the face of adversity. Nevertheless, each person in his/her particular way, manifests the effect of the violent experience. The manifestations of the impact may be unobtrusive or the effects may severely pervade a person's social functioning, in either the short term or the long term.

All forms of violence are disruptive, and detract from the quality of life. The impact of violence contradicts the commonly-held values of personal, family, and societal well-being.

What follows is a brief overview of some of the effects of violence on the individual *per se* and on society in general.

Violence can injure and destroy

Violence can result in human injury and destruction, which can result directly from war, capital punishment, and other violent physical confrontations which occur on an interpersonal and intergroup level, such as murder, armed robbery, assault and battery, and riots. Temporary or permanent harm may occur and people may even be killed. Violence also leads to destruction of property, which has economic consequences for private citizens, private financial institutions such as insurance bodies, and government. In the words of Lauer (1989: 184) 'the fear generated by crime means that everyone loses'.

Violence can restrict lifestyles

Violence can result in restricted lifestyles in varying degrees. A high incidence of armed robbery, housebreaking, and theft leads to the extensive use of security devices on private premises such as dwellings, and commercial and industrial premises. Fear of interpersonal violence such as rape and the victimization of persons living alone or attacks on elderly persons, in their homes or on the street, leads to the restricted movement and activities of such persons. Forms of structural violence, such as detention, also curb freedom of movement and environmental stimulation, as do riots.

Violence evokes fear

Whereas violent crime, riots, and acts of interpersonal violence such as physical abuse are obviously injurious physically, fear, an ever-present element in violent interactions, is injurious to mental health.

Fear is a general emotional response to violence, whether aroused by an interpersonal incident, or an intergroup violent event, or repeated incidences of the same form of violence, or an impacting of several forms of violence. Fear of further physical violence or death is common. Widespread violence can also result in pervasive fear in society. Widespread fear affects all, even those who have not been directly affected as victims.

As Lauer (1989: 182) points out, the cost of psychological damage is difficult to assess, but the victim of violence experiences some trauma. Some kind of negative emotional reaction such as nervousness, anxiety, anger, outrage, shame, humiliation, self-blame, despair, or fear accompanies the trauma of violence.

Widespread violence leads to pervasive fear in a society — a fear of being a victim of violence. Freedom from fear, one of the four basic freedoms proclaimed by Roosevelt (Lauer, 1989: 353) constitutes one of the 'freedoms' presently championed by the Five Freedoms Forum in South Africa.

Fear of violence not only erodes the fabric of interpersonal and inter-group relationships, but can also lead to the disruption of social networks and the depletion of communities, who seek escape from violence or the threat of violence by moving out of a specific neighbourhood, community, or country.

Violence damages relationships

Violence, whether interpersonal or intergroup, damages relationships. Polarization may occur, or the fear of further harm can reinforce a relationship, as happens in forms of domestic violence such as wife battery, child physical and sexual abuse, and elder abuse.

Caring, trusting, and intimate interpersonal relationships are in the first instance fostered in the home between spouses, between parent and child, and between members of the nuclear family and those of their families of origin, within a structure balanced by power relations. All family violence negates caring, and abuses power which in turn damages trust and interferes with healthy family closeness. Star (1987: 469) maintains that 'once the violence barrier is broken, abuse becomes part of the repertoire of family interactions' — an item incorporated into interpersonal relationships outside the family as well as into intergroup relationships. In this way violence cuts across the family function.

Violence dehumanizes

Lauer (1989: 480–1) names a number of aspects of the 'maladaptive' dehumanization that occur in wars as identified in research, which apply equally to other violent interpersonal and intergroup confrontations:

1. Increase in emotional distance from others.

2. Decreased sense of responsibility for one's own actions.

3. Increased concern with procedures rather than with human needs.

4. Lack of resistance to group attitudes and pressures.

5. Feelings of helplessness and alienation.

No form of violence has as great a dehumanizing impact as war in any of its forms. It inverts value systems and makes maiming and killing socially acceptable.

War impacts on both people and the physical environment, because it always involves some environmental destruction, as well as psychological disruption on a massive scale, not only touching the victims and perpetrators, but extending beyond to the significant people in their lives. Moreover, whereas war in the past involved opposing armies in battle, civilian populations are tending more and more to become involved in formally declared wars, or wars of liberation, with equal traumatizing effect.

Whereas young adults and adults were the combatants in previous armies of war, children feature prominently in liberation struggles, thereby being robbed of their childhood. In South Africa today, children have 'emerged from the shadows to invade the arena and the history books usually reserved for adults' in 'the struggle' (Burman, 1986: 4). It has been confirmed that in Mozambique, an estimated 10 000 children under the age of fifteen years have been combatant-trained by the resistance movement, and in many instances forced to kill (Institute for Research Development, 1990: 1).

Violence alienates

In whatever context it occurs, violence alienates. Alienation becomes widespread when there is an escalation of violence in society. For example, a high incidence of violent crime creates an atmosphere of distrust in society, lowers social morale, and creates widespread social disorganization (Lauer, 1989: 184). The same is true of the impact of an escalating spiral of institutional violence and counter-violence, and in particular political violence.

Violence causes psychological disruption

Violence is traumatic in any guise. Whether one is a victim or witness, violence makes an emotional impact. As an event outside of the ordinary realm of experience the traumatic effects of violent manifestations can surface immediately and may linger for months or years, or may present themselves as aftershock. Victims may suffer mild emotional trauma, or may suffer psychological damage. Aftershock appears after the traumatic event, and its symptoms can make it look like an entirely unrelated condition (Slaby, 1989). People can also relive the original violent experience in frightening and realistic detail. This response is called post-traumatic stress disorder (PTSD) and it is a major element of after-shock. Slaby (1989) has coined the term 'aftershock' to describe any significant delayed response to a traumatic event, whether this reaction is manifested by anxiety, depression, substance abuse, or PTSD.

Burgess and Holmstrong (1974) have identified two phases of reaction common among rape victims which may equally apply to victims of other forms of violent crime or physical abuse: an initial acute phase of disorganization, and a long-term phase of reorganization. Emotional reactions manifested in the acute phase range from fear, humiliation, and embarrassment, to anger, revenge, and self-blame. Emotional reactions associated with the long-term phase of reorganization include helplessness, nightmares, the development of phobias (such as a fear of being indoors/outdoors or of being left alone), and sexual fears.

Similar emotional reactions are documented by Lauer (1989: 182) in respect of crime victims, and by Slaby (1989: 39–40) in his description of the emotional features accompanying aftershock. Further features mentioned by these authors are nervousness, panic attacks, depression, shame, rage, guilt, withdrawal, and sadness associated with loss.

Anxiety is a pervasive reaction in all violent manifestations, and is related to a feeling of having little or no control over the episode, its possible or certain re-occurrence, or over a prevailing widespread violent situation. The response embodies frustration, in that the victim's fate is in the hands of another, temporarily or in the long term, leaving him/her powerless. Notions of unfairness and injustice are embodied in feelings of frustration.

Empirical evidence points to victims of violence feeling disempowered and fearing for their survival in the face of repeated and prolonged violence, thereby losing their ability to predict that their responses will have an effect on what happens to them. Learned helplessness, a phenomenon featuring in the battered-woman syndrome, emerges as one such response.

Trauma victims concentrate on survival and when the danger from repeated violence is still present, their thoughts, feelings, and reactions are regulated by the need to reduce the violence threat (Lystad, 1986; Seligman, 1975; Walker, 1979 & 1984).

Denial is another powerful reaction to violence. This response can feature as numbness, or can extend to amnesia. Desensitization to the manifestation, if repetitive, features as a coping behaviour. Desensitization also serves the purpose of denying the deleterious effects of violence. The desensitizing process not only denies the existence of feelings a person may have in relation to self and the event, but may also centre on denying feelings for the plight of another, which results in blunted empathy.

The longer acute emotional symptoms persist, the more chronic and serious they become, leading to psychological disruption, whereby the symptoms themselves become problematic.

Intense, persistent feelings may be acted out in antisocial behaviour, or may result in mental breakdowns leading to hospitalization. In the final instance intense, unresolved emotional reactions to violence may result in suicide.

Violence thus causes psychological injury to its victims which can be measured and diagnosed using the traditional Diagnostic and Statistical

Manual of Mental Disorders (DSM–III), published in 1980 and revised in 1986–7, and which has listed qualifying variables for Acute, Chronic and Delayed PTSD (Lystad, 1986: 77; Slaby, 1989: 34–7).

Violence leads to moral atrophy

Desensitization leads to moral atrophy, whereby people no longer question violent actions because moral principles no longer apply, and the individual is absolved of the responsibility of making personal moral choices. Kelman (1973, cited by Holdstock in Chapter 12), points out that in such circumstances, people learn to look to official definitions of actions — authorization — rather than to their human consequences in assessing the legitimacy of the actions. This extends the notion of learned helplessness to include moral helplessness.

Moral atrophy results in dehumanization, as is illustrated in the following example of a currently frequent occurrence in the townships of Natal:

About 20 youths, most apparently in their late teens, were chasing a man aged about 19 or 20.

He fell down and they swooped, punching him. He got up and ran into a parked minibus taxi with passengers, but his pursuers caught up with him. They dragged him out and punched him.

He fell again. His tormentors punched, stoned and jumped on him. By now his face was covered in blood.

I and the many adults who saw the attack winced at every blow, but uniformed schoolchildren looked on as if they were watching a soccer match.

The nightmare went on. Relentlessly, the youngsters drew knives and stabbed the man.

A youngster produced a bush knife. With all his might he hacked the victim on the head six or seven times.

Amazingly, the man managed to stagger towards the station, followed by the group, gathering in numbers all the time, hurling stones at him.

Suddenly a gunshot came from the group.

'They are now shooting him. They are going to kill. Only God knows what's happening in kwaMashu, this is no longer a place to live in,' a woman beside me wailed.

I cannot be sure what happened to the man after he ran towards the station. Police later said a body had been found in the area, but had no further details (*The Star*, 25 January 1990).

Violence can be perpetuated

In a similar vein the impact of violence administered in the form of aggressive discipline experienced in the classroom, a small-scale society, or in other similar societal structures, such as institutions of care, or punitive institutions like reformatories and prisons, inculcates and perpetuates the use of violence as a conflict-resolution technique from one generation to the next.

On the domestic front children witness parent abuse, and they themselves can fall victim to a similar plight. The research of, among others, Straus *et al.* (1980) and Walker (1984) suggests that modelling of parents' behaviour is a powerful way to pass violence as a strategy down to the next generation.

Burgess (1984) found one common factor in empirical studies. This was the lack of social competence in abusing adults and some of the abused children. He postulates that what largely determines whether or not an abusive style continues from parent to child is the peer socialization experienced by the child. If the abused child is rejected by peers, he or she loses a further model from which to learn less destructive social skills.

FROM UNDERSTANDING TO ACTION

An understanding of the nature of violence can lead to its reduction. It cannot be denied that violence presents itself as a social problem rather than only a personal one. It is invasive and even when manifested on an interpersonal level within the sanctity of the family, it affects the stability of society.

Currently violence is a public issue in South African society, and solutions for its manifestations, whether occurring within families, the community, protective institutions, or in the society at large, require collective action. Collective action implies a multi-dimensional approach to reduce violence.

To strike appropriately at the core of violence it is necessary not to confuse conflict with violence. Van der Merwe (1989) emphasizes this difference, pointing out that in order to change a society for the better, it is not a matter of eliminating conflict, but violence. Conflict denotes a conflict of interest, a difference of opinion, and is in itself not bad; but the tendency to equate conflict with violent manifestations, reinforces violence as an acceptable means of conflict management and resolution.

Intervention needs also to be comprehensive, and must incorporate integrated multi-disciplinary action. Its focus must be the person in transaction with his/her environment, both the primary environment consisting of the family, and the wider environment, the community, and the larger society with its multiple institutions.

Mindful of the ecosystems paradigm, interventive strategies must be appropriately pitched along the promotive/preventive/curative/rehabilitation continuum.

The present economic, political, and socio-cultural stratification of South African society, which is based on gross entrenched legal inequality, promotes manifestations of structural violence in person-environment transactions. Thus the thrust of promotive intervention would be structural reform. The social structure requires fundamental change to reduce inequalities. Similarly, the political structure requires change to introduce political equality. The economic structure 'would certainly require political intervention to ensure a fairer distribution of the wealth and resources of the country' (Van der Merwe, 1989: 7).

Van der Merwe (1989) argues that it is normal for any society to protect its vested interests and that the moral force within the establishment in South Africa is not strong enough to bring about change willingly. He therefore proposes negotiation and non-violent coercion as a means by which to achieve reconstruction.

Fundamental societal reform will result in the empowerment of presently disadvantaged socio-cultural groups and individuals. Empowerment will not automatically lead to a reduction in conflict, nor to a decrease in violent manifestations of conflict in person-environment transactions. Therefore, preventive interventive strategies will have to incorporate large-scale mediation between conflicting people and groups. Educational programmes to teach people conflict resolution and management skills, and self-assertiveness skills which will replace violent strategies, and thus slowly rebuild fragmented relationships and re-fashion maladaptive modes of communication within families, groups, and communities, must be introduced in existing educational, health, and welfare organizations.

The most powerful educational tool is the transactional patterns of political and societal leaders. If political leaders can model constructive conflict resolution modes of behaviour, violent strategies will fall into disfavour. Moreover, should the non-violent strategies prove successful, trust in leaders will be fostered which will reinforce non-violent means of resolving conflict. Hopefully non-violent transactions on the societal level will filter through to the intra-family level.

Legislation which protects the interests of vulnerable persons and groups in society comprises a form of promotive and preventive intervention. In South Africa incisive legislation is required to equalize opportunities and resources for all its peoples. Laws are also required which will adequately protect persons discriminated against because of gender or age against abusive transactions on the domestic scene. In similar vein, child-protection legislation requires amendment to appropriately and adequately provide for and protect homeless children and children in institutions and group care.

A primary thrust in intervention to combat violence is to attend to the family unit because of its central importance in the socialization of children into non-violent behaviour.

Slaby (1989) cites research which has shown that a stable family environment can sustain victims of traumatic events, and can prevent the manifestations of aftershock developing into pathology. Not only has South African society been divided, but so also have families. Families have been structurally divided by apartheid legislation, which has subjected their members to economic, physical, and emotional hardship, which could in itself be construed as violence.

Many children in this country have no normal family life and know only fear and violence. In the words of Chikane (1986: 337) 'to be born into an apartheid society is to be born on a battlefield' — a scenario which promotes violence as a survival strategy in the face of apartheid and security and emergency laws, over and above a struggle for survival for some in the face of poverty, hunger, inadequate housing, split families, and an unresponsive educational system. In consequence, the traditional family structure in many instances has been affected by a relocation of the parental seat of power and authority to the children. Thus intervention to promote family stability must begin with structural societal change, to be further addressed on the preventive, curative, and rehabilitative levels. For, the world of today's township children is extremely violent. The impact of violence on their lives will extend into their transactions as they grow up into the adults of tomorrow and the creators of future families. Indeed it may take a number of generations, despite appropriate intervention, to stabilize family life in South Africa on a broad scale.

In the opinion of Chuenyane (1989) the country should not be surprised to see a sharp increase in domestic violence, child and spouse abuse, illegitimacy, homicide, suicide, and a general decline in morale and respect for authority as the township 'children of violence' grow into adulthood.

All types of violence, whether between individuals, between groups, or between nations share two features: violence tends to evoke counter-violence; and violence in one setting or relationship tends to spread to others. The problem of reversing the escalating spiral of violence and the spread of violence is also basically the same everywhere (Glaser, 1986).

Goodness-of-fit between persons and environments, characterized by minimal violence, requires that the basic needs of persons are adequately met within relatively stable families supported and supplemented by adequate and appropriate health and welfare resources; that benign social controls — including adequate and appropriate legal protection — act to stabilize person-environment transactions; that non-violent conflict resolution and management procedures are known and called upon; and that the teaching of personal skills to adults and children in formal and informal education becomes a priority. Personal skills to be taught include those of communicating, forming, and maintaining relationships, asserting oneself without harming another, managing or resolving conflict, negotiating, and, above all, skills pertaining to the roles of spouse and parent.

REFERENCES

Bandura, A. (1983) 'Psychological Mechanisms of Aggression'. In *Aggression: Theoretical and Empirical Reviews*, Vol. 1, edited by R.G. Green & E. J. Donnerstein, New York: Academic Press.

Bandura, A. & Walters, R. H. (1963) *Social Learning and Personality Development,* New York: Holt, Rinehart & Winston.

Bartol, C. R. & Bartol, A. M. (1986) *Criminal Behaviour — A Psychosocial Approach,* Englewood Cliffs: Prentice-Hall, Inc.

Bothuis, H. (1982) 'Violence on the Road — A New Approach'. In *Crimes of Violence in South Africa,* edited by J. van der Westhuizen, Pretoria: University of South Africa.

Burgess, A. W. & Holmstrong, L. L. (1974) 'Rape Trauma Syndrome', *American Journal of Psychiatry,* 131, September, 981–6.

Burgess, R. L. (1984) 'Social Incompetence as a Precipitant to and Consequence of Child Maltreatment', paper presented at the Third International Victimology Conference, Lisbon, 10–18 November.

Burman, S. (1986) 'The Contexts of Childhood in South Africa: An Introduction'. In *Growing up in a Divided Society: The Context of Childhood in South Africa,* edited by S. Burman & P. Reynolds, Johannesburg: Ravan Press.

Burman, S. & Reynolds, P. (1986) *Growing up in a Divided Society: The Contexts of Childhood in South Africa,* Johannesburg: Ravan Press.

Central Statistical Services (1989) *Bulletin of Statistics,* 23(4), December, Pretoria: Central Statistical Services.

Central Statistical Services (1988) *Crimes: Prosecutions and Convictions with Regard to Certain Offences,* Report No. 00-11-01, 1987/88, Pretoria: Central Statistical Services.

Chikane, F. (1986) 'Children in Turmoil: The Effects of the Unrest on Township Children'. In *Growing up in a Divided Society: The Contexts of Childhood in South Africa,* edited by S. Burman & P. Reynolds, Johannesburg: Ravan Press.

Chuenyane, M. (1989) '"Children of Violence" Will Grow up Violent', *The Star,* 21 September 1989.

Deutsch, M. (1973) *The Resolution of Conflict,* New Haven: Yale University Press.

Eberstadt, N. (1988) 'Poverty in South Africa', *Optima,* 36, March, 20–33.

Folberg, J. & Taylor, A. (1984) *Mediation: A Comprehensive Guide to Resolving Conflicts without Litigation,* San Francisco: Jossey-Bass.

Freeman, M. D. (1971) *Violence in the Home,* London: Gower.

Gil, D. G. (1986) 'Sociocultural Aspects of Domestic Violence'. In *Violence in the Home: Interdisciplinary Perspectives,* edited by M. Lystad, New York: Brunner/Mazel, 124–49.

Gil, D. G. (1970) *Violence against Children,* Cambridge: Harvard University Press.

Glaser, D. G. (1986) 'Violence in Society'. In *Violence in the Home: Interdisciplinary Perspectives,* edited by M. Lystad, New York: Brunner/Mazel.

Goldstein, J. H. (1975) *Aggression and Crimes of Violence,* New York: Oxford University Press.

Hart, S. N. *et al.* (1987) 'The Challenge: To Better Understand and Combat Psychological Maltreatment of Children and Youth'. In *Psychological Maltreatment of Children and Youth,* edited by M. R. Brassard *et al.,* New York: Pergamon Press.

Human Sciences Research Council Sports Investigation (1982), 'Sport in the RSA', Report of the Main Committee, Pretoria: HSRC.

Institute for Research Development (1990) *Bulletin,* 2(2), March, Pretoria: Institute for Research Development.

Lauer, R. H. (1989) *Social Problems and the Quality of Life* (4th edn.), Dubuque: Wm. C. Brown Publishers.

Laurence, P. (1990) 'Violence: Issues not Clear Cut', *The Star,* 5 April 1990.

Lystad, M. (ed.) (1986) *Violence in the Home: Interdisciplinary Perspectives,* New York: Brunner/Mazel.

McClintock, F. H. (1963) *Crimes and Violence,* New York: MacMillan.

Roux, H. O. (1982) 'The Incidence of Prison Violence and Strategies for Dealing with Violent Offenders'. In *Crimes of Violence in South Africa,* edited by J. van der Westhuizen, Pretoria: University of South Africa.

Roy, M. (1977) *Battered Women: A Psycho-sociological Study of Domestic Violence,* New York: Van Nostrand Reinhold.

SAIRR (South African Institute of Race Relations) (1989) *Race Relations Survey 1988/89,* Johannesburg: SAIRR.

SAIRR (1988) *Race Relations Survey 1987/88,* Johannesburg: SAIRR.

Seligman, M. E. P. (1975) *Helplessness: On Depression, Development and Death,* San Francisco: W. H. Freeman.

Slaby, E. (1989) *After-shock: Surviving the Delayed Effects of Trauma, Crisis and Loss,* New York: Villard Books.

Star, B. (1987) 'Domestic Violence', *Encyclopaedia of Social Work,* Vol. I, Silver Spring: NASW, 463–76.

Steele, B. & Pollack, C. (1968) 'A Psychiatric Study of Parents who Abuse Infants and Small Children'. In *The Battered Child,* edited by R. Helfer & C. H. Kempe, Chicago: University of Chicago Press.

Steinmetz, S. K. (1986) 'The Violent Family'. In *Violence in the Home: Interdisciplinary Perspectives,* edited by M. Lystad, New York: Brunner/Mazel.

Steinmetz, S. K. (1977) *The Cycle of Violence: Assertive, Aggressive, and Abusive Family Interaction,* New York: Praeger.

Steyn, C. (1989) 'Discussion of the Research Strategies Used by the HSRC Family Murder Research Team — Theory, Hypotheses and Practical Implications', paper presented at the HSRC Seminar on Family Violence, Pretoria, 29 September 1989.

Storr, A. (1970) *Human Aggression,* Pelican Books.

Straus, M. *et al.* (1980) *Behind Closed Doors: Violence in American Families,* Garden City, N Y: Anchor/Doubleday.

Toch, H. (1969) *Violent Men: An Inquiry into the Psychology of Violence,* Chicago: Aldine Publishing Co.

Van der Merwe, H. (1989) *Pursuing Justice and Peace in South Africa,* London: Routledge & Kegan Paul.

Van der Westhuizen, J. (1982) 'The General Nature and Incidence of Crimes of Violence'. In *Crimes of Violence in South Africa,* edited by J. van der Westhuizen, Pretoria: University of South Africa.

Van Zyl Slabbert, F. (1989) *The System and the Struggle: Reform, Revolt and Reaction in South Africa,* Johannesburg, Jonathan Ball Publishers.

Walker, L. E. A. (1986) 'Psychological Causes of Family Violence'. In *Violence in the Home: Interdisciplinary Perspectives,* edited by M. Lystad, New York: Brunner/Mazel, 71–97.

Walker, L. E. A. (1984) *The Battered Woman Syndrome,* New York: Springs.

Walker, L. E. A. (1979) *The Battered Woman,* New York: Harper & Row.

Walter, E. (1969) *Terror and Resistance: A Study of Political Violence,* London: Oxford University Press.

Part 2

Violence in society

Introduction

That South Africa is a particularly violent society is indisputable. Simply by being a part of the society, the lives of all are touched — and tarnished — by violence: perpetrating it, legally or illegally; being a victim of it, directly or indirectly; and being a witness to it, first-hand or via the media. The nation has been caught up in a destructive pattern of violence, both repressive and revolutionary, and in the process many South Africans have come to accept violence as an ordinary, normal, and legitimate solution to conflict.

The second part of this book seeks to document the nature of this violence in society, to analyse some of its possible causes and consequences, and to suggest means of ameliorating it. First, the bitter political violence that has come to characterize this country is examined. Consideration is then given to how societal violence is reinforced by the legally-sanctioned violence of corporal and capital punishment. Thereafter, two illustrations are offered of how generally-held attitudes in society serve to sanction, reinforce, or excuse violence at the interpersonal level. The two examples are those of rape, and violence in sport.

In Chapter 2, the nature of the political violence ravaging South Africa is discussed and dissected. Political violence is viewed as any act of destruction which impacts on the power relations of society. Its main incidence is two-fold — violent action by the white group to enforce and maintain an unjust social order, and reactive violence by others, mainly black, against the injustice and domination of whites who attempt to impose apartheid.

In this situation of civil war, or low-intensity conflict, different strategies are utilized by opposing parties. The white power group has over time acted to militarize society, so that there has been the spread of militarization as an ideology and the expansion of the influence and power of the military as a social institution enforcing apartheid advantage and disadvantage. On the opposing side, violent response to state coercion has been viewed as a 'people's war', legitimated as the only remaining response to state oppression, or as 'meeting the repressive violence of the state with the revolutionary power of the people'.

While it is true that in early 1990 President De Klerk took steps to reduce the role and power of the military, and that the African National Congress (ANC) agreed to partially suspend acts of violence by its military wing, Umkhonto we Sizwe, the apparatus of violence on both sides remains intact, even if temporarily under-used: the security legislation and legislation protecting the military and the police remains in force, as does the military organization of the South African Defence Force (SADF); similarly, Umkhonto we Sizwe remains on 'hold', ready to be reactivated.

While the principal protagonists on the stage of violent action, the state and the ANC, are warily testing each other's sincerity in exploratory moves towards negotiation, other players in the violence have not been inactive: for example, 'vigilantes' and 'comrades' still violently oppose each other in some townships, and in Natal the battles between Inkatha and the United Democratic Front (UDF) have resulted in increasing bloodshed and destruction.

All of these aspects are reflected in Chapter 2, which attempts to provide a conceptual framework within which to understand the nature of South African political violence and the mechanisms and philosophies which undergird it. Also identified are the agents of violence and the means by which violence is expressed. From the state, these embrace capital punishment, including the execution of people found guilty of political crimes (temporarily suspended at the time of writing); the use of 'death squads', either official or unofficial — which are under the scrutiny of the Harms Commission at the time of writing; 'legal' police killings in the control and dispersion of riotous and potentially riotous crowds; detention without trial in terms of emergency and security legislation, and sometimes also the torture of detainees; and, allegedly, arson and armed attacks against anti-apartheid organizations and their premises. From 'resistance' organizations, there have been assassinations of state agents and 'collaborators', arson and armed attacks against security and civilian targets, and the horrifying 'necklacing' of black political collaborators, persons suspected of witchcraft, and others.

But what is the part played by the law in enabling violence, especially violence by the state? The emergency and security legislation protects many police and military actions, yet other non-emergency legislation exists that is part and parcel of the ordinary law regulating the functioning of people in society, and which reinforces violence as an acceptable and justified retaliation by the state against individuals who have committed a crime. Put simply, there are 'ordinary' laws which enable the state to model to its citizens the use of violence as a means of responding to anti-social, criminal behaviour.

These laws, their application, and their consequences are the focus of Chapter 3, where the use of corporal and capital punishment is examined. South Africa is one of a shrinking number of countries which purportedly subscribe to Christian and westernized values, yet which exercise institutional violence, or violence sanctioned by the criminal law. Corporal punishment is authorized for a wide range of offences, and can be applied under prescribed circumstances to adults as well as juveniles. Capital punishment — the death penalty — is also applicable as a legal punishment for an unusually broad list of offences, so much so that until 1989 South Africa was amongst the world leaders in legal killings. Although the execution of persons sentenced to death was temporarily suspended by President De Klerk in early 1990, and although the practice of capital punishment is currently under official review, it remains an integral feature of the criminal justice system.

Two issues concerning corporal and capital punishment in South Africa merit special note, since both are related to the pattern of political violence mentioned earlier.

First, there exists evidence to suggest that both corporal and capital punishment are more likely to be applied to blacks than to whites. In the case of corporal punishment, this may in part be due to a dearth of alternative resources for the punishment of blacks; in apartheid South Africa, discrimination and inequality extend into the means of disciplining offenders too. In the instance of capital punishment, statistics suggest a racial bias in the handing down of death sentences. Africans are most likely to hang, and, moreover, most of them are from backgrounds of poverty and social disadvantage.

Second, there is extensive evidence to suggest that both corporal and capital punishment are increasingly used as means of control in times of social and political upheaval. For example, changes were made to the criminal law in 1986 to permit rebellious behaviour to be met by physical violence, in that whipping was made a competent sentence for offenders convicted of public violence. In the same way, during the 1980s the courts determined that the doctrine of 'common purpose' could be extended to include murder convictions for participants in acts of public violence in which murder occurred.

Three conclusions emerge from these facts: whipping and executions seem to have become a basic part of state repression in South Africa; legal violence is used to 'control' public violence, so that violence begets violence; and state actions exemplify to South Africans a policy and practice that negates bodily integrity and the sanctity of life.

While there is no empirically-validated direct causal link between the violent nature of the South African state and interpersonal violence between South African people in their day-to-day living, there is sufficient evidence to suggest very strongly that such a link exists. Chapters 4 and 5 explore this circumstance, first through a discussion of rape, and then through a consideration of violence in sport.

In Chapter 4, rape is examined as a crime of violence. Twenty thousand rapes are reported to the police in South Africa each year, and since it is reliably estimated that only 5 per cent of rapes are officially reported, the actual number is possibly up to twenty times greater.

Based upon information obtained from interviews with rapists themselves, the chapter shows that rapists are 'normal' men, and that most were known to their victims prior to the act. While much of the study makes horrifying reading, some of the author's conclusions are highly pertinent to understanding this form of interpersonal violence. Although there are often personal experiences that may incline a man to rape, the act of rape is facilitated by social circumstances in two ways. First, South Africa is a sexist society, with certain qualities being ascribed to ideal gender roles, for example, men being dominant and assertive, and women being weak, docile, and submissive. These values are modelled to many men in their family of origin and in the mass media, and are reinforced by peer-group interaction. Second, and complementing the former situation, there is a widespread societal attitude that the physical violation of rape is 'not serious' and that it is 'invited' by the victim.

It thus becomes possible for a rapist to 'justify' his act of violence by perceiving the meeting of his sexual tension as more important than any rights of his female victim, who in any event is degraded in his mind into an object to serve his sexual gratification. Because the victim is unwilling, violent force is used, and coercion serves as a means of resolving tension and fulfilling desire. The nature of the rapist's act reflects in many ways the nature and values of his social environment: resolving tension through violence is typical of broader South African society.

Chapter 5 deals with sport, ostensibly 'a pleasant pastime, an amusement, a diversion', and widely regarded as having the potential to encourage self-discovery and self-fulfillment. Yet sport is also universally acknowledged to have the purpose of training sportspersons to develop attributes needed for socially-approved life roles in other, less playful contexts, a sentiment encapsulated in the statement that 'Waterloo was won on the playing fields of Eton'. Hence, sport has other functions besides play and recreation, and these are explored in detail in the chapter.

Violence in sport can be introduced by competitors, officials, spectators, administrators, sponsors, the media, the government, or any party with some form of active or passive interest, but it cannot survive without condonation, approval, or support. Condonation can be reflected in ways such as little or no action by officials to penalize sports violence; approval may be evinced by spectator applause for 'blood' and adulation of players who win 'at all costs', even if part of the cost is violence; and support may be shown by the violent player's family, peers, coaches, and public when they justify the use of violence in sports such as rugby with sentiments such as 'it's a man's game' ... 'it separates the men from the boys'.

In the chapter, the nature and extent of known violence in South African sport is documented, and theories which can assist to explain it are analysed and evaluated. Three of the conclusions which may be drawn from the chapter have significance for the understanding of violence in South Africa. First, violence in sport is learned behaviour, and it survives principally because it is positively reinforced overtly or tacitly, and not sufficiently punished. Second, while the level of violence in some sports, such as rugby, is dangerously high, in other sports — for example soccer — the level of violence is low by international standards, and gross spectator violence is minimal in comparison with many other countries. Third, the paradox of high violence in some sports and little violence in others may be explained by a closer examination of them. Rugby, which Dr Danie Craven says is 'being ruined by violence', is an amateur activity, mainly white, and is characterized by an acceptance of violence to the extent that it is seldom punished in any serious way. Soccer, on the other hand, is professionally-organized, multiracial, and heavy penalties are imposed for any violence which occurs. Can it be that rugby, a mainly white activity that has been raised to the level of a near-religion by the South African ruling group, is violent because it is not only a ritualized substitute for warfare, but also a means of training young males for their dominant role in society and, in South Africa, for the coercion which they will be required to exercise in enforcing and perpetuating white hegemony?

Amongst the principal themes running through Part 2 of this book are that violence is accepted as being normal and ordinary in South African society at both macro and micro levels; that violent behaviour is almost always learned behaviour; that violence, when used, generates more violence; and that the unjust arrangement of South African society is perhaps a major root cause of much of the violence: the perpetuation and enforcement of apartheid advantage and disadvantage requires violence to sustain it, and stimulates reactive violence in opposition to it. Moreover, the injustice of apartheid permeates down to all levels to contaminate and pervert social organization, the quality of life, and the values of all South Africans, black and white.

2 Political violence

J. Cock

Political violence is increasing in South Africa and is a current distinguishing feature of both state repression and resistance to the state. An estimated 3 500 people have died in incidents of political violence between 1984 and early 1989.[1] This violence is classified very differently by different people. Some refer to it as terrorism or criminality, or the inevitable outcome of genetic programming or tribal enmities. Others view such violence as acts of war. Commenting on the bomb explosion in August 1988 at Hyde Park Corner, Johannesburg, one of the country's richest shopping areas, Harry Schwartz said:

> This blast, in one of the country's richest shopping centres, brings the war to the Northern Suburbs. It also brings home to the people in our upper echelons the reality of South Africa, and makes us conscious that we live in a society which is terrorized (*The Sunday Star*, 14 August 1988).

This quotation highlights a number of key questions. Are African National Congress (ANC) bombings acts of terrorism, or are they part of a war of liberation? Does the present violent conflict in contemporary South Africa indeed constitute a 'war'? What are the main forms and agencies of violence in this conflict? These are crucial questions in any discussion of political violence in contemporary South Africa.

VIOLENCE AND TERRORISM

The phrase 'political violence' is used in this chapter to mean acts of destruction that impact on power relations in society. 'Terrorism' is used here to mean a strategy of political violence that involves systematic acts of destruction aimed at altering or maintaining power relations through spreading extreme fear. Terrorism is usually defined as political violence exercised by one's opponents.[2] Other definitions are anchored in a distinction between military and civilian personnel. For example:

> Terrorism is acts of intimidation, injuring unarmed, presumably innocent civilians (Said, 1988: 50).

> Terrorism is political violence directed against non-combatants (Craig Williamson, interviewed on 'Network', SABC-TV, 11 September 1988).

The notion of 'non-combatants' and 'civilians' rests upon a precise demarcation of the battlefield. This is difficult to draw in revolutionary situations.

Terrorism is also said to operate outside of international law and definitions of human rights:

> Terrorists kill and maim defenseless men, women and children, while freedom fighters seek to adhere to international law and civilized standards of conduct (George Bush, quoted in *Weekly Mail*, 13 January 1989).

In this sense, terrorism is anarchic and devoid of moral content. Rich argues that it is the features of amorality and unpredictability of terrorism that distinguish it from 'guerrilla warfare':

> In its assumption that the use of armed force against state power is a logical extension of existing political objectives, guerrilla warfare exhibits a far greater degree of predictability and political morality than terrorism (Rich, 1984: 80).

VIOLENCE AND WAR

The ANC presents its strategy of 'armed struggle' as a form of guerrilla warfare. The ANC has been described as:

> … the most Quixotic guerrilla organization of modern times. Its leadership endorses violence, but with manifest reluctance and an aversion to terrorist tactics … (Davis, 1987: 203).

'Armed struggle' is said to be one phase of a much wider strategy of political mobilization culminating in the notion of 'people's war', which the ANC adopted at its Kabwe Conference in 1985. The ANC leadership has often argued that this 'people's war' is informed by moral considerations. Firstly, in relation to the purpose of the war:

> We are fighting a war of liberation against the apartheid regime and against colonialism of a very special type. We have continuously restrained the oppressed people from allowing themselves to be put into a position where they will find themselves fighting a racial

war (Jacob Zuma, giving evidence on commission in London, *The Star*, 7 October 1988).

Furthermore, the leadership has repeatedly affirmed that the methods to be employed in this 'war of liberation' must be informed by moral restraints, which exclude attacks on civilian targets:

> The National Executive Committee [NEC] hereby underscores that it is contrary to our policy to select targets whose sole objective is to strike at civilians. Our morality as revolutionaries dictates that we respect the values underpinning the humane conduct of war (NEC statement quoted by Kasrils, giving evidence on commission in London, *New Nation*, 6 October 1988).

Oliver Tambo has signed a protocol of the Geneva Convention binding the ANC to avoid attacks on civilian targets and to 'humanitarian conduct of the war'. This is said to be the first time a guerrilla group has ever done so (Davis, 1987: 122).

Moral considerations are sometimes cited by members of the ANC's military wing, Umkhonto we Sizwe (MK) — Spear of the Nation, to underline their status as 'soldiers' as opposed to 'terrorists': 'I am a soldier trained to shoot other soldiers. I was trained in guns, the weapons of soldiers' (Interview with an awaiting trial prisoner, 1988). Asked if he would place a bomb in a shopping centre and risk killing civilians if ordered to do so, this informant replied, 'The ANC would not give such an order. They told us we should not hurt civilians' (Interview, 1988).

Nevertheless, the bombing of civilian or 'soft' targets occurred on an increasing scale in 1988, as did attacks on military and police targets.

In a recent treason trial, Brigadier Hermanus Stadler maintained that the ANC cannot be regarded as being at war with the South African government. Instead, the government is facing a 'revolutionary onslaught' (*The Star*, 2 August 1988). In another treason trial, Brigadier Stadler said that South Africa was at war with Angola, but that inside South Africa, only acts of terror took place. He said that the security police regarded 'these acts of terror as criminal actions and not actions of war. There is a definite difference between terror and war' (*The Star*, 29 November 1989).

In a different court case in 1988, the state did describe itself as at war. In this case, the state's argument was that the South African Defence Force (SADF) was beyond the reach of the courts and outside the law. In this application, the End Conscription Campaign (ECC) brought a Supreme Court action against the SADF to restrain it from illegally harassing the organization. Lieutenant-General Jan van Loggerenberg, former Chief of Staff (Operations) and now Chief of the Air Force, said in an affidavit that the SADF was on a 'war footing' (*Weekly Mail*, 2 September 1988).

While Hannah Arendt's 1970 definition of war as the 'massification of violence' implies a simple relation between war and violence, it is clear that the conflict in South Africa does not easily fit into other conventional definitions. For example:

> Warfare is socially organised physical coercion against a similarly organised opponent (Kaldor, 1982: 263).

> War is an open armed conflict in which: regular, uniformed forces are engaged, on at least one side; the fighters and the fighting are organised centrally to some extent; and there is continuity between armed clashes (Kidron & Smith, 1983: 6).

MK and the SADF are not 'similarly socially organized opponents'. Nor is there 'continuity between armed clashes'. Much of the violent confrontation is episodic. Clearly one of the sites of struggle in contemporary South Africa is the definition of the struggle itself.

In this chapter the conflict in South Africa is understood as a low-level civil war, or a situation of 'low intensity conflict'. Low intensity conflict is one point along a spectrum which includes conventional war through to nuclear, or high intensity, war. War is thus viewed along a continuum of violent conflict.

However, the term 'low intensity conflict' may also be used to describe a counter-insurgency strategy. This is a military strategy; a blueprint to defeat liberation movements without engaging in a full-scale conventional war. It involves the mobilization of resources at political, economic, and ideological levels.

This mobilization of resources has occurred in South Africa. The impetus to this process is increasing resistance to minority rule and the apartheid system. From about 1975, SADF personnel referred to a 'total onslaught' against the South African state. The state's response of 'total strategy' provided the basis for legitimizing an increasing military involvement in all spheres of decision-making. In this sense total strategy was the launch-pad for the militarization of South African society.

SOUTH AFRICA AS A MILITARIZED SOCIETY

'Militarization' implies a distinction between three related phenomena:

1. The military as a social institution; a set of social relationships organized around war, and taking the shape of an armed force.

2. Militarism as an ideology. The key component of this is an accep-
    tance of organized state violence as a legitimate solution to conflict.
    Other components involve a glorification of war in terms of which
    actors and encounters are portrayed in heroic terms, and an accep-
    tance of what has been called 'military values' — hierarchy, dis-
    cipline, obedience and the centralization of authority (Merryfinch,
    1981: 9).

3. Militarization as a social process that involves a mobilization of
    resources for war at political, economic, and ideological levels.

These phenomena are closely related. Militarization involves both the
spread of militarism as an ideology and an expansion of the power and
influence of the military as a social institution.

Some writers have tried to conceptualize this expansion in notions of
the 'military-industrial-technological-bureaucratic complex' (Eide &
Thee, 1980), or the 'military-industrial complex'. Williams refers to this
as:

> … an organised grouping of arms production, military research and
> state-security interests which has, in effect, moved beyond the
> control of civil society, and is the true contemporary form of the
> state itself (Williams, 1985: 224).

Other writers are critical of concepts which attempt to delimit the
problem. For example:

> We speak of 'the military-industrial complex' or of the 'military
> sector' or 'interest' of the arms lobby. This suggests that the evil is
> confined in a known and limited place: it may threaten to push
> forward but it can be restrained, contamination does not extend
> through the whole societal body (Thompson, 1982: 21).

This notion of contamination is the crucial insight in Thompson's
analysis. He concludes that '… the USA and the USSR do not have
military-industrial complexes, they are such complexes' (Thompson,
1982). Similarly, Bahro has lamented that 'our whole social organism is
riddled by the disease of militarism' (Bahro, 1982: 89).

It is tempting to analyse South African society in terms of these concepts
of 'contamination' and 'saturation'. However, one of the difficulties with
this approach is that the notions become too broad and inclusive to have
any analytical usefulness. 'Militarization' becomes a kind of 'hold-all' into
which everything negative and repressive about South African society is
thrown.

The approach followed here is to ground analysis in a particular social
process — militarization. The SADF has played a crucial part in the

mobilization of resources for war that this involves. This is clear at political, economic, and ideological levels.

At the economic level, militarization is indicated by an until recently expanding armaments industry and growing links between the SADF and the private sector. The pressure of an arms embargo and increasing sanctions stimulated the development of Armscor, which is now the third largest corporation in South Africa, and the fifth largest arms producer in the world (*The Star*, 7 November 1988). There are important links between the SADF and private industry through a reliance on Defence Force contracts and institutional co-operation in apparatuses such as the Defence Manpower Liaison Committees set up in 1982 to discuss the allocation of human resources, and the National Key Points Committee that oversees the protection of non-military installations that are considered vital for state security. Furthermore, South Africa's defence budget has risen in recent years and now absorbs a large percentage of total government expenditure. According to Frankel, 'Since the beginning of the eighties, roughly 20 per cent of total government expenditure has been fed into the Defence Force' (Frankel, 1984: 73). In June 1987 the defence budget was increased by 30 per cent over that of 1986 to R6 683 billion. Most analysts agree that the real total is much larger. One estimate is that the total security force expenditure is closer to R15 billion, or about 28 per cent of the national budget (*Weekly Mail*, 15 July 1988).

At the ideological level, militarism is hegemonic in South Africa. Militarism involves 'a set of attitudes and practices which regards war and the preparation for war as a normal and desirable social activity' (Mann, 1987: 35). This ideology is promoted through the state-controlled education system and the state-owned radio and television networks. It is linked to consumerist militarism, which is evident in the popularity of war toys, games, parades, displays, and films which glorify military encounters and power. The effect is to encourage South Africans to accept and share the state's definition of and solutions to conflict.

At the political level, militarization is indicated by the increasing use of the SADF to protect white minority rule, and in the power of the military in decision-making. It is generally agreed by analysts that the military have come to be positioned at the centre of state decision-making. For example, Frankel maintains that:

> ... militarization is always measured by the appearance of soldiers as public decision-makers, and the growing influence of the South African military is finally, and perhaps most importantly, reflected in the penetration of top government institutions by Defence Force personnel, on either a formal or informal basis (Frankel, 1984: 103).

Vale took this further in 1988 to argue that the military constituted an extra-parliamentary government which actually ruled South Africa (*The Star*, 12 February 1988).

However, the militarization of the state may be open and explicit, or it may take more indirect, 'subterranean' forms. In the latter case, 'the armed forces do not occupy the front line in the political sense. They do not govern directly, but exercise rather tight control over the formal holders of power' (Lowy & Sadler, 1985: 9).

In the South African case, this control has until recently operated through the National Security Management System (NSMS). The most significant site of power within the NSMS has been the State Security Council (SSC), which, until recently, replaced the cabinet as the most influential decision-making body (Grundy, 1987). The NSMS gave the military direct influence in decision-making down to local government. At a regional level this operated through Joint Management Centres (JMCs), which co-ordinated local strategies to deal with potential security problems. Eleven out of twelve JMC chairmen were SADF officers. There were 60 sub-JMCs which worked alongside the Regional Service Councils (RSCs), and 350 mini-JMCs at the local level. The bottom level was the Local Management Centre headed by the South African Police (SAP) station commander and the SADF company commander. Thus the reality was a massive network of some 500 secret committees operating under the control and direct chairmanship of the police and Defence Force. However, President De Klerk has recently down-graded the SSC to the level of a cabinet sub-committee, and moved to dismantle the NSMS structure.

The SADF has increasingly been used to maintain minority rule and the apartheid system. In this process of repression, the Defence Force has come to be an important agency of political violence.

AGENCIES OF VIOLENCE

During 1984–6, violence escalated in many of South Africa's black townships. The immediate trigger event was the implementation of the tricameral parliamentary system, which came into force in September 1984, and incorporated 'coloureds' and Indians, but excluded Africans altogether (Baynham, 1987). The SADF was sent into a number of townships, ostensibly to contain this violence. During 1985 alone, 35 000 troops were used in townships throughout the country. In October 1984, army units joined the police in patrolling Soweto. This was followed by Operation Palmiet, when 7 000 soldiers sealed off the township of

Sebokeng, carrying out house-to-house searches and making at least 350 arrests. This represented a strategic shift away from a reliance on the police force alone to maintain what the state called 'law and order'. Since that time, the SADF has been used extensively in internal repression in diverse areas of black experience such as health, housing, labour, and education. The army has been employed in evicting rent defaulters in an effort to break the rent boycott, and has occupied classrooms in an effort to break the schools boycott. In August 1985, 800 children, some only seven years old, were arrested after a curfew was declared forcing Soweto children to stay inside classrooms during school hours. In 1986, this was enforced by the occupation of black schools by white soldiers, and 'stories of children even having a military escort to visit the lavatory were not uncommon' (Hawarden, 1987). The SADF has been deployed to guard polling booths, invade health clinics to identify the injured, and maintain beach apartheid; and in forced removals, monitoring demonstrations, suppressing resistance to homeland independence, organizing student registration at Turfloop University, and strike-breaking.

There is a good deal of evidence of SADF violence directed against township residents generally, and young people particularly, during the 1984–6 period. The Detainees' Parents Support Committee (DPSC) reported a pattern which involved soldiers picking children off the street at random, and holding them for several hours in military vehicles or in remote areas of veld. The children have described being beaten with fists and rifle butts and even being subjected to electric shock treatment.

During this period, the SADF often acted together with the SAP. Their activities were indistinguishable to many township residents as they fused in a pattern of indiscriminate violence. One Crossroads squatter commented:

> Today's army is lions. They hate a person. If one of the police or army come towards you, you are so scared. You know that the first thing they may do is beat you up and then shoot you (*Out of Step*, May 1987).

It was the arbitrary and indiscriminate nature of the violence that intensified the spread of extreme fear:

> In our streets, one day it's all right. The next day you can cross the street when a Casspir [police vehicle] comes round the corner, and you'll die. It's like Beirut (A Soweto resident, quoted in *The Sunday Star*, 8 September 1985).

The degree to which the SADF and the SAP were linked in this period in suppressing black resistance is an important indicator both of the level of violent conflict in this society and of the role of the SADF within that conflict. This role changed in 1986 as surrogate forces in the shape of vigilantes and municipal constables came to be the agents of violence and fear.

Vigilantes first emerged in 1985 as organized and conservative groups acting violently against anti-apartheid forces (Haysom, 1989). Their violent actions have been markedly to the advantage of the South African state. However:

> ... it is virtually impossible to establish the actual links between vigilantes and the state, more so under the emergency restrictions which effectively permit vigilante activity to go unreported. Nevertheless there is growing evidence which suggests tacit and active approval by the state for vigilante groups (Levin, 1987: 26).

Such evidence relates to diverse areas, such as Crossroads, Kwanobuhle, and Queenstown, as over the past years vigilante attacks on progressive community organizations and leaders have become common across the country. The effect of vigilante groups is to disorganize and destabilize such organizations and individuals. Haysom (1989) points out that this effect holds whether the police actively sanction and support the vigilantes, or whether they appear incapable of curbing or reluctant to curb vigilante activities.

The violent actions of the 'Witdoeke' vigilante group in Crossroads is well known, and their open support from the police is well documented (Cole, 1987). Another case study which illustrates how vigilantes operate violently without legal consequences is the community of Leandra, a black township on the East Rand. Residents had been involved in a grassroots campaign to prevent their forced removal, which enjoyed such popular support that the authorities were forced to negotiate with one of the residents' association leaders, Chief Mayise. Vigilante attacks culminated in a mob assault on Chief Mayise's house in January 1986, during which he was hacked to death. To date, no one has been prosecuted for this killing. This illustrates how vigilante groups disorganize and destabilize opposition through spreading violence and extreme fear.

The reliance on vigilantes as a disorganizing force represents a shift away from a reliance on the SADF and the SAP to suppress black resistance. It is crucial to appreciate that this shift is part of a military strategy — a strategy of counter-insurgency (McCuen, 1966; Saul, 1987). The vigilante phenomenon illustrates both the neutralization of opponents and the use of surrogate forces that are key elements of this strategy. However, the use of surrogate forces also extends to new forms of policing.

This involved two new police forces deployed in 1986 at the height of the uprising against the apartheid state. An additional 16 000 'kitskonstabels' (special constables) and municipal policemen were added to the police force.

These hastily trained black policemen were deployed in large groups in all areas where resistance was strong. From the beginning they used excessive violence. Their brutality created an atmosphere of fear that was aimed not only at activists but at intimidating entire communities. The behaviour of the new police is characterized by an arrogant disregard for the law (Catholic Institution for International Relations (CIIR), 1988: 13–14).

A township resident describes them as follows: '... they are the dogs of the SAP doing all their hunting and watching' (CIIR, 1988: 19).

In some communities the new police forces established what the CIIR publication describes as 'a reign of terror'. The violence involved both systematic torture and beatings. For example, Mr VB of Duncan Village (an African township near East London) was bundled into a van driven by a municipal policeman and, in his own words:

I was taken into a building where I was instructed to lie on my stomach. Three policemen wielding metal bars then struck me on the back. When they hit me, I tried to jump up. I grabbed one of them and pleaded with him to help me as I did not know where the firearm was. Another one grabbed me by the throat and choked me. I lost consciousness. When I woke up I was lying beneath a tap with water running over me.

After more interrogation, Mr VB was burned with cigarettes on the arm and foot (CIIR, 1988: 61).

Clearly, the effect of this type of violence is to spread extreme fear. This fear becomes widespread when the pattern of violence is arbitrary, and seems to be directed not only against anti-apartheid activists, but also against ordinary township residents, as this statement by a Duncan Village resident shows:

One day I came home late from work. It was 6.30 pm. A taxi stopped near my house and a woman got out. She was carrying a lot of parcels and as she passed my house some 'greenflies' [municipal police] stopped her. They just started beating her with sjamboks. She cried out to them, 'What have I done? I have come from work'. They gave no reply. The 'greenflies' saw that I was watching this, and they told me to go inside my house. The woman had dropped her parcels and her groceries were lying all over the street ... you just can't send your children to the shop after half-past six any more. It seems that is how they want to control the townships. They want the people off the streets (CIIR, 1988: 53).

This arbitrary and indiscriminate pattern of violence that generates widespread fear is also reported from Bhongolethu, a black township outside Oudtshoorn. It has been reported that 'a feeling of constant fear of assault by constables was widespread' (CIIR, 1988: 37). Similar reports come from Van Eyk, who writes of 'a campaign of terror' being waged by black policemen against township residents in Valhalla Park and Elsies River, and who states:

> We heard detailed eye-witness accounts from ordinary people: men, women and children being sjambokked viciously for no other reason than being outside their homes; of a young woman seriously wounded by buckshot while trying to get into her own yard, of a boy shot dead at point blank range (Van Eyk, 1989: 19–20).

When the fear of arbitrary imprisonment is added to a fear of assault, the effect is to freeze anti-apartheid activity. A municipal policeman interviewed in the Eastern Cape is reported to have said, '… now everyone is afraid of going to jail without any reason, no one is causing trouble' (CIIR, 1988: 1).

During the period 1984–6, many black South African townships were re-constituted into what Walzer (1978) has termed 'zones of terror'. Within these areas, relationships were structured around violence and fear. It is important to note that the violence and fear was largely confined to these areas. Outside the townships, power relations followed the conventional rules of authority for most people not involved in anti-apartheid activities.

However, the SADF, the SAP, vigilantes, municipal policemen, and kitskonstabels have not been the only agencies of violence and fear. In 1988, Pietermaritzburg was described as 'the battleground in a war' (Van Holdt, 1988: 16). The 'war' has been fought between Inkatha and United Democratic Front (UDF)/Congress of South African Trade Unions (Cosatu) supporters, and between September 1987 and February 1989 there were 668 deaths (*The Citizen*, 10 February 1989). Both sides have been implicated in many violent acts, and it is clear that both groupings have considerable grassroots support. However, there have been numerous affidavits filed in court applications suggesting SAP support for Inkatha vigilantes. Despite the numerous affidavits filed against Inkatha office-bearers alleging arson, assault, and murder, and also despite the granting of court interdicts against such office-bearers, most of the respondents have not been arrested or charged. Chief Gatsha Buthelezi now speaks of a 'black civil war', but the state also has to take responsibility for the banning and restricting of UDF organizations and individuals, which made peace negotiations impossible (*New Nation*, 12 January 1989).

These restrictions were intensified by the South African government's declaration of a state of emergency in 1985. The Emergency Regulations were intended to break the spiralling cycle of violence, but many analysts agree that such restrictions, added to conditions of extreme material deprivation, underlie much of the violence in Natal.

It has been estimated that 70 people were killed, 150 injured, and 60 houses damaged in violence in the Inanda and Inanda-Newtown area between April and December 1988, and in January 1989 township residents in the region were reported to be 'happy' that the army had been sent into the area because this had afforded them some protection (*The Star*, 23 January 1989). At the same time, it was reported that the main obstacle to ending the violence in the area was that 'meetings were not allowed'. As one resident explained: 'We were told by the army people that a meeting of more than five people is illegal, so we can't get together to talk about possible solutions' (*The Star*, 23 January 1989). In response to this, the National Organization of Women called for a concerted effort to provide adequate housing, schools, health services, and employment opportunities; to bring action against vigilantes; and for the unbanning and lifting of restrictions on UDF and Cosatu so that they could be involved in efforts to end the violence (*The Star*, 23 January 1989). This emphasis on negotiation and the improvement of material conditions points us towards the only possible solutions to the present pattern of political violence.

There are two main agencies of 'resistance violence' in contemporary South Africa. It has been estimated that the ANC has 8 000 to 10 000 trained guerrillas in Umkhonto we Sizwe (*City Press*, 12 January 1986; Davis, 1987; Lodge, 1983). Much ANC guerrilla violence has been directed against military and collaborationist targets. These have included some elaborate and spectacular missions, such as the bombings at the Sasol oil-from-coal plant, the rocket attack on Voortrekkerhoogte military base, and the explosions at the Koeberg nuclear power complex, which caused damage in excess of $40 million (Davis, 1987). However, in an analysis of the six-year period following the 1976 Soweto uprising, Lodge found that only 2 per cent of guerrilla attacks were aimed at SADF targets. By contrast, 37 per cent involved sabotage of key economic objectives such as railway machinery and industrial facilities, and 17 per cent involved assaults on government buildings and police stations (*Rand Daily Mail*, 21 December 1982, cited by Davis, 1987: 147).

The second agency of resistance or counter-violence is 'the comrades', mainly unemployed township youth. They have tried to neutralize state control of the townships, and have perpetrated some cruel acts of political violence in the name of the liberation struggle. These acts have included the burning and stoning to death of suspected informers and 'collaborators'. There were almost 400 'necklace' murders between 1984 and 1987, and some of the perpetrators were amongst those on 'death row' in early 1989.

One of these was Paul Tefo Setlaba, a member of the Colesberg Youth Organization, who was sentenced to death on 10 December 1986 for his role in the burning to death of a woman who broke the Colesberg consumer boycott. Setlaba was reported as having undergone a 'personality change' after his friend was shot by police in July 1985 (Black Sash, 1989: 20). Setlaba was detained under the Emergency Regulations for five months in 1986. Apparently this detention affected him a great deal: 'It was when he needed to support his girlfriend who was carrying his child, and he could not go to look for work' (Black Sash, 1989). In his judgment in Setlaba's case, Mr Justice Kannemeyer said that in September 1985 a consumer boycott was being observed by the black community in Colesberg. On 21 September, Mrs Julia Dilato bought some meat from a butchery in defiance of the boycott. When she took the meat back to the township, she was stopped by the 'comrades', who were enforcing the boycott. The meat was thrown to the ground and stamped on. Mrs Dilato reported this incident to the police, and thereafter she was considered to be an 'impimpi' (informer). On 24 September her house was stoned, and on 2 October she was set upon by a group of people on her way to work. Petrol was poured over her, she was set alight, and burned to death.

This horrifying incident highlights a number of important themes. Firstly, it points to the violent and punitive action taken in some townships to enforce political compliance. Such action was common during the 1985 consumer boycott of white-owned shops. Many of the victims of these tactics were African women who were subjected to cruel treatment. For instance, a case was reported of a woman who went into town and bought fresh meat, and who was made to eat it raw. Another was made to swallow a whole bottle of cooking oil (Cock, 1987: 139). Secondly, the Setlaba case illustrates a worrying aspect of state violence. The trial, which took place in Graaf-Reinet, lasted only three days. This has raised doubts among many legal people about the adequacy of the legal process involved in the death penalty.

An increasing number of death penalties involve political offences. According to official figures, a total of 101 people were sentenced to death for 'unrest-related incidents' in the period 1985–8. Among the Black Sash's small sample of people on death row in early 1989, almost half (47 per cent) had been found guilty in cases widely regarded as politically-related. Some of those hanged have been members of Umkhonto we Sizwe, and there have been pleas that such persons should be treated as prisoners of war in terms of the Geneva Convention.

One of this category on death row in early 1989 was the Messina trialist and MK guerrilla, Mthetheleli Mncube. He told the court that he had acted as a soldier. When he was captured by SADF soldiers, he had expected to be treated as a prisoner of war. Instead, he was stripped, put in the back of a truck, and the dead bodies of his shot comrades were piled on top of him. When he was transferred to another open truck shortly afterwards, he broke the shoe-laces with which his hands were tied, grabbed a rifle lying near him on the back of the truck, and fired into the cabin, killing two policemen. He said that any other soldier would have done the same in the circumstances (Black Sash, 1989: 30). Both Messina trialists said that when they originally left South Africa their intention had been to join the ANC to further their education. Both had changed their plans after commando raids on neighbouring African countries, which they believed to have been staged by the SADF. Mncube was in Matola, Mozambique, in 1981 when ANC men staying near him were killed in a raid.

One case where the imposition of the death penalty was considered by the judge was that of the 'Bethal trial', when Ebrahim, Dladla, and Maseko were sentenced to long terms of imprisonment. Ishmael Ebrahim's story will be used as a case study to point to some of the main forms of political violence in contemporary South Africa.

A CASE STUDY: ISHMAEL EBRAHIM

Ebrahim, one of the most senior members of the ANC to go on trial in recent years, was sentenced in January 1989 to twenty years imprisonment. He had been active in anti-apartheid politics since his early teens. He participated in the defiance campaigns of the early 1950s and was a delegate to the Congress of the People at Kliptown in 1955, at which the historic Freedom Charter was adopted. At this time, his political orientation was determinedly non-violent and he was a great admirer of Gandhi. The Sharpeville Massacre in 1960, when sixty-nine peaceful protesters were shot down by the police, and the banning of the ANC were key influences on him. His commitment was to 'the establishment of a free democratic society', but 'the banning of the ANC removed our hopes of achieving this through peaceful, non-violent means. A chapter closed in our history. We decided to fight rather than surrender. We decided to meet the repressive violence of the state with the revolutionary violence of the people' (Court statement).

It was at this point that Ebrahim joined Umkhonto we Sizwe. He was first convicted in 1964, when he was found guilty on three charges of sabotage: 'I was arrested in 1963, detained and tortured, and finally tried and sentenced to 15 years'. After his release from Robben Island, he was banned and heavily restricted. 'I was under constant police harassment and found it difficult to live a normal life. In 1980 I left South Africa illegally and went into exile.' In 1986, he was allegedly abducted by South African state agents from Swaziland.

> I was kidnapped from a foreign state by the South African security forces. At that point I was carrying an Indian passport, issued to me by the government of India. The lack of any judicial restraint has given the security forces of apartheid a free hand to continue their abductions with impunity. The violation of the borders of the neighbouring state, of its independence and sovereignty, is itself a great offence against international law and has in the past resulted in countries going to war. Kidnapping people and forcibly bringing them across the border fences into South Africa is an act of state terrorism (Court statement).

He said his abduction took place four days after the murder of a close friend, allegedly by the SAP, and the kidnapping from Swaziland of a Swiss couple, a Swazi woman, and a registered South African refugee. He asked:

> Are these abductions and murder not acts of state terrorism? We in the ANC never advocated a policy of murdering or abducting South African personnel abroad. Yet it is now the accepted policy of the South African security forces to assassinate and abduct the opponents of the apartheid regime in foreign lands (Court statement).

He said that his abduction was followed by police torture through the use of electronic sound 'to the point where I nearly lost my mind'.

On trial, he told the court that the use of violence was 'a painful necessity ... but there was no other way out. One hated the racist system and knew it was violent and found oneself forced to use force'. As a member of the ANC, he said that he supported all four pillars of the struggle — 'one of them, the armed struggle, inevitably involves violence and, in its ambit, includes white farmers on the borders, because they have become part and parcel of the defence machinery' (Court statement). The judge said that he did not impose the death sentence because no one had been killed by the landmines placed in these border areas.

The Ebrahim case points us to a number of different kinds of political violence.[3]

FORMS OF VIOLENCE
Capital punishment

This form of state violence has increased in recent years, although there was a decline in 1989. Amnesty International maintains that the death penalty was used in South Africa on 'an unprecedented scale' in 1987. In that year a total of 164 people were hanged, which represented a substantial increase from 115 in 1984, 137 in 1985, and 121 in 1986 (*Weekly Mail*, 1 December 1987). South Africa is a world leader in using the death penalty. The 1987 total was four times more than Iran, and thirty-two times more than China, both countries with much larger populations (Black Sash, 1989: 5). According to Lawyers for Human Rights, about 700 people were executed in South Africa between 1983 and 1988 (*New Nation*, 6 October 1988). Capital punishment is examined in detail in Chapter 3 of this book.

Death squads, assassinations, and disappearances

The murder and disappearance of prominent anti-apartheid activists, and the fact that their killers have not been brought to court, has provoked speculation that there are 'death squads' operating in South Africa. These are a familiar feature of some Latin American states, such as Colombia, El Salvador, Guatemala, and Peru. They are a means of obscuring the responsibility of the terrorist state for the violent acts it commits.

The assassination of apartheid's opponents outside the country is increasing. The assassinations go back to the parcel bomb which killed Abraham Tiro in Botswana in 1974, and include the attacks on Joe Gqabi, who was gunned down in his Harare home in 1980, Ruth First, and others. However, Moss has suggested that:

> … in the last few months action against opponents of apartheid — in particular ANC members — appears to have changed from random slaughter to a sustained campaign; from individual covert hits to generalized policy — a policy that would dovetail exactly with the statement: 'Wherever the ANC is, we will eliminate it' [a statement made by Magnus Malan on 19 February 1988]. Every

twelve days since the beginning of the year there has been at least one armed attack on an ANC member living outside South Africa (Moss, 1988: 25).

Death squads may be operating not only against ANC leaders in Europe and elsewhere, but in this country as well. Since the murder of the sociologist Rick Turner a decade ago there have been a number of unsolved political crimes. These include the killings of a number of anti-apartheid activists, such as four community leaders from Cradock (Matthew Goniwe, Fort Calata, Sparrow Mkhonto, and Sicelo Mhlawuli) in 1985, Fabian Ribeiro and his wife, who were killed in Mamelodi in 1986, and the Institute for a Democratic Alternative for South Africa (IDASA) director, Eric Mntonga, who was murdered in 1987. The DPSC worker Sicelo Dhlomo was killed mysteriously in 1988, along with ten other anti-apartheid activists, and in 1989, David Webster was assassinated. No one has yet been charged with the killings mentioned, but it is widely believed that the victims may have been killed by state agents acting in terms of the state's counter-revolutionary strategy as expressed by Major-General C. J. Lloyd, when he said, 'Sometimes you have to take out the revolutionaries if they are controlling the people' (*Christian Science Monitor*, 11 May 1988).

Substantiation for the existence of death squads operating within the state mechanism came in late 1989 from ex-policemen who claimed to have been part of such squads. Butana Nofamela, a convicted murderer on death row, admitted to involvement in another murder, that of Durban civil rights lawyer Griffiths Mxenge, who was assassinated at Umlazi Stadium in 1983. Nofamela claimed that the leader of the death squad concerned was former police captain Dirk Coetzee, and that a member was David Tshikalange. Coetzee and Tshikalange fled the country, but admitted their involvement, and, moreover, Coetzee alleged the complicity of senior police officers. Nofamela has been charged with the murder of Mr Mxenge, but no others have yet been charged with him, although warrants of arrest have been issued for Coetzee and Tshikalange. The allegations made by the ex-policemen were investigated by the Free State Attorney-General, Jim McNally, who reported his findings to the State President. The State President, after weeks of delay, appointed an independent judicial commission of inquiry into the allegations.

In addition to known deaths, there have also been a number of 'disappearances' of anti-apartheid activists, such as the Anglican Bishop of Lebombo, Denis Sengolane, who was reported missing in 1988, and at least three trade unionists. A recent disappearance is that of Stanza

Bopape, who was in detention when, according to the police, he escaped from custody.

At present, it is extremely difficult to prove connections with the state in many unsolved murders and disappearances. This also applies to Ebrahim's alleged kidnapping from Swaziland. Lured outside his home on the pretext of helping an individual with car trouble, Ebrahim was seized and brought to Pretoria in a sequence of events that strongly suggests state responsibility or sanction.

There have also been a number of assassinations of state agents. For example, a number of black policemen have been shot. This number includes Sergeant Chapi who, at the time of his death in 1978, was described in press reports as 'the most feared policeman in Soweto'. He allegedly played a prominent role in crushing the 1976 uprising (*New Nation*, 2 February 1989). On trial, the alleged killers of Chapi refused, as MK soldiers, to plead or to recognize the jurisdiction of the civilian court.

There have also been assassinations of state witnesses in political trials. What is distinctively different about these assassinations, as compared to the assassinations and disappearances of most of the anti-apartheid activists mentioned above, is that the killers are usually brought to court.

Legal police killings

Police killings have made South Africa notorious since 1961, when sixty-nine African protesters against the pass system were shot by the police in what has come to be widely known as the 'Sharpeville Massacre'. This was followed by the Soweto revolt, initiated on 16 June 1976, when around 10 000 students in Soweto protested against Bantu Education and met with police violence. Some sources put the death toll on that day at twenty-five, while others placed it nearer a hundred (Hirson, 1979: 184). The Soweto protest became an uprising that lasted a year, during which some 700 African people were killed. This was followed by the police shootings at Langa near Uitenhage, where twenty-one people were shot dead in March 1985.

South African police may shoot to kill in the defence of persons or property, to prevent the escape of certain subjects, or to effect the dispersion of a riotous and dangerous crowd. Police shootings have increased in South Africa in recent years. In 1987 more than 1 000 people were wounded or killed by the   SAP (*The Sunday Times*, 3 April 1988). Between September 1984 and May 1987, of the 2 517 civil unrest fatalities in South Africa, the security forces had killed 1 002 — 40 per cent of all deaths (Riordaan, 1988: 6).

Detention without trial

This way of 'neutralizing' political opponents is a familiar strategy of counter-insurgency, and has been used in many different social contexts. In South Africa, detention without trial has been lawful since the 1960s, but in recent years the numbers of people detained without trial has increased dramatically.

> From an estimated 1130 detentions in 1984, the figure rose to over 8,000 in the first seven month emergency period 1985/6. Since June 1986 approximately 30,000 people have been detained (DPSC, 1987: 101).

Altogether, an estimated 51 000 detentions took place between August 1984 and 1988, which is over 60 per cent of all the detentions which have occurred in South Africa since 1960 (Human Rights Commission, 1988). In January 1989, about 1 500 people were estimated to be in detention under the Emergency Regulations (*New Nation*, 2 February 1989).

Many of these detentions have involved extremely lengthy periods. For example, Christopher Ngcobo was detained on 15 June 1986. On that date:

> Christopher Ngcobo was asleep in Room 263 when about 200 men covered by balaclavas and brandishing rifles, surrounded Glynn Thomas dormitory in the middle of the night. They stormed the hallways of this residence for black students at the University of the Witwatersrand, forcing the monitor at gunpoint to open up rooms with his pass key. The security forces roused the sleeping students, tore off their blankets, and marched several of them, including Mr Ngcobo, into waiting vans (*The Christian Science Monitor*, 23 June 1988).

The violent and frightening circumstances of his arrest are significant. Christopher Ngcobo is one of some 200 people who spent over two years in detention. He was released in early 1989 with severe restriction orders.[4]

The main target of detention has been the UDF, where ordinary members as well as leadership figures have been detained. It is in this sense that detention has been random as well as prolonged. It does not seem to have been aimed at extracting information, as 'interviews with some 200 detainees [from the Eastern Cape] revealed that many were never questioned' (Roux & De Villiers, 1988).

The effectiveness of this destabilization strategy depends on the fear associated with detention without trial. This fear is well-founded given that approximately seventy detainees have died while in custody — the most well-known case being Steve Biko in September 1977. Many detainees are held in solitary confinement, which is an acknowledged form of torture. However, the forms of torture documented in South Africa extend further than isolation.

Torture

Torture is an important element of modern 'counter-revolutionary war'. Trinquier (one of the architects of the 'pacification' programme in the Casbah in Algiers) emphasized the necessity of this:

> Torture is not only considered as a means of obtaining information on clandestine networks, at any price, but also as a means for destroying every individual who is captured, as well as his or her sense of solidarity with an organisation or community (Trinquier, cited by Mattelart, 1979: 415).

Thus torture is an effective instrument of social atomization, a function which may be more important than obtaining information. As a destabilization strategy, this theory draws upon what Hitler wrote on psychological warfare in *Mein Kampf*: 'Our strategy consists in destroying the enemy from inside, and making him the instrument of his own conquest' (Quoted by Mattelart, 1979: 423). Guilt and isolation dislocate the individual from any sense of identification with the group. The outcome is an exaggerated individualism and sense of aloneness — it is in this sense that social organizations are fragmented and social relations atomized.

Torture is widely used in South Africa to achieve this. A study done at the University of Cape Town established that 85 per cent of a sample of 175 ex-detainees had suffered torture (Foster *et al.*, 1987). Among the forms of physical torture that have been detailed are assault, electric shock, suffocation, and immersion in cold water (DPSC, 'Memorandum on Security Police Abuses of Political Detainees', quoted in *The Star*, 1 August 1988). Ebrahim reported being subjected to a continuous pattern of electronic sound which 'almost destroyed his nervous system' (Interview with key informant, January 1989). The incidence and nature of torture of detainees is dealt with in detail in Chapters 14 and 15 of this book.

Arson and armed attacks

There have been numerous arson attacks in recent years. During the 1984–6 period particularly, hundreds of businesses, homes, churches, halls, some government offices, and cars and buses were destroyed in townships throughout South Africa. At least 2 000 people, many of them under the age of eighteen, are presently serving sentences for 'public violence', which often involved such attacks (US Report on Human Rights, quoted in *Weekly Mail*, 10 February 1989).

There have also been arson and bomb attacks on the homes of anti-apartheid activists and the headquarters of anti-apartheid organizations. In 1988 there were three serious attacks on such organizations, which significantly disrupted their work. In August 1988, a powerful bomb shattered the interior of Khotso House in Johannesburg, which housed the offices of the South African Council of Churches (SACC), the Black Sash, and other anti-apartheid organizations. In October 1988, a fire raged through Khanya House in Pretoria, the headquarters of the Southern African Catholic Bishops Conference (SACBC), after an explosion. In November, a firebomb exploded in the head office of the National Union of South African Students (Nusas), destroying files and causing considerable damage. To date, no one has been charged with these offences.

There is also an increasing pattern of armed attacks against the South African security forces — especially members of the SAP or municipal police. According to official statistics, a total of 238 of these guerrilla or terrorist attacks took place in the first ten months of 1988, compared with 234 during the whole of 1987, 230 in 1986, 136 in 1985, and 44 in 1984. This means that there was a 640 per cent increase in the number of attacks; from 3,6 per month in 1984 to 23,4 per month in 1988 (*Weekly Mail*, 23 December 1988).

In the month of January 1989 alone, 5 black policemen were killed and 36 wounded in AK-47 and hand-grenade attacks in Reef townships. The most dramatic attack took place in Katlehong on the East Rand, when four grenades were hurled at a group of 95 parading municipal policemen. One policeman was killed and 35 others were injured (*The Sunday Times*, 29 January 1989). According to the Minister of Law and Order, in the period February 1988 to January 1989 there was an increase of 215 per cent in the use of limpet mines, which were used in 139 ANC attacks. In the same period, there were 74 hand-grenade attacks, and 34 involving the use of AK-47 rifles. According to the Minister, a total of '284

ANC terrorists and collaborators had been arrested, and 48 killed by the security forces' (*The Citizen*, 10 February 1989).

A pattern has also emerged in which civilians, rather than security forces or security installations, have been the targets of bomb attacks. It is not clear who has been responsible for some of these attacks, such as a car bomb aimed at civilians leaving a rugby match, or limpet mines at a restaurant, sports club, amusement arcade, and art gallery. White right-wingers and MK cadres operating in defiance of discipline have been suggested. Davis (1987: 19) suggests that the ANC's decision to transfer combat responsibilities and to forego the benefit of close supervision 'brought the greater likelihood of home-grown soldiers carrying out attacks in the ANC's name but contrary to ANC guidelines'. The case of Andrew Zondo, sentenced to death for the Amanzimtoti bomb which killed five passers-by, illustrates some of the experience of the latter group (Meer, 1987).

'Necklacing'

This weapon of terror involves placing a motor-car tyre around the neck of a victim, filling it with petrol, and setting it alight. It has been described as 'the most singular and spectacular form of murder in living memory' (Ebersohn, 1987: 39). There were almost 400 necklace murders between 1984 and 1987, and another 200 people were burned to death (SAIRR, 1988: 23). The necklace murder is an African phenomenon, both perpetrators and victims being black.[5] Victims have included community councillors, policemen, suspected informers and collaborators, and women suspected of witchcraft. In a single 24-hour period, twenty aged and infirm women from the village of Makgadi in Sekukuniland died by the necklace. The 'necklace' has become a symbol of political violence in South Africa, a focus of attention in which the increasing pattern of state violence has become obscured.

A 'terrorist state'?

The scale of state violence is such that it raises the question of whether or not South Africa is a 'regime of terror' or a 'terrorist state'. The phrase 'terrorist state' appears to involve a contradiction in terms. 'Terrorism' is usually defined as illegitimate violence, and the source of legitimacy is conventionally defined as the state. However, Van der Vyver has argued that 'South Africa is now solidly in the grip of state terror violence' (1988: 70), and Riordaan (1988: 4) has similarly described the state strategies of repression as 'state terrorism'. However, it is important to note that if the

South African state maintains its authority largely by the spread of fear through an organized and sustained policy of violence, this is not practiced on a scale that is comparable to the situation in the South American countries that have been termed 'terrorist states'. The scale and intensity of terror is not comparable to the situation in El Salvador, for instance, where in 1980 there were over 10 000 killings of trade union leaders, peasant activists, teachers, students, professors, and journalists.[6]

CONCLUSION

In conclusion, it must be emphasized that we are clearly caught up in a spiralling pattern of repressive and revolutionary violence. This spiral is evident in some individual case histories, such as those of Sefala, Mncube, and Ebrahim, all of whom had witnessed or been subject to various forms of state repressive violence before turning to resistance violence. In this spiralling process, violence comes to be accepted as a legitimate solution to conflict.[7] This acceptance threatens to destroy our humanity; to erode our capacity for human/humane responses:

'I went into Lindile's yard and observed what was happening. I saw that people were attacking a man I knew as Peti. I saw that he was full of blood, I saw him fall. The people who were attacking him were the Comrades. Mtutu was hitting the deceased with a sword, so was Lunga Petros. Boy-boy had a small knife, he was stabbing the deceased. After a while it was obvious that the deceased would not be getting up again. The Comrades then left. We also went into one house and I had breakfast' (Court document, quoted by Riordaan, 1988).

This is a particularly clear example of brutalization. However, there is a very real danger that all of us will feel overwhelmed by the violence in our society, and withdraw into a kind of survival mentality. This involves an emotional anaesthesia, a disengagement from others, a retreat from social involvement into a private defensive core.[8] In South Africa, at present, the normalization of violence and atrocity threatens to blunt our human sensibilities.

The only solution to this escalating spiral of violence is in finding the courage to deal with its causes. The only hope for peace is in intervention to break the vicious circle of structural, reactive, and repressive violence. The starting point must be to eliminate the material inequalities and injustices upon which our society is structured. Even government spokespersons admit the violence-deprivation nexus:

If we are honest with ourselves we must admit that some of the violence which is seen in South Africa is due to the frustration which a large majority of the population experiences because their expectations are not satisfied (The Deputy Minister of Health, Dr M. H. Veldman, quoted in *The Star*, 5 August 1988).

This deprivation has itself been conceptualized as a form of violence. For instance, Galtung (1969: 168) maintains that 'violence is present when human beings are being influenced so that their actual somatic and mental realizations are below their potential realizations'. This 'structural violence' is equated with injustice and discrimination: 'The violence is built into the structure and shows up as unequal power and consequently unequal life chances' (Galtung, 1969).

Two indicators point us to the extent of this inequality in South Africa, income distribution and infant mortality rates. Whites, who constitute less than one-sixth of the population, earn nearly two-thirds of the income; blacks, who account for nearly two-thirds of the population, earn a quarter (Wilson & Ramphele, 1989). Nearly two-thirds of black people live below the minimum living level, fixed in 1985 at R350 per month (Wilson & Ramphele, 1989), and Simkins (1986) has estimated that more than 80 per cent of blacks in the reserves and homelands live in dire poverty.

Secondly, inequality is clearly indicated by infant mortality rates. While these have improved considerably in the last decade, Simkins has calculated that for 1980 the infant mortality rate per 1 000 births was 20 and 15 for white male and female babies respectively. For Africans, the equivalent rates were 96 and 76 (Simkins, 1986). Urban areas in South Africa were predictably better than rural ones, with Soweto having 25,5 infant deaths per 1 000, compared with 130 in rural Transkei (Zille, 1986).

Breaking the chain of political violence in which we are all caught up involves eradicating this structural violence on which apartheid is based. In concrete terms, this means providing the mass of South Africa's people with access to well-paid jobs; adequate pensions and social services; decent housing, health services, and education; and proper sanitation and clean water. This can only be achieved by massive redistribution of power and resources within a new political dispensation — a non-racial democracy.

It seems appropriate to conclude this chapter by quoting the words of a prominent 'specialist in violence', as Laswell termed military men, the former head of the SADF, General C. J. Viljoen: 'South Africans must be prepared to accept certain levels of discomfort, disruption and even violence in their everyday lives' (Quoted in Hough, 1984: 6). In this process of 'acceptance', some of us reading this chapter are in danger of losing our freedom, property and even lives. All of us are in danger of losing our humanity.

NOTES

1. According to Riordaan, there have been 3 400 deaths in the four years from September 1984 to 1988 (1988: 2). The South African Institute of Race Relations (SAIRR) estimates that there were 2 987 deaths from political violence between the outbreak of violence in September 1984 and the end of 1987 (SAIRR, 1988: 22). According to the 1987 Report of the South African Police tabled in Parliament, there were 10 129 cases of 'public violence' during 1986 and 1987 (SAIRR, 1988: 22). Clearly there are difficulties involved in the construction of these figures, which refer to both their reporting and labelling as 'political violence', 'public violence', 'incidents of unrest', and so forth.

2. Walther (1969: 4) points out that ever since the French Revolution, 'terrorist' has been an epithet to fasten on a political enemy. Most definitions are partisan and unsatisfactory: '... the disputes about a comprehensive, detailed definition of terrorism will continue for a long time ... and will make no notable contribution towards the understanding of terrorism' (Laquer, 1987: 24).

3. Much of this violence is obscured by state censorship of the media, and public support for official violence. 'The result: the war being waged behind the myriad images of protest has gone unnoticed by vast numbers of South Africans and foreigners alike' (Davis, 1987: x). Furthermore, 'violence by the state is strangely absent from most discussions of the problem of violence' (Archer & Gartner, 1978: 219). These authors point out that 'Public support for official violence is so pervasive that the definition of violence is itself affected. In a 1979 survey [in the USA] for example, 30% of a national sample said that "police beating students" was NOT an act of violence, and an astonishing 57% said that "police shooting looters" was NOT an act of violence ... The same survey asked respondents what violent events were of greatest concern to them. Even although the survey occurred during the Vietnam war, only 4% of those interviewed mentioned war' (Archer & Gartner: 221).

4. The Human Rights Commission reports that since 1988 the state has resorted to these more sophisticated methods of silencing its opponents. They point out that restriction orders are more often the rule than the exception when detainees are released (*New Nation,* 19 January 1989; see also Chapter 14).

5. The one exception to this pattern was the case of Henry Burt, the first white man convicted of murdering a black man by the 'necklace method'.

When sentencing him to death, the trial judge said that the necklace method was chosen 'specifically to cast suspicion on black persons' (Black Sash, 1989: 32).

6. Nor is it comparable to the Argentine during the years of the military junta, when 'the scope of state terror ... embraced whole neighbourhoods and a broad array of occupational groups in the cities, towns and countryside. Peasant victims were found in mass lime graves in the countryside; workers' bodies were strewn at busy bus stops or floating down the Mapocho; students dropped from helicopters into the ocean; 30,000 dead, many times that number arrested and tortured' (Petras, 1987: 321).

7. This is the key component of militarism, the ideology that remains hegemonic in South African society.

8. Lasch sees this siege mentality infiltrating all aspects of cultural, social, and political life in advanced capitalist societies. It is a mentality that he attempts to describe in his concept of the 'minimal self'. He writes, 'People have lost confidence in the future. Faced with an escalating arms race, an increase in crime and terrorism, environmental deterioration and the prospect of a long-term economic decline, they have begun to prepare for the worst, sometimes by building fallout shelters and laying-in provisions, more commonly by executing a kind of emotional retreat from the long-term commitments that presuppose a stable, secure and orderly world' (Lasch, 1985: 16).

REFERENCES

Aitcheson, J. (1988) 'Numbering the Dead; Patterns in the Midlands Violence', paper presented at the ASSA Conference, Durban.

Archer, D. & Gartner, R. (1978) 'Legal Homicide and its Consequences'. In *Violence — Perspectives on Murder and Aggression,* edited by I. Kutash *et al.,* New York: Jossey-Bass, 219–32.

Arendt, H. (1970) *On Violence,* London: Allen Lane.

Bahro, R. (1982) *Socialism and Survival,* London: Heretic Books.

Baynham, S. (1987) 'Political Violence and the Security Response'. In *South Africa in Crisis,* edited by J. Blumenfeld, London: Croom Helm, 107–25.

Black Sash (1989) 'Inside South Africa's Death Factory', unpublished report.

Chapkis, W., (ed.) (1981) *Loaded Questions: Women and the Military,* Amsterdam: Transnational Institute.

CIIR (Catholic Institution for International Relations) (1988) *Now Everyone is Afraid. The Changing Face of Policing in South Africa,* London: CIIR.

Cock, J. (1987) 'Trapped Workers: Constraints and Contradictions Experienced by Black Women in Contemporary South Africa', *Women's Studies International Forum,* 10(2), 133–40.

Cole, J. (1987) *Crossroads,* Johannesburg: Ravan Press.

Davis, S. (1987) *Apartheid's Rebels. Inside South Africa's Hidden War,* New Haven: Yale University Press.

DPSC (Detainees' Parents Support Committee) (1987) 'A Year of Emergency, A Year of Repression', *Review of African Political Economy,* 40, December, 96–103.

Ebersohn, W. (1987) 'Ring of Fire', *Leadership, South Africa,* 6(1), 39–42.

Eide, A. & Thee, M., (eds.) (1980) *Problems of Contemporary Militarism,* London: St Martin's Press.

Encloe, C. (1983) *Does Khaki Become You? The Militarization of Women's Lives,* Boston: South End Press.

Fanon, F. (1963) *The Wretched of the Earth,* New York: Grove Press.

Foster, D. *et al.* (1987) *Detention and Torture in South Africa,* Cape Town: David Philip.

Frankel, P. (1984) *Pretoria's Praetorians. Civil-Military Relations in South Africa,* Cambridge: Cambridge University Press.

Galtung, J. (1969) 'Violence, Peace and Peace Research', *Journal of Peace Research,* 6(3), 167–91.

Grundy, K. (1987) *The Militarization of South African Politics,* Oxford: Oxford University Press.

Grundy, K. (1983) *Soldiers Without Politics. Blacks in the South African Armed Forces,* Berkeley: University of California Press.

Hall, P. & Roux, M. (1988) 'Life After Detention', *Sash,* 31(1), 44–5.

Hawarden, J. (1987) 'Apartheid Education 1986', paper presented at the International Conference on Education Against Apartheid, Lusaka.

Haysom, N. (1989) 'Vigilantes and Militarization'. In *War and Society. The Militarization of South Africa,* edited by J. Cock & L. Nathan, Cape Town: David Philip.

Hirson, B. (1979) *Year of Fire, Year of Ash. The Soweto Revolt: Roots of Revolution?,* London: Zed Press.

Horowitz, I. L. (1973) 'Political Terrorism and State Power', *Journal of Political and Military Sociology,* 1, 147–57.

Hough, M. (1984), *Institute for Strategy Studies Review,* August.

Human Rights Commission (1988) 'A Free Choice. Memorandum on Repression and the Municipal Elections', Special Report SR1.

Kaldor, M. (1982) 'Warfare and Capitalism', *Exterminism and Cold War,* London: Verso.

Kidron, M. & Smith, D. (1983) *The War Atlas,* London: Pan Books.

Laquer, W. (1987) *The Age of Terrorism,* London: Weidenfeld & Nicholson.

Lasch, C. (1985) *The Minimal Self. Psychic Survival in Troubled Times,* London: Pan Books.

Laswell, H. (1941) 'The Garrison State', *American Journal of Sociology,* 46, 455–68.

Levin, R. (1987) 'Class Struggle, Popular Democratic Struggle, and the South African State', *Review of African Political Economy,* 40, 7–21.

Lodge, T. (1983) *Black Politics in South Africa Since 1945,* London: Longmans.

Lowy, M. & Sadler, E. (1985) 'The Militarization of the State in Latin America', *Latin American Perspectives,* 12(4), 7–40.

Mann, M. (1987) 'The Roots and Contradictions of Modern Militarism', *New Left Review,* 162 (March/April), 35–51.

Mattelart, A. (1979) 'Notes on the Ideology of the Military State'. In *Communication and Class Struggle, Vol. 1: Capitalism and Imperialism* by A. Mattelart & S. Siegelaub, Cornell: Cornell University Press.

McCuen, J. (1966) *The Art of Counter-Revolutionary War. The Strategy of Counter-Insurgency,* London: Faber & Faber.

Meer, F. (1987) *The Trial of Andrew Zondo,* Johannesburg: Skotaville.

Merryfinch, L. (1981) 'Militarization/Civilization'. In *Loaded Questions: Women and the Military,* edited by W. Chapkis, Amsterdam: Transnational Institute.

Moss, G. (1988) 'Politics with a Price on its Head', *Work in Progress,* 53, April, 24–7.

Petras, J. (1987) 'The Anatomy of State Terror: Chile, El Salvador and Brazil', *Science and Society,* 51(3), 314–38.

Randle, M. (1981) 'Militarism and Repression', *Alternatives,* VII, 61–144.

Rich, P. (1984) 'Insurgency, Terrorism and the Apartheid System in South Africa', *Political Studies,* XXXII, 68–85.

Riordaan, R. (1988) 'Murder by Proxy — the Modernization of South Africa's Security Juggernaut', paper delivered at the Conference on State Terrorism, Michigan State University.

Roux, M. & De Villiers, M. (1988) 'Restructuring Apartheid: Terror and Disorganisation in the Eastern Cape', paper presented at the Conference of the Association of Sociologists in Southern Africa, Durban, July 1988.

Said, E. (1988) 'Identity, Negation and Violence', *New Left Review,* 171, October, 46–50.

SAIRR (South African Institute of Race Relations) (1988) *Race Relations Survey 1987/88,* Johannesburg: SAIRR.

Saul, J. (1987) 'Killing the Dream: The Role of the Counter-Revolutionary Guerrilla in the Militarization of the Third World', paper presented at the Conference on Militarization in the Third World: The Caribbean Basin and South Africa, Queens University, Belfast.

Scruton, R. (1987) 'Notes on the Sociology of War', *British Journal of Sociology,* XXXVIII(3).

Simkins, C. (1986) 'Household Composition and Structure in South Africa'. In *Growing Up in a Divided Society,* edited by S. Burman & R. Reynolds, Johannesburg: Ravan Press.

Smith, D. & Smith, R. (1983) *The Economics of Militarism,* London: Pluto Press.

Swilling, M. & Phillips, M. (1988) 'Reform, Security and White Power; Rethinking State Strategy in the 1980s', paper presented at the ASSA Conference, Durban.

Thompson, E. P. (1982) 'Notes on Exterminism, the Last Stage of Civilization', *Exterminism and Cold War,* London: Verso.

Van der Vyver, A. D. (1988) 'State Sponsored Terror Violence', *South African Journal on Human Rights,* 4(1).

Van Eyk, J. (1989) *Eyewitness to Unrest,* Johannesburg: Taurus.

Von Holdt, K. (1988) 'Vigilantes versus Defence Committees', *South African Labour Bulletin,* 13(2), 16–27.

Walther, E. (1969) *Terror and Resistance. A Study of Political Violence,* New York: Oxford University Press.

Walzer, M. (1978) *Just and Unjust Wars,* London: Allen Lane.

Webster, D. (1987) 'Repression and the State of Emergency', *South African Review 4,* Johannesburg: Ravan Press.

Williams, R. (1985) *Towards 2000,* Harmondsworth: Penguin Books.

Wilson, F. & Ramphele, M. (1989) *Uprooting Poverty. The South African Challenge,* Cape Town: David Philip.

Wiseman, J. (1988) 'Militarism, Militarization and Praetorianism in South Africa, *Africa,* 58(2), 231–3.

Zille, H. (1986) 'Beginning Life in an Apartheid Society'. In *Growing Up in a Divided Society,* edited by S. Burman & R. Reynolds, Johannesburg: Ravan Press.

3 Legal violence: corporal and capital punishment

J. Sloth-Nielsen

INTRODUCTION

In the face of international abhorrence of brutal physical punishments, the South African legal system has retained two forms of punishment which elsewhere are regarded as archaic and barbaric: whipping and the death penalty. This chapter will focus upon these controversial sanctions and the legal structures that enable their imposition. It is important to note at the outset that in considering flogging and the practice of execution, one is concerned with authorized or legal violence; violence against the individual which is sanctioned by the state in retaliation for the commission of a crime. In consequence, what is ultimately at stake is the articulation of state policy towards bodily integrity and towards the sanctity of life. Since both whippings and hangings are routinely imposed in response to the perpetration of crime, it is apparent that the legal structure endorses the notion that the infliction of physical injury is an appropriate response to infringements.

From this perspective, it will be argued that the reduction or abolition of corporal penal sanctions would demonstrate a commitment by the state to non-violent practices, and would show the states's recognition of the inviolable right to physical integrity possessed by each citizen.

AETIOLOGY: A HISTORICAL OVERVIEW

Penal practice has for centuries been characterized by the use of brutal and inhuman practices. In previous eras punishment was inevitably a public spectacle, comprising the infliction of pain to an offender's body in a variety of imaginative ways. Quite understandably, physical punishment was simply introduced into a world already accustomed to the infliction of physical injury and suffering. Private retaliation had often been violent. So, too, was the formal penal system developed by states during medieval times to replace private vengeance. Attitudes to violence remained essentially the same and became entrenched within the penal structure (Spierenburg, 1984). Until dramatic changes occurred during the middle of the eighteenth century, criminal punishment was typified by the twin features of publicity and physical violence. 'The standing gallows, built in stone and situated at the outskirts of town ... signified to town residents and travellers alike that here was a "city of law"'. Similarly, the mutilation of corpses, and exposure of bodies to the public gaze symbolized that the authority of the ruler extended beyond death itself (Garland, 1987).

The legal and penal system that was adopted at the Cape of Good Hope in the early settler period closely resembled counterpart systems in Europe and (later) in Britain. Records of trials held at the Cape during the eighteenth and nineteenth centuries show that people were sentenced to a range of cruel physical sanctions, such as being drawn and quartered (pulled apart by four beasts), hanged, burned, and drowned.

Dramatic changes in penal philosophy occurred in Europe during the course of the eighteenth century. These shifts were partly a product of the industrial revolution, but they also reflected a growing concern with humanitarian considerations fostered by the Age of Enlightenment. Society no longer needed to enforce law and order in so public and overt a manner. What was required for the new economic order was a disciplined and compliant workforce. Thus, the prison developed as the major alternative to formerly brutal practices. The accent shifted from the infliction of physical suffering upon offenders, to a new disciplinary penal regime, when the focus would be the soul of the criminal. Foucault (1977), the major revisionist biographer of the changes that occurred in the development of the prison from the mid-eighteenth century onwards, has shown how the twin themes evident in former punishment practices became transformed: the public mode of punishment became private, and instead of corporal infliction of violence, imprisonment became the norm.

In the development of the South African penal system, changes occurred regarding the decline in corporal punishment and emergence of the prison that paralleled developments on the continent and in Britain (Van Zyl Smit & Offen, 1984). However, the South African position diverged in a number of significant ways. For example, in 1960 it was pointed out that whipping of offenders had been abandoned in almost the whole of the civilized world, and that the South African legislation's authorization of flogging was exceptional (Kahn, 1960). It has been argued (Sloth-Nielsen, 1989) that themes unique to South African history explain this phenomenon. It is perhaps instructive to explore briefly aspects of those particular features of South African penal history, for a historical dimension can contribute to a more meaningful understanding of the continued use of violent punishments in the criminal justice system today.

Firstly, the colonial experience of slavery resulted in the widespread practice of flogging slaves. When slavery was abolished in the 1830s, Master and Servant laws that were enacted to compel erstwhile slaves to remain with their owners retained corporal punishment as the sanction for a number of offences. Generally these offences were disciplinary in nature (neglect of duty, disobedience, and desertion), and flogging was therefore essentially a non-disruptive form of labour control. Whippings were also still publicly punitive, that is, they served as a lesson to other workers. This was particularly effective in outlying frontier areas, where access to formal justice was difficult to procure.

Secondly, South Africa's colonial status rendered whipping an ideologically acceptable form of punishment to white settlers. Particularly in Natal (which was known as 'the whipping province'), whipping played a prominent part in the punishment of African offenders (Peté, 1986). The colonists maintained that physical coercion was the one thing that the child-like, savage, black person could understand.

Imprisonment alone was not a sufficient punishment for the black person — he/she had to be taught that the white person was master. While British administrators repeatedly sought to curtail flogging in the colonies, whites here 'stubbornly defended their right to impose this form of punishment freely' (Peté, 1986). In a debate in the Natal Legislative Council in 1876, which centred on the proposed abolition of whipping for offences under the Master and Servant Ordinance 2 of 1850, one speaker articulated a view which was indicative of the paternalist ideology of the times: '… a kaffir liked a master who was masterful' (Peté, 1986). The underlying idea that a black person responds only to the imposition of physical pain has found expression as recently as 1949. The 'liberal' Lansdown Commission of Inquiry on Penal Policy (UG47/47) recommended that whipping be retained as a sentence in South Africa chiefly because this punishment was a deterrent 'of special efficacy' for Africans who had not yet emerged from an 'uncivilized state' (Lansdown Commission of Inquiry, 1949: para. 484). These considerations go a considerable way in explaining the tenacious grip that corporal punishment has had in the evolution of our penal system.

However, South African penal history also reveals the unique feature that corporal punishments have tended to be utilized increasingly in times of social and political upheaval (Sloth-Nielsen, 1989). Frequently this has been evidenced by legislative changes to the sentencing structures to allow for added opportunities to impose corporal punishments. It has been alleged that the state responds to threats to its hegemony by resorting to physical violence (Sloth-Nielsen, 1989).

In 1952, for example, the newly elected Nationalist government ignored the recommendations of the Lansdown Commission of Inquiry of 1949 (which proposed restrictions on the imposition of corporal punishment). Instead the government adopted legislation which made whipping a compulsory sentence for certain offences. In just one year (mid–1957 to mid–1958) 18 542 adult offenders, most of them black, were sentenced to a whipping in terms of the new legal provisions. As Kahn (1960) has shown, the courts were forced to embark on an orgy of whipping, and despite repeated protestations from the bench and the magistracy, it was only in 1965 that the government relented and quashed the mandatory whipping provisions. This period (the 1950s) corresponded to the rise in black political organizations, which by 1965 had been effectively crushed. In 1976 and 1977, after widespread civil unrest in South African townships, publicity was given to the fact that many black school children were whipped for participating in politically motivated activities (Midgley, 1982). When resistance surfaced again in 1986, the law was amended to extend legal whipping provisions. New offences were added to the list for which corporal punishment was a competent sentence. These were the offences of public violence, sedition, arson, and malicious damage to property. It was the commission of this spectrum of criminal offences that represented the challenge to state authority in the townships (Sloth-Nielsen & Itsikowitz, 1986). Once again the state responded by re-emphasizing through changes to criminal law that rebellious behaviour would be met by physical violence.

Similarly, the legislation permitting the imposition of the death penalty was amended in 1957 to extend the range of offences for which the death penalty could be imposed. Offences such as childstealing, kidnapping, robbery with aggravating circumstances, and housebreaking with aggravating circumstances, which had never before attracted the ultimate sanction, were now capital crimes. More recently, the numbers of inmates on death row have been swelled by those sentenced to death for their participation in mob killings in unrest-torn townships between 1984 and 1988. The courts have extended the doctrine of common purpose (which imputes the liability of the actual perpetrator to all active members of a crowd, whether or not the individual crowd member actually dealt any fatal blows to the victim) to support murder convictions and subsequent death sentences for participants in the township violence. Controversial cases such as that of the Sharpeville Six (*S v Safatsa* 1988, (1) SA 868 (AD) and the Upington 14 (*S v Khumalo*, KS 110 186 (NC)), where multiple death sentences were imposed, have fuelled public perceptions that the death penalty is part and parcel of the authorities' response to political turbulence.

It would appear, therefore, that it is important to consider historical, structural, and political aspects of South African society in explaining the continued importance of corporal punishments here, when brutal and violent penal sanctions have been abolished in most parts of the civilized world. While there has been some reform this century in this country with respect to violent punishment (particularly in respect of the limits that have been imposed on whipping), the recent increases in the use of the death penalty and flogging is a matter for concern. Not only does it indicate a criminal justice system further and further removed from internationally accepted human rights norms, but it signals a disturbing lack of commitment to upholding the standard that a state opposed to personal violence should set.

INCIDENCE
Corporal punishment

Currently the Criminal Procedure Act 51 of 1977 provides for two forms of whipping that can be imposed as a sentence. The first relates to juvenile offenders (i.e. those under the age of twenty-one years) who may be sentenced to seven strokes with a cane no more than one metre long and nine millimetres in circumference. This punishment is restricted to use on male offenders, and must be administered in private. The parents or guardian of the child may, however, be present when the cuts are given. Generally cuts are administered by a policeman in the court building or in the police station, and a district surgeon must first certify that the juvenile is fit to receive a whipping.

Adult whipping for male offenders may be imposed for a number of offences which are specified by the Criminal Procedure Act 51 of 1977. These offences include robbery, assault with intent to do grievous bodily harm, indecent assault, housebreaking, theft of (or out of) a motor vehicle, murder, arson or malicious injury to property, and public violence or sedition. Once again the maximum number of strokes that may be imposed is pegged at seven and it has recently been laid down that whipping may not be imposed together with a prison sentence unless all or part of that prison term is suspended. No adult older than thirty years may be subjected to a flogging, although the Prisons Act 8 of 1959 provides that persons up to the age of forty years may be whipped for disciplinary offences committed during a period of imprisonment. Adult whippings are imposed in a prison (in terms of section 36 of the Prisons Act) and the maximum specifications of the rod to be used are 125 millimetres in length and 12 millimetres in circumference.

More than 40 000 people were whipped in South Africa in the period 1987–8, according to the figures provided in Parliament by the Minister of Justice. This means that on average 112 people a day were sentenced to undergo corporal punishment for the twelve months between July 1987 and June 1988, most of them juveniles. These figures exclude whippings imposed on prisoners for disciplinary infractions, and whippings imposed on juveniles in reformatories (who are sentenced to undergo corporal punishment in terms of the internal disciplinary codes of these institutions). The Annual Report of one such school, Porter Reformatory in Cape Town, reveals that 481 sentences of corporal punishment were imposed upon pupils in 1988 (Porter School Annual Report, 1988). Whipping as a legal sanction authorized by both legislature and courts is therefore arguably the most frequent and pervasive manifestation of state violence upon individuals in South Africa today.

It must be conceded that throughout this century there has been a vast amelioration of the law and practice relating to flogging. While a sentence of a hundred lashes was not unknown at the end of last century, the legal maximum has progressively decreased to the present number of seven strokes. Except in the instance of a juvenile whipping, no one may be subjected to a whipping more than twice and, once again with the exception of juveniles, a second whipping may not be imposed within a period of three years of the last sentence of a whipping.

The judicial response to corporal punishment has been to show increasing distaste for the practice of flogging, and the Supreme Courts of South Africa have been at pains to reduce the opportunity for imposing whippings on a sentence. For example, they have found it to be unsound to couple a whipping with a long term of imprisonment (*S v Sele* 1985, (3) SA 1039 (O)), and undesirable to impose a sentence of whipping where the crime was not one which was aggravated by the use of violence (*S v Maisa* 1968, (1) SA 271 (T)). In *S v Khumalo and Others* 1965, (4) SA 565 (N), Judge Fannin described whipping as a punishment of a particularly severe kind. 'It is brutal in its nature and constitutes a severe assault not only upon the person of the recipient but also his dignity as a human being.' He was of the opinion that some of those who are whipped 'may well suffer physical and mental after-effects out of all proportion to the gravity of the offence for which they have been punished'. In *S v Motsoesoana* 1986, (3) SA 850 (N), one of the presiding judges termed corporal punishment a 'brutal and degrading form of punishment'. Similar indictments have been heard from a number of other judges concerning corporal punishment.

Thus, while juvenile whippings in particular are frequently described as 'moderate corrections', this euphemism cannot conceal the fact that whipping is a perpetration of physical violence imposed as a legitimate sentence at the behest of the courts. Despite the amelioration brought about in the manner of its infliction, corporal punishment remains a severe and degrading punishment. This was graphically illustrated by Mr Justice Gubbay in the recent Zimbabwean case *S v Ncube, S v Tshume, S v Ndhovu* 1988, (2) SA 702 (ZSC). He described the usual process thus:

> Once the prisoner is certified fit to receive the whipping, he is stripped naked. He is blindfolded with a hood and placed face down upon a bench in the prone position. His hands and legs are strapped to the bench, which is then raised to an angle of 45 degrees. The … calico square is tied over his buttocks and the kidney protector secured above his buttocks at waist level. The prisoner's body is then strapped to the bench. The cane is immersed in water to prevent splitting. The strokes are administered to one side across the whole of the buttocks. It is within the power of the officer administering the strokes to determine their strength, timing and to some extent, their placement upon the buttocks. A second stroke upon the same part as an earlier stroke undoubtedly causes greater pain than were it to be placed elsewhere (*S v Ncube, S v Tshume, S v Ndhovu*, 1988 at 714A-C). [This sets out the procedure for adults who are flogged.]

The Zimbabwean court proceeded to reject corporal punishment as a legitimate sentence for adults — it is contrary to the provisions of the Zimbabwean Constitution which outlaws inhuman or degrading punishment or treatment. The court pointed out that the administering of whipping is attended by acute pain and much physical suffering and that, irrespective of the extent of regulatory safeguards, it is a procedure easily subject to abuse in the hands of a sadistic and unscrupulous prison officer who might be called upon to administer the punishment (*S v Ncube, S v Tshume, S v Ndhovu*, 1988 at 722A-D). Simply because there is an aura of official procedure in imposing a sentence of corporal punishment, just because a certificate of medical fitness to be flogged is required, and solely because the number of strokes and the type of rod used are carefully measured does not mean that corporal punishment becomes in essence anything other than 'one human being inflicting violence upon another human being'. To quote Mr Justice Gubbay again, whipping 'by its very nature treats members of the human race as non-humans ... Whipping does not accord [the offender] human status' (*S v Ncube, S v Tshume, S v Ndhovu*, 1988 at 772C).

Not only have southern African judges evidenced their distaste for the practice of whipping. Academic writers have argued strenuously that corporal punishment is a severe punishment that is brutal in nature. Midgley (1975), who studied the operation of the juvenile justice system utilizing the 898 cases heard by the Cape Town juvenile court in 1968, found that 57 per cent of those convicted (331 offenders) were sentenced to be whipped. Even numbers of strokes were most commonly imposed, and most offenders received six strokes. Midgley points out that 'if in excess of 4 strokes a whipping will often cause bleeding and scarring ...'. He alleges that whippings were 'imposed for all types of offences, for all age and ethnic categories, irrespective of whether the offender was legally represented or not and irrespective of previous convictions'. Young children were not exempted since the youngest child who was whipped was only nine years old. More frequently, however, the children who were sentenced to undergo corporal punishment were over the age of twelve. In addition, it seemed as though corporal punishment was imposed on the offenders in this sample in a racially discriminatory pattern: while 60 per cent of all 'coloured' offenders were whipped, corporal punishment was imposed on only 12 per cent of the white offenders.

More recently, the service organization National Institute for Crime Prevention and the Rehabilitation of Offenders (NICRO) found in a 1987 study conducted in two magisterial divisions in the Cape, that corporal punishment accounted for 47,5 per cent of the sentences imposed upon all first offenders who appeared in a juvenile court. It was thus the most commonly used form of punishment for those children who were first-time offenders. In this sample, children as young as ten years old were subjected to a whipping. A disturbing feature of this study is the suggestion once again that there may be racial disparity in the imposition of corporal punishment. The degree to which the sentence of cuts was used in comparison to other types of sentence varied between races. Where whites were found guilty, 16,3 per cent were sentenced to cuts while in the instance of African offenders this proportion was 71,6 per cent. For 'coloured' juveniles, the percentage sentenced to a whipping was 56,8 per cent. In a study conducted in the Durban/Umlazi area in 1980/1, similar conclusions were reached. It was found that race was a 'significant factor when considering whether a juvenile is likely to be whipped and how many cuts will be administered. A whipping seems to be a sentence more likely to be imposed on blacks [Africans] and "coloureds" than on Asians and whites.'

It is likely that this racial disparity is partially explained by the then lack of suitable sentencing alternatives for race groups other than white. Until recently, for example, there were no custodial institutional options for Africans in the Western Cape. Similarly, there is a historical discrepancy in the availability of social services (which would enable a sentencing officer to utilize more welfarist-oriented sentencing options) for different racial groups (Hutchinson, 1983). Nevertheless, amid persistent allegations of racial bias in the sentencing process, and given the empirical evidence of racial differentiation in the imposition of whipping cited above, the provision of better social services to African and 'coloured' offenders is probably not the full answer to the question of whether discriminatory practices occur in the use of corporal punishment. This is a matter which warrants further attention, since indications of racial discrimination in the imposition of whipping constitute a further fundamental objection to the continued use of this form of punishment. Corporal punishment can be designated cruel not only because of its inherent physical brutality, but also as a consequence of the violation of the fundamental principle of equality before the law.

The empirical studies referred to above have all indicated that whipping (for juveniles in particular) is regarded here as the panacea for all delinquency, borne out especially by the ready recourse to whipping as a sentence for first offenders. The extensive use of corporal punishment in South Africa stands in stark contrast to the standards for the treatment of both juvenile and adult offenders currently embodied in international instruments. The European Convention on Human Rights, for example, brands whipping as an inhuman and degrading punishment. The United Nations Standard Minimum Rules for the Administration of Juvenile Justice (the Beijing Rules adopted in the General Assembly in 1985) lay down the rule in Article 17 that juveniles shall not be subjected to corporal punishment for the commission of any crime. Similar commitments are to found in Article 7 of the International Covenant on Civil and Political Rights, and the Convention against Torture and other Cruel, Inhuman or Degrading Treatment or Punishment. In this light, then, the incidence of judicial flogging in this country should occasion alarm.

The death penalty

The large number of people that South Africa executes annually has led to an international outcry. The Amnesty International survey of executions world-wide carried out between 1985 and mid-1988 revealed that during this period more people were executed in this country than in any other country in the world save Iran (Amnesty International Report, 1989: 264). It has been calculated that for the decade 1978–88, 1 335 people were executed in South Africa. At the beginning of 1990 there were some 289 people on death row awaiting the death sentence (*Weekly Mail*, 17 November 1989). The accommodation on death row has recently been extended to provide for the increase in the number of prisoners awaiting hanging.

Currently of immediate concern to those perturbed by the death penalty in South Africa are a range of legal problems affecting death penalty trials. These flaws not only augment the numbers sentenced to die unnecessarily, but also raise serious doubts about the fairness of the death penalty in this country. Some of these arguments merit closer examination.

The South African legal structure is unjustifiably wide in its elaboration of crimes for which the death sentence is a competent verdict. Not only is murder included, but also treason, rape, robbery with aggravating circumstances, and even housebreaking with aggravating circumstances. In addition, serious anomalies have arisen with regard to the mandatory death penalty for the crime of murder. The Criminal Procedure Act provides that unless the offender is under the age of eighteen, or unless extenuating circumstances are found to have been present during the commission of the crime, the court has no option but to sentence an accused to death for murder. The greatest majority of sentenced prisoners on death row are persons who have been convicted of murder and sentenced in terms of the mandatory provisions. For example, in a statistical survey carried out in the Cape Provincial Division, it was found that of the 136 death sentences imposed between 1986 and 1988, 118 sentences were imposed for the crime of murder (Murray *et al.*, 1989). A crucial objection to the mandatory provision is that the notion 'extenuation' is narrowly defined to include only factors which affect the accused's moral blameworthiness at the time of the commission of the crime. The accused's previous convictions, or, alternatively, un-blemished record, may not be presented to the court until after the judgment has already been pronounced. Similarly, evidence of the character of the accused, or the encouraging prospect of rehabilitation, is irrelevant to the enquiry into extenuation. Ordinarily these factors would be highly relevant to sentencing. Procedurally, a further problem arises in that the accused is forced to bear the onus of proving the presence of extenuating factors. This is an arduous burden, particularly given the poor quality of legal representation that many accused facing capital charges enjoy. In practice, it appears that it is only rarely that fresh evidence is introduced to advance the accused's case that extenuating circumstances exist. Preliminary research undertaken in the Cape Supreme Court in 1988 indicates that in only 10 per cent of the cases surveyed was separate expert evidence led in extenuation (Davis, 1989). It has been suggested that were the death sentence to become a discretionary matter for the judge to decide (rather than mandatory), and were the concept of extenuation and the accused's burden of proving it to be jettisoned, the result would be a dramatic reduction in the number of those sentenced to die (Kahn, 1989).

Linked to problems arising from the law enabling the imposition of the death penalty are concerns about the trial process in capital cases. Generally, undefended persons who are charged with crimes where the death penalty is a possible outcome are provided with *pro deo* counsel, who are paid by the state. Very often the legal professionals who accept *pro deo* assignments are junior and inexperienced members of the legal fraternity. They are not assisted by attorneys in the preparation of evidence for the trial, and virtually no funding is provided to enable *pro deo* advocates to engage expert witnesses to testify during the extenuation phase of the trial. Grave doubts have been voiced about the adequacy of representation that accused in many capital cases experience. Counsel appear only in the Supreme Court trial itself, while the accused may have pleaded earlier in the magistrate's court without the benefit of legal advice, and there provided an extensive and binding statement regarding the commission of the crime. Consequently, counsel's ability to prepare a defence is limited by the statements made at the earlier proceedings. Furthermore, it is alleged that *pro deo* counsel are often ill-prepared for trial, and that trials where these counsel are involved are on average shorter in duration than trials where private counsel are engaged (Black Sash, 1989). A study conducted in the Cape Supreme Court in 1983 substantiates these assertions (Van Zyl Smit & Isakow, 1986). Of all accused who were tried in this division of the Supreme Court (including those who were not sentenced to death) in this sample, 50 per cent saw the advocate that had been assigned to them on the day of the actual trial for the first time. A further 18,9 per cent saw counsel only one day before the trial. The researchers found that only

10 per cent of *pro deo* counsel in their sample spent longer than an hour in total consulting with their clients. There were other, more quantitative indications revealed by the study that relationships between client and advocate were less than ideal. The organization Lawyers for Human Rights reports that accused often withhold important information from *pro deo* counsel due to lack of trust (Currin, 1989). The poor relationship between representative and client must necessarily impinge upon the quality of defence.

There is at present consensus in many quarters that as long as accused facing capital charges continue to be defended by the *pro deo* system of assigning advocates, a substantial danger exists that innocent people may be hanged, or that mitigating factors affecting the sentence may not come to light. Judges themselves have on occasion expressed unease about the quality of defence in the most serious cases they are called upon to try. Mr Justice Leon, formerly Judge in Natal, remarked that while he was presiding he 'always tried to do his best to see that justice was done, but that there is a limit to what the court can do. One cannot assume the role of counsel' (Leon, 1989).

While the problems attached to the *pro deo* system could possibly be redressed by a properly-funded legal defence team to assist defendants in capital trials, the thorny issue of differing judicial attitudes towards execution is less easily resolved. This issue was highlighted recently in a study undertaken in the Cape Provincial Division between 1986 and mid-1988 to illuminate the trial process leading to execution (Murray *et al.*, 1989). Information was collected regarding the frequency with which different judges imposed the death penalty, given the total number of criminal cases (for which the death sentence was a competent verdict) that each judge tried. A significant disparity amongst individual judges in handing down the ultimate sentence was revealed by this survey. For example, three judges heard only 15 per cent of the cases in the sample, yet they sentenced to death 51 per cent of the accused in the sample. On the other hand, from amongst the judges who did impose the death penalty, another group of three judges had tried 32 per cent of the criminal cases but had sentenced only 12 per cent of the condemned people. One judge handed down the death sentence in 44 per cent of the cases that he heard, while another, who tried almost twice as many criminal cases, did not sentence any accused to death during the period under review.

The authors of this research explain the disparity amongst individual judges in handing down death sentences on two levels. Firstly, some evidence exists that allocation of particular cases to individual judges takes place in the organization of Supreme Court workloads. It could be alleged, in response to the disparity in the use of the death penalty, that 'some judges are routinely assigned to cases where the death penalty is more probable, while their brethren are allocated less serious trials'. However, the authors show that whatever the motive for such allocation might be, an untrammelled discretion to appoint judges is fundamentally unacceptable as a basis upon which to assign death penalty cases to judges for trial. Any system permitting intervention before the trial in order to influence its outcome is inapposite in the context of the death penalty, which is a morally problematic penalty. Because the decision as to which judge receives which case 'involves the uncontrolled determination of ... factors which are vague, imprecise and irrelevant', differential allocation of capital cases is inappropriate. If the special allocation of serious cases to certain judges were to be advanced as the explanation for sentencing disparity amongst individual judges, the current system could be rejected as a violation of the principle of equality before the law.

Secondly, however, and more importantly, the significant difference amongst judges in sentencing accused to death raises the question of the influence of judicial penal philosophy and, more particularly, a judge's personal view on capital punishment. It is well known that some judges are strongly opposed to the death sentence while others defend its role as a punishment. There is a wealth of evidence, from judges and researchers alike, that attitudes to penal policy are an important factor in explaining differing sentences. This raises serious doubts about the potential for a fairly-imposed death penalty system in South Africa. If the ultimate fate of the accused is to depend on which judge hears the case, then it is inevitable that the death penalty is going to operate in an arbitrary and discriminatory manner.

Indeed, it has been a key assertion in the public campaigns that have developed around the death penalty in South Africa that the death sentence is imposed not only arbitrarily, but also in a racially discriminatory manner. This argument was first propounded by the late Dr Barend Van Niekerk in an academic article, in which he cited the results of an attitudinal survey amongst advocates to poll their views on the possible influence of racial considerations in the imposition of the death penalty. A significant number of the replying advocates (almost 50 per cent) believed that 'justice as regards capital punishment is meted out on a different basis to the different races' (Van Niekerk, 1969).

Statistics are frequently cited to support the proposition that while many blacks are hanged for murdering whites, few whites who are convicted of intra-racial murder or rape are executed. For example, of the 81 blacks convicted of murdering whites between June 1982 and June 1983, 38 were executed. Of the 52 whites sentenced for murdering whites over this period, only one was executed, while none of the 21 whites convicted of murdering blacks was hanged (*Weekly Mail*, 17 November 1989). Alleged racial bias in the imposition of the death penalty has repeatedly been raised regarding the imposition of the death penalty in the United States. The likelihood of the death penalty being imposed is disproportionately higher when the offender is black and the victim is white, than with any other combination of victim's race and offender's race (Radelet & Vandiver, 1986). However, the charge that race is a significant factor in the imposition of the death sentence is hotly disputed in South Africa, and a typical response to statistical studies that focus on the racial issue is that what appears to be racial disparity on the face of it is actually an illusion of discrimination, because other factors distinguishing one homicide from another are obscured by stark statistics. In the only sustained analysis of the many variables (including race) that affect the imposition of the death sentence in South Africa, it was concluded that in the Durban and Coast Local Division of the Supreme Court, where the survey took place:

> ... racial factors *per se* do not play the part frequently attributed to them, in the imposition of the death penalty ... . The race of the victim though at first examination, a highly significant factor, drops out as a variable with a high explanatory power when the compounding effects of other variables are removed (Olmesdahl, 1983).

It should be noted, however, that the methodology utilized by this researcher has been subjected to sustained criticism (Murray *et al*, 1989) and the conclusions he reached may be seriously flawed. Indeed, it is a moot point as to whether the 'death row egg can ever be unscrambled to reveal the effect of race upon any particular sentence' (Bruck, 1987). Nevertheless, while judges in South Africa are drawn exclusively from the ranks of the white race, and while most trialists are black, the perception is not going to abate that racial factors play some part in death penalty practices. In a racially polarized society it may prove to be impossible to ever allocate death sentences in a colour-blind way.

Even though it cannot be accepted as proven that the death sentence is imposed in a racially discriminatory manner, recent personalized accounts of the life histories of typical death row defendants tend to reinforce the assertion that the death sentence is reserved overwhelmingly for those from disadvantaged social groups in our society. In the sample profiled in the Black Sash Research Report (1989), 85 per cent of death row prisoners grew up in families which struggled financially. Overcrowded living quarters were an indicator of a disadvantaged youth. The majority of prisoners in the sample were raised by single parents or by other relatives. The vast majority in the sample suffered disrupted schooling patterns, and most received no further skills training or education after leaving school. Ninety per cent in the sample were black. The conclusion is inescapable that the high incidence of executions in this country is part and parcel of the systematic social destructiveness of apartheid.

EFFECTS ON INDIVIDUALS, FAMILIES, AND SOCIETY
Corporal punishment

Reference has already been made to the brutal physical effects of even a 'moderate' whipping. The Viljoen Commission of Inquiry into the Penal System in 1977 endorsed the view that whipping of adults constitutes a brutal assault, not only upon the person of the recipient, but also upon his dignity as a human being. The charge that corporal punishment is offensive because it is humiliating and degrading has repeatedly been at the core of legal decisions abroad overruling corporal punishment as a penalty. One of the most important decisions was that of the European Court of Human Rights in *Tyrer v United Kingdom* (1978). Tyrer (aged fifteen) argued that the birching imposed on him as a sentence by a juvenile court on the Isle of Man contravened Article 3 of the European Convention on Human Rights to which the United Kingdom was a signatory. The article forbad the use of inhuman and degrading punishment. In its judgment the Court considered that, in order for a punishment to be degrading, the humiliation or debasement inflicted must attain a particular level, and although Tyrer's birching did not have severe or long-term effects:

> … his punishment — whereby he was treated as an object in the power of the authorities — constituted an assault on precisely that which it is one of the main purposes of article 3 to protect, namely a person's dignity and physical integrity (*Tyrer v United Kingdom*, 1978: para. 33).

Moreover, the psychological effects of corporal punishment upon an individual are possibly as harmful and serious as the potential physical consequences. There is a good deal of evidence to suggest that a receiver of severe physical punishment 'may model his behaviour on that of the punisher when he wishes to cope with or control the behaviour of others'

(Van Zyl Smit & Offen, 1984). In other words, administering flogging may well lead to an escalation of violence and aggression in the offender. Support for this concept is provided in detail in Chapter 12 of this book. In addition, there is no evidence that corporal punishment actually deters either the receiver or others. Rather, it tends to 'weaken the sense of shame on which the hope of improvement depends … What results is a psychological resistance to change and an entrenching of the initial attitudes expressed'. Researchers and committees who have examined recidivism rates and corporal punishment have concluded that whipping has no beneficial consequences, since offenders are more likely to be reconvicted than when other sentences were imposed (Van Zyl Smit & Offen, 1984).

The detrimental consequences of whipping can be examined from a societal level too. There is evidence to suggest that whipping actually increases the violence of a society. The hypothesis is encapsulated in the maxim 'violence breeds violence' (Van Zyl Smit & Offen, 1984). That whipping may perpetuate the levels of violence in a society is borne out by studies of the sentencing practices of 'peoples' courts', the structures that sprang up in the unrest-torn townships in 1985 and 1986. Instances have been documented of an increase in violent sentences, particularly lashings, imposed by these courts as a direct response to rising levels of police use of whipping in unrest situations (Schärf & Burman, 1989). The implication is that brutal practices, initiated by state officials, created a climate in which recourse to personal violence against others became an authenticated mode of dispute settlement (Sloth-Nielsen, 1989).

Moreover, whipping as a judicial sanction tends to legitimate the state's use of violence. The implications of this concern were spelt out by the European Court of Human Rights in the Tyrer case: in its judgment the Court noted that corporal punishment was:

> … institutionalized violence, that is, violence permitted by the law, ordered by the judicial authorities of the State and carried out by the police authorities of the State. The institutionalized character of this violence is further compounded by the whole aura of official procedure attending the punishment … (*Tyrer v United Kingdom*, 1978, para. 33).

It must be remembered, too, that corporal punishment is likely to brutalize the individual policeman or prison warder administering the strokes. Policemen should not be mandated by society to use the cane, whether privately below the courtroom, or publicly in the streets (Sloth-Nielsen, 1989). There is but a thin line between legitimate and authorized flogging in one context, below the courtroom, and the appropriate response to delinquency in the context of the policing of township violence. Is the structure of our penal system not partly responsible for the many allegations of extra-legal police whipping during township funerals, rallies, and meetings? It is probable that were corporal punishment to be abolished as an authentic form of punishment in South Africa, the state's commitment to the values of decency and human dignity would have a far-reaching and beneficial ripple effect on the levels of violence in this society.

The death penalty

The death penalty is the premeditated and cold-blooded killing of a human being by the state.

> No matter what reason a government gives for killing prisoners and what method of execution is used, the death penalty cannot be detached from the movement for human rights and in particular the right to life (Amnesty International, 1989).

Central to the notion of human rights is that they may not be abrogated, even if a person has committed the most atrocious of crimes: '... human rights apply to the worst of us as well as the best of us' (Amnesty International, 1989). Amnesty International show that whatever the method of killing used, execution always constitutes a cruel physical and mental assault upon a person. In South Africa, the method of execution employed is death by hanging. Writing in the *Rand Daily Mail* in June 1978, Dr Chris Barnard (the famous heart surgeon) described this method of killing as 'slow, dirty, horrible, brutal, uncivilized and unspeakably barbaric'. He detailed the process involved:

> The man's spinal cord will rupture at the point where it enters the skull, electro-chemical discharges will send his limbs flailing in a grotesque dance, eyes and tongue will start from the facial apertures under the assault of the rope and his bowels and bladder may simultaneously void themselves to soil the legs and drip onto the floor ... .

The process of death is not instantaneous, since it may take up to twenty minutes for the pulse to stop beating. On occasion, the prison authorities have had to use teargas on condemned people who resisted the walk from death row to the gallows (Black Sash, 1989).

The cruelty of the death penalty is not only related to the execution itself. The very experience of being on death row is inhuman and brutal. It is clear from interviews with those who are living on death row, and from those who have been released (through reprieve or after having had the death sentence overturned on appeal) that living in a place 'whose sole purpose is to preserve those who live there so that they may be executed' (Vogelman, 1989) is a traumatic experience. The lights are never turned off in the cells, and elaborate precautions are taken by the prison authorities to prevent suicide by the prisoners. Nevertheless, it has been reported that suicide fantasies amongst the inmates are common, and suicides have occurred (Vogelman, 1989). It has also been alleged that sleeping pills and tranquillizers are dealt out extensively to death row prisoners. Vogelman maintains that a cause of terrible anguish and pain are the visits received from family members, since the condemned are 'upset about being unable to take emotional and financial care of family members' after death. But possibly most painful is the constant reminder of the transient nature of life on death row. Friends receive notices of executions and disappear. This occurrence reinforces the reality of impending death. When a prisoner is finally given notice of his/her fate, the prisoner is called to the lobby of death row, after packing up his/her belongings. At this stage it is often not clear what the outcome of an appeal or a reprieve petition has been. When the prisoner is called, then he/she is unsure about what his/her fate is to be: execution or reprieve. This is needlessly cruel.

Upon receiving a notice of execution, the prisoner is moved to another section of death row, known as the 'Pot', where the last week of life is spent. A well-documented feature of life in the 'Pot' is the continuous singing of the condemned people. Hugh Lewis, in *Bandiet: Seven Years in a South African Prison*, described the routine of the week preceding an execution thus:

> The first thing you notice as you come into Central is the singing, the sound of the condemneds. Up behind the huge sign in the hall saying 'Stilte/Silence', the condemned sing, chant, sing through the day and, before an execution, through the night. At times, the chant is quiet, a distant murmur of quiet humming, softly. Then it swells, you can hear a more strident, urgent note in the swell, sounding through the prison, singing the hymns that will take them through the double doors into the gallows ... . Condemneds, waiting their turn, singing their fellows through their last nights.

After the execution, death row is once again quiet. Prisoners who have since been released from the death cells maintain that the effect of an execution is to render the other prisoners sad and morose. Accounts of these prisoners' experiences of the process of execution suggest that it may take them years upon release to recover from the ordeal of being on death row (Vogelman, 1989).

The cruelty of execution is thus not restricted to the prisoner's death agonies but extends to all those touched or involved by the process, including other prisoners, and their families. In a petition to the State President in July 1989, calling for clemency for death row prisoners and an end to capital punishment, family members of executed prisoners said:

> We have experienced first-hand the anguish, torment, the sense of helplessness and the anger experienced while waiting for a loved one to die. We have all experienced the deep feelings of futility and anger when our husbands, brothers and sons have been hanged ... . The killing of our family members has caused immeasurable suffering and torment (*South*, 3 August 1989).

Moreover, those attendant upon an actual hanging — the hangman, prison warders, and doctors present — are arguably as deeply affected by the barbarous procedure. Mr Chris Barnard, South African retired executioner who oversaw the executions of some 1 500 condemned people during his career, reported that if he could have his life over again, he would not undertake executions, he felt it was inhuman to watch people die (*Huisgenoot*, 13 April 1989). He also gives an indication of the anxiety and psychological stress felt by a participant in an execution. 'Daar was nagte dat skrikwekkende en deurmekaar drome my nat van die angsweet my laat wakker skrik het' (*Huisgenoot*, 13 April 1989).[1]

Finally, it has been asserted that the practice of capital punishment demeans society at large.

> The taking of life in the name of the law does not engender respect in the citizen for human life. We must not in this way deny the infinite value of the human personality (Kahn, 1989).

Empirical studies and recorded crime rates of countries which have abolished the death penalty have failed to show that the death penalty reduces crime in any way. The argument that the death sentence deters has been widely discredited. Obviously the death penalty incapacitates a prisoner permanently, preventing him or her from repeating the crime, but dangerous offenders can be successfully contained by incarceration, without resorting to the death sentence. An important consequence of imprisonment, rather than execution, is that mistakes can be rectified should the person later be acquitted. The fallibility of the death penalty system has repeatedly been evidenced by persons being freed who have previously been sentenced to death. Given the shortcomings of the trial process in South African capital hearings alluded to above, the death penalty 'is too arbitrary and enormous a punishment to be part of a civilized system of criminal justice' (Davis, quoted in *The Argus*, 17 June 1989).

ENDING VIOLENT PUNISHMENT

Both corporal and capital punishment should be abolished in South Africa. Concerning the former, the time is long overdue that serious consideration be given to the development and extension of alternative sentencing strategies for juveniles. Young offenders are frequently whipped due to a desire to avoid imprisoning them, yet to satisfy the need to impose some punitive alternative. Clearly the solution lies in the expansion of creative sentencing options. Adult whipping, already limited by judicial guidelines detailing the special circumstances which must exist before this form of flogging may be imposed, should also be ended. If the objects of sentencing are to punish the criminal, to reform him, to deter him from committing further offences, and to deter others from committing similar offences, then these aims can be achieved by the imposition of other established punishments (*S v Khumalo and Others* 1965, (4) SA 565 (N)). There is no evidence that flogging is beneficial to either the individual or to society, and modern conceptions of justice and humanity have led to its abolition in many other countries. A commitment by the legislature to uphold the dignity and physical integrity of all subjects would be a progressive move towards eliminating institutionalized violence.

The same considerations hold true for the future of judicial killing. Execution is a calculated and cold-blooded form of eliminating offenders, and the South African system is a particularly 'savage' system of capital punishment (Mureinik, 1989). The sheer numbers of those sentenced to death, the apparent arbitrariness by which those selected to live or die are distinguished, and the inhuman experience of living on death row itself bears testimony to the brutality of the death penalty system in South Africa. The death sentence is a relic of a barbarous past age and has no place in a civilized legal system. As an interim measure, the Society for the Abolition of the Death Penalty in South Africa called for a commission of inquiry into the death penalty in South Africa to be appointed, and a moratorium on all executions until that report has been finalized. While this request has not yet been heeded, a variety of influential lobby groups have added their voices to the campaign for reform. It is likely that a judicial inquiry would find the current death penalty system seriously flawed, susceptible to error, and unreasonably wide-reaching. Only total abolition would eliminate the elements of inconsistency, fallibility, arbitrariness, and brutality associated with judicial executions.[2]

Ultimately, however, legal abolition of capital punishment will depend on a civic and governmental commitment to respect the sanctity of human life. Andrei Sakharov, the dissident Russian, has provided a useful moral creed for the abolition of the death penalty:

> I regard the death penalty as a savage and immoral institution which undermines the moral and legal foundations of a society. A state, in the person of its functionaries, who like all people are subject to influences, connections, prejudices and egocentric motivations for their behaviour, takes upon itself the right to the most terrible and irreversible act — the deprivation of life. Such a state cannot expect an improvement in the moral atmosphere in its country. I reject the notion that the death penalty has any essential deterrent effect on potential offenders. I am convinced that the contrary is true — that savagery begets only savagery (Quoted in Amnesty International, 1989).

NOTES

1. 'There were nights when frightening and confused dreams woke me with a start and had me in a cold sweat.'

2. On the occasion of the opening of Parliament on 2 February 1990, the State President announced a moratorium on executions, pending the introduction of far-reaching changes in the administration of the death penalty in South Africa. A Criminal Law Amendment Bill (B93–90) published in consequence of the announcement embodies fundamental reforms to the death penalty system. Briefly summarized, the imposition of the death penalty would become discretionary in all cases where the death penalty is competent. The mandatory death sentence for murder where no extenuation is found to be present, and the onus of proof which rests on the accused to prove extenuating circumstances, would fall away. The Bill envisages that the death penalty would only be imposed after a judicial determination of all aggravating and mitigating factors. In addition, each death sentence would be reviewed automatically by the Appellate Division of the Supreme Court. The Bill provides further that the cases of people currently on death row will be reassessed according to the new criteria.

   It should be stressed that although the reform proposals are welcome, as they augur the possibility of a dramatic reduction in the number of hangings in South Africa, fundamental objections remain. In particular, the fallibility, arbitrariness, and brutality inherent in the application of the death penalty will not be eliminated by the new measures.

REFERENCES

Amnesty International (1989) 'When the State Kills ...', Report, London: Amnesty International.

Black Sash (1989) 'Inside South Africa's Death Factory', Research Report.

Bruck, D. (1987) 'On Death Row in Pretoria Central', *The New Republic*, 13 and 20 July.

Currin, B. (1989) 'Lawyers for Human Rights and the Campaign Against Capital Punishment in South Africa', *South African Journal of Criminal Justice*, 2, 231.

Davis, D. (1989) 'Extenuation — an Unnecessary Halfway House on the Road to a Rational Sentencing Policy', *South African Journal of Criminal Justice*, 2, 205.

Foucalt, M. (1977) *Discipline and Punishment: The Birth of the Prison*, Harmondsworth: Penguin Books.

Garland, D. (1987) 'The Punitive Mentality: The Socio-historic Development and Decline', *Contemporary Crises*, 10, 305.

Harcourt, B. J. D. (1983) 'Sentencing the Juvenile Offender'. In *Criminal Justice in South Africa*, edited by M. C. J. Olmesdahl & N. C. Steytler, Cape Town: Juta & Co. Ltd.

Hutchinson, D. (1983) 'Juvenile Justice'. In *Criminal Justice in South Africa*, edited by M. C. J. Olmesdahl & N. C. Steytler, Cape Town: Juta & Co. Ltd.

Kahn, E. (1989) 'How Did We Get Lopsided Law on the Imposition of the Death Penalty for Common Law Crimes? And What Should We Do About It', *South African Journal of Criminal Justice*, 2, 137.

Kahn, E. (1960) 'Crime and Punishment', *Acta Juridicia*, 191.

Leon, Hon. R. (1989) *South African Law Journal*, 106, 42.

Midgeley, J. (1982) 'Corporal Punishment and the Death Penalty: Notes on the Continued Use of Corporal Punishment with Reference to South Africa', *Journal of Criminal Law and Criminology*, 73, 388.

Midgeley, J. (1975) 'Children on Trial', NICRO Report.

Mureinik, E. (1989) *South African Law Journal*, 106, 48.

Murray, C. M. *et al.* (1989) 'The Death Penalty in the Cape Provincial Division 1986–1988', *South African Journal of Human Rights*, 5, 154.

NICRO (National Institute for Crime Prevention and the Rehabilitation of Offenders) (1987) 'Juvenile First Offenders in Cape Town and Athlone', unpublished report.

Olmesdahl, M. C. J. (1983) 'Predicting the Death Sentence'. In *Criminal Justice in South Africa*, edited by M. C. J. Olmesdahl & N. C. Steytler, Cape Town: Juta & Co. Ltd.

Peté, S. 'Punishment and Race: The Emergence of Racially Defined Punishment in Colonial Natal', *Natal University Law and Society Review*, 1(2), 99.

Radelet, M. & Vandiver, M. (1986) 'Race and Capital Punishment: An Overview of the Issues', *Crime and Social Justice*, 25, 94–113.

Schärf, W. & Burman, S. (1989) 'Informal Justice and People's Courts in a Changing South Africa', unpublished report.

Sloth-Nielsen, J. (1989) 'Corporal Punishment: The Past and the Future', paper presented at the Conference Towards Justice? Crime and Social Control in South Africa, Cape Town.

Sloth-Nielsen, J. & Itsikowitz, I. (1986) *South African Journal on Human Rights,* 4, 224.

Spierenburg, P. (1984) *The Spectacle of Suffering,* Cambridge: Cambridge University Press.

Van Niekerk, B. (1969) 'Hang By the Neck Until You Are Dead', *South African Law Journal,* 86, 475.

Van Zyl Smit, D. (1984) 'Public Policy and the Punishment of Crime in a Divided Society: An Historical Perspective on the South African Penal System', *Crime and Social Justice,* 21–2, 146.

Van Zyl Smit, D. & Isakow, N. (1986) 'The Decision on How to Plead: A Study of Plea Negotiation in Supreme Court Criminal Matters', *South African Crime and Criminology,* 10, 3.

Van Zyl Smit, D. & Offen, R. (1984) 'Corporal Punishment: Joining Issue', *South African Crime and Criminology,* 8, 69.

Vogelman, L. (1989) 'Living on Death Row', *South African Journal of Human Rights,* 15, 183.

4 Violent crime: rape

INTRODUCTION

Rape takes on many forms. This chapter will use the term within the framework of sexual coercion in which a woman is a victim, and a man is the perpetrator. This is, of course, not always the case, but heterosexual rape is by far the dominant form of sexual violence.

Rape in South Africa has reached epidemic proportions. It occurs in all spheres of society and all women are potential victims. Women's fears of rape have begun to affect their basic day-to-day decisions and reduce their quality of life. Restrictions on movement, behaviour, and dress are imposed in order to elude the rapist. Precautions, however, are not always a reliable safeguard, for the woman's attacker is often the man she least suspects to be a rapist. Contrary to public opinion and to what many believe, the rapist is not a stranger who is psychotic, or a sex maniac who lurks in dark alleys waiting for his victim. He is in most cases a friend, an acquaintance, a date, a father, or a husband. The rapist is usually what society calls 'the normal man'.

There are a sufficient number of these 'normal men' to make rape an incident which, according to official statistics, occurred approximately 16 000 times annually during the 1980s. By 1988 the official annual figure for rape was 19 368 (*The Star*, 19 April 1989). With regard to the official racial breakdown of these figures, there were 819 white rape victims and 18 549 black. Unofficially, based on the premise put forward by the National Institute of Crime Prevention and the Rehabilitation of Offenders (NICRO) that only one in twenty rapes is reported, the figure is about 380 000 a year. This means that on average approximately 1 000 women can expect to be raped a day in South Africa.

The world of academia has told us very little about rape and rapists. The important reason expounded for rape having received so little organized notice is that a crime only attracts attention when the actual and potential victims have sufficient resources and power to summon such attention (Clark & Lewis, 1977). It is therefore no coincidence that the increasing attention paid to rape is historically linked to the growth of the feminist movement in the late 1960s. Some of the most compelling insights into rape first appeared in feminist publications at this time.[1] Most were articles, not detailed studies, dealing with the feelings and reactions of the victim, and often including strong attacks on official and public attitudes towards rape and rape victims (Clark & Lewis, 1977). The 1970s and 1980s saw more comprehensive reports on the rape victims's ordeal — her fear, embarrassment, humiliation, anger, desire for revenge, guilt, and depression (Kanin & Parcell, 1977; Katz & Mazur, 1979; Kilpatrick *et al*, 1981; Bart, 1981). Yet, throughout this period, the men responsible for making victims of rape were to a large extent ignored. While this chapter focuses primarily on the rapist — his experience and the factors which contribute to his crime — aspects of the victim's experience and behaviour will also be addressed.

Many researchers of the rapist have avoided speaking to or interviewing him, but instead have tended to try to understand him theoretically, from a knowledge of patriarchy, sex roles, and the victim's account of her experience (Connell & Wilson, 1974; Hill, 1982; Brownmiller, 1975). This information is of use, but nevertheless inhibits a comprehensive understanding of the rapist because it ignores his actual experience.

There are innumerable difficulties involved in interviewing rapists. A central research problem is obtaining subjects. The South African prison authorities are generally reluctant to allow rapists to speak to non-prison medical practitioners and investigators. Rapists who have not been charged are unlikely to come forward and volunteer information for fear of being reported. Such factors make sample sizes small, preventing the presentation of large-scale demographic details and profiles.

Furthermore, presuming that the prison authorities do permit one to interview convicted imprisoned rapists, difficulties in obtaining reliable information exist. Imprisoned rapists are likely to tell the researcher what they believe she/he wants to hear, since they are of the opinion that this will positively affect their possibility of early release.

Another problem is sample selection. Rapists who are studied are normally men who have been convicted. Since the majority of rapists are likely to be undetected, and those that are charged are generally from a working-class background, samples of convicted rapists are generally unrepresentative of the rapist population.

Despite these difficulties, it is crucial that such research continue. Developing an understanding of the rapist is central to the formulation of a science of rape. By accomplishing the latter, better preventive measures can be devised so as to significantly limit the incidence of rape in our society.

This chapter is based on interviews with nine rapists who all lived in Riverlea, a 'coloured' township on the south-western border of Johannesburg. Five of the rapists had been convicted of rape. Four only admitted to rape in the course of the interview. The nine rapists were part of a larger sample of twenty-seven subjects, nine of whom had been involved in physical assault but not rape, and nine who had not committed any violence against persons. Thus there were three groups of subjects: a rape group, a physical assault group, and a non-violent group. The criterion for the rape group was that the man must have coerced a woman into having sexual intercourse with him. Although rape should encapsulate all forms of sexual coercion, this definition (which is similar to the current legal one) was adopted because a standardized behaviour would make comparative analysis easier.

THE RESEARCH STUDY

Riverlea, the setting

In 1985, Riverlea had an official population of close on 12 000 people. Recent unofficial estimates put the figure around 25 000. Riverlea's residents seem to divide their community into two sections — the areas below and above the railway line. Living conditions are very different in these areas. Above the line there is more affluence and some streets are distinctively middle class. Below the line there is overcrowding, houses are small and of poor quality, there is considerable unemployment, and the incidence of alcoholism, drug abuse, gang fights, and domestic violence is high. The subjects interviewed were drawn from this area.

Like the educational standard of the subject sample in the study, the majority of Riverlea's residents have an education level between standards five and eight. The low level of education in the community is reflected by only a half a percent of its population having a post-matric qualification, while only 10 per cent have attained a matric. The educational profile of Riverlea's residents helps to partly account for why only approximately one per cent of the population engage in senior white-collar work, such as managerial work. Most of the population are involved in manual labour, and there is a reported unemployment figure of 10 per cent. The latter, according to social service workers in the area, is an underestimate.

Demographic details of the subjects

All the subjects had similar educational backgrounds, age levels, marital status, and occupations. Most had, as earlier mentioned, completed between a standard five and standard eight education. The average age in the non-violent group was almost twenty-nine years, while in the other two groups, the average age was approximately twenty-four and a half years.

The majority of subjects in all groups were unmarried, but most of the men in each of the groups had children. Most of the subjects were manual labourers, and unemployment was found in each of the groups. All except one member of the non-violent group reported being members of Christian denominations.

THE AETIOLOGY AND NATURE OF RAPE

Just as it is impossible to put forward the same set of causes for every man raping, one cannot assert a prototype of a rapist. Common features do exist, but the biographical details are different. Furthermore, some men rape only in certain circumstances and contexts. Their offences are disparate in nature. Some rapes are of longer duration and more violent than others, while some rapes involve lone rapists, and others gangs. The former is the major focus of this study. Despite all the differences between rapists, two generalizations about rapists can be made. Firstly, they have a strong desire to assert their power through coercion, and secondly, they are unable to perceive women as people (Fremont, undated).

To make the study of rape and the rapist's behaviour more coherent, a feminist analysis, which views society and the attitudes and behaviour of men and women within an economic, political, and cultural totality, has been employed. Feminism is not only about women, as popular ideology suggests; it is about women and men, and their intra-relationships and inter-relationships. This chapter adopts a feminist position which does not hold biology as the over-determining factor in the behaviour of the sexes. It thus rejects the radical feminist, conservative, and sexist biological thesis of human development. Such theories posit, for example, that in relation to violence men are naturally more aggressive, and women intrinsically more passive. Instead, this chapter adopts a framework supported by both socialist and liberal feminists that human conduct is largely socially constructed.

In tackling the question of why men rape, three primary interconnected theories emerge. The first is that of sexist ideology and the rapist's imbibation of all the qualities assigned to the male sex role. The second is the shocking picture of our society as a 'rape culture' in which rape is tacitly accepted. This is evidenced partly through patriarchal institutions and structures in our society, sexist interpersonal relations, the great importance society attaches to male power and aggression, and the social, economic, and political factors that lead to violence. Finally, there is the postulate of rape as a mechanism of social control. Rape, like other forms of sexist behaviour, dehumanizes women and accentuates their forced subservience to men.

A detailed presentation of the individual, social, and personal factors which make up the aetiology of rape are beyond the scope of this chapter. Therefore, only a few central features will be focused on. As suggested, the ideology of sexuality and current norms of sexual behaviour are primary contributing factors to rape. For example, in dating many men tend to measure the success of their sexual encounters on a physical intimacy scale. On this scale, sexual intercourse is the ultimate achievement. This often means that if a particular point in erotic intimacy is reached on one occasion, the man expects to gain ground in the next. It is this belief that often leads, for example, to 'date rape'.

Within the domain of sexual practice, the institutions of (for instance) pornography and prostitution also help to encourage rape. Prostitution, like much of pornography, helps to contribute to the image of the woman as a docile object, and the man as a sex-hungry, domineering subject. With reference to hard-core pornography, to which many of the subjects in this study had access, much of it promotes the notion that sexual aggression is erotic and desirable.

Language is also not without its contribution. Although the cardinal function of language is to facilitate communication, its importance extends far beyond this. It mirrors the prevailing culture, and teaches and abets the attitudes which helped create it (Schulz, 1975). Language in a sexist society therefore comprises of words which are distasteful to many women (and some men). Very often, sexist language objectifies women. They become less human — they become 'chicks' and 'birds'. An excellent example of the reification of women is encapsulated in a rapist's description of his participation in a gang rape with thirteen other men, in which a woman was severely assaulted and raped for two hours:

You can't get your satisfaction out of this woman lying there like a piece of pole in front of you. A woman you rape will never give her best.

He and his mates had not assaulted, raped, defiled, and humiliated another human being, they had used a 'piece of pole'.

As will be illustrated in this chapter, rape is primarily an act of power, and the rapist's desire to assert his power can be linked to a number of economic, social, and political factors. Of these, only work will be concentrated on. Work is of central importance because men fix much of their identity around their occupation (Tolson, 1977) — 'an ideal man should do a man's job'.

Thus unemployment, a condition with which anywhere between two to four million men in South Africa are familiar, and which has become an increasing problem in Riverlea, is likely to threaten the personal identity of a mass of men. Instead of perceiving their situation as a fault of the economic system, many see it as a personal failing.

Dissatisfaction with work is another condition all too common among men. This dissatisfaction manifests itself in resentment, boredom, and a feeling of powerlessness. Negative attitudes and feelings about work amongst men from Riverlea can be linked to some or all of the following: poor wages; dangerous work conditions; racism; the absence of control over work conditions; and perseverance, despite being dissatisfied, because of the difficulty of finding alternative employment.

Passive acceptance, heightened dependence, and powerlessness, particularly because they run counter to a masculine sense of self, provide a strong foundation for frustration. The level of frustration is based on the strength of the person's desire to achieve the frustrated goal (e.g. work satisfaction), and the degree to which the goal is interfered with (e.g. boring work, racist supervisor) (Miller, 1941). According to Miller's (1941) frustration-aggression hypothesis, frustration often leads to aggression, but the resulting aggression is not necessarily directed against the immediate source of frustration. This may be due to the source's superior power, and the great risks involved. For instance, a male worker's fear of losing his job might prevent him from directing his aggression at the immediate source of his hardship, his boss, and redirect it to another less dangerous source. Dollard *et al.* (1939) have called this occurrence 'displacement'.

If men do not always aggress against the source of frustration, who do they aggress against? In many respects, the perfect victim is a woman. For what is required is someone the man can overpower and control without too many negative economic or social consequences, someone who cannot challenge his physical strength, and someone who can reaffirm some of his lost masculine feelings. A no-nonsense mechanism of doing this is physical assault and rape. The latter provides short-term relief to frustration, alters self-conception positively, and can be justified by social norms.

Since unemployment and extreme frustration in the working place are more likely to be experienced by the working class, are men who live below the railway line in Riverlea more likely to rape than the middle-class men who live above it? In more general terms, do working-class men have more potential to rape than middle-class men? This question cannot be answered empirically, since no data has been collected on the occupational and economic status of rapists. And even if this data was available, statistics would be skewed because middle-class rapists are less likely to be apprehended or convicted. Their economic power, for example, often means that victims who share the same work environment are less likely to report them. The perceived social power of the middle-class rapist may also result in women, particularly working-class victims, believing that the police and the courts will be sympathetic to the offender.

Having said that working-class men are more likely to be disenchanted with their occupational lives than their middle-class counterparts, it does not mean that the latter do not experience work dissatisfaction. They do. They feel disenchanted by not receiving promotions, or by insufficient financial remuneration. The competition in white-collar and business jobs can be fierce, and not all are winners. One result is that non-achievers feel inadequate and need to regain a sense of power. This, like their working-class counterparts, they may do at the expense of women.

There are numerous men, whether blue-collar or white-collar workers, who are dissatisfied with their work and do not rape. It is therefore important to understand the issue of occupational disenchantment within the context of other contributing variables. Just as it is improbable that a man will rape solely because he is politically dissatisfied and feels powerless, it is unlikely that he will rape solely because he is unhappy in the workplace. To rape, he will also need to feel inadequate in other spheres of life, and to objectify the woman, feel aggressive towards her, and see violence and coercion as a means of resolving tension and fulfilling desire.

Resolving conflict and problems through violence has long been a major part of South African culture. Violence played a significant role in African tribal society and in white colonial settlement, and it is currently a popular method of resolving conflict and achieving certain goals in the family, in sexual relationships, in the school, in peer groups, as well as in the industrial relations and political sphere.

Within a small community like Riverlea, violence is strongly intertwined with a machismo ethos. It is often a bestower of esteem and respect. A statement by one rapist illustrates this point:

> I felt proud of myself. You see we have a small township and if that thing [massive fist fight] happens in our township, then I feel like a bit of a hero because I started the whole thing. It was a good feeling.

A primary venue for violence in Riverlea is the family. Both the norm of male dominance and notions of family privacy frequently make male violence a sanctioned activity within the family (Marsden, 1978).

Using Bandura's (1965, 1971) theory of modelling, it becomes apparent that the violent behaviour of adults provides boys with a model to relate to. This is especially significant in relation to woman, since the violence boys witness is, more often than not, directed against their mothers. Their mother's response often fits the traditional mode of behaving — passive and accepting. Said one rapist, 'She just used to take it all the years. It's like this and, I must accept it.' The experience of parental conflict and the effects of sex role socialization help to reproduce this mode of relating in adulthood. As Melani and Fodaski (1974: 85) put it:

> We find, in the early lives of many convicted rapists, an indication of great parental friction, with a violent father abusing an ineffectual mother. The culturally established images of male aggressiveness and female weakness, learned from the parents and approved by society in general, are thus duplicated symbolically and physically in the explosive act of rape.

Observation is not the only method for learning about violence, some children learn about it through being victims of it themselves. Results yielded from the author's study indicate that while none of the subjects of the non-violent group were severely beaten, most of the rapists and physical assaulters had experienced physical and psychological abuse as children. Many of these violent childhood encounters occurred with their fathers. One rapist remarked: 'He would hit us with his fist and with his belt until we had blue marks.'

Removing a child from a violent environment does not necessarily inhibit the possibility of violent behaviour in adulthood. If a boy is raised in a violent family and culture, is punished through violence, and is seldom responded to with love, it is to be anticipated that he will at a later stage resort to violence. The boy learns that violence is a plain sailing method to get what he wants and to control the behaviour of others.

Besides witnessing the violence perpetrated against his mother, another reason for the boy later directing his aggression towards women is his perception and experience of his mother (Bradbury, 1982; Pleck, 1979). The mode of relating to his mother changes from absolute dependency and intimacy at the time of birth to a perception of her as servant and nurse — a somewhat inferior person. The boy learns that he is in a position to both dominate and be dominated. Sons dominate because they have been given some special status. They are taught the naturality of demanding from their mothers, and later from their girlfriends, lovers, and wives, nurturance and physical sustenance. Thus if a woman challenges him, does not demonstrate affection, or does not confirm his image of manhood, it conflicts with his perception of her as satisfier and nurturer. To overcome these anxieties, and reassert his masculinity, the man responds in a sexually aggressive fashion (Bradbury, 1982).

Another possible reason for the rapist expressing his aggression towards women is past anger for maternal neglect. Deprived of care and nurturance, the boy feels unloved, unspecial, and inadequate. To overcome his deprivation, he becomes greedy for attention and love. To ensure that he does not feel unspecial he might for instance be loud, abusive, be the joker and do things which gain him acclaim. Many of the latter actions may be directed towards women. Rape being an extreme behaviour is able to compensate for extreme insecurities and deprivation, and satisfy intense needs. By raping, the perpetrator feels special since he receives the complete attention of his victim. And because he can coerce the woman into having sex, he feels powerful and strong. He is thus able to remove himself from boyish memories of inadequacy and weakness.

The boy's conceptualization of his mother as the 'other' and inferior sex results in his rejection of any of the qualities associated with her. To be 'like a woman' is a disgrace. To inhibit this possibility, it is essential that men control and dominate those who are feminine. Tweedie (in Levine and Koenig, 1983: vi) states:

> A boy, reared by a woman, perceives that he is not as she is, that he must reject his beloved to gain himself, that paradise must be lost to achieve manhood. Whatever the beloved is, he must not be. Is she emotional? Then he must be unfeeling. Is she gentle? Then he must be aggressive. Is she kind? Then he must be unkind. His earliest model, from whom his earliest comfort came, must be obliterated. Many men manage this difficult transition and confine its injuries to themselves. Others, rapists among them, do not. The

necessary split is too painful, the interring emotion too grievous. Who do they blame for the murder of their souls, unconsciously? Women.

Rape is thus in part an act fuelled by the historical experience of the family, which leads to rage, vindictiveness, and revenge. In terms of the rapist's perceptions, it is a 'repayment in kind for childhood injuries received' (Tweedie, in Levine and Koenig, 1983: vii).

While having stressed the importance of familial and sub-cultural factors in contributing to rape, to understand the crime purely within this framework would be a mistake. The crime of rape is a reflection of the values of both the specific and broader culture. Thus, to view rape only as part of the violence that plagues the sub-cultures of working-class and black people would make it difficult to explain why middle-class white men, who are from communities where the incidence of violence is lower, rape. Therefore, while a familial and sub-cultural theory of rape is useful in explaining rape, the purpose and aim of sexual violence must not be placed in a social vacuum. As Wilson (1983: 67) points out:

> ... rape represents an act of machismo and sadistic domination, not only in the ghetto but also outside of it. It is not the subculture alone that is violent: our whole culture is suffused with beliefs in male supremacy, dominance and aggression.

The eulogization of violence as an appropriate tool to get what one wants means that the committal of violence often does not result in social censorship, but rather provides additional social status to the perpetrator. Since violence is void of social embarrassment, tacit social permission is granted. Within such a setting and considering women's inferior status, 'attacks on women are as certain ... as death and taxes — more certain than taxes, since some manage not to pay' (Shapiro, 1979: 469).

Sexuality and rape myths

Probably the most popular belief and myth about rape is that it is a sexual act, committed for sexual gratification by men who, in the face of women's sexual provocation, have lost their normal self-control. Men's sexual appetites are supposedly sufficiently volatile for a woman's dress, presence, or actions to trigger off exceptionally lustful behaviour. Women are expected to be conscious of this, especially if they choose to be sexually intimate but do not want to have sexual intercourse with a man. They are expected to impose certain limits so as to curb the man's powerful sexual drives. Of this scenario, Medea and Thompson (1972: 45) state:

We would prefer to establish that, if women flirt they are not inviting rape. If they kiss a man goodnight, they are not inviting rape. Even, and this should raise a few male hackles, if they should be guilty of 'teasing' a man, they are not inviting rape.

The myth that men's sexual cravings are uncontrollable is part of the fiction surrounding rape, and is used by many men to explain their behaviour. This myth has penetrated the minds of rapists and public alike. Said one rapist:

There is a thing as a rape. I mean look, you get guys that get tempted, something runs away with their mind ... They see a girl walking with a mini and he goes and rapes her. You find with guys its in them.

Besides devaluing men's responsibility for perpetrating rape, the above statement points to the belief that rape is a sexually spontaneous act, inflicted upon an unknown victim. Findings from studies (Amir, 1971; Bell, 1981; MASA, undated) show otherwise. At least half of rapes involve men known to the victim and take place in the victim's home. In these familiar situations, the vast majority of rapes are planned and premeditated.[2]

Related to the issue of spontaneity is the assumption that because men are overwhelmingly attracted to a woman's physical beauty, they find it difficult to contain their sexual drive. Rapists in the author's study did not mention this motivation. While some men are attracted to women purely on the basis of their looks, and prefer to rape stereotypically attractive women, this form of admiration is not sufficient for them to rape. The need to conquer and control is the primary contributing factor. Based on the rapist's idiosyncrasies, he may choose to assert his power and coercion in relation to 'physically beautiful' women because his conquest will be of greater value. Are stereotypically beautiful women therefore more vulnerable to attack? This question cannot at present be answered since no data has been collected on the rapist's perception of his victim's physical appearance. However, what is clear is that all sorts of women are raped, including those normally viewed as conventionally unattractive — like very old women.

In the light of the above, structural theories focusing on the sexual nature of rape should be viewed with caution. For example, a study by Svalastoga (1962) attributes a higher incidence of rape in certain societies to an excess of males in the sex ratio, since a surplus of men makes the 'hunt' for sexual partners more tense. Theories of sexual access rest largely on the concept of relative deprivation and deviance. Individuals evaluate themselves partly on the basis of comparison with others.

Within the framework of sexual access theory, men without sexual partners are envious of men who do have partners. This then becomes a source of frustration and displeasure. Rape becomes a means of resolving this frustration and taking what is not available through legitimate avenues (Chappell *et al.*, 1977).

Lester's (1974) study, cited in Deming and Eppy (1981), brings the validity of the sexual access theories into question. He found no relationship between sex ratio and the incidence of rape. Further other studies (Deming & Eppy, 1981; Medea & Thompson, 1972; MASA, undated) indicate that the majority of rapists were involved in a consenting sexual relationship at the time of their rape. These findings were partly substantiated by the author's study — the majority of rapists had sexual access to a consenting partner at the time of their rape.

The notion that women enjoy rape does not only derive from media romanticization of rape, but also from sexual ignorance regarding female sexual arousal. If a man believes that women relish male sexual aggression, as many do, he will not see rape as harmful. When this is coupled with the perception that the central feature of sexual intercourse is satisfaction of a man's physical needs, it is no surprise to find that many rapists conceptualize sex as an act of aggressive passion devoid of mutual tenderness.

Another major factor tied up with sex is feelings of sexual and masculine inadequacy. Both may be the result of anxiety about sexual competence. Masculinity's strong association with the virility mystique has negative implications for men who do not comply with it. To overcome their insecurity, an over-identification with sexual and aggressive behaviour may occur (Deming & Eppy, 1981). In rape this may manifest itself in the offender forcing his victim to respond sexually, and to tell him that 'he is wonderful'.

In a war situation, where very real dangers of combat exist, as occurred for many South African men in Angola and Namibia in the 1980s, insecurity about masculinity can be further exacerbated. The insecurity of some men in war situations is such that they are extremely vulnerable to conformity pressure. This can lead to participation in army gang rapes. Komisar (quoted by Herman, 1979: 6) gives an example of this:

> In 1966, an American patrol held a 19 year-old Vietnamese girl captive for several days, taking turns raping her and finally murdering her. The sergeant planned the crime in advance, telling the soldiers during the mission's briefing that the girl would improve their 'morale'. When one soldier refused to take part in the rape,

the sergeant called him 'queer' and 'chicken', another testified later that he joined in the assault to avoid such insults.

In everyday heterosexual behaviour, sexual and masculine insecurity is most often magnified by sexual rejection. To defend against the failure of sexual conquest, some men prefer not to initiate sexual relations. Others cope by dismissing the rejecting woman as 'a nothing' or through lying about their sexual exploits. Among rapists, a popular method of coping with the fear and the occurrence of sexual rejection is not taking 'no' for an answer, or deceiving themselves that the woman's 'no' means 'yes'. In the context of sexual rejection rape 'represents a response arising out of the chaos of a beleaguered self image' (Chappell *et al.*, 1977: 231).

THE RAPE

As stated earlier, research into the rapist's behaviour and feelings during and after the rape has been minimal. In an investigation of these areas in this section, the rapist's experiences will be detailed, so that the rapist's feelings and attitudes throughout the offence can be better ascertained and understood.

Events leading up to rape

Rapists tend to exploit situations in which women are vulnerable to attack. This may mean raping women who are psychologically and economically powerless, physically disabled, mentally retarded, sleeping, very young, or very old (Selkin, 1975). Rapists in this study took the opportunity of raping adult women who were hiking, standing alone, intoxicated, being sexually intimate, or in need of an escort home. The common threads running through the rape situations described in this study are that the victims were alone, and that they were not in a position to defend themselves.

According to the rapists, many of the rapes were preceded by the woman being in a sexually intimate situation with another man or the offender himself. An example of the former is the rapist who waited for a friend to finish having sex with a 'girl', and then proceeded to rape her with the assistance of another friend:

> There was a girl, we were in the same standard. I also heard she was a girl who mucks around. We went to another friend's flat. He was busy with her and I watched through the louvre doors — and I see the guy busy and then he's finished. Then one of my classmates comes with me ... and held her legs ... and I had sex with her.

Superficial sexual encounters were the final precursor to other rapists' rapes. Many men expect to have sexual intercourse if the woman expresses sexual affection. Women's refusal to go 'all the way' is therefore frequently a forerunner to men's use of force and coercion.

Location

The majority of rapes are perpetrated in relatively safe environments where the victim is alone and the rapist will not be seen or interrupted. In this study, the most common location for rape was the victim's or rapist's home. Approximately 55 per cent of rapes were committed in these locations. The second most common place was large open spaces. Just over 44 per cent of rapes were committed in the veld or parks distant from highly populated areas.

These findings closely approximate those of other research. Amir (1971) found that 50 per cent of all rapes occurred in the victim's home, and 19 per cent in the assailant's home. Other figures for rapes occurring within all types of homes (rapist's, victim's, and other homes) are the following: Macdonald (1971) — 58 per cent; Medea and Thompson (1972) — 57 per cent; and Peters *et al.* (1976) — 51,9 per cent. The conclusion drawn from these statistics is that both public and domestic locations may be perilous. The myth that the home is a safe place, and that women can escape rape by avoiding dark alleys, should be laid to rest.

As indicated, a sizeable proportion of rapes are planned. This inevitably influences the location of the rape. In the example described below, the rapist's immense desire for 'sexual gratification' did not make him rape the 'girl' on the dance floor. He managed to control his sexual urges, and at the same time think about finding a private place:

> We [friends] went to the disco and I left my girlfriend at home. I danced with this one girl and without me trying anything, she was keeping me warm and I thought this is my chance. The first thing in my mind is sex. I danced a few numbers and took her out. Then I remembered a nice place, no one is there, it's not in town, it's past Eldorado Park. We went outside under a tree; there was no one around. I then took her, she had no chance.

In the above case, the woman appears to have been sexually assertive. But 'sexual liberation' from feminine passivity is not an unambiguous advantage for women. For while women now supposedly have the right to choose whom they want to have sex with and when, they are still trapped by society's double standards of respectability. When women walk late at night, hitchhike, or go to discos or shebeens by themselves, they may be called 'loose', and regarded as easy, even 'fair', targets. These were the insinuations the victim, in the case cited above, had to endure. Medea and Thompson (1972: 45) write:

> A woman can say 'no' all day, but if she has gotten herself into what, by Victorian standards, is a compromising situation, she will not be believed. At the present time, the rapist has the best of both worlds — women who are taking more risks, and a society which says that if they take those risks they deserve whatever they get.

The rapist's experience

In the interests of clarity, the rapist's experience has been broken up into component parts, although these are clearly interconnected. They include: the rapist's pattern of interaction, which tends to involve the threat of force, actual force, and various other manipulatory techniques; the rapist's responses to his victim's behaviour; the type of language which the rapist uses; his sexual behaviour during the rape; the length of the rape; and the rapist's feelings during the rape.

Patterns of interaction

When men have power over women, the possibility of rape exists. During rape, power may be expressed in different ways. Tedeschi *et al.* (1973) describe two different patterns of interaction used to gain power in a two-person encounter. Both of these patterns were employed by rapists in this study. The first is an open method of coercion whereby the assertion of power is not concealed. The second mode of interaction involves manipulation. With this method, the power seeker's intent is disguised. Rapists in this study tended to favour the open method of coercion, using either the threat of force or force itself. At times, however, this mode of interaction was interspersed with manipulatory techniques.

Threat of force

Instilling fear is an effective means of ensuring compliance. Rapists instil fear by making a variety of threats which focus on the victim's social and physical vulnerability. The threat of physical assault is the most recurrent. A rapist in the present study commented:

> I will say 'ek sal jou slaan' [I will hit you], then she sorts of gives in … I've done it, say about three or four times.

To give more weight to their threats of physical injury, some rapists display and make use of weapons:

> When we got to the veld, I took out my gun and fired a shot into
> the air to frighten her. She was frightened because she could see
> that it wasn't a toy.

The exhibition and use of violent weapons serve another purpose —
that of validating masculinity and power. By demonstrating to his victim
his ability to handle aggressive armoury, the rapist engages in traditional
machismo behaviour, and at the same time illustrates his domination
over the woman. In this case, firing into the air displayed a lack of
concern about the gun's noise. This would have increased the victim's
fear and feelings of helplessness, for the rapist's confidence that he
would not be heard meant he believed her screams for assistance would
be futile, and it certainly meant they would not halt his sexual assault.

Other intimidatory tactics employed by rapists include the threat of
incarceration, and attacks on the victim's social respectability. Both these
mechanisms were successfully utilized by one rapist:

> She had to give in, because she knew if she's not going to give in,
> then I'm not going to let her go home, because I'm going to keep
> her there the whole night. I just told her, 'if you not going to give
> it, I'm not going to let you go home. You'll sleep right here'.
>
> I wanted to rape her, but then I took on second thoughts and
> thought 'no'. I know her and she knows me, let me rather talk nicely
> … I told her you must not come with your 'shit' here. You must
> give me, otherwise it's bad and I'm going to tell everybody. You
> know, just making up stories.

Besides his distorted conception of what it means to rape or to 'talk
nicely', the rapist's statement reveals his ability to make use of society's
double standards. He appeared to have such confidence in society's
prejudiced sentiments about women who find themselves in intimate
sexual situations, that he used the threat of societal exposure to gain
further control over his victim. If anyone's respectability is endangered,
it should have been his for raping his victim, and not the victim's for being
raped. Thus men's power over how women are perceived, and more
specifically their ability to cast a shadow on women's social respectability, were partly responsible for this rape.

Threats and overt intimidation are central components of rape.[3] Those
who deny the reality of rape, and jokingly claim that 'a pencil cannot be
inserted through a moving doughnut', fail to comprehend this. They do
not realize that the victim faces menacing threats, and that by the time
sexual intercourse occurs, she 'has been terrorized into co-operating with
her assailant or is immobilized with fear' (Selkin, 1975: 71). A lack of
physical resistance by the victim is not indicative of ambivalence towards

her assailant, as some defence attorneys want to argue. It is reflective of fear.

Use of physical violence

The majority of rapists do not stop at threats and actually employ physical force. Amir (1971) has estimated that in over 85 per cent of reported rapes, the victim had to endure some sort of physical violence. Roughness was used in over 25 per cent of the cases; non-brutal beatings in just under 25 per cent; brutal beatings in more than 20 per cent, and choking in close to 12 per cent. Van Ness (1984) reports that the majority of youth rape offenders used guns or knives to coerce their victims. Clearly, if sadistic threats instil fear, then actual violence terrorizes the victim even further.

One of the most common constituents of 'rough' behaviour is the forceful removal of the victim's clothes. For the victim, exposure of her naked body to a terrifying, hating attacker is a source of great humiliation. In addition to setting the tone for more gruesome violence, aggressive removal of the victim's clothes indicates the rapist's determination to accomplish his goal. A statement from a rapist substantiates this:

> I wanted to have sex — she didn't want to have sex with me. She was fighting back crossing her legs. And then I pulled off her boob tube and she pulls it up and I go and pull it off again. Eventually I got it down and then I struggle opening up her legs and all that.

In a second case, the woman had initially physically demonstrated her liking for the man. Yet he still found it necessary to use physical force. It appears that violence was used in order to guarantee completion of the sex act. This may be because the rapist, perhaps on the basis of previous experience, feared rejection. Alternatively, he may have believed that since the woman had consented to some sexual intimacy, he was entitled to her complete sexual submission.

Many rapists used moderate forms of violence: 'holding her down with my hands'; 'grabbing her by her tits'; 'keep her hand and pull down her panties'. There seems little doubt that if the victims in these cases had resisted more resolutely, moderate violence would have turned into brutal violence. In these instances, the process of rape had already begun, and the rapist was determined that no obstacle would prevent him from having sexual intercourse. One rapist's rape encounter exemplified this. After threatening and grabbing his victim by 'her tits', he still faced resistance. He described his response to his victim's continued unwillingness:

> How are you going to get that sexual excitement out of her, if she
> is not willing to have sex with you ... You know how you get it,
> you become cross — I smacked her.

Some rapists do not even come close to the display of physical affection
and use violence immediately. A simple 'no' to sexual advances is
sufficient to galvanize some rapists into brutalizing their victims. Said
one:

> I was forced to do it because I couldn't control myself ... Lots of
> times, I have used a lot of force. If I talk to a girl and she doesn't
> want to have sex with me ... I would start hitting her.

The rapist's use of violence in response to female sexual rejection does
not only serve to rid him of anger; it is also a declaration to his victim that
no matter what she may do, he is still a 'man', still sexually and physically
dominant. Through force he illustrates to her that she really does desire
him — for despite her refusals, she is nevertheless having sex with him.
The rapist's impatience at not receiving instant sexual gratification further
stimulates his violent behaviour. His socialized method of achieving
instant solutions to problems is through violence. A rapist commented:

> A few kicks and smacks ... is the quickest way. It's useless taking
> a cherrie out and then sit the whole night and treat her nice. If you
> are going to take her, what's the point, you are still going to be
> arrested.

Sadly, because of the convergence of sex and male domination in our
society, acts of force within the sexual arena are not always perceived as
aggression. Medea and Thompson (1972: 12) assert that:

> Killing and hitting are seen as real acts of aggression by one person
> against another, regardless of whether they are taken to court; they
> are acts which may provoke revenge. Strangely, however, in the
> case of rape that connection — that it is an act of aggression
> regardless of whether or not it is prosecutable — is not made. It is
> not made in the mind of the rapist. Sometimes it is not made in the
> mind of the victim. It is seldom made in the minds of the people
> the victim will have to deal with after the attack.

Often it is only when the rapist engages in physical brutality, such as
sticking sharp objects into his victim's vagina, or hitting, punching, and
kicking her, that the rapist, the victim, and the public will classify rape
as an aggressive act.

Any discussion about mechanisms of coercion and physical violence
in rape must examine the phenomenon of gang rape.[4] In the present
study approximately 44 per cent of rapists had engaged in gang rape.
The phenomenon of gang rape provides clues to men's brutal treatment

of women. A brief description of one gang rape will give the reader some sense of the ruthlessness of this crime:

> One night, we saw two women standing at the gate. While we were talking with these two women, these fourteen 'ouens' [young men] came up. We were all under the influence of liquor and we just decided at the same time that we are going to rape them. The one ran away, so there were about thirteen of us that rape the one woman ... She was very 'dead'. They fucked her up, blue eyes and all ... because she didn't want to take her pants off.

Another feature of gang rape (although it also occurs when there is an individual rapist) is making the victim's boyfriend or husband watch the offence. A report in *Business Day* of 17 April 1989 highlighted one gruesome incident: The offence occurred near the isolated Nasrec centre in south Johannesburg. It began about 10.30 p.m. when a couple in a parked car were held up by four men armed with guns. The couple were forced out of the car and the woman was gang raped while her companion was held at gunpoint. A short while later, another (second) couple who were driving past were forcibly stopped by the gang. The woman in the second couple was forcibly raped by one of the gang members. The gang then forced (probably under threat of assault, or murder of his partner) the man in the second couple to rape the woman who had initially been gang raped. Afterwards the gang chased the second couple away, locked the first couple in the boot of their car, and drove off in another car.

Making a man watch the rape of his wife or sexual partner has two primary purposes. Firstly, it makes the husband or the boyfriend part of the rape by having to 'passively' observe it. Secondly, it is an illustration of the rapist's greater power relative to the other man, since the man is perceived as incapable of safeguarding and controlling 'his woman'. This type of rape serves to affirm the rapist's masculinity while destroying that of another man (Griffin, 1971). In the process the position of a woman as the property of a man, and as a sexual object to be used and abused becomes flagrantly conspicuous.

What makes the gang rape unique is that even though it is a situation 'in which no brutality, no threat even, would be necessary to subdue the victim', sadistic violence occurs on a large scale (Medea & Thompson, 1972: 36). Excessive force and debasement in rape point to other needs besides sexual gratification (Deming & Eppy, 1981). Thus, in studying the gang rape syndrome, one discovers conformity pressure and the participant's need to prove his sexual competence and physical strength to the others involved in the rape. This desire stems from insecurities about masculinity and sexual prowess. An example in the present study was the rapist who was concerned about the size of his penis during a gang rape: 'I was thinking about, I wonder whether she feels the difference inside her, you know big and small.' Sexual anxiety of this sort may precipitate overcompensatory behaviour, resulting in intense degradation of the victim.

The victim's behaviour and the rapist's response

More often than not, the victim does not passively accept her assailant's attack. She resists before and during the rape, or both. Her resistance may be related to her age, physical strength, experience of violence, and her confidence. According to Katz and Mazur (1979) young girls are inclined to struggle less than adolescents and adults; working-class women, who are often more familiar with violence, tend to resist physically more than their middle-class counterparts, who are frequently strangers to violence and have been socialized to be 'ladies'; and women who are assertive and confident in day-to-day social situations resist the rapist more fiercely. While these factors are of some significance, the primary factor determining the victim's resistance is the rapist's actions. In turn, his behaviour is influenced — to a lesser degree — by the victim's behaviour. From rapists' descriptions of their victims' resistance as described in this study, four broad categories of resistance have been identified: attention-seeking tactics; non-cooperation tactics; psychological tactics; and physical resistance.

Judging from an American study of victims' descriptions of resistance strategies during rape, rapists in this study have given a fairly consistent portrayal of their victims' resistance (*Psychiatric News*, 1975). The American study published in *Psychiatric News* reported that:

> Eighteen per cent [of victims] tried to determine possible alternatives, such as how to escape or wondering whether the assailant would panic; over half [57 per cent] used a verbal tactic such as trying to talk themselves out of the situation, stalling for time, reasoning with the assailant by trying to change his mind, trying to gain sympathy from the assailant, using flattery, attempting to strike a bargain, feigning illness, threatening the assailant, trying to change the assailant's perception of the woman, joking and using sarcasm; and 22% employed the physical techniques of attempting to flee the scene, or fighting with the assailant. Naturally some victims used a combination of these strategies.

Before delving into the four categories of victims' resistance, it must be stressed that resistance in this study has been discussed within the context of completed rapes. There are many accounts of successful resistance which have been documented elsewhere. One study, for example, claims that in one-third of situations involving sexual aggression the victim emerged victorious (Denver Anti-Crime Report, undated). Successful resistance was primarily achieved through yelling (15 per cent), physical resistance (18 per cent), and fleeing (24 per cent).

Attention-seeking tactics

'She would shout "Oh no, no"', was how a rapist characterized his victim's resistance. Shouting, screaming, and yelling are the most common attention-seeking tactics. They are often the tactics first employed by the victim. In general, the rapist responds to his victim's verbal protestations either by verbally reassuring her that the situation is not as menacing as it seems, or by using physical force to silence her. In doing this the rapist may also shift some responsibility for the act onto his victim. As one rapist stated:

> She did scream, but the way I was handling her was to say you must not go on like this. You're actually making me do it to you now.

Attention-seeking tactics appear to be successful only in public places. In other circumstances, they are largely ignored by the rapist. The development of hand-held gadgets which produce extremely loud sounds may be of use in scaring the rapist off. However, the high price of such technology makes it inaccessible to most working-class women. Interestingly, none of the rapists in this study reported that any of their victims had protection gadgets.

Non-cooperation tactics

These tactics can involve refusing to remove clothing, or not assisting with the insertion of the penis into the vagina. Non-cooperation does not cause many difficulties for the rapist. He either tears the woman's clothes off or beats her up until she removes them. With regard to penetration, the rapist proceeds without the victim's assistance. He often makes penetration easier for himself by wetting his victim's vagina with his saliva, which he applies with his fingers.

Psychological tactics

Strategies that fall within this category include reasoning with the rapist, frightening or disgusting him, or trying to gain sympathy from him. The

most assertive of these strategies is the victim's attempt to induce fear in
the rapist through threats:

> She said, she is going to tell her mother. She was still at school, she
> was 17. She said she will tell her friends. I said no man, what's she
> worried about her friends for.

In this example, the rapist went on to threaten her with physical assault
and to rape her. Other rapists were similarly unmoved by the victim's
endeavours to evoke sympathy. Said one rapist, 'She did it, but not
willingly. She kept telling me she was still a virgin and she is young and
she is at school'. He did take some notice of her plea, however: 'I didn't
want to do her harm, so I said she can keep my magazine [of the gun]'.
He proceeded to 'pomp her [have intercourse] about three times'.

Begging and straightforward appeals for understanding also had little
effect on the rapists studied. In one rape described by a rapist, a woman
was forcibly grabbed and pushed into a van by nine men. After they
began physically assaulting her, she repeatedly requested that they
release her. According to one of the rapists, she was saying, 'please guys,
I don't know you. My mommy is going to shout and things like that. I
can't go with you'. Her pleas fell on deaf ears. Six of the nine men brutally
raped her.

A more sophisticated strategy employed by one victim was to attempt
to evoke both sympathy and disgust in the rapist. Unfortunately, her
gambit failed, as the rapist responded even more aggressively.

> She came out with the story, she's sick and she has got a period.
> So I said to her, 'you mustn't speak shit with me'. I just wanted to
> have sex with her and she didn't have a period.

The question often asked by victims and concerned public with regard
to incidents such as the above is why does the rapist not respond to his
victim's pleas? This is related to two other questions — 'How could men
do this?' and 'Are the perpetrators ridden with guilt after the act?'

Much of the substance to the answers to these questions lies in the
rapist's objectification of his victim, which is an essential ingredient of
rape. For individuals to rape or to engage in extreme violence, it is
necessary that they perceive their victims as less than human. By
dehumanizing the rape victim, the rapist ensures that she loses her status
as a feeling, thinking human being who has the right to make her own
choices, including the right to say no. Feelings of guilt may be true for
some perpetrators, but for many, including those interviewed in the
present study, guilt is limited or non-existent because they have raped a
pathetic, disgusting creature unworthy of human respect. This attitude
helps to explain why in the process of the rape the victim's crying or

pleading meets with little response. At times such behaviour can increase the victim's dehumanization, since in the rapist's eyes she has become more pathetic — she is now a 'snivelling bitch'.

Although psychological tactics employed by the victim are not always successful in making herself more human and preventing rape, Storaska (1975) upholds them as the best rape prevention method. He believes that women can almost always avert rape by adopting strategies based on a personality assessment of the rapist. Strategies include complimenting the rapist on his personality or physical build, engaging in lengthy conversations, being vulgar (burping, urinating, defecating, vomiting), informing the rapist one has a venereal disease or Aids, or behaving in a bizarre fashion to defuse his sexual responses.

Physical resistance

None of the rapists told of victims who maintained concerted physical resistance throughout the rape. However, 55 per cent did report some form of physical rebuff from their victims. One rapist stated:

> So when I started pulling down her panties, she started pushing my hands away. So I asked her why she's doing that, doesn't she want to have sex with me. So she says, no she doesn't, she's not that kind of person, she only just fucks around. Like me, I got 'naar' [annoyed], so I forced her.

Another form of resistance, which only temporarily bothered the rapists, entailed the victim crossing her legs and pushing him away from her body. The rapist sometimes meets the victim's attempt to push him away by lying on top of her with increased weight, and by using more violence. This response was also employed by a rapist who had to deal with biting and scratching — 'she started getting excited and biting … scratching too … so I just stayed on top of her'. Of course, rapists do not always behave so calmly when confronted with this type of resistance. Said one rapist:

> They bite you, here on the chest, so you have to smack her and so on … After that she must be scared … she had to give in.

Physical resistance does not necessarily inhibit the rapist's will to continue with the act. In fact, it can have the opposite effect. Fifty-five per cent of the rapists in this study said they became more 'excited' when their victims resisted. This may be because resistance provided the opportunity for heightened use of aggression and force. One answer to the question 'Did her struggling excite you?' took this form:

> You enjoy it more having to struggle first. When other girls just say okay just come, you don't enjoy yourself like that. You have to struggle first and she has to make you hot.

The fact that rapists find resistance titillating again illustrates that the pleasure of raping lies in the assertion of power, and not merely the achievement of sexual orgasm. Broth (in *Time*, 5 September 1983) reports that a rapist told him:

> You know I could get all the sex I wanted because my brother ran a chain of massage parlours. But if they were giving it to me, I wasn't in control. I wanted to take it.

However, rapists do not always enjoy continual resistance. Eighty-eight per cent of rapists in this study wanted their victims to resist less. How is this apparent contradiction explained? It appears that while the victim's resistance does increase the rapist's sexual excitement, this excitement does not match the gratification provided by a more co-operative victim. Ideally, the rapist craves a victim who resists slightly: her struggling enables him to conquer her and experience corresponding feelings of power and control. At the same time, he can interpret the weakness of her resistance as a signal that she really desires him sexually. Considering that none of the victims vigorously physically resisted rape, it was not surprising to discover that 66 per cent of the rapists believed that their victims were 'playing hard to get' or enjoyed the rape experience. One rapist stated:

> I was holding and opening her legs ... but afterwards I don't think this could be rape ... because she didn't really fight back. She did say, no she doesn't want to do it, but maybe she did.

The question of whether women should be uncooperative and physically resist rape has been widely debated. Those favouring active revolt point to the many cases where potential victims have successfully resisted rape through attention-seeking tactics and physical resistance (Clark & Lewis, 1977). Those opposed to this position express concern that active resistance might provoke additional violence (Finkelhor & Yllo, 1982; Medea & Thompson, 1972; Russell, 1975; Selkin, 1975). A gruesome illustration of the violence that resistance can provoke is given by Wood (1974). She quotes Lear (1972) who speaks of a 37-year-old woman who required 120 stitches in her face and head after resisting a man who tried to rape her in New York's Central Park. A detective said of this case:

> We've been looking for this guy for a long time. Two years ago we picked him up for attempted rape, and it was a throw-out in court; no corroboration. Now we have this poor woman, who fought like

hell and didn't get raped. The guy has been indicted for assault in the first degree. She's scarred for life. And you know what she says now? She says she wishes she hadn't fought, and maybe he wouldn't have cut her up the horrible way he did.

It is on the basis of such incidents that Storaska (1975) suggests that if resistance is to be employed, it should be done through manipulatory or psychological means rather than physical techniques.

It emerges from this study that active resistance is unlikely to be effective in rape locations which are private, or with rapists who are extremely violent from the start of the rape. In these situations, psychological tactics may be more successful. However, in more public locations, active resistance may scare the rapist, who wishes to avoid detection. This does not apply in gang rapes, where there may be public support for the offence. *Time* (3 September 1983) detailed one such disturbing case:

Last March, a 21 year old mother of two walked into Big Dan's tavern in New Bedford, Massachusettes, to buy a pack of cigarettes. A man in the bar threw her to the floor, stripped her and hoisted her onto a pool table, where he and three companions took turns raping, sodomizing and beating the woman. Other patrons cheered the rapists on, screaming, Go for it! Go for it!

This emphasizes the complicity and guilt of those men who did not rape, but cheered and further encouraged the actual rapists to continue with their humiliation of their victim. What is indeed frightening about such an incident is that the rapists felt that they did not need to employ any caution in concealing their rape. The presumption was that all the men would support them. This incident, more than most, reveals the meaning of a sub-culture and culture of rape.

A noticeable feature of both a culture and sub-culture of violence is the 'shared commitment to violence and a shared concept of aggressive masculinity' (Deming & Eppy, 1981: 364) in homosocial relations. In Riverlea, for example, gang fights and gang rapes are not exceptional occurrences. Considering the high level of alienation and conflict within the community, this is not surprising, since gang rapes provide a rationale for solidarity and an interaction based on male bonding and masculine validation (Brownmiller, 1975).

The rapist's speech

It is not only a rapist's violent behaviour that can damage a woman emotionally. Verbal abuse can be equally damaging. The rapist's insulting language intensifies the victim's humiliation. His words reinforce his derogatory perception of her: she is nothing more than a 'juicy little bitch'.

The rape perpetrated by one rapist provides a good example of how verbal behaviour is used to debase. He admits that what he said to her could not be termed 'talking — it was more like making fun of her'. Says the rapist of the incident: 'She was sitting in the van and five of us were laying there in the back, watching her and shouting about her body.'

Demeaning comments were also a component of a rape in which another rapist participated. The rape took place in the victim's house. Immediately prior to the rape, the victim was voluntarily having sex in her bedroom with one of the rapist's friends while he and two other friends sat in the lounge. No longer able to be left out of what was going on in the bedroom, the informant and his two friends entered and proceeded to rape the woman, assisted by the man with whom she had been having sex. As if to add to her humiliation, this man declared in the midst of the rape: 'you can give my round to the others, I mean it's still a cock.' This statement reflected the woman's position as a sexual object. It portrays her as unfeeling and undiscriminating. She is presumed to be indifferent to whom the penis belongs.

Earlier mention was made of verbal threats as a means of coercion. Occasionally this strategy leads to unexpected consequences. Instead of immobilizing the victim, threats may engender hysteria. The rapist often chooses between physical aggression and reassurance to deal with the victim's emotional protestations. In the case described below, the rapist tried to reassure his victim that their sexual encounter would soon be coming to an end:

> It was sore, you know how the first time a girl does it, she can't take it. She started crying and I just kept it in and said it's going to be over now my dear.

Ignorance of women's sexual responses and feelings is so widespread that rapists are prepared to suggest to the victim that her rape experience 'will be nice'. These rapists have so confused domination and sexual affection, that they are able to conceive of themselves as lovers. For them the line between sex and violence is extremely thin.

The rapist's sexual behaviour during the rape

The majority of rapists did not give any detailed account of their sexual behaviour during the rape. Those that did appeared to have incorporated a substantial amount of aggression and defilement into their sexual activity. For instance, one rapist who participated in a gang rape stated:

> Then she gave in and we had sex. She was bleeding afterwards, I think it was because of the way I was forcing it in. Also I think it was her first time.

Yet it is the very use of aggression and physical force that often inhibits the rapist's sexual enjoyment. To have their masculinity validated, rapists have to believe that their victims want them sexually. Thus when co-operation is lacking and force prevalent, rapists may feel cheated and unsatisfied.

What does this mean for the rapist's sexual behaviour during the rape? In this study, none of the rapists made any mention of erections or orgasms. Consequently, all information on this issue is drawn from the work of other researchers. Literature on the subject is sparse, however. Some rapists complain that they have difficulty obtaining erection and orgasm (Levine & Koenig, 1983). Many rapists have problems in maintaining an erection when they believe they are involved in a rape, rather than a seduction. Clark and Lewis (1977) have provided some statistics on the frequency of erection and orgasm among rapists. In 61,9 per cent of cases, no mention was made of orgasm. Only 7,0 per cent of rapists gave an unqualified confirmation of orgasm. Over 20 per cent admitted to not having achieved orgasm, and 10,2 per cent to having it with difficulty. Thus, in 33 per cent of reported rape cases, the rapist had problems with orgasm. According to Paske (1982: 53):

> ... generally in psychiatric literature sexual dysfunction as a whole is correlated with psychological mood, states of anxiety, depression and anger as well as with conflicts regarding sex — viewed as negative or dirty, as dangerous, etc. These same factors are prominent characteristics of rapists.

It should also be noted that in over half of the cases studied, problems with orgasm were associated with difficulties with erection (Clark & Lewis, 1977). Unfortunately, this involves a bitter irony for the victim. It is precisely because the rapist is unable to achieve erection or orgasm that the victim's forcible confinement can be prolonged. In this extended period, she has to endure further humiliation, and sometimes degrading sexual acts.

Another irony of the rapist's sexual dysfunction is the legal consequences it may have for the offence. The rapist's defence team may assert that since no sperm was found in the woman's vagina, rape could not have occurred (Paske, 1982: 57). It is in the light of this that Paske comments:

'The lack of sperm in the alleged victim's vagina does not preclude the possibility that she was indeed raped.'

Duration of the rape

No information was forthcoming regarding the exact duration of rapes. Some rapists reported raping their victims for 'two hours' and 'a whole night'. The length of these rapes could be the consequence of problems with erection or orgasm, or prolonged desire to debase the victim.

The rapist's feelings during the rape

The rapist's primary feelings during the rape have already been documented. Feelings of sexual enjoyment, sexual exasperation, power, control, and insecurity have all emerged. Other emotions also feature.

A rapist's statement, 'I felt nothing at the time. I just wanted to have sex', sheds light on his divorcing sex from any emotion, as well as his objectification of the woman. The victim had become objectified to the extent that he was concerned only with his self-gratification. The cost of his gratification, in terms of his victim's pain, was of no significance to him. This callous disregard for, and dehumanization of, the rape victim can be contrasted with the way some rapists treat women for whom they feel affection. According to one rapist:

> I don't feel anything for her and won't worry about her and what time she has to go home … it's just straight sex, when you come, you are finished. But with a cherrie that I am moving with, I dance with her, cuddle her, it's more romancing with her.

The two quotations cited below reveal rapists' principal feelings to be of power, control, and strength. This bears out one of the central contentions of this study, namely that the primary motivation for rape is the offender's need for power, which he attains through sexual conquest:

> I feel strong … It feels good to make a girl scared … It feels good because she is listening to you.

> I felt … I was the best, I had put her down … [also] it made me feel even better … to know I am a man because a woman is bowing down to you.

Thus far, some of the reasons for why men rape and how they feel while raping have been explored. But how does the rapist feel when the rape is over? In briefly examining this, greater insight can be obtained into the rapist's perceptions of the crime, as well as the reasons for so few women reporting rape.

The aftermath of the rape

Most rapists in the present study were calm immediately after the rape. They made no attempt to flee the scene of their crime.

Some even escorted their victims back to their homes or to the discotheque where they were previously. The rapists' behaviour immediately after the rape suggests that they are unaware of their victims' feelings towards them. Most of them do not acknowledge the brutality of their offence. They tend to perceive their actions as being beyond reproach, or perhaps as a slight misdemeanour. The fact that a rapist can walk his victim home, or take her back to a disco, without extreme fear of legal or social reprisals, may point to a perception that he has done nothing criminal or harmful. It may also be indicative of his confidence that his victim will not report the attack.

Rapists' feelings after raping can be divided into three basic categories: the no guilt and indifferent feelings; the 'slight regret' feelings; and the remorseful feelings. The rapist may experience different feelings after different rapes. Most rapists fall into the first two categories, largely because of their sexist attitudes and behaviour.

The type of rapist who escapes guilt feelings entirely is one who objectifies women excessively. For such a rapist, the concept of rape is inconceivable because women are not self-determining individuals with the right and ability to choose. One rapist remarked: 'Once you have finished with that [sex], you feel nothing for that girl. Once you have come, you think nothing about her.'

Rapists with slight regret feelings recognize their use of coercion in the rape, and feel slightly perturbed by such coercive behaviour. Said one rapist:

> I felt shit and thought hey, why did I do it? I went to her and spoke about it but then I told her 'it's your own fault and you know … it won't be the last'.

The rapist indicated his awareness that intercourse achieved through coercion is morally reprehensible. But his insensitivity and superficial awareness prevent the development of a long-term sense of concern and guilt. This rapist preferred to escape responsibility for his actions by blaming his victim, and he repressed the recognition of his violence by suggesting that his conduct would continue in the future.

The rapist's slight regret (which soon turns into no regret) can be traced to a number of sources. Firstly, there is the desire to see his victim again. This applies particularly when his victim is his girlfriend, lover, or wife. The second reason for the rapist's self-condemnation is his fear that his victim will report the crime to the authorities. Another motivating factor may be his social conscience. Even though his peer group and his cultural context may support his conduct, he is aware that there is a small section of his community (e.g. church officials) who regard rape as wrong. However, these small sectors cannot be expected to influence the rapist sufficiently to change his sexually aggressive behaviour.

Only one of the rapists in the study had any remorse after the rape. He had raped three times, but his guilt was reserved for the one victim who he said came from 'a respectable family'. Unlike the sexually promiscuous women who were his two other victims, the respectable woman was perceived as having feelings and sensations.

The lack of remorse and guilt after the rape suggests that offenders do not classify their own behaviour as rape and that they are unaware of the devastating effects of their actions, and are somehow able to rationalize their crime. This does not mean that all rapists remain unperturbed by the incongruity between their attitudes and their behaviour. In fact, most rapists engage in a process of rationalization in order to deal with their (slight) regret or guilt. This process of rationalization further indicates rapists' prejudiced attitudes and feelings towards women. A belief in rape myths, described earlier, is a primary factor in assisting rapists to deny responsibility for their offence.

Rapists also vindicate their behaviour by asserting that alcohol and drugs made them uncharacteristically aggressive and sexually uncontrollable. While alcohol and drugs do act as disinhibitors of behaviour, and thus can be seen as contributing factors to the offender's aggression, his choice of women as a target of his aggression is guided by his attitudes — and those of his society — about women, sex, and violence.

There are a number of psychological mechanisms through which rapists justify their conduct. A primary one involves social comparisons. According to Festinger (1954) people do not compare themselves randomly to others; they tend to draw comparisons with people they see as roughly similar to themselves. A rapist who has reservations about his conduct may therefore ask members of his peer group for their opinions and change his attitude in the direction of the norm. Because friendships are usually based on similarities, the rapist's peer group probably has sexist views and believes the common myths about rape. Consequently, after speaking to his peer group, it is less likely that the rapist would be conflict-ridden about his behaviour.

POLICE AND COURT TREATMENT OF RAPE CASES

Within and after the rationalization period, the rapist may become perturbed by the possibility of arrest and conviction. An awareness of this possibility determines the behaviour of some rapists during and after the offence. However, most rapists were not particularly concerned about the consequences of their conduct, and some took it for granted that their victims would not report the rape. Some of the reasons for the victim's reluctance to report the rape are dealt with below.

The police attitude towards the victim sometimes puts the rapist at an advantage. According to Robin (1977), in Western countries police advice and behaviour towards the victim is often guided by the 'slum sex code' which is a moral appraisal of the victim. For example, if the victim was drunk, is black, or is suspected of moral promiscuity, then her report is less likely to be believed. Police may also be less sympathetic to victims wanting to prosecute in cases where there has been little physical violence, and where a prior sexual relationship has existed between her and the assailant.

In an interview with the author in May 1989, Lieutenant-Colonel Frans Malherbe, the Witwatersrand police liaison officer, asserted that the police attitude towards the complainant is irrelevant, since they are obliged to investigate all complaints. It was only the public prosecutor, he said, who could decide whether to charge someone, or alter the charge to a lesser charge, such as indecent assault.

While noting the obligation the police are under to investigate all complaints, the question is how much time they put into their investigations. While official policy does not determine which victim's complaints should receive more attention, the police may be influenced by their social and political views when investigating certain complaints. According to a study conducted in the United States in the late 1960s, police believe that 80 to 90 per cent of the rapes reported to them are not really rapes. There has been no local research to establish whether this statistic holds true for South Africa, but if such official attitudes do exist, then the rapist need not be overly anxious of incarceration.

Police questioning, which reflects police attitudes, may equally provide the rapist with a measure of indirect protection. Insensitive questions asked of the victim — 'Did you enjoy it?' — serve to inhibit victims from reporting rape. In a 1981 'Opinion Finder' feature of a popular South African magazine, *Darling*, seventy-nine respondents stated that police were insufficiently sympathetic towards rape victims. This view of the police attitude may help to explain why, in the same survey, 58 per cent of women said they would not go to the police if they were raped.

If a victim does report the offence to the police, her insensitive treatment may continue. She will be taken to the district surgeon or a hospital, where she is often left alone for lengthy periods. She frequently becomes nauseous as she is prohibited from washing the semen or blood from her body. The rape victim may also, according to Levett, have to deal with an unsympathetic attitude from the district surgeon since 'there are some district surgeons [in South Africa] who readily express the belief that many women complain of rape falsely' (Levett, 1981: 78).

In contrast to the victim, the apprehended rapist may receive lenient treatment from the police. This occurs particularly when, according to one rapist, 'it's a policeman that knows you or likes you'. Familiarity with the local police is not unusual in the context of small communities like Riverlea, where residents and the police often consort and fraternize.

Of course, not all police treat rapists and victims in these ways. This is an important point to note, since police conduct may be stereotyped and distorted so that understanding of rape and the non-reporting of the offence may be incomplete or skewed. There are many in the police force who act with care and concern and work long hours to apprehend the rapist. Unfortunately, the treatment accorded by the police to some rape victims, and occasional reports of policemen themselves raping, negate much of this good work.

If the rapist is apprehended and charged, the law affords him good protection. For example, Section 197 of the Criminal Procedure Act 51 of 1977 provides that 'An accused who gives evidence at criminal proceedings shall not be asked or required to answer any questions tending to show … that he is of bad character'. If the accused challenges the complainant's character, then the accused may lose the protection accorded to him and questions may be put to him to indicate that he is of bad character. This procedure changes substantially when the person is accused of perpetrating a crime of an 'indecent nature'. In the rape situation, the accused is entitled to acquire information about the complainant without endangering the protection granted to him in terms of Section 197. The implication of this, says Hoffman (1970), is that testimony regarding sexual history cannot be used against the alleged rapist, but can be used against the complainant to demonstrate the probability of her consenting to sexual intercourse.

The court's emphasis on consent seems to be rooted in the notion that women lay false charges of rape. To prevent unjust prosecution, courts demand corroboration of the victim's testimony. Corroboration is confirmation by additional evidence that the defendant is the rapist; that penetration took place; and that the complainant did not give her consent.

The circumstances of most rapes make it likely that the victim will correctly be able to identify the rapist: more frequently than not, the victim and the rapist are not total strangers. In addition, the relatively long duration of the rape gives the woman the opportunity to observe the rapist. It takes time for the victim's clothes to be removed. In general, it would seem that rape victims have a greater opportunity to take note of the rapist's identity than do victims of other direct contact crimes such as mugging. Taking these factors into account, the question arises as to why corroboration of identification in rape cases is regarded as more essential than in other crimes, such as mugging, for example.

When the harrowing ordeal of police questioning, medical examination, and court cross-examination is combined with the social embarrassment of being raped, the unofficial figure that only one out of twenty rape victims report the offence to the police becomes more understandable.

CONCLUSION

Man's wish to dominate, which may be expressed through rape, is not instinctual. Controlling and domineering behaviour is learnt from family modes of relating, the media, sexist sexual institutions and activities, and society's glorification of 'strong-armed' masculinity and docile femininity. Since the cause of rape is social, physiological solutions such as castration miss the point. What is required are social strategies. Thus, transformation of prevailing social relations can only come about through a change of social structures and ideologies.

In a transformed society where personal development is not assigned according to class, race, or sex, the possibilities of egalitarian relationships abound. No longer would women be thought of as sexual objects, or human beings in the service of man. No longer would their lives be restricted by discriminatory economic, social, and sexual practices. In a society void of sexual conceptualizations of women and male dominance, rape would become a decreasing phenomenon.

At present, however, rape remains a slightly improper act. The reason for this lies not only in the prevalence of sexist ideology and rape myths, but also in the thin line separating sex and violence. What distinguishes rapists from other men is that for them there is no line. They perceive of sexually violent behaviour and seduction as one and the same thing. For them, sexual activity is tied up with force, as well as with power and domination.

Like the images of pornography, men too associate sex with mastery over another human being. Feelings of ascendancy achieved through sex help to relieve the fear of not being considered a 'real man'. Rape is therefore not only the conquest of a woman, but of the offender's own fears about his virility, his courage, and his masculinity.

Trying to fulfil the expectations of manhood often means that sexual activity is likely to be impoverished by separation from feelings of affection. Endearment in love-making and sexual liberation requires sex role liberation (Russell, 1975). Only when men do not believe their role to be hegemonic and commanding, and regard women as people, can heterosexual relationships be sensual, relishing, and refreshing for both partners. Such a realization among men would help to destroy the myth that women look for and enjoy rape, and would go a long way towards making sexual violence an aberration in our society.

The revision in the standards of masculinity and femininity that are taking place today does not alter prevailing heterosexual relations substantially. Men wearing perfume, earrings, tight pants, platform shoes, and long hair does not readily tamper with the older, inbred attitudes of dominance, possessiveness, and competitiveness. As Hoch puts it:

> True, men no longer fight duels the way they did in the age of gallantry, and for the educated 'middle' classes even fist-fights between rugged individualists have gone somewhat out of style. But competition for women and status is still with us; only now it tends to be fought in terms of a consumption ethic of cars and clothes and credit cards. This kind of competition, this pressure to prove himself 'more of a man' than the next fellow, will be with us as long as the present economic system with its hierarchical social classes and status (Hoch, 1979: 144).

The objectification of women, male competition, and the virility mystique makes the man brought up in squalid living conditions just as much a potential rapist as the academic, the intellectual theatre-goer, the politician, and the business executive.

What of the changes in femininity? Even in the midst of greater economic opportunities which have provided women with a modicum more autonomy and independence, the all too powerful socialized feminine traits of acquiescence, passivity, and submissiveness persist. Thus many women 'prefer' not to have a more autonomous kind of fulfilment, and continue to rely on the acquisition of a lover, a husband, or family to give them their sense of identity and social respectability.

Their dependence on men devalues their worth, for in order to maintain a relationship with them, they must often yield to men's authority and gratify their needs, even when unwilling. This ideology of unquestioning acceptance plays a large part in men not being able to take 'no' for an answer in sexual encounters.

Women's position as potential rape victims becomes increasingly precarious as sexism continues to pervade our society, and as men continue to feel a sense of powerlessness. Therefore, as the years proceed, it is to be expected that the amount of rapes in South Africa will begin to far exceed the current unofficial figure of 380 000 per annum, or the official figure of six rapes daily. To break out of this spiral of sexual violence, a concerted effort must be made to develop a science of rape, to implement the conclusions of this science, and to actively work towards the establishment of an egalitarian and democratic society.

NOTES

1. The popular reaction to rape began with an article by Susan Griffin in *Ramparts* magazine in 1971. The article, titled 'Rape — The All American Culture', was a powerful attack on society's beliefs about rape and rape victims (Clark & Lewis, 1977).

2. Amir's study (1971) contends that of reported rapes, 71 per cent were premeditated, 11 per cent were partially planned, and only 18 per cent were impulsive acts.

3. Amir (1971), for example, reports that in 87 per cent of the cases, the rapist either possesses a weapon or threatens the victim with death.

4. In the United States it is estimated that one in four rapes are gang rapes (a statistic revealed in the 1988 film *The Accused*).

REFERENCES

Achilles Heel, (1982) 'Masculinity and Violence', 5.

Althanasiou, R. *et al.* (1982), 'Sex', *Psychology Today,* July, 339–52.

Amir, M. (1971) *Patterns in Forcible Rape,* Chicago: University of Chicago Press.

Bandura, A. (ed.) (1971) *Psychological Modeling: Conflicting Theories,* Chicago: Aldine-Atherton.

Bandura, A. (1965) 'Influence of Models. Reinforcement Contingencies on the Acquisition of Imitative Responses', *Journal of Personality and Social Psychology,* 589–95.

Bart, P. B. (1981) 'A Study of Women Who Both Were Raped and Avoided Rape', *Journal of Social Issues,* 37(4).

Bell, R. R. (1981) *Contemporary Social Problems,* Homewood: Dorsey Press.

Bradbury, P. (1982) 'Sexuality and Male Violence', *Achilles Heel,* 5.

Brownmiller, S. (1975) *Against Our Will: Men, Women and Rape,* New York: Bantam Books.

Chappel, D. *et al.* (eds.) (1977) *Forcible Rape: The Crime, the Victim and the Offender.* Cited in 'The Sociology of Rape' by M. Deming & A. Eppy, *Sociology and Social Research,* 65(4), 357–80.

Clark, L. & Lewis, D. (1977) *Rape: The Price of Coercive Sexuality,* Toronto: Women's Press.

Cleaver, E. (1972) *Soul on Ice,* New York: Dell-Delta/Ramparts.

Connell, N. & Wilson, C. (eds.) (1974) *Rape: The First Sourcebook for Women,* New York: Plume.

Court, J. H. (1979) 'Pornography and Rape in South Africa', *De Jure,* October, 236–41.

Coward, R. (1982) 'Pornography: Two Opposing Feminist Viewpoints', *Spare Rib,* Issue 119.

Davis, A. Y. (1982) *Women, Race and Class,* London: Women's Press.

Deming, M. B. & Eppy, A. (1981) 'The Sociology of Rape', *Sociology and Social Research,* 65(4), 357–80.

Deutsch, H. (1944) *The Psychology of Women,* London: Grune & Stratton.

Dollard, J. L. *et al.* (1939) *Frustration and Aggression,* New Haven: Yale University Press.

Donnerstein, E. (1980) 'Aggressive Erotica and Violence Against Women', *Journal of Personality and Social Psychology,* 39(2), 269–77.

Edwards, S. (1981) *Female Sexuality and the Law,* Oxford: Martin Robertson.

Farady, A. (1982) 'On the Other Side of the Billboard ...: Pornography, Male Fantasies and the Objectification of Women'. In *On the Problem of Men,* edited by S. Friedman & E. Sarah, London: Women's Press.

Faust, B. (1980) *Women, Sex and Pornography,* Harmondsworth: Penguin Books.

Festinger, L. (1954) 'A Theory of Social Comparison Processes', *Human Relations,* 7.

Finkelhor, D. & Yllo, K. (1982) 'Forced Sex in Marriage. A Preliminary Report', *Crime and Delinquency.*

Firestone, S. (1979) *The Dialectic of Sex,* London: Women's Press.

Freeman, J. (ed.) (1979) *Women: A Feminist Perspective,* New York: Mayfield.

Fremont, J. (undated) 'Rapists Speak for Themselves', publisher not known.

Friedman, S. & Sarah, E. (eds.) (1982) *On the Problem of Men,* London: Women's Press.

Geis, G. & Geis, R. (1981) 'Rape in Stockholm: Is Permissiveness Relevant?', paper presented at the meeting of the Pacific Sociological Association, Anheim, California.

Gellers, R. J. (1972) *The Violent Home,* New York: Sage.

Gluek, B. (date unknown) 'Final Report. Research Project for the Study and Treatment of Crimes Involving Sexual Abberations'. Cited in 'The Psychology of the Rapist and His Victim' by L. Melani & L. Fodaski.

Graser, R. R. 'Marxist Criminology: A Critical Consideration', *South African Journal of Criminal Law and Criminology,* 4.

Greer, G. (1971) *The Female Eunuch,* London: Granada.

Griffin, S. (1971) 'Rape: The All American Culture', *Ramparts,* 10(3), September.

Groth, A. N. (1979) *Men Who Rape: The Psychology of the Offender,* New York: Plenum Publishing Company.

Herman, D. (1979) 'The Rape Culture'. In *Women: A Feminist Perspective,* edited by J. Freeman, New York: Mayfield.

Hill, T. (1982) 'Rape and Marital Violence in the Maintenance of Male Power'. In *On the Problem of Men,* edited by S. Friedman & E. Sarah, London: Women's Press.

Hoch, P. (1979) *White Hero Black Beast,* London: Pluto Press.

Hoffman, C. H. (1970) *Law of Evidence,* Durban: Butterworth.

Kanin, E. J. & Parcell, S. R. (1977) 'Sexual Aggression: A Second Look at the Offended Female', *Archives of Sexual Behaviour,* 6(1), 67–76.

Katz, S. & Mazur, M. (1979) *Understanding the Rape Victim,* New York: John Wiley & Sons.

Kaye, H. E. (1979) *Male Survival: Masculinity Without Myth.* Cited in *White Hero Black Beast,* by P. Hoch, London: Pluto Press.

Kilpatrick, D. G. *et al.* (1981) 'Effects of a Rape Experience: A Longitudinal Study', *Journal of Social Issues,* 37(4).

Komisar, L. (date unknown) *Violence and Masculine Mistique,* Pittsburg: Know, Inc.

Kuhn, A. & Wolpe, D. (eds.) (1978) *Feminism and Materialism,* London: Routledge & Kegan Paul.

Levett, A. (1981) 'Considerations in the Provision of Adequate Psychological Care for the Sexually Assaulted Woman', unpublished paper.

Levine, S. & Koenig, J. (eds.) (1983) *Why Men Rape,* London: W. H. Allen.

Lips, H. M. (1981) *Women, Men and the Psychology of Power,* Englewood Cliffs: Prentice-Hall, Inc.

MacDonald, J. M. (1971) *Rape Offenders and Their Victims,* Springfield: Thomas.

MacKellar, J. (1975) *Rape: The Bait and the Trap,* New York: Crown Publishers.

Marsden, D. (1978) 'Sociological Perspectives on Family Violence'. In *Violence and the Family,* edited by J. P. Martin, Chichester: John Wiley & Sons.

Martin, J. P. (ed.) (1978) *Violence and the Family,* Chichester: John Wiley & Sons.

MASA (undated) 'Rape, the Full Story', publisher not known.

Medea, A. & Thompson, K. (1972) *Against Rape,* London: Peter Owen.

Melani, L. & Fodaski, L. (1974) 'The Psychology of the Rapist and His Victim'. In *Rape: The First Sourcebook for Women,* edited by N. Connell & C. Wilson, New York: Plume.

McIntosh, M. (1978a) 'The State and the Oppression of Women'. In *Feminism and Materialism,* edited by A. Kuhn & D. Wolpe, London: Routledge & Kegan Paul.

McIntosh, M. (1978b) 'Who Needs Prostitutes? The Ideology of Male Sexual Needs'. In *Women, Sexuality and Social Control,* edited by C. Smart & B. Smart, London: Routledge & Kegan Paul.

Miller, N. E. (1941) 'The Frustration-Aggression Hypothesis', *Psychological Review,* 48, 337–42.

Millet, K. (1970) *Sexual Politics,* New York: Avon Books.

Paske, A. T. (1982) *Rape and Ritual,* Toronto: Inner City Books.

Peters, J. J. *et al.* (1976) 'The Philadelphia Assault Victim Study', final report submitted to the National Council on Mental Health, Washington.

Pleck, J. (1979) 'Man's Power with Women, Other Men, and Society: A Man's Movement Analysis'. In *The Women Say, The Men Say,* edited by E. Shapiro, New York: Dell.

Reeves, S. P. (1981) 'The Socio-cultural Context of Rape: A Cross-cultural Study', *Journal of Social Issues,* 37(4).

Renvoize, J. (1979) *Web of Violence,* Harmondsworth: Penguin Books.

Robin, G. D. (1977) 'Forcible Rape: Institutionalized Sexism in the Criminal Justice System', *Crime and Delinquency,* 23(2), April.

Russel, D. E. H. (1975) *The Politics of Rape,* New York: Stein & Day.

Satchwell, K. (1981) 'Women and the Law'. In *NUSAS Law Directive,* compiled by Students' Representative Council, University of Cape Town.

Schneider, D. J. (1976) *Social Psychology,* Manila: Addison-Wesley.

Schultz, M. (1975) 'The Semantic Derogation of Women'. In *Language and Sex: Difference and Dominance,* edited by B. Thorne & L. Henley, Rowley: Newbury House.

Selkin, J. (1975) 'Rape', *Psychology Today,* 8.

Shapiro, L. (1979) 'Violence: The Obscene Fantasy'. In *Women: A Feminist Perspective,* edited by J. Freeman, New York: Mayfield.

Smart, C. & Smart, B. (eds.) (1978) *Women, Sexuality and Social Control,* London: Routledge & Kegan Paul.

Spender, D. (1980) *Man Made Language,* London: Routledge & Kegan Paul.

Storaska, F. (1975) *How to Say No to a Rapist ... and Survive,* New York: Random House.

Svalastoga, K. (1962) 'Rape and Social Structure', *Pacific Sociological Review,* 5, 48–53.

Tedeschi, J. T. *et al.* (1973) *Conflict, Power and Games: The Study of Interpersonal Relationships,* Chicago: Aldine.

Thorne, B. & Henley, N. (eds.) (1975) *Language and Sex: Difference and Dominance,* Rowley: Newbury House.

Tolson, A. (1977) *The Limits of Masculinity,* London: Tavistock.

Van Ness, S. R. (1984) 'Rape as Instrumental Violence. A Study of Youth Offenders', *Journal of Offender Counselling, Services and Rehabilitation,* 9(1–2), 161–70.

Wallace, D. & Wehmer, G. (undated) 'Contemporary Standards of Visual Erotics', *Technical Reports,* 6.

Weiss, K. & Borges, S. (1977) 'Victimology and Rape: The Case of the Legitimate Victim', *Issues in Criminology,* Fall, 71–115.

Wilson, E. (1983) *What Is To Be Done About Violence Against Women,* Harmondsworth: Penguin Books.

Wood, P. L. (1974) 'The Victim in a Forcible Rape: A Feminist View'. In *Rape: The First Sourcebook for Women,* edited by N. Connell & C. Wilson, New York: Plume.

5 Violence in sport

M. Siff

INTRODUCTION

The issue of violence in sport is one of universal concern. In the South African context, however, the analyst is compelled to question whether or not violent behaviour in sport differs significantly in nature and degree from that in other countries. The premise here is that the extensive scale of reported violence in other walks of South African life will be reflected in sport. Since sport is a microcosm of South African society in many respects, such as goal-orientation, group dynamics, management, productivity, competitiveness, law enforcement, status, and reward, it should offer valuable insights into the macrocosmic society in which it operates. In this context, the national or most popular sports should then furnish the most representative correlations between violence in society and violence in sport.

For sport to be regarded as one of the various complementary indicators of general societal violence, this limited premise needs to be expanded considerably. In particular, the following questions have to be addressed:

☐ To what extent is sport an indicator of violence in society?

☐ Is sport in South Africa more or less violent than in other countries, and more or less violent than other aspects of South African society?

☐ Are certain sports more conducive to violence?

☐ Does sport breed violence, or diminish it by acting as a 'healthy' outlet for stress and as a means of 'building character'?

☐ To what extent is violence in sport influenced by coaches, sports administrators, spectators, and the media?

This list of questions is by no means complete, nor is this chapter aimed at providing definitive answers to them. Instead, it has been compiled to demarcate the scope of violence in sport and the extent to which it is inextricably woven into the entire fabric of society. It is naïve to imagine that clear-cut statistical interrelations can be found among fairly discrete factors which may influence the emergence of violent behaviour in sport.

At the outset, it is important that an adequate definition of violence be formulated. Without such a definition, it is relatively meaningless to attempt to answer any of the above questions. For instance, it would be extremely difficult and entirely misleading to examine the incidence and degree of violence in boxing or wrestling without such a definition. The very nature of these two sports is one of violent physical contact, and what may be defined as violence in cricket and soccer may be regarded as a normal part of the sporting transaction in these contact sports.

Violence, therefore, has to be defined and examined within the framework determined by the rules of the game, the laws of society, and the acceptable standards of interpersonal behaviour as tacitly laid down by society and the participants in each sport.

DEFINITION AND SCOPE OF VIOLENCE IN SPORT
Sport as ritualized combat

Sport has often been regarded as a latter-day heir to primitive warfare. Teams in many ways are analogous to hunting bands or miniature armies, whereas individual sports have certain links to jousting and duelling. It is of interest that jousting was usually synonymous with chivalry and adherence to specific rules designed to distinguish 'fair play' from 'foul play'. This is not to eulogize the violence of medieval jousting as gentlemanly and civilized; on the contrary, foul play was just as prevalent then as it is now in sport. Violence in jousting and duelling, unlike in modern sport, at least served the valuable purpose of maintaining essential levels of military preparedness.

Instead of concentrating on the veracity of the military origins in sport, it is more appropriate to recognize that the immediate recreational antecedents of modern sport made definite attempts to eliminate the existence of unacceptable levels of violence on the field of combat or play. At the same time it is relevant to note that the medieval combatants had their own unwritten code of conduct toward one another.

Violence then fell into two neatly distinguished classes: legally accepted violence necessary for executing the game competently and fairly, and illicit violence falling outside the rules of the game. Games and, ultimately, sports thus developed a system of laws like those of society.

However, transgression of the laws of the land is regarded as criminal activity, whereas the violation of sporting laws did and does not carry the same stigma. Today's stress on law enforcement in sport is entirely similar to police attempts to reduce the incidence of criminal acts in society in that in both cases this method fails to address the causes of undesirable behaviour, although it often succeeds in protecting the innocent from injury and death.

The parallels between the jousts of old and some modern sports are obvious, the differences between them often being ones of degree rather than of nature. Thus, an initial definition of violence in sport would distinguish between legal and illegal violence, where violence would be regarded as synonymous with aggressive physical contact.

To some critics, this distinction is tenuous. George Orwell, for instance, considered that:

> Serious sport has nothing to do with fair play. It is bound up with hatred, jealousy, boastfulness, disregard for all rules, and sadistic pleasure in witnessing violence; in other words, it is war minus the shooting.

Sporting violence as territorialism

Some researchers have postulated that sporting violence is often the product of human defence of territory, primarily in the case of team sports in which defence or attack of territory is the basis of the game. Like the animal protecting its home territory against the privations of marauding rivals, so the sportsperson is presumed to protect home grounds against the invasion of opposing teams. In his book *The Territorial Imperative*, Robert Ardrey popularized the concept of humans as territorial creatures, a theme which has readily lent itself to extrapolation into the realm of sport.

Some research on a limited number of sports suggests that a team displays more violence when it has to invade an 'away' ground. Other research, based on the assumption that home grounds are defended more vigorously, directly contradicts this finding. A closer analysis of the raw data frequently reveals that a significant number of displays of violence cannot readily be related to territorial factors.

Often violent behaviour is not characteristic of the team, but of certain individuals, some of whom regularly manifest violent behaviour on both home and away grounds throughout the season. Rarely is a distinction made between reactive and instrumental aggression by each player responsible for acting violently, largely because of the difficulty in studying press reports or films to identify the personal motives of players.

In an analysis highly pertinent to this issue, socio-psychologist Elliot Aronson stresses that:

> ... although it is true that many animals ... will attack an animal who invades his territory, it is a gross oversimplification to imply, as some popular authors have, that man is likewise programmed to protect his territory and behave aggressively in response to specific stimuli ... The same physiological stimulation can produce widely different responses, depending upon learning (Aronson, 1972).

It is relevant to note that territorial theory assumes that entire teams perceive a 'home' field as entirely equivalent to their residential territory. While this may be true of the home where one spends a considerable portion of one's life and invests much of one's lifetime savings, it is not necessarily true of a sportsfield where a player spends but a few hours a week training on his or her 'home' ground. Powerful identification with territory is not merely instinctive. It is largely the result of propaganda involving the manipulation of player perceptions by coaches, managers, sponsors, and other interested parties. Individuals or groups first have to perceive a particular tract of land as their special territory before any valid assumptions can be made about territorial influence on aggression.

The home-versus-away territory theory often ignores the important fact that in many team sports each team, like an opposing chess player, is allocated a particular half of the field. In other words, half of an 'away' ground becomes the temporary 'home' territory for a visiting team and, simultaneously, the temporary 'away' territory for the home team, as decreed by the rules of the game. What then becomes vital to a definitive territorial analysis is whether or not violence is more frequent when the opposing team frequently and effectively invades 'your' half of the field. Even an accurate count of the instances of violence in each half would not necessarily produce any significant data confirming the territorial hypothesis. Instead it might lend support to the frustration-aggression model, since violence might increase if a team is frustrated in invading opposing territory or in being incapable of efficiently defending its own territory. Territorial invasion at its most fundamental level may readily be interpreted as a threat to personal or group safety needs, according to Maslow's hierarchy of needs.

The demonstration of violence on the sports field also depends on the severity of the legal, social, and financial penalties imposed on offenders.

Certainly in South African rugby the penalties generally constitute little more than nuisance value to offenders and teams. It is rare or unheard of for a rugby player to be banned for an entire season or for life for deliberate use of excessive or continued violence. Fear of incurring penalties which could adversely affect the individual or the team may confound the validity of data being collected to prove the territorial-aggression hypothesis.

Furthermore, researchers have learned that the outcome of aggression has a vital influence on the manifestation of violence. If aggressive behaviour is overtly or covertly encouraged, approved, or rewarded, participants and spectators of violence tend to be more aggressive. For instance, the association of rugby aggression and violent physical supremacy with manliness in the eyes of many in South African society clearly constitutes exactly this type of tacit reward. It should not be surprising then that more violent behaviour occurs in rugby than in any other sport in this country.

The influence of the sports field should also not be ignored. Berkowitz (1968) has shown that the mere presence of an object or setting associated with violence can increase aggression in frustrated or angered individuals. The perception by players of any territory as violent or hostile would be more important to the production of violence than the mere fact that the field is 'home' or 'away' territory. In this context of setting, the attitude of spectators and referees towards the 'home' and 'away' teams then might have a significant effect on the display of violence by both opposing teams.

Some researchers, drawing on the finding in a limited number of sports in specific countries that 'away' games are lost more frequently than home games, maintain that territorialism is enhanced on 'away' fields because of the greater likelihood of successful invasion by opponents, and consequent Maslovian fear of team safety, leading to frustration-aggression. Territorial cues *per se*, however, might not be the most influential factors in increasing the incidence of violence. Unfamiliarity with the field and other environmental factors might be sufficient to increase player anxiety and the likelihood of losing. Fear or apprehension of the unknown or inadequately known, rather than fear of losing control of territory, might be more fundamental to the effect of 'away' territory on player aggression.

Thus it may be concluded that attribution of violence to human territorial instinct is based on premises and findings which have not scientifically excluded the possible primacy of other causes. Territorial factors may well compound or precipitate the display of violence, but it is unlikely that human behaviour is governed predominantly by territorial instinct.

Play and work

While sport in many cases is the ritualized substitute for warfare, it also has its origins in two other basic human activities: play and work. Play is one of the characteristics of all animal development and when formalized in the human setting, can give rise to games, sports, and dance. Some of it is goal-directed, while some of it is random, hedonistic, or supplementary to more cerebral activities. Yet other derivatives of play, such as gymnastics, trampolining, dance, and diving, have aesthetics as their primary goal and are more process-centred than goal-centred. We would expect violence to be rare in these situations, particularly since high levels of aggression would be detrimental to the sophisticated degree of motor skill required by these activities.

Individual or group

Unlike warfare, play may be indulged in on an individual or group basis. This observation immediately identifies one of the limitations of theories of violence in sport founded on the assumption that sport is ritualized warfare. Sport is also the product of unsinister natural play and work, with the same potential for self-discovery, self-fulfilment, and self-development. It might be tempting to analyse the occurrence of violence in sport on the basis of whether a particular sport emerged originally from play or from warfare. Caution needs to be exercised in this regard, however, because modern archery, fencing, and equestrianism are among the most chivalrous of all sports, despite their militaristic origins.

A further distinction could then be made for individual versus team sports. Individual sports may involve one individual locked in sporting conflict against another individual, or individuals trying to outperform one another by running, throwing, lifting, or carrying out some activities which can be measured.

We would then be led to recognize that some forms of violence in sport may not be aimed against an opponent, but against oneself. Aggressive frustration at personal error and failure to perform adequately would then manifest itself, for instance, in the self-directed, implement-throwing tantrums of tennis and amateur golf.

The absence of violence against another human thus does not necessarily imply that violence is absent from sport. The identification of violence in sport has to take into account both violence against others and self-directed violence. The effect of either form of violence on the individual and society may be equally harmful, as is the case with self-administration of drugs and alcohol. The effect of violence on the individual, after all, is ultimately what determines its emergence in society.

The scope of violence in sport

The definition of violence in sport encompasses other forms of behaviour including aggressiveness and assertiveness, often to the extent that the competitive sports participant is unable to distinguish among them. Aggressiveness is invariably regarded as the *sine qua non* of élite level performance. The 'all costs' in the expression 'winning at all costs' usually includes astute infringement of the rules and the use of illicit violence.

Any analysis of violence in sport needs to consider violence and aggression as inseparable, although violence would more accurately be defined to be a form of aggressive behaviour accompanied by a vigorous physical act intended to injure, damage, or destroy.

In this sense, it would be more appropriate to commence any realistic evaluation of violence in sport by defining the scope of violence to include any act of aggression aimed at inflicting physical or mental harm on oneself or an opponent. Violence may then be subdivided further into violence accepted within the rules of the game, and violence prohibited by the rules of the game and the legal system of the land. Competitors are governed by both sets of laws, whereas spectators are governed only by the laws of the land.

On this basis the laws of sports such as boxing and the martial arts permit high levels of legitimate violence, whereas those of non-contact sports such as athletics, golf, and swimming, with their origins mainly in play, exclude any forms of violence.

Finally, within the framework of sport as a recreational pursuit characterized by fair play, both of these forms of violence must include manifested violence or threats of violence. Such threats are characterized by the display of aggressive language, gestures, or behaviour suggesting that physical violence is the next logical consequence for one's opponent.

Off the field of play, these threats are not necessarily confined to implied harm to a player or the family of a player unwilling to lose a match at the behest of a financial backer. They may also take the form of competitions and financial or political boycotts. This type of threat may affect not only the athlete, but also the school, racial group, university, or country, as has often been the case in South Africa.

In analysing sporting violence within the bounds of this extended definition, we need to appreciate that the perpetrators of violence may be anyone directly or indirectly involved with the sports event in question — violence may be introduced into sport by competitors, officials, spectators, administrators, governments, sponsors, the media, or anyone else with some form of active or passive interest in the sport.

Aetiology and theories of violence in sport

Sports psychologists have identified two basic types of violence or aggression in sport: *reactive* and *instrumental.* Reactive, or hostile, aggression is the result of spontaneous emotional anger or frustration and is aimed primarily at injuring an opponent. Instrumental aggression, on the other hand, is behaviour intended not only to injure, but also to achieve a specific performance goal.

In cricket, for instance, instrumental aggression by a fast bowler would take the form of body-line or head-line bowling aimed at physically intimidating the batsman and forcing him to play an injudicious stroke. Unlike the reactive aggression displayed by the rugby player throwing a punch in response to continual harassment by an opponent, the bowler's instrumental aggression is directed at the dismissal of the batsman.

The main difference between these two classes of aggression is that reactive aggression is always an emotional response to anger, frustration, fear, or pain. It is more physiological than cerebral. To the casual observer, however, the distinction between the two types of aggression may not be clear.

The underlying reasons for violence in sport are not entirely clear, although theorists usually discuss them in terms of three broad models: human instinct, frustration-aggression, and social learning. These models, of course, are modest elaborations upon the well-known nature–nurture debate which is prevalent in all theorizing about animal behaviour in general.

Instinct theory maintains that aggression is an innate human characteristic inextricably associated with drive or motivation. The periodic violent expression, or catharsis, of accumulated aggression is considered to be an integral part of behaviour. In this context, the vigorous physical activity and violence of sport are regarded as the healthy sublimation of stored aggression. Research, however, reveals that aggression in sport tends to breed further aggression.

Frustration-aggression theories posit that aggression is the result of frustration of effort aimed at fulfilling specific needs. Aggression, however, is not the inevitable consequence of frustration. It is simply one of several possible types of behaviour which also include anger, anxiety, grief, depression, and embarrassment.

Both instinct theory and frustration-aggression theory may be explained on the basis of the various theories of human needs and motivation.

Maslow (cited in Tellier, 1978) for instance, hypothesized that, in order of priority, all humans exhibit the following *hierarchy of needs*: physiological (food, warmth, sex, and other biological functions), safety, social, ego-status, and self-actualization. These needs create basic drives which impel us to produce specific types of behaviour, including aggression. The desire to fulfil these basic needs, as well as any frustration experienced in attempting to fulfil them, presumably could cause aggression and violence.

In the case of sport, safety and ego-status needs would appear to be the most influential in determining the appearance of aggression. Deeper analysis, however, reveals that all needs, except perhaps self-actualization, might be implicated in the production of sports violence. The need for social acceptance might precipitate violent behaviour if the players and supporters of a particular sport overtly or covertly approve of aggressive play. Acquisition of a reputation for aggression and 'toughness' would then automatically enhance one's social standing in that sport.

It is also not often appreciated that physiological needs include the need to touch and to be touched, the need to satisfy all the senses, and the need to enjoy kinaesthetic or bodily movement processes which characterize much of the early development of the infant. It is in this realm that masochistic-type behaviour is often exhibited by many individuals, albeit in covert or heavily disguised, more socially acceptable form. This includes the perverse pleasure experienced in striking an opponent in martial combat and in the intense stimulation experienced in violent physical contact.

That these para-masochistic processes may be more universal than commonly accepted is suggested by research into the nature of the sex act. This is supported by evidence that highly stressful sexual practices, such as flagellation and biting, are commonly enjoyed by perfectly normal humans. Some sex theorists maintain further that the orgasm is the result of excessively intense arousal caused by simultaneous imposition of almost intolerable levels of pain and pleasure.

A vast proportion of the public displays vicarious enjoyment of pain or pleasure experienced by others, as is clearly evidenced by crowds gathered at the scene of a gory motor-car accident or by spectators shouting for blood at boxing, wrestling, and karate ringsides. The fact that many of the highest-rated television series in this country include considerable amounts of aggression, violence, and human suffering provides further corroboration for the contention that masochistic-sadistic traits are fairly widespread among the population.

The universality of these traits in social, political, religious, and sporting contexts throughout history might easily lead one to conclude that masochism, sadism, and violence are basic human qualities. Regrettably, there is more than adequate evidence that this type of deviate behaviour is common among players and spectators in several sports such as rugby, soccer, ice hockey, water polo, boxing, wrestling, and karate. The tacit support given by television companies, producers, and networks to violence further compounds the problem. It would appear that much of our population has not progressed beyond the stage of fulfilling the most basic physiological needs which characterize early primitive and infan-tile development.

Besides Maslow, there are other analysts, such as McLelland and Vroom (both cited in Tellier, 1978), who have proposed models to explain human drives. Several of them maintain that there are only two inherent needs: the *need for pleasure* and the *need to avoid pain.*

The validity of this model recently has gained support from neurophysiological research which has revealed the presence of 'pleasure' and 'pain' centres, as well as natural opiates ('pleasure chemicals') in the brain. These biochemicals tend to be produced when a person is exposed to physical or mental stress and appear to be part of the adaption mechanisms for survival. Other research reveals the presence or absence of specific neurotransmitters in the brains of in-dividuals displaying uncharacteristic or aggressive behaviour. It would not be surprising if future researchers discovered that violence in sport is strongly related to particular biochemical profiles in the perpetrators. It is unlikely, however, that chemicals would prove to be the cause of violence; rather, they probably would be important mediators associated with the complicated process linking environmental stimulation to motor production of violent action.

McLelland (cited in Tellier, 1978) contends that all other needs beyond pleasure and pain avoidance are learned. On this basis, he categorizes these acquired needs as follows: achievement, power, and affiliation, all of which clearly are central to sporting performance. Both the drive to achieve these needs as well as any frustration experienced in pursuing them could precipitate violent behaviour. Spectators as vicarious participants in the event could also experience stresses similar to those experienced by players and could react violently against supporters of the opposing team.

Further useful insights into human drives are offered by Vroom (cited in Tellier, 1978) who developed an *expectancy theory of motivation*. He proposed that 'motivational force' depends on two factors:

☐ the perceived attractiveness of the goal or outcome; and

☐ the perceived probability of achieving the goal of outcome (i.e. the personal belief that success is likely).

In other words, the strength of the motivational force depends on the product of these two factors. For numerical calculations, perceived attractiveness (valence) is rated from -5 (extremely undesirable) to +5 (extremely desirable), while belief in success is rated on a scale from -1 (total disbelief) to +1 (total belief).

In applying this theory to understanding violence in sport, one must understand that a player who perceives instrumental aggression as essential to achievement of a goal, while believing that the goal is attainable by such means, is more likely to manifest violence than a player who does not entertain these beliefs. Frustration of any player whose violence is based on his /her beliefs in aggressive play is certain to generate additional violence. If a significant number of players in both teams believe in the match-winning value of violence, then the climate for producing extensive violence becomes even more apparent.

Conversely, if players believe that instrumental or reactive violence is likely to result in highly unattractive consequences such as large penalties, fines, suspension, or legal action, then it is less likely that violence will be prevalent. Furthermore, if players entertain a strong and realistic belief in winning by legitimate means, then the probability of violence becomes considerably reduced.

If players believe that behaviour in sport is an essential part of overall behaviour as civilized, ethical, or religious humans, then violence will be perceived as unattractive under all circumstances. This illustrates clearly that the most fundamental aspect of Vroom's model is perception. This is the foundation of all learning; namely that so-called reality is a perceptual construct based on subjective interpretation of environmental stimuli. It is, therefore, vital that the role of coaches, administrators, educators, media, and parents be appreciated in creating or reinforcing perceptions of aggression or violence in sport. Unless the formal and informal educators in society create the perception that violence is abnormal and unacceptable in sport, it is unlikely that violence will ever disappear from sport.

The nature of violence suggests that it be analysed more extensively in terms of *arousal theory*. Yerkes and Dodson (1908), soon after the turn of this century, learned that there is an inverted-U shaped relationship between performance and level of arousal (Fig. 5.1).

Aggression and violence are characterized by high levels of arousal, so the display of aggression by some sports participants may serve under certain circumstances to raise inadequate performance to the optimal zone in the region of the turning point of the curve. Local rugby Springbok, Naas Botha, and several tennis legends such as John McEnroe are striking examples of sportspersons whose performance often improves with aggression deliberately produced in response to irritation, frustration, or harassment. It is important to note, however, that excessive aggression, or over-arousal, can lead to deterioration in performance.

According to frustration-aggression theory, this can lead to greater aggression and initiate a vicious cycle of increasing violence and deteriorating performance.

More recent research has shown that the exact shape of the arousal curve depends on individual personality factors such as degree of extraversion/introversion and task factors such as degree of difficulty. For example, the curve for complex tasks usually exhibits a much sharper and more clearly defined peak, which implies that small changes in arousal level can effect major changes in performance. Again, this tends to support the observation that violence is less frequently displayed during the execution of intricate skills in sports which require optimal levels of concentration or during phases of complicated play. Thus displays of aggression and violence are more common during the phases preceding and following any complex activity.

Social learning theory contends that aggression is behaviour learned by individuals in adjusting to their environment. Other individuals influence the acquisition or rejection of aggressive behaviour by responding with negative or positive reinforcement. Due to the exaggerated emphasis placed on aggressiveness and winning in most sport, the opportunity for learning aggression in sport is extremely high. Research generally reveals that social learning theory offers the most plausible explanation for much of the violence in sport, as well as the public perception of its acceptability in particular sports.

The modern setting necessitates that we also add the category of *chemical modification of behaviour* to these models. For example,

Figure 5.1: The relationship between performance and arousal

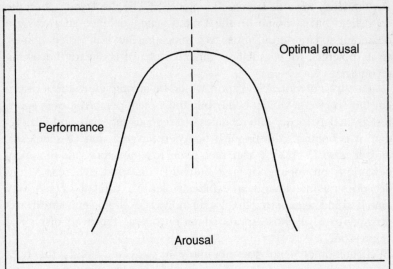

some of the drugs commonly used to enhance sporting performance, such as stimulants and anabolic steroids, may be associated with increases in the level of aggression. It is interesting to note that anabolic steroids apparently were first used as performance modifiers by the Nazis in the Second World War, not to increase muscle bulk, but to enhance the level of aggression in their soldiers. Today scientists are once more examining the effect of anabolic and androgenic substances on mood change.

The scale of substance abuse in sport has not been thoroughly studied anywhere in the world, but it is common knowledge among the participants in the strength and contact sports that anabolic steroids are extensively used, even among schoolchildren. In sports such as bodybuilding and powerlifting, professional boxing, rowing, water-polo, and American football, where drug testing is rare, it has been estimated that in excess of 75 per cent of the top participants regularly use anabolic steroids. If these estimates are even approximately accurate and the aggression-enhancing character of these drugs is confirmed, then the implications for the escalation of violence in sport are grave.

This problem is by no means confined to overseas athletes. For instance, the author has been informed personally of anabolic usage by local sportspersons from field athletics, body-building, powerlifting, weightlifting, rugby, soccer, triathlon, and swimming. Even casual gym users are regularly using anabolic steroids. The implications here are that any tendency towards increased violence will be displayed not on the sportsfield but at home. In the United States, defence attorneys are beginning to cite steroid abuse as a mitigating factor in violent crimes, so its potential for stimulating general violence is already becoming recognized.

An analysis of violence in sport would be incomplete without distinguishing between violent behaviour and violent personalities in sport. Just as anxiety theory differentiates between anxiety-state and anxiety-trait, it is helpful to distinguish between *violence-state* (V-state) and *violence-trait* (V-trait). V-state then refers to a transitory state of violent behaviour producible by any individual in sport, whereas V-trait describes the individual who exhibits violence as a regular personality trait. It would be expected that V-trait individuals should gravitate to and possibly excel in those sports which encourage the overt display of aggression.

Recognition of V-trait does not imply the correctness of the theory of innate aggression. Instead, it suggests that aggressive behaviour can be socially learned to the extent that it becomes an integral character trait and cannot readily be eliminated. It may be inferred further that groups of individuals or entire sports may develop V-trait behaviour, so that violence becomes a personality trait of certain sports such as rugby, professional wrestling, boxing, and karate. Whether this behaviour extrapolates from the sport to daily life is not known, but it would be useful to analyse the possible relationship between convicted violent criminals and their sporting profiles.

In South Africa, the search for such a correlation would have to be confined to the white population, since a considerable portion of the black population does not have access to formal sport. Would a wider availability of sport create attractive goal-directed opportunities, which could reduce the likelihood of reactive violence manifesting itself in other walks of life? One must conclude that better provision of sporting and recreational facilities *per se* would not reduce the incidence of violence in society. However, a reduction of violence in sport could be achieved if the players, coaches, and officials associated with each sport displayed those qualities of discipline, respect, self-control, altruism, and integrity which characterize a true sense of fair play in sport.

INCIDENCE AND EFFECTS OF VIOLENCE IN SPORT

The incidence and effects of violence in local sport may be assessed on the basis of a survey of reports in the mass media, analysis of sports injuries, or by a scientific survey conducted in every South African sport. Up to the present, no definitive study of violence in all South African sports has yet been undertaken. Such a study would indeed constitute a useful contribution to sociology in this country.

This chapter, therefore, has had to rely on media reports, interviews with sports officials, published articles on sports injuries, and discussion with sportspersons. In doing so, it has focused largely on the questions posed in the introduction.

Media information is generally fairly extensive on top-level play in the high profile or large spectator sports such as rugby, soccer, boxing cricket, golf, motor racing, and tennis. Since sports such as these are widely televised, the violence in them is witnessed by a considerable proportion of the public and therefore exerts a powerful influence on the acceptance or rejection of violence, according to the social learning theory discussed earlier. Serious accidents and physical violence are generally replayed on numerous occasions on television, thereby reinforcing pre-existing public attitudes towards sporting aggression.

In some cases violence ignored by officials and players as part of 'robust play', but exposed by television, forces action to be taken against offenders. Prominent rugby players, for instance, have been withdrawn from provincial or national teams as a consequence of adverse television coverage.

Violence in rugby has long been accepted as a normal part of the game and it was not until the advent of television in South Africa that public opinion began to force administrators to take more serious action against violent players. Concurrent medical focus on rugby injuries, stimulated by the emergence of sports medicine as a discipline, has acted as a further stimulus for re-examining the rules and control of rugby. Newspaper headlines condemning 'thugby' and the incidence of death and paraplegia in rugby has led to some parents forbidding their sons to play this sport.

Rugby, nevertheless, continues to be regarded as the national sport among much of the white population, and still produces the highest prevalence of player violence. It is noteworthy that violence is not confined to matches. Medical statistics reveal that the number of injuries sustained in practice games is second only to those produced in matches against overseas tourists. Here the cause often lies both in reactive and instrumental aggression, with reckless tackling, kicking, and punching commonly being in evidence.

The persistence of violence in rugby and its growth at school level, evidenced by the occurrence of three deaths and eleven serious spinal injuries among schoolboys during the first six months of 1989, has compelled the South African Rugby Board to change some of the official rules and pressurize referees to enforce them more strictly. In addition, it has expanded its educational programmes, with coaching and refereeing clinics being conducted extensively at all levels from school to national.

Dr Craven, President of the South African Rugby Board, however, remains dissatisfied with progress, maintaining that rough play and assault on officials 'is ruining rugby, ruining referees, and ruining our image' (*The Star*, 29 May 1989). Aggressive behaviour and serious neck injuries associated with wheeling and collapsing the scrums have forced him to propose replacing many of the scrums with tap kicks. In addition, he considers that better law enforcement would become possible with the introduction of a two-referee system.[1]

Springbok rugby players have also recently revealed that anabolic steroid use is not uncommon in local rugby. Overseas, the Irish Test lock, Willie Anderson, tested positive for steroids after the 1988 Five Nations International against Wales. As has been the case in American football, the problem of substance abuse will escalate in rugby, especially if professionalism is allowed in the game. The possible relationship between enhanced aggression and steroid abuse does not auger well for rugby, particularly as it is unlikely that regular drug testing will ever be introduced into non-Olympic or professional team sports.

The situation regarding violence in soccer is quite different, since this sport includes a professional league and officials generally are far more diligent in applying the law to players and officials. Fouls are common, but penalties are equally common, with players regularly being removed from the field or suspended from playing for one or more matches. There is no real equivalent in rugby of soccer's colour card system for robust play, and sanctions against violent rugby are rare or minimal.

The rugby attitude of 'taking it like a man' has a profound effect on players or officials instituting any action against their peers. This attitude is proliferated from primary school upwards, so player acceptance of violence at senior level is not surprising. Its acceptance is indelibly ingrained in players but if similar violence were exhibited off the sports field it would result in criminal prosecution. Even within the rules of the violent sport of boxing, such behaviour could result in instant disqualification. It is clear that rugby coaches have a major responsibility in minimizing the emergence of violence in their sport, as do coaches in all sport.

Fortunately the escalation in spectator violence which is evident in British soccer has not occurred in South Africa, despite the potential for intergroup conflict created by the country's apartheid laws. Soccer regularly attracts larger and more racially mixed crowds than other sports, yet the average scale of spectator violence is generally lower than in British and South American soccer. In fact, spectator violence is more frequent at rugby and cricket matches.

This problem, however, should not be laid at the feet of sport, as it is often associated with alcohol abuse. The extensive promotion of South African sport by distillers and brewers does little to alleviate the situation, especially as much of the media advertising of beer deliberately links beer drinking with masculine assertiveness in sport.

This link is further reinforced by the social rituals of sport which decree that players should relax with an after-match or after-practice beer. It is in this setting that regular consumption of alcohol by youngsters in South Africa frequently begins. The universality and social acceptability of alcohol consumption emphasizes that the influence of the latter should not be excluded from any study intended to examine a possible relationship between drugs and sporting aggression.

Further findings and observations may be summarized as follows:

☐ Violence in local sport is lower than in society as a whole and therefore cannot be regarded as a reliable indicator of general violence in South Africa.

☐ Violence in sport among participants or spectators is not higher than in other countries. There is, however, a disturbing increase in the level of spectator violence and intimidation of officials in school sport, especially rugby.

☐ Interracial violence is rare in local sport, particularly in soccer, the most popular team sport in South Africa. On the contrary, interracial harmony in soccer and athletics is especially evident. The opposition to so-called mixed leagues in rugby, especially at school level, suggests that this harmony would not readily transpose to all sports, particularly where the controlling officials support apartheid politics.

☐ There is widespread reluctance of players to lay charges of assault against opponents who not only transgress the laws of the game, but also the laws of the land. This is especially evident in rugby, where manliness is associated with the ability to withstand injury and insult.

☐ Violence in sport is far less among females than males, both here and overseas, although it is sometimes apparent in sports such as women's hockey. However, in predominantly female physical activities such as dance, displays of aggressive behaviour are common among mothers of participants. This seems to parallel the aggressive behaviour of fathers at school rugby matches.

☐ There has been an increase in levels of overt aggression in local provincial cricket, apparently following an international trend among players. As in tennis, this aggression has often been directed against umpires and the media. The gentleman's game nowadays would appear to be professional golf rather than cricket, both here and overseas.

☐ Despite the fact that boxing has the acknowledged primitive goal of inflicting serious physical harm on an opponent and that deaths occur periodically in local boxing, extensive financial investment decrees that it is unlikely that this violent sport will be barred here or overseas. Apparently it will continue to attract the attention of V-trait individuals as participants, officials, and spectators.

☐ Despite the violence demanded by boxing, self-control is often more evident in this sport than in karate, which purports to instil prescribed maxims of conduct at every practice. An interesting phenomenon almost unique to karate is the prevalence of aggression of instructors or higher graded exponents towards relative novices.
   Late-comers to class are often 'punished' in military fashion by having to perform medically inadvisable exercises such as repetition 'bunny-hops' on the haunches. Lower graded belts who score unexpected points against higher graded colleagues are often 'put in their place' by being overpowered by physical violence. Instructors invariably attempt to emulate the Japanese Samurai image of calculated ruthlessness and strict feudal lines of verbal commands, the lack of humour, the aggressiveness of posture and gesture, and the denial of pain.

☐ Many of the injuries treated by sports medical doctors and physiotherapists are not caused by intentional violence in sport. A considerable number of these injuries are self-induced in activities such as athletics, recreational jogging, 'aerobics', and several other individual sports.

In some cases these injuries may be attributed to an aggressive, masochistic fervour to improve fitness or performance, but in most instances they are the result of deficient technique, accident, over-training, and inadequate rest. In boxing, wrestling, basketball, rugby, soccer, and most contact sports, however, there is a clear causal relationship between aggressive play and injury.

☐ Much of violence associated with South African sport does not appear on the sports field. Instead, the main combatants are administrators and politicians who have been drawn into the arena of sports boycotts.

The emergence of sports boycotts as a powerful force followed the Nationalist government's ill-advised and aggressive stand against allowing Basil d'Oliveira, 'coloured' former South African cricketer, to tour the country as a member of the English team. During the same era South Africa was not invited to send a team to the 1964 Olympics. Next, a threat by forty countries to boycott the 1968 Mexico Olympics influenced the International Olympic Council to again withdraw its invitation to South Africa. Finally, South Africa was expelled from the Olympic body in 1970.

Despite government comment to the contrary, there is little doubt that these boycotts exerted a profound influence on hastening the advent of integrated sport in South Africa.

☐ South Africa has in a limited way aggressively countered these boycotts by organizing tours by very well-subsidized rebel teams from overseas. These measures have been relatively successful in breaking the sports boycott in the case of rugby, and until recently in cricket, but they have not adequately compensated for the desire of teams to test their ability against official international teams. In addition, aggressive overtures to the government by anti-apartheid groups using the motto 'no normal sport in an abnormal society' have resulted in an impasse.

☐ Sport is continuing to flourish here among blacks and whites, and many world class performances are still being produced. The struggling smaller sports have virtually resigned themselves to exclusion from the Olympics for the foreseeable future and are unlikely to pressurize the government any further to dismantle apartheid. The violent threats made for years by black power groups against black sportspersons participating in apparently white-dominated sports seem to have abated. Black athletes have become dominant in distance running.

Many South African sports have accepted that outside competition, though highly attractive, may not be an indispensable motivator in producing excellence. They recognize that sports elsewhere in the world, such as American football, flourish despite the absence of international competition. Lucrative financial rewards and extensive local leagues at all levels are increasing. It would appear that aggressive sporting boycotts from overseas may have outlived their useful lifespan and additional manœuvres outside the realm of sport will have to stimulate the integration of sport.

☐ Local sanctions imposed against right-wing clubs, schools, municipalities, and individuals who aggressively oppose integrated sport, however, will probably assume a more prominent role in the sporting community.

The above analysis of the incidence of violence in local sport does not pretend to be definitive or complete, as the data base available is confined largely to sports, competitors, and events more frequently in the public eye or within the field of experience of the author and his colleagues in sports administration, competition, or medicine. Most studies of local violence in sport are of a preliminary nature and do not address the extent of the problem in lower leagues, in female sport, or among schoolchildren in all sectors of the population.

Furthermore, other than the official medical records of serious boxing injuries, accurate figures on the annual injury rate caused by violent play are virtually non-existent. Medical experts are currently pressing for such records to be kept in rugby, although these statistics are intended to prevent the recurrence of injury to high-risk individuals, rather than the incidence of violence. Nevertheless, the registration of injuries and their causes in rugby and other major sports would provide a valuable source of information of patterns of violence in sport.

PREVENTION OF VIOLENCE IN SPORT

Founder of the modern Olympics, Baron de Coubertin, at the outset of his idealistic sporting venture in 1896, stressed that:

> ... athleticism can occasion the most noble passions or the most vile ... It can be chivalrous or corrupt, vile, bestial. One can use it to consolidate peace or prepare for war.

His fears and aspirations have both been realized and, in addition to our inheriting his gift of the Olympics, we have been bequeathed the task of controlling its negative concomitants such as violence.

Success in achieving this goal of diminishing or preventing violence in sport relies on selecting the appropriate countermeasures from a list such as the following:

☐ Modification of the rules of the game to minimize the occurrence of violent play.

☐ Stricter enforcement of existing rules.

☐ Implementation of stricter penalties against all forms of violence.

☐ Invoking the laws of the land to penalize violent behaviour displayed on the sports field.

☐ Education of players and officials in the desirability of following an ethical code of non-violence and fair play.

☐ Education against violence in general, commencing at home, reinforced at school, and continuing into adulthood.

The control of violence in sport needs to be based on an understanding of how attitudes towards violence may be changed. Since the days of Pavlov, conditioning of behaviour has been an important part of research in psychology, with reward and punishment serving as key components in the process. In social psychology, behaviour modification may be explained in terms of 'reinforcers', where a reinforcer may be defined as anything following a particular action so as to modify the probability of the same action being repeated. Reinforcers may be positive ('reward') or negative ('punishment'). The former induce one to repeat the same action, whereas the latter produce the opposite effect.

The following major types of reinforcers are commonly recognized (Leith, 1982):

☐ social reinforcers;

☐ performance reinforcers;

☐ internal reinforcers;

☐ material reinforcers; and

☐ token reinforcers.

As discussed earlier, *social reinforcers* provide a powerful stimulus for imprinting specific patterns of behaviour. Overt or covert acts of approval or disapproval from parents, peers, coaches, educators, spectators, the media, and other influential associates of the athlete can serve to promote or diminish violent behaviour. If violence is to be eliminated from sport, it is essential that society, particularly in the form of the coach and immediate family, reinforces non-violent, holistic behaviour rather than winning at all costs.

Although it is also vital that suitably severe penalties be invoked to make violence as undesirable as possible, it needs to be remembered that individuals often deliberately display socially unacceptable behaviour to attract what Erik Berne has termed 'strokes', even if they are negative. Attention-seeking, as part of the process of satisfying social and ego-status needs, may be the underlying reason why a particular individual behaves violently in sport. Leith (1982) contends that the mere attention accorded the athlete by public punishment may be more rewarding than the coach or referee's negative social reaction. Accordingly, he stresses that the coach should positively reinforce constructive behaviour rather than merely punishing or negatively reinforcing aggressive behaviour.

Some athletes may have such an intense need for attention that they will display the trappings of aggression and violence without actually indulging in violent exchange with opponents. For example, some powerlifters, cricketers, tennis players, and karate competitors will often shout violently, curse, or 'punch the air' to attract attention rather than to achieve effects such as enhanced concentration or stronger muscle contraction.

The competitor is able to distinguish between violent behaviour and what might be termed pseudo-violent display, but spectators and younger sports aspirants often are not. Consequently, the novice in certain sports may confuse violence with aggressive posturing. Often the opponent may not be able to distinguish between the two and may react with actual violence to counter what is interpreted as a physical threat. It is important, then, that athletes be made aware of the possible detrimental effects of displaying pseudo-aggression, as it could readily be misconstrued to be true aggression rather than a need for attention.

Two types of *performance reinforcers* are recognized: intrinsic and extrinsic. Intrinsic performance reinforcers refer to the bodily sensations evoked through what was discussed previously as the kinaesthetic sense. It was pointed out that these sensations may be produced by the 'feeling' of landing a punch, throwing an adversary, or tackling an opponent. While such actions may be part of the game, it is important that the coach does not in any way reinforce the value of the violent aspects of the process. Instead the coach needs to show the athlete how to appreciate the intrinsic reward offered by the efficient, flowing, or aesthetic execution of any physical task.

Extrinsic performance reinforcers have their source outside the athlete and include external information given on performance rather than on behaviour. Most frequently this appears in the form of feedback from the coach or comments from peers and spectators. As extrinsic performance reinforcement is related to social reinforcement, the same comments apply as for the latter: positive reinforcement of constructive performance is more important than mere negative reinforcement of aggressive performance.

Internal reinforcers comprise two distinct types: self-control and vicarious. The former refers to internalized causes of behaviour, in particular the athlete's perception of the actions of himself/herself and others. He/she may rationalize that spectators or peers will regard him/her as a coward unless he/she displays aggressive, and in the case of men, 'masculine', behaviour. According to attribution theory, he/she may attribute certain ulterior motives to his/her opponents and internally justify his/her aggression. The theory of cognitive dissonance reveals how an athlete can perpetrate hostile actions which clash seriously with his/her ethical, religious upbringing if he/she reasons that there are extenuating circumstances or exceptions to the rule. Since this behaviour is learned, the offending athlete needs to be taught more suitable ways of understanding and responding to the actions of others.

Vicarious internal reinforcement refers to the modification in behaviour produced in an athlete by observing the behaviour of others. Since imitative behaviour characterizes the learning process of children and less self-actualized adults, it is vital that violent actions be eliminated, condemned, or appropriately punished whenever they are witnessed in sport. The media have a special duty in this regard. Responsible journalism and photo-journalism need to be defined more clearly to include how violent behaviour should be presented for public consumption. This would always emphasize the negative role of violence played in sport and how it lowers the quality of life for society at large. The South African Police would do well to appreciate that any violent crowd control administered by them produces a similar vicarious effect in generating further violence in the informal 'sport' of police versus the people.

Material reinforcers refer to tangible rewards in the form of pay, prizes, team colours, and trophies. While there is an abundance of such rewards for winning, there are still too few instances where fair play and exemplary behaviour are materially rewarded. There are even fewer instances where a person is denied awards of team or national colours for violent behaviour. Society has acquired the perception that excellence of play far overrides all other factors in sport. Just as many believe that politics and sport do not mix, so they also believe that litigation and sport do not mix.

In the same way as Ben Johnson was stripped of his 1988 Olympic medal for steroid use, so other sportspersons need to be stripped of their colours for persistent violent play. Athletes need to realize that excellence of performance warrants award only if it is coupled with fair play and ethical play. It would be highly desirable for the future of true sport that all sports participants be required to sign a Hippocratic Oath for Sport, in which one of the Articles of Declaration states that 'I recognize that I shall receive no award whatsoever if I contravene any of the Articles of this Oath'.

It has to be recognized by administrators, sponsors, and parents that, just as violent play needs to be punished, so exemplary behaviour has to be rewarded in the form of financial bonuses, badges, trophies, and bursaries. Unfortunately, academic institutions still tend to award sports bursaries to the most prominent athletic applicants rather than lesser athletic applicants of superior moral fibre. It would be preferable to award such bursaries biannually and make continuation thereof incumbent upon exemplary behaviour in sport or any social settings associated with sport.

Token reinforcers, unlike material reinforcers, provide intangible reward in the form of points, ratings, and recognition that serve to satisfy the need for status in particular. Like material reinforcers, they may be used to reward or punish. Token reinforcement may be linked to material reinforcement by awarding colours, cash bonuses, or trophies for the accrual of a specific minimum number of points by any athlete.

Selection of suitable measures to eliminate violence in sport depends on examining the phenomenon on a global and a local level with the aim of identifying if there is a necessity for invoking specific local measures.

In the South African setting, sincere steps need to be taken by individuals and the government to diminish the potential for the growth of violence created by the apartheid mentality. In this respect, the problem of the increasing fanaticism of the aggressive right-wing parties needs to be given priority attention. With regard to sport, should any of their retrogressive acts gain a significant foothold, there can be little doubt that aggressive overseas and local boycotts will escalate enormously.

At present, it is remarkable that there is little interracial conflict in sport and that its existence is confined mainly to the influential administrators. This is more a tribute to the positive qualities of competitive sports participants who compete in the interests of sporting excellence rather than political prominence. The lesson here is that the solution to politically inspired aggression in sport may lie more in the hands of the participants than the administrators or politicians. Laying the blame on the authorities alone may then be seen to be evasion of personal responsibility for the future of non-violent sport.

At a general level, the implementation of approaches based on humanistic education represents the idealistic solution to eradicating violence from sport. Their successful application would ensure the eventual limitation of sporting violence to the inevitable persistence of certain aberrant personalities. Even Aristotle acknowledged: 'For argument based on knowledge implies instruction and there are people whom one cannot instruct.'

Obviously, parents, the teaching profession, and coaches have a vital role to play in this process. One of their most important tasks is to focus on the rewards associated with the process and not merely the outcome of sport. Winning at all costs needs to be underplayed, but healthy competition to the benefit of all participants must be emphasized. At the same time, the image of 'manliness' associated with aggressive action in sport such as rugby must be eliminated and replaced by an association of 'manliness' with all-round moral fibre.

It is unlikely, however, that a significant enough percentage of the population will rapidly ascribe to these ideals and it will be necessary to invoke sufficiently strong rules and penalties aimed at making violence as unattractive as possible in sport.

The battle-cry of 'no normal sport in an abnormal society' needs to be extended to emphasize that normality and non-violence in sport is not feasible in a society rendered abnormal not only by aggressive separation of its races, but also by a distorted concept of the nature and role of sport in society.

It is especially important to appreciate that the goal of society and sport is to enhance overall quality of life via structured and unstructured human interaction. The aphorism of 'a sound mind in a sound body' and the South African motto 'Unity is Strength' are central to attainment of this goal. They both refer to the centrality of unification.

When sports competitors, individuals, and politicians in our country begin to implement the sentiments implicit in these idealistic words, both violence in sport and violence in society will eventually assume a less dominant role in South Africa.

NOTE

1. In May 1990, the South African Rugby Board introduced several ex-
    perimental rule changes into schoolboy rugby, including measures
    designed to make scrumming safer.

BIBLIOGRAPHY

Aronson, E. (1972) *The Social Animal,* New York: Viking Press.

Bandura, A. *et al.* (1961) 'Transmission of Aggression Through Imitation of
    Aggressive Models', *Journal of Abnormal and Social Psychology,* 63,
    575–82.

Berkowitz, L. (ed.) (1968) *Roots of Aggression: A Re-examination of the
    Frustration-Aggression Hypothesis,* New York: Atherton Press.

Carrol, R. (1980) 'Football Hooliganism in England', *International Journal of
    Sport Sociology,* 15(2), 77–92.

Gilbert, B. & Twyman, R. (1983) 'Out of Hand in the Stands — Spectator
    Violence', *Sports Illustrated,* 58(4), 62–74.

Kahn, M. (1966) 'The Physiology of Catharsis', *Journal of Personality and
    Social Psychology,* 3, 278–98.

Kelly, B. & McCarthy, J. (1979) 'Personality Dimensions of Aggression: Its
    Relationship to Time and Place of Action in Ice Hockey', *Human Relations,*
    32(3), 219–25.

Lefebre, L. & Passer, M. (1974) 'The effects of Game Location and Importance
    on Aggression in Team Sport', *International Journal of Sport Psychology,*
    5(2), 102–10.

Leith, L. M. (1982) 'Aggression Controls in Sport'. In *Sport in Perspective,*
    edited by J. T. Partington *et al.,* Ottawa: Coaching Association of Canada
    and Sport in Perspective, Inc.

Leonard, W. (1980) *A Sociological Perspective of Sport,* Minneapolis: Bur-
    gess.

Lewis, J. (1982) 'Fan Violence: An American Social Problem', *Research in
    Social Problems and Public Policy,* 2, 175–206.

Luxbacher, J. (1986) 'Violence in Sport', *Coaching Review,* March/April,
    14–17.

Mayer, K. (1976) 'The Physiology of Violence'. In *Psychology of Sport —
    Issues and Insights,* edited by A. C. Fisher, New York: Mayfield.

Meaney, P. (1984) 'Aggression in Sport', *Sports Coach,* 7(4), 27–30.

Reeks, D. (1983) 'Violence in American Sports', *Olympic Message,* 6, 97–103.

Roadberg, A. (1980) 'Factors Precipitating Fan Violence: A Comparison of
    Professional Soccer in Britain and North America', *British Journal of
    Sociology,* 31(2), 265–76.

Rushall, B. & Siedentop, D. (1972) *The Development and Control of Behaviour
    in Sport and Physical Education,* Philadelphia: Lea & Febigzer.

Russel, G. & Drewryt, B. (1976) 'Crowd Size and Competitive Aspects of Aggression in Ice Hockey: An Archival Study', *Human Relations,* 29(8), 723–35.

Schneider, J. & Eltzer, D. (1983) 'The Structure of Sport and Participant Violence', *Arena Review,* November, 1–6.

Scott, J. P. (1978) 'Sport and Aggression'. In *Sport Psychology — An Analysis of Athletic Behaviour,* edited by W. Straub, New York: Movement Publications.

Siff, M. C. (1990) *Professional Communication,* Johannesburg: Lex Patria.

Smith, M. D. (1983) 'What is Sports Violence? A Socio-Legal Perspective'. In *Sports Violence,* edited by J. Goldstein, New York: Springer-Verlag.

Smith, M. (1975) 'Sport and Collective Violence'. In *Sport and Social Order: Contributions to the Sociology of Sport,* edited by D. Ball & J. Loy, Reading: Addison-Wesley.

Snyder, E. & Spreitzer, E. (1983) *Social Aspects of Sport,* Englewood Cliffs: Prentice-Hall, Inc.

Tahmindjis, A. (1986) 'Violence "Down Under"', *Coaching Review,* March/April, 21–4.

Tellier, R. D. (ed.) (1978) *Operations Management,* New York: Harper & Row.

Terry, P. & Jackson, J. (1985) 'The Determinants and Control of Violence in Sport', *Quest,* 37(1), 27–37.

Part 3

Domestic violence

Introduction

Because the family is a microcosm of society, the prevalence of violence in a particular society is invariably linked to high levels of domestic violence. Therefore an understanding of violence in the home lends itself to a better grasp of violence in the wider societal context. Indeed, the family can be regarded as a 'cradle' of violence because experiences of violence in childhood and in family life are invariably socialized into a cycle of violence, manifested inter-generationally within families, and perpetuated within the wider society in many forms.

In pursuit of understanding violence in the family, Part 3 of this book explores questions about the nature, causes, and incidence of six different kinds of violence occurring within families.

Of the six phenomena documented, three, those of the physical and sexual abuse of children, and familicide, are currently more actively and widely addressed in South Africa because of growing public awareness, stimulated largely through the media. Others, like wife abuse and abuse of the elderly, receive little attention, and tend to remain hidden, partly due to persistent societal prejudices against women in the case of wife abuse, and in the case of elderly abuse, partly due to ignorance about the existence of such phenomenon, or to a fear of growing old.

Emotional abuse remains the least understood and exposed, because its effects are insidious, and are not necessarily visible in the form of physical scarring.

The emotional abuse of children, which is examined in Chapter 6, refers to parental acts which can kill a child's ability to feel empathically, thereby rendering him/her unable to make emotional contact with others and unable to feel deeply for them. The presentation utilizes a social-cultural model of child abuse which locates its aetiology within the broader society, and which depicts how values, norms, social structures, and institutional arrangements generate abuse.

The thesis is developed that racial attitudes held in white households towards the child-minder, the black nanny, are damaging, and therefore abusive to the child, because they blunt the growth of empathy. The development of the thesis is further guided by the 'emic' perspective, a perspective which argues against ethnocentrism, and which seeks to understand practices and behaviours within the context in which they occur. It facilitates empathic entry into the frame of the other, and an understanding of the meaning and significance of behaviours within that context.

This untraditional, insightful exposition of emotional abuse of some children on the domestic scene is pertinent to the wider South African arena, in that the white household often provides the only venue where a young child comes into close contact with a black person, in the form of the domestic worker, the nanny.

It is in the home that values are inculcated into family members, and especially young children — to be manifested elsewhere in attitudes and behaviour.

In support of the argument that blunted empathy feeds racial attitudes, thereby retarding altruism and concern, the exploitive circumstances of the black child-minder are examined, stressing the imbalance of power relations between the white employer and the black domestic; an imbalance reinforced for children by parental explanations, which in themselves can be damaging to the child. For these explanations, which reinforce attitudes and behaviours in the child, strengthen the belief of the child that people are classified into categories, and internalize the notion that the world operates in terms of domination and subordination — a notion which in itself can breed violence.

Blunted empathy, a significant consequence of emotional abuse, which depicts a form of violence in an adult-child relationship, tends to facilitate violence in other such relationships as is illustrated in Chapters 7 and 8, in which the physical and sexual abuse of children receive attention. Whereas emotional abuse may occur without the direct use of physical force, the view is expressed that emotional abuse accompanies all forms of physical abuse.

The physical abuse of children by their parents cuts across the parental nurturing function. No wonder that initially there was a reluctance on the part of medical practitioners and magistrates, who enforce child care legislation, to face this unpleasant reality.

Indicators of physical abuse, a description of the kinds of injuries inflicted, the causative factors of such abuse, and strategies for intervention form the content of Chapter 7. The majority of injuries, whether superficial or internal, tend to be inflicted on children within the birth to three-year age category. To be remembered is that physical abuse of children occurs in all population groups across social strata, in cities and country areas alike. For educational purposes illustrations of the various physical injuries which can be inflicted are included in the chapter. It is stressed that all children under the age of three years presenting with a serious injury or burn should be considered victims of child abuse. Taking the history of the injury is a procedure to be delicately handled, as fear and at times loyalty can motivate a child to corroborate an untruthful history of the injury given by the parents.

The legal consequences of physical abuse are prescribed in the Child Care Act 74 of 1983. Immediate action is an essential element in intervention, as is team effort, because no single profession can alone plan and execute an intervention plan in physical abuse.

Preventive intervention is accentuated, and among the causative factors described, aggressive discipline is lifted out. Harmful parenting practices highlight the need for extensive preparation for parenthood. For, parenthood preparation fosters an understanding of the needs of children which is manifested in their behaviours, and helps parents to pitch their own expectations of their offspring within the behavioural parameters of the latter's developmental status. Education for parenthood is one form of attack against the inter-generational perpetuation of child physical abuse, where the abused in turn becomes the abuser.

Whereas the perpetrators of physical abuse on a child are commonly one or both parents, or a substitute primary care-giver, the perpetrator in sexual abuse can be a relative, in which case it is referred to as incest, or a non-family member. As with physical abuse, it occurs across the spectrum of families in society. Although it is an age-old phenomenon, its public exposure is of recent origin, as is explained in Chapter 8.

Non-family sexual abuse can take the form of child prostitution, sex rings, child pornography, and sexual abuse in children's homes. In incest the second member of the abuse dyad can be a parent of the child, a sibling, a grandparent, or another relative. Multiple incest refers to incestuous relationships between different family members within the same family.

Secrecy surrounds sexual abuse within a family, a secrecy based on fear — fear of reprisal, and/or fear of family disintegration. Thus moral values become split, and maintaining the lie to keep the secret becomes the ultimate virtue — the first response identified in a typical pattern of behaviour in sexual abuse, referred to as the Child Sexual Abuse Accommodation Syndrome.

Unless the victim receives therapeutic help, intense anger and resentment towards both parents are harboured life-long — anger towards the perpetrating parent for the exploitation and betrayal, and anger against the other parent for lack of protection.

A sexually abused child is at severe risk of further abuse by other persons in the environment, and is usually poorly-adjusted socially, finding it difficult to establish and sustain relationships.

The long-term effects of child abuse do not remain contained within the victim or the victim's family, but extend to the wider society. This poses a challenge to helping professionals to intervene timeously in the lives of the victim and the family as a whole. It also demands a societal response which extends beyond the public hysteria customarily evoked by the media. A response must also address the offender, and be based on the consideration of certain options, which in themselves present dilemmas in intervention, such as the criminalization of the offender or not.

In many instances the perpetrator of wife abuse is found to have been abused in childhood, a conclusion emerging from the content of Chapter 9 which documents wife abuse — the abuse women suffer at the hands of male partners in intimate relationships. This chapter is the first of three which examine further forms of family violence, the other two being familicide and the abuse of elderly persons.

Wife abuse in South Africa, as in many other countries world-wide, is a pervasive problem. It is a multi-determined phenomenon, best understood as one of the many forms of violence which women suffer by virtue of their vulnerability and relative disadvantage within the broad social structure. A very broad stance is taken in defining wife abuse in this chapter. It includes physical, sexual, and/or psychological force, coercion, emotional humiliation, degradation or torment, verbal assault, and economic deprivation or exploitation.

Although a direct link is made in the presentation between the level of violence in society and the prevalence of wife abuse, the ultimate cause of the phenomenon is explained in terms of the patriarchal structuring of gender relationships, with the inequality between women and men encoded in a variety of linguistic, legal, institutional, and economic practices. Traditional stereotypes of masculinity are empowering of individuals, while traditional stereotypes of femininity reinforce women's sense of powerlessness and vulnerability. The contention is that it is precisely these concepts which make women the obvious targets in domestic abuse.

Examination of the dynamics of violent relationships of this kind reveals three stages in a cycle of violence in wife battery, a cycle based on social learning theory. A stage of tension-building accompanied by minor battering incidents is followed by acute battery and assault, and finally contrite loving behaviour is demonstrated by the abusive partner, a stage which reinforces the cycle. Loss or fear of loss features prominently in the maintenance of an abusive intimate relationship.

Previously, the theories of wife abuse have tended to focus on the personality factors of abused women only, a matter rectified in contemporary literature. Research has suggested a high correlation between wife abuse and early impairment in attachment formation in the abuser, and has also revealed that a high percentage of abusive men were abused as children or had witnessed their fathers abusing their mothers, thereby internalizing a sense of violence as a norm, leading to the perpetuation of the phenomenon.

Because the effects of wife abuse extend not only to the victim and the perpetrator, but also to their children and their extended family and further into the wider society, multi-dimensional intervention is advocated on both curative and preventive levels.

At present in South Africa recourse to the law holds limited options for a battered wife, none entirely satisfactory. She may seek or lay a charge of assault against her abuser; or she may seek a peace order in terms of the Criminal Procedure Act 57 of 1977, restraining her husband from assaulting her; or she may seek a Supreme Court interdict restraining her abusive husband, a costly exercise. A final recourse may be legal separation or divorce. A policy of non-interference in 'domestic disputes' seems to operate, and therefore of crucial importance would be reform of the criminal justice system to truly protect battered women. Only when wife abuse is legally sanctioned as a crime, and the necessary machinery is instituted to adequately protect women and give them effective recourse to the law, will a comprehensive system of intervention evolve.

Although a tardiness is discernible in comprehensively addressing wife abuse, this seems not to be the case with familicide, the form of family violence examined in Chapter 10.

Extensive financial resources are facilitating research into this violent phenomenon, a brand of family violence uncommon elsewhere, and in South Africa most commonly found in white Afrikaans-speaking families.

Some writers have referred to familicide as an 'extended suicide' in which the head of a household kills all the family members and then himself/herself as an act of saving them from some feared situation or fate — regarding it as an act of salvation, or 'aggression in the service of attachment'.

Four possible causal factors, gleaned from current literature, are lifted out in the chapter. Familicide has been linked with psychopathology;

with a specific type of vulnerable, dependent personality unable to bear a financial crisis or the loss of a love object; with the current violence in South African society; and with facets of the Afrikaner national character such as a supposed authoritarianism in a patriarchal family, and a firm belief in happiness in the hereafter.

To date, no reliable profile has been constructed of the perpetrator of a family murder, because of the difficulty in collecting conclusive, first-hand evidence in a situation in which the main actors have died.

In this discussion on familicide, an argument is developed which places its cause primarily on a predominant, all-encompassing, yet warped sense of responsibility which is felt by a provider in the family.

An interesting, as yet unique postulation links this right to determine the lives of family members with guardianship and responsibility, factors mooted to be operating within the ideology of apartheid — an ideology which subscribes to uncalled for interference into, and uncalled for regulation of, the lives of race groups other than white.

The chapters in Part 3 thus far provide enough evidence to conclude that the home can be a very dangerous place and that individuals may have more to fear from close members of their own families than from total strangers. And so it is also in the case of elderly members of a family, as demonstrated in Chapter 11.

The phenomenon of elder abuse appears even more hidden than child physical and sexual abuse. The reasons cited for this family secrecy include the reluctance of elderly persons to report cases of violence, because such action may leave them destitute. Their limited mobility and their increasing isolation, which keep them out of the sight of members of the public or of professionals, may be further reasons.

The abuse, ill-treatment, neglect, and victimization of older persons is a growing phenomenon as more persons live beyond their economically productive years and become increasingly dependent on others, especially family members, for help and support. The extent of care and attention required by an infirm elderly person, and which may provoke abuse, is encapsulated in the following profile of a victim:

> An elderly female, aged between 70–80 years, chronically ill, immobile, incontinent and/or aphasic, with limited financial resources, living in a confined space, whose social interaction has been severely curtailed. Constant supervision is necessary day and night as is assistance with daily living activities.

That a dependent elderly person can be a source of emotional, physical, and financial stress to adult family members who may be untrained, unwilling, and financially unable to provide the extent of care required, is self-evident. Moreover, the care-givers themselves may be elderly and experiencing increased health and financial problems — all factors conducive to potential abuse. The abuse of an elder may also be part of a recurring pattern of violence in the family's history, enacted over several generations.

Sexual abuse, misuse of medicine, physical injury or constraint, malnutrition, personal neglect, and financial exploitation are all forms of abuse inflicted on elderly persons. A growing form of abuse experienced by persons who live alone in the community is criminal victimization, which holds serious material, social, and psychological consequences for such persons.

In South Africa, the welfare and public sectors have been slow in recognizing the extent and significance of the suffering elderly people endure at the hands of family members. It is therefore appropriate that intervention receives detailed attention in the chapter. Much-needed guidelines for the care-giving family are given, and the provision of outside support for the family and respite care for the care-giver are emphasized. Also emphasized is adequate legal provision for elderly persons living in the community.

Further themes recur throughout Part 3 alongside those of the cycle of violence, and the inadequacy or inappropriateness of services and statutory provision. These relate to issues inherent in formulating definitions of the different types of domestic violence, and a plea is made that cognizance be taken of social and cultural influences in such an exercise.

Highlighted also is the lack of research, and in consequence a lack of statistics by which to correctly determine the incidence of domestic violence.

Finally, repeated calls are made for appropriate intervention and adequate resources. Multi-disciplinary intervention on both a micro and macro level is promoted, with an emphasis on prevention; as is the provision of adequate, co-ordinated services.

Interventions of this calibre would educate families and their individual members and the public at large about the subtleties of emotional abuse; the psychological and physical needs of children and elderly persons; and the nature and consequences of family stress, which may lead to the abuse of different members of the family, and which may in some instances culminate in a family murder.

6 Violence against children: emotional abuse

G. Straker

ETIC AND EMIC PERSPECTIVES OF ABUSE

Conventional wisdom has it that human nature compels parents to rear their young with tenderness and care. The disturbing frequency with which neglect and abuse occur has done little to shake this belief but it has at least forced the recognition that child abuse and neglect are well within the repertoire of human behaviour (Korbin, 1980).

What precisely it is that constitutes child abuse and neglect remains a thorny issue. These definitional problems increase when the focus shifts from neglect and physical or sexual abuse to emotional abuse. There is no standard for childrearing from which deviations may be measured. There is a wide diversity across nations and groups in modal patterns of childrearing. The rights accorded to children, the conditions considered necessary for healthy development, and even the degree to which childhood is recognized as a developmental stage are all contested in the literature (Eisenberg, 1981; Levett, 1988).

Most studies on the subject have been carried out on Western nations which have no claim to reflect pan-human traits. Indeed as Korbin (1980) points out, Western nations, contrary to our own beliefs, may be seen by others to be at the extreme end of the continuum for non-indulgence. Infants are expected not only to sleep in their own beds, but in a separate room to their mothers, a practice which is an anathema to many non-Western societies (Eisenberg, 1981). Similarly, our demands regarding toilet training and achievement, especially with regard to the pre-school child, may be perceived by others as exceptionally harsh.

This perception and evaluation of the practices of one group by another is termed the 'etic' perspective. It is a problematic perspective as it evaluates practices and behaviours from the outside, often without due regard to the context in which they occur. The 'emic' perspective, in contrast, attempts to understand practices and behaviours within the context in which they occur. It attempts empathetically to enter the frame of the other and to understand the meaning and significance of behaviours within the groups in which they occur.

The emic perspective argues against ethnocentrism. In multi-cultural societies it acts to protect minority groups from attempts by the dominant culture to eradicate, through punishment or education, practices which it does not understand, without regard for the significance of these practices for the socialization of children within a particular culture (Korbin, 1980). The following examples illustrate this point.

In the first example Korbin (1980) cites the case of a woman in London who was arrested for child abuse because she had cut the faces of her two sons with razor blades. It transpired that this woman was a member of an East African tribe where children without such markings would never be accepted into adult society. To have failed to have marked her children would have been regarded by her own group as emotional abuse or neglect.

Similarly, Korbin (1980) cites the case of an American anthropologist in New Guinea who was regarded with horror by the local people for failing to pick up his new-born child as soon as it cried. Not only did they regard this as cruel in terms of the child's immediate well-being, but they believed that in the long term a child could die through being left unattended for too long. The villagers, in order to avert this catastrophe, applied their own form of protective custody and began to pick up the child themselves.

A further example of the need for the emic perspective derives from a source closer to home. A young boy who had a bad infection was circumcised in a local hospital in Johannesburg. He and his parents were mortified, and his parents accused the staff of child abuse for depriving the boy of his rite of passage to adulthood through ritual circumcision.

From the above, it is clear that childrearing practices have to be understood within their cultural context. However, the argument for cultural sensitivity should not be read as an argument for extreme cultural relativism. It is neither possible nor desirable when considering children to suspend all judgements concerning their humane treatment. The etic perspective, while problematic and of necessity itself culture-bound, is vital. Behaviours that from the outside seem harmful towards children cannot simply be accepted without further exploration because of the cultural realizations advanced to justify them (Eisenberg, 1981).

If children are to be protected, and this in itself is a value judgement, then judgements concerning both what constitutes harm to children and what behaviours promote this have of necessity to be made. Nowhere in the arena of child abuse and neglect are value judgements more apparent than in the area of emotional abuse.

DEFINITION OF EMOTIONAL ABUSE

There is general agreement in the literature that the term emotional abuse defies precise definition (Wald, 1982). Emotional abuse has encompassed notions such as chronic parental indifference and rejection, verbal abuse, sarcasm, intimidation, and harassment (Child Welfare League of America, 1973; Douglas & Besharov, 1981; Goldstein *et al.*, 1974).

It has been described as parental acts which cause the destruction or impairment of a child's competence, and more broadly as parental acts which deny the child the normal experiences of being loved, wanted, and secure (Garbarino, 1976; Whiting, 1976). Definitions have varied according to the stress they have placed on intentionality, the weight they have given to the acts of the parents, and the importance of the impact of these acts upon the child.

Given the range of definitions in the area of abuse and the complexities of the issues, researchers such as Gelles (1977) have argued that we should give up the attempt to define these terms. He argues that:

> The term child abuse is a political concept which is designed to attract attention to a phenomenon which is considered undesirable or deviant. As a political term 'child abuse' defies logical and precise scientific definition (Gelles, 1977, cited in Douglas & Besharov, 1981: 388).

The author is sympathetic to this argument and accepts that given the degree to which the term child abuse is bound both historically and culturally, a universally agreed upon definition is unlikely to emerge. Nevertheless, it would seem undesirable that the attempts to refine definitions in the area should be abandoned. For the moment, however, it is accepted that the term child abuse is a political one 'designed to attract attention to a phenomenon which is undesirable'.

For the purposes of attracting such attention, a modification of the definition of emotional abuse advanced by Fortin and Reed (1984: 117) will be used in this chapter to attract attention to a form of emotional abuse which is endemic in South Africa. This definition states that emotional abuse refers to any parental acts which 'can kill a child's spirit, his ability to feel deeply and to make emotional contact with others'.

The focus in this chapter is not only on those parental acts which kill the child's ability 'to feel deeply and to make emotional contact with others' but also on those ideologies and structural relations common in South African homes which have the same effect. Specifically, the focus is on the employment, under apartheid, of child-care workers and the implications this has for the child's developing capacity for empathy.

In choosing to locate the aetiology of emotional abuse within broad social structures, the author is following what has been termed the socio-cultural model of child abuse (Gelles & Cornell, 1983). This model is one of three main models used in the literature to explain the aetiology of child-abuse; the other two being the medical intra-individual model, and the socio-psychological model.

AETIOLOGICAL MODELS OF ABUSE

The medical intra-individual and the socio-psychological models

The *medical intra-individual model* attempts to locate the causes of abuse within the individual. It emphasizes, for example, alcoholism, mental retardation, and sociopathy. It is the model most frequently associated with psychological research by lay people. In reality, however, the international literature indicates that it is not as frequently used to explain abuse as are the socio-psychological or socio-cultural models. Its main use seems to be to sensitize physicians to the possibility of abuse occurring in families where these pathologies exist, rather than serving as an explanatory system for the abuse itself (Gelles & Cornell, 1983).

In contrast, the *socio-psychological model* has been used world-wide in attempts both to explain and to understand the causes and the consequences of abuse. In this model the causes of abuse are located within family interactions and family systems. Parental disharmony, domestic upheavals, as well as the family contexts of, for example, poverty and social mobility are emphasized. In its stress on contexts, this model is similar to the socio-cultural model which also embodies some of these concepts. However in its analysis the latter model places greater emphasis on the family context than on the family itself.

The socio-cultural model

The *socio-cultural* model is the most widely applied model in the international literature on child abuse and neglect (Gelles & Cornell, 1983). It stresses values, norms, social structures, and institutional arrangements in the aetiology of abuse.

It locates child abuse within the broader society. It shows its relationship, *inter alia*, to social class, to the availability of day-care centres, the quality of care available for premature and congenitally impaired infants, and the availability of contraceptives and free abortions.

It also explores the relationships between culturally legitimized patriarchy, authoritarianism, and abuse in the family. Clearly this model is applicable to the aetiology and transmission of the form of emotional abuse to be described in this paper, which is emotional abuse which blunts the child's capacity for empathy. The contention is that this occurs through the exposure of the young child to the common practice of employing black child-care workers under conditions which communicate the notion that human exploitation is legitimate and that a class of people are inferior as human beings. That black child-care workers under apartheid are indeed employed under conditions which are exploitative and which underline their powerlessness in the broader social system is amply demonstrated in the following section.

THE BLACK NANNY AND THE DEVELOPMENT OF EMPATHY IN CHILDREN

The status of a black nanny in a white home

The term 'nanny' is one used by both adults and children to describe a woman employed to look after children. The practice of hired mothering goes back centuries and is a product of societies which are highly differentiated by class (Wulfsohn, 1988). In South Africa, where class distinctions are enforced and maintained along racial lines by repressive legislation, the nanny in a white home is almost always black. She is also frequently illiterate and poorly educated, both because of the poor quality of education offered to blacks and because domestic work attracts less skilled individuals (Kuzwayo, 1985).

Lacking in education and skills and operating in a society where there are high levels of unemployment, the black nanny is open to extreme exploitation. In her work on maids and madams, Cock (1980) describes this exploitation, as well as the extreme dependence black women feel with regard to their white employers. Domestic workers are not only dependent on their employers for their livelihood, but they frequently reside on the property where they work. Loss of employment for domestic workers therefore often means not only a loss of income, but the loss of their abode as well.

Furthermore, until the recent repeal of the pass laws, loss of employment also often meant loss of the right to remain in a particular residential area.

Because the child-care worker frequently lives at the site of her employment, her private life as well as her work life comes under the scrutiny and control of her employers. The times that she is allowed visitors, whether they can spend the night, whether her own children can stay with her, and many other personal and intimate aspects of her life are monitored by her employers (Cock, 1980).

From this it is clear that the black nanny operates in a situation which underlines her powerlessness, a powerlessness of which she is acutely aware. The degree to which this awareness will translate itself into particular child-rearing styles is, however, dependent on many factors, especially the parents' preparedness to delegate to the nanny real authority in the upbringing of the children. Even when this authority is delegated, however, the children know that this authority is derived and that their parents are the final arbiters in conflicts. This has implications both for children's perception of the nanny's authority and her freedom to exercise it. That the authority she is delegated is usually limited is confirmed both by the author's own observations and the comments of black workers themselves, which indicate that the delegation of absolute authority by parents to the nanny is the exception rather than the rule (Kuneine, 1985; Whisson & Weil, 1971). The rule seems to be that the black nanny is expected to take a great deal of responsibility for the well-being of the child but without concomitant authority and without the right to cultivate a relationship with the child based on emotional reciprocity and mutual obligation. Given that emotional reciprocity and mutual obligation in relationships are the foundation stones for the development of empathy and concern in the young child, this creates a situation which is damaging. The encouragement of relationships which are based on the antithesis of reciprocity and mutual obligation, and which are founded on an enduring sense of entitlement, impair the child's ability to feel deeply and to make emotional contact with others. The child thus becomes emotionally abusive.

The development of empathy in children

The notion that the development of empathy depends upon the establishment of relationships of emotional reciprocity and mutual obligation is substantiated both by psychological theories and empirical studies. The developmental theories of the object-relations school are relevant in this regard (Kohut, 1983; Winnicott, 1974). The basic premise of this school is that the original subjective state of the child is one of symbiotic fusion with the caretaker. There is little recognition that the caretaker is a source of need gratification. Rather, the infant exists in a state of primary omnipotence, believing that he/she is the source of his/her own need gratification. It is only through a long, slow process of disillusionment, when the child fails through personal endeavours to meet his/her own needs, that the child gives up this omnipotence and develops a sense of separateness from the caretaker, along with a sense of concern for her as an independent person. This process needs to be gradual and if the child's omnipotence is shattered too early by insensitive parenting, it is argued that this will impair the child's ability to truly separate and to develop concern.

While most object-relations theorists have focused on the detrimental effects of disabusing the child of notions of omnipotence too early, there has been more recently a focus on the potentially negative effects of failing to do this through mothering which continually anticipates the needs of the child, thereby denying the child's sense of separateness. Caretakers involved in this form of mothering often have anxieties about separation themselves and need to keep the child very close to them, using them as an extension of the self, and rejecting the child's attempts to move away (Kohut, 1983; Mahler *et al.*, 1975).

Whether theorists focus on the negative effects of disabusing the child of a sense of omnipotence too quickly or of not doing so sufficiently, all are agreed that for a healthy development to occur such disillusionment is necessary. Furthermore, all are agreed that the ability to perceive the other as a separate human being with needs distinct from one's own underpins the development of concern in an interpersonal context (Klein, 1948; Kohut, 1983; Mahler *et al.*, 1975; Winnicott, 1974). Although the object-relations theorists' views pertain largely to the infant and very young child, the principles they describe apply to the older child too.

A corollary of these principles is that any ethos which undermines the perception of the other as having distinct needs, and encourages the use of the other as an extension of the self beyond the age-appropriate time, will impair the child's developing sense of concern. Certainly the conditions under which child-care workers in South Africa are employed encourages the perception of them as extensions of the self, and certainly the little empirical evidence we have to date indicates that from a young age children fail to develop a sense of concern for their black child-care workers (Bhana & Bhana, 1975; Wulfsohn, 1988).

The view that the perception of others as separate is essential to the development of empathy is not only a basic premise of object-relations theorists, but of most workers in this area, including the cognitive-development theorists.

Cognitive-development theories of empathy

From observational studies of infants it is postulated that a purely emotional response to the distress cries of others is innate and can be observed from birth (Hoffman, 1983). However, the intuitive emotional distress response is elaborated upon and fine tuned through social feedback as the child's cognitive capacities expand. There are three stages in the cognitive-emotional growth of empathy (Hoffman, 1983). The first stage refers to the intuitive emotional response to distress already described and spans the ages from birth to about two years. The initiation of the second stage occurs at about two years and is complete at about six years. The second stage is the one of greatest concern in this chapter. During this stage the child comes to realize that others are separate from the 'self' and as such they have inner states which are distinct. The cognitive capacity which underpins this realization is the ability to take on the perspective of the other via role-taking. Through taking the role of the other the child is able to make a clearer assessment of the other's needs, which then facilitates an appropriate response to them. The ability to refine the assessment of the other's inner state is, however, dependent on feedback from the other concerning the accuracy of the attributions made by the child. This ability to assess the inner state of the other is further honed by the provision of opportunities for the child to role-play the perspective of the other.

From the earlier description of the black nanny's structural position in the home it is clear that she is already hampered both in regard to providing opportunities for role-playing and in providing emotional feedback, the essential ingredients in the development of empathy. The direct expression of many emotions by the child-care worker is discouraged in her site of employment. Her powerless position dictates that she should be grateful for her job. The expression of anger and resentment concerning exploitative conditions experienced daily would jeopardize her position as would the too frequent expression of sorrow. The ideal employee is a grateful one. Yet the direct expression of emotion is vital to the facilitation of empathy in the developing child.

As regards role-playing, which is an essential factor in the development of empathy, it is known from social learning theory that children are less likely to identify with and imitate low-status models (Bandura, 1969). Given the low status of the nanny, children would not tend to enter role-plays from which they could learn about her perspective on life. This tendency not to identify with the nanny also interferes with the child's capacity for concern in yet another respect.

In addition to her caretaking duties most child-care workers are expected to contribute substantially to household tasks (Wulfsohn, 1988). The performance of these tasks by a low-status individual both devalues the tasks themselves and lessens the need for family members, including children, to be engaged in such tasks. Yet there is convincing evidence in the literature that it is precisely such participation in household duties and responsibilities which promotes altruistic and pro-social behaviour, of which empathy is a component.

Whiting and Whiting's (1975) classical cross-cultural study on pro-social behaviour found that children who showed the most pro-social behaviours were those in cultures where they were expected from a very early age to participate in household chores and to take on family responsibilities. Similarly they found that first-born children who are usually expected to take on more household responsibility than youngest children or only children also showed a greater incidence of pro-social behaviours. From this the Whitings (1975) concluded that children who have the most experience with being helpful in the house and participating themselves in caretaking showed the most pro-social behavior. Conversely, the children with the least experience showed the least pro-social behaviour. Given that in white homes the explicit function of the nanny is to relieve both mother and child of household responsibilities and that children are not encouraged to imitate the nanny, it would seem fair to infer that white children in South Africa would be less experienced than most in taking the kind of household responsibility shown by the Whitings to promote concern and empathy for others.

That white South African children do indeed denigrate household tasks and resist participating in them is amply demonstrated in the following section, which looks at empirical studies on children's attitudes to their black child-care workers.

Empirical studies of child – nanny relationships

There is a dearth of literature in this area (Feldman, 1988; Wulfsohn, 1988). Furthermore, what little research does exist tends to examine the child's relationship with the domestic worker as a secondary rather than as a primary focus. Both Feldman (1988) and Wulfsohn (1988) designed studies aimed to fill this gap.

Feldman (1988) studied the attitudes to the nannies of twenty-eight white, middle-class to upper-class children, aged eight to eleven years. She used a modification of Bronfenbrenner's Parent-Child Questionnaire as well as an open-ended interview. Her findings at the first level of analysis were paradoxical. On the one hand they revealed that the nanny's 'sense of protectiveness and sensitivity to the child's needs are perceived by the child as the domestic's most striking characteristics' (Feldman, 1988: 53). However, despite this, and the fact that nannies were found to spend an average of seven hours per day with their charges, Feldman's (1988: 54) results revealed that the majority of her sample seemed to regard the nanny as 'merely a companion — someone to pass the time with, to relay one's daily activities to and of course to help in instrumental tasks'. She was not really seen as a 'friend in the true sense of the word' and she was not afforded the status of a confidante. Presumably too, she was not afforded the status of an independent person with needs of her own, although this cannot be assumed as none of Feldman's questions really tapped these dimensions. However, Feldman's (1988) study gives indirect support to the idea that the nanny was not seen as an independent person. Its main finding was that the children's perceptions of their nanny centered on her responsiveness to their own personal needs.

Wulfsohn (1988), like Feldman (1988), did not specifically assess either the child's perception of the nanny as a separate person or the child's capacity for empathy with her. Her sample comprised fifty English-speaking five-year-old children and she assessed the quality of their relationship both with their nannies and with their mothers. The specific relationship dimensions she studied were intensity of involvement and the positive or negative quality of the relationship. Wulfsohn (1988) also studied the mother's perception of the child's relationship with the nanny and the mother's reported closeness to the nanny. Following comprehensive statistical analyses of her data as well as in-depth qualitative analysis, Wulfsohn's (1988: 161) final conclusion was that:

> In the majority of cases the nanny was found to be a peripheral, shadowy figure, as viewed both by the child and the mother ... She

does not feature strongly in the child's emotional world and for the most part is experienced as a stranger with whom there is no emotional involvement.

Wulfsohn's study may be criticized in that on some of the measures the child's perception of the nanny was not assessed independently but only in comparison to the perception of the mother. However, this was not true of all the tests, and in addition the dismissiveness which was found to characterize the child's relationship with the nanny in Wulfsohn's test findings were confirmed by her informal *in vivo* observations. The following vignettes pertaining to three children illustrate this (Wulfsohn, 1988).

> When the child came into the house, she took off her wet shoes and handed them over to the nanny without looking at or greeting the nanny (p. 172).

> Not once did this child glance in the direction of its nanny, who was vacuuming in the same room in the course of the testing (p. 173).

> The child snatched her leotard from her nanny without any sign of appreciation or recognition for the time the nanny had spent hunting for it at the whining demand of the child (p. 173).

In addition to these observations, comments made spontaneously to Wulfsohn (1988) both by the children and their mothers confirmed the finding that the nanny's status in the home was one of a 'non-person' or at least an inferior person. They also confirmed the child's denigration of household tasks. These comments included the following:

> When I ask my child to clean up his mess he tells me that he's not a nanny.

> When my child has to tidy up, she responds, 'Anna will do it; she's just the maid'.

The disrespect the children had for the nanny was shared by their mothers, some of whom commented as follows:

> My daughter knows the nanny can't sit with us at the table and sit on the same furniture — my children have been brought up that way (p. 170).

> When we're eating at the table and her sister asks the *girl* to come and sit with us, she tells her sister that the nanny may not come and sit with us at the table (p. 170).

> We don't take the *girl* on holiday. I need a break from her, too, because she does sometimes intrude on our family life. Also it's

such a hassle to organise her special food, you know like boys-meat and mealie-meal (p. 173).

I don't talk to Blacks much, I don't think it's a good idea (p. 172).

Thus far in this chapter the focus has been on the structural position of the child-care worker and how this in itself creates a situation which dictates against the development of empathy and concern in the child. However, the above quotations from the mothers in Wulfsohn's study add a new dimension to the discussion. They indicate clearly how mothers, through direct statements about child-minders, convey both their lack of empathy for them and their more generally racially prejudiced attitudes. Doubtless both these features of the mother's relationships to the child-minders are conveyed through a variety of behaviours other than the direct statements quoted above. These behaviours reinforce the direct statements and are observed and imitated by the children. In this way the mother reinforces the lack of empathy encouraged by the structural relationship between child and nanny and provides the justification in racial terms for the nanny's position in the house. The concern of this paper is not, however, the development of racial prejudice *per se*. Therefore, only those aspects of the development of racial prejudice which would interact with the impairment of the development of empathy will be considered further.

THE INTERACTION BETWEEN LACK OF EMPATHY AND RACIAL PREJUDICE
Blunted empathy underpins racial prejudice

The mechanisms which impair the development of empathy have been outlined in some detail earlier but bear recapitulation. They include a lack of mutual obligation which impairs the development of the sense of separateness crucial to the development of empathy. They also include a lack of emotional reciprocity which impedes the child from receiving feedback concerning the accuracy of the emotional states attributed to the child-care worker. The difficulties created by this lack of feedback are, in turn, increased by the child's tendency not to enter the nanny's world or to identify with her. This tendency is promoted both by the child-care worker's low status and the low status accorded to the tasks she performs.

There are, however, further psychological processes which act to blunt the child's empathy and to increase the racial prejudice it underpins. As has already been mentioned, empathy is dependent both on identification, which involves the perception of others as similar to oneself, and on the ability to appreciate simultaneously their separateness and difference. Similar processes underpin the development of racial tolerance. Conversely, racial prejudice is promoted both by a failure to identify with and see others as similar to oneself and by a failure to discriminate between members of alternate groups, thereby not perceiving their individuality and uniqueness.

In discussing this phenomenon in relation to the development of racial prejudice, Katz (1976) spoke of the 'acquired distinctiveness of cues' as well as the 'acquired equivalence of cues'. Katz's basic argument was that racial labelling affects the individual's ability to make refined perceptual differentiations. She argued that the association of distinctive labels with particular groups enhances the ability to distinguish between groups, but diminishes the ability to make distinctions within groups. That is, labels lead to a distinctiveness of cues between groups but an equivalence of cues within groups.

Katz demonstrated this notion in an experiment in which children were required to discriminate between pairs of Caucasian, Negro, and green faces. She argued that if other-race faces are more difficult to discriminate between because of their relative unfamiliarity, then the green faces and other-race faces should be equally difficult to discriminate between. If, on the other hand, other-race faces are more difficult to discriminate between not because of their unfamiliarity, but because the group has been given uniform racial labels, then green-face learning should be easier. Katz found that for children of both race groups green faces were easier for them to discriminate between than other-race group faces.

As children were even less familiar with green faces than with other-race faces, Katz (1976) postulated that the green faces were easier to discriminate between because they had not acquired stereotyped labels to describe them. She postulated further that her findings reflected adult society's tendency to magnify differences between groups and to de-individuate members within alternate groups through racial labelling.

Given the above it seems clear that the way to improve children's perceptual differentiation *vis-à-vis* other races does not lie in simply increasing contact between groups. In fact cue equivalence, which in lay parlance is the notion that 'all blacks look alike', could be increased rather than decreased by simply increasing contact without due regard to the context within which this contact occurs. Contact with black child-care workers under conditions of apartheid is one such context which could act to increase rather than decrease cue equivalence.

Writing about the dilemmas facing black domestic workers in general, Whisson and Weil (1971) of the Domestic Workers Union postulated that white households are the crucible of racism because within them children are exposed to intense personal contact with blacks in a situation which encompasses a strict hierarchy and a stratification of authority. This contact is the only one the child is likely to have with blacks, as apartheid mitigates against personal contact with blacks in more equal contexts. Encapsulated in this statement, which is based on an intuitive understanding of the problem from within, is a confirmation of Katz's (1976) conclusions. This statement also contains the notion that broadening contact between blacks and whites might paradoxically facilitate more prejudice and less empathy if it occurs only in contexts such as that of domestic work. Certainly studies which have examined the epidemiology of racial prejudice confirm this notion. In these studies racial prejudice was found to be at its height in areas where there was a high rather than a low chance of casual contact with blacks from a more deprived lower socio-economic class, for example, in the rural south of the United States (Chesler, 1972).

It is beyond the scope of this chapter to explore all the possible explanations which have been advanced to explain the findings of these epidemiological studies. It is sufficient for present purposes to simply comment that intergroup interaction in contexts of unequal status has been shown to be related to high levels of prejudice, which in turn is related to low levels of empathy for the group against which the prejudice is held. Further, there is evidence that the institutional arrangements which ensure this inequality are themselves more likely to be the cause than the consequence of racial prejudice, although obviously there is reciprocal interaction between the two. These institutional arrangements and unequal relationships which contribute to racial prejudice are also those advanced by the author to stunt the development of empathy. It is to the development of empathy that attention is now returned.

Blunted empathy retards altruism and concern

As mentioned earlier, Hoffman (1983) postulated three stages in the development of empathy. The first two stages refer to the development of empathy on an individual, personal basis. That is, they refer to the development of empathy for persons to whom the child relates directly to in her/his immediate family and world.

The third stage refers to the development of a sense of empathy for people in general. It heralds the development of altruism and concern in a broader sense. The resolution of this third stage is dependent upon the negotiation of the previous two stages. If the child has not developed a sense of empathy for the child-care worker on a personal level, the chances of developing a more general sense of concern for her and for those perceived to be like her will be diminished.

Furthermore, race is the marker the child is most likely to use in determining who is similar to and who is different to the child-care worker. Firstly, racial cues are distinct and very easy to identify, and secondly, racial cues are used by others in the family to categorize and describe. Thus the probability that race will be used as a marker by the child is great and once it is used this tendency will be reinforced by the society in general.

RETURN TO THE ETIC PERSPECTIVE

It has been argued in this chapter that the employment of child-care workers under apartheid blunts the child's capacity for empathy with regard to the child-care worker and those like her. In terms of Fortin and Reed's (1984: 117) definition of emotional abuse, namely that emotional abuse refers to parental acts which 'can kill a child's … ability to feel deeply and to make emotional contact with others', it has been argued that this constitutes emotional abuse.

Whether or not the reader accepts the legitimacy of this will depend on a number of factors. Firstly, it will depend on the reader's stance in relation to Gelles' (1977: 388) statement that 'The term child abuse is a political concept which is designed to attract attention to a phenomenon which is considered undesirable or deviant'.

It will also depend on the reader's view regarding the legitimacy of the etic perspective which justifies labelling that which may be normative within a culture as psychopathological. Racial prejudice and the lack of empathy which underpins it is normative among most white South Africans. It is supported by the legislature and communicated and endorsed by all the state apparatus, including the schools, and until very recently the church. It is obvious, therefore, that it will be taught both directly and indirectly through the family, which is a primary vehicle for the socialization of children into a particular culture.

To argue that this constitutes emotional abuse may be seen by many to be stretching the concept too far. However, as pointed out earlier, there is a tradition in the child abuse literature which locates abuse within broad social structures and which focuses on, for example, authoritarianism and patriarchy as particular instances of ideologies which promote the abuse of women and children.

It is granted that in these discussions, most authors do not argue that patriarchy *per se* is abusive. They rather argue that it creates an ethos which promotes 'abuse'. In this chapter the argument with regard to child-care workers is taken further and it is proposed that unequal power relations in white homes, reinforced by parental explanations of them, are in and of themselves damaging to the child in a way which may be construed to be abusive. The argument is thus extended beyond that which is customary in the child abuse literature in its consideration of, for example, patriarchy and authoritarianism, although it is not extended beyond arguments in much of the feminist literature. This extension may nevertheless be considered to be unacceptable, especially in the light of evidence which suggests that in certain situations the same power relations which have been posited to be destructive may serve to promote a sympathy for, and understanding of the nanny.

One such situation would be that in which parents consciously provide explanations of the nanny's plight in terms which locate blame in the broader social structure that impinges on her rather than in terms of her race. A second set of circumstances in which sympathy may develop are those where the child's relationship with the mother is defective and the child compensates through a transfer of attention to the nanny. In these circumstances the child's relationship with the nanny may well promote rather than stunt emotional development including the development of empathy, despite the context of this relationship.

These facts may be seen to mitigate against the argument that the employment of child-care workers under apartheid is in and of itself abusive. However, the author would argue that even in the exceptional instances described above, the distorted power relations in the home would impact upon the child's capacity for empathy, albeit in a different form to that described in this chapter.

Sandler and Sandler (1978), writing in the area of object-relations, point out that the child internalizes total transactions between subjects and objects and that in the child's inner world the concrete persons in the position of subject and object alternate. Thus the child who is abused, for example, internalizes a total pattern of abusive relations including a victim and a perpetrator. Internally this child then identifies both with the victim and the perpetrator and not only with the victim. The enactment of this identification in the multi-generational transmission of abuse, where the abused becomes the abuser, is well documented

(Kempe & Kempe, 1978). Thus, children who identify with exploited child-care workers for the reasons stated above may not automatically be exempted from an impairment in empathy. The principle of classifying people into categories will have been internalized as will the notion that the world operates in terms of domination and subordination.

These principles will impact upon the individual's style of relating. For example, it may translate itself into a style of relating to those perceived as the aggressor which lacks empathy and which has as its primary motive revenge and the acquisition of power rather than the promotion of equal relationships. Thus the inner form of the object-relations internalized in this individual may well be similar to that of the child who lacks empathy for the nanny. Obviously though, the valence in relation to the content of the object-relations will differ for them both. In the case of one it will primarily be the aggressor not the nanny for whom empathy is lacking, and in the case of the other the reciprocal will apply. However, the former pattern, by virtue of its juxtaposition to the normative one, contains the greater possibility of change.

Be this as it may, instances such as that described above remain the exception rather than the rule. What may well be normative, however, when considering the impact of the nanny on the child, is an improvement in the child's cognitive development and life opportunities as a result of the employment of the child-care worker (Shmukler, 1977). The child-care worker releases the mother to work and to improve the socio-economic status of the family. She also releases from household chores mothers who are not bread-winners, so they have the opportunity to spend more time with their children during which time they may stimulate them cognitively and emotionally. This will have obvious gains for the white child. The accompanying loss in empathy, particularly as this may well be a loss which is not a general one but rather a loss which is restricted along racial lines, may, from an emic perspective, seem to be a small price to pay for these advantages.

However, the thrust of this exposition has been the justification of the etic perspective. From this perspective the author believes that there is little doubt that in most instances the employment of child-care workers under conditions of apartheid is destructive with regard to the child's developing abilities 'to relate meaningfully and to make deep contact' with a large sector of humanity, and that it is therefore abusive within the parameters set out by Fortin and Reed (1984). In arguing that this practice is abusive and that it does indeed contribute to killing the 'child's ability to relate meaningfully to others and to make contact with them', the following quotation, with which this chapter concludes, pertains. It is from a five year-old child in Wulfsohn's study and typifies the response of many of her subjects.

> When Catherine baths my brother and me I can see her titties. I try and pull her clothes away. I splash her with water. She gets cross with me so I smack her on her titties. It doesn't matter: she's just the maid (Wulfsohn, 1988: 158).

In this quotation the child's perception of the nanny as powerless is clearly revealed as is his derogatory attitude towards her in this position.

Revealed too is his position of power which enables him to be abusive toward her with impunity. Thus he inserts himself once more into the destructive cycle so commonly associated with child abuse in which the abused becomes the abuser and perpetuates the endless cycle of abuse. This is obviously a highly undesirable phenomenon and one that will persist until such time as the balance of power in South Africa is sufficiently radically altered so that children are protected from those forces which infringe upon their humanity and their capacity for empathy for the majority of the country's population.

REFERENCES

Bandura, A. (1969) *Principles of Behaviour Modification,* New York: Holt, Rinehart & Winston.

Bhana, K. & Bhana, A. (1975) 'Colour Concept Attitudes among Indian Pre-School Children as a Function of Black Nannies', *Journal of Behavioural Science,* 2, 115–20.

Chesler, M. (1972) 'Desegregation and School Issues', *Integrated Education,* New York: CWLA.

Child Welfare League of America (CWLA) (1973) *Standards for Child Protective Services,* New York: CWLA.

Cock, J. (1980) *Maids and Madams,* Johannesburg: Ravan Press.

Douglas, J. & Besharov, J. (1981) 'Toward Better Research on Child Abuse and Neglect: Making Defunctional Issues an Explicit Methodological Concern', *Child Abuse and Neglect,* 5, 383–90.

Eisenberg, L. (1981) 'Cross-Cultural and Historical Perspectives on Child Abuse and Neglect', *Child Abuse and Neglect,* 5, 299–308.

Feldman, N. (1988) 'Primary School Children's Perceptions of their Domestic Workers', Honours Dissertation, University of the Witwatersrand.

Fortin, P. & Reed, S. (1984) 'Diagnosing and Responding to Emotional Abuse within the Helping System', *Child Abuse and Neglect,* 8, 117–19.

Garbarino, J. (1976) 'The Elusive Crime of Emotional Abuse'. Cited in 'Diagnosing and Responding to Emotional Abuse within the Helping System', by P. Fortin & S. Reed, *Child Abuse and Neglect,* 8 (1984) 117–19.

Gelles, R. J. (1977) 'Violence toward Children in the United States'. Cited in 'Toward Better Research on Child Abuse and Neglect: Making Defunctional Issues an Explicit Methodological Concern' by J. Douglas & J. Be-sharov, *Child Abuse and Neglect,* 5 (1981), 383–90.

Gelles, R. J. & Cornell, C. P. (1983) 'International Perspectives of Child Abuse', *Child Abuse and Neglect,* 7, 375–86.

Goldstein, J. *et al.* (1974) *Beyond the Best Interests of the Child,* New York: The Free Press.

Hoffman, M. (1983) 'Affective and Cognitive Processes in Moral Internalisation'. In *Social Cognition and Social Behaviour: Developmental Perspectives,* edited by E. T. Higgins *et al.,* New York: Cambridge University Press.

Katz, P. (1976) 'The Acquisition of Racial Attitudes'. In *Toward the Elimination of Racism,* edited by P. Katz, New York: Pergamon Press.

Kempe, R. S. & Kempe, C. H. (1978) *Child Abuse.* The Developing Child Series, New York: Fontana Open Books.

Klein, M. (1948) *Contributions to Psychoanalysis,* London: Hogarth Press.

Kohut, H. (1983) *The Restoration of the Self,* New York: International Universities Press.

Korbin, J. (1980) 'The Cultural Context of Child Abuse and Neglect', *Child Abuse and Neglect,* 4, 3–13.

Kuneine, S. (1985) 'Domestic Bliss? Not for "Nanny"', *City Press,* October 20, 3.

Kuzwayo, E. (1985) *Call Me Woman,* Johannesburg: Ravan Press.

Levett, A. (1988) 'Psychological Trauma: Discourses of Childhood Sexual Abuse', Ph.D. Thesis, University of Cape Town.

Mahler, M. *et al.* (1975) *The Psychological Birth of the Human Infant,* New York: Basic Books.

Sandler J. & Sandler A. (1978) 'On the Development of Object-Relationships and Affects', *International Journal of Psychoanalysis,* 59, 285–96.

Shmukler, D. (1977) 'Origins and Concomitants of Emotional Play in Young Infants', Ph.D. Dissertation, University of the Witwatersrand.

Wald, M. (1982) 'State Intervention on Behalf of Endangered Children — A Proposed Legal Response', *Child Abuse and Neglect,* 6, 3–45.

Whisson, M. G. & Weil, W. M. (1971) *Domestic Servants: A Microcosm of the Race Problem,* Johannesburg: South African Institute for Race Relations.

Whiting, L. (1976) 'Defining Emotional Neglect: A Community Workshop Looks at Neglected Children', *Children Today,* 5, 6–10.

Whiting, B. B. & Whiting, J. W. M. (1975) *Children of Six Cultures: A Psychocultural Analysis,* Cambridge: Harvard University Press.

Winnicott, D. W. (1974) *The Child, The Family and The Outside World,* London: Pelican Books.

Wulfsohn, D. (1988) 'The Impact of the South African Nanny on the Young Child', Ph.D. Thesis, University of South Africa.

7 Violence against children: physical abuse

W. S. Winship

A BRIEF HISTORICAL OVERVIEW

The classic paper by Kempe *et al.* entitled 'The Battered Child Syndrome' documented the first recognition by the medical profession of child abuse as a major cause of injuries and death in children. In this paper the authors reported on a survey conducted in the United States which covered 779 cases. Of these, 302 were gleaned from the one-year records of seventy-one hospitals and 477 from the records of District Attorneys. In the opinion of Krugman (1985) this total figure was probably exceeded in an eight-hour period in the United States in 1985.

In South Africa the first medical discussion of child abuse took place during the Congress of the South African Paediatric Association in Pretoria in 1974 and it was not until 1976 that the first multidisciplinary team was formed in Durban with the specific task of managing this complex problem. The original team was made up of social workers from child welfare agencies; doctors, nurses, and social workers from the hospitals; and senior staff from the state welfare department.

Great difficulty was encountered in convincing medical practitioners that child abuse occurred and many still find it hard to believe that parents could so injure their children, even when faced with obvious evidence. The same reluctance to accept evidence has been experienced in the magistrates' courts.

In 1976, 36 cases of child abuse were recognized in Durban compared with 412 cases in 1988. Public awareness as well as the co-ordination of the various professions caring for children have resulted in this dramatic increase in the recognition of serious childhood disorder in all centres in South Africa. Contrary to previously held misconceptions, physical abuse of children occurs in all population groups and among both urban and country dwellers.

Today all major hospitals have medical staff trained in the recognition of injuries which are not accidental and most centres have multidisciplinary teams to investigate and manage the total problem. Child Protection Units of the South African Police were first introduced in Durban in 1978, and became represented on the hospital multidisciplinary team. Similar units have now been established in all major centres. In Durban there are also a court and police subcommittee which collaborate on the handling of problem cases.

No single profession is capable of handling the problem of child abuse. Doctors can suspect that injuries have not been acquired accidentally but their treatment stops at the management of the injury. Social workers have the difficult problem of investigating the social circumstances and arranging the management of abused children and their families. The police conduct investigations where a criminal charge appears appropriate; the courts give judgment; and psychologists deal with the family disorder. However, all must work together if each case is to be treated appropriately with the object of ensuring that no further injury to the child will occur, and providing for that child a chance to attain adulthood as a satisfactorily functioning adult.

INDICATORS OF CHILD ABUSE
Age

In the author's experience the majority of severe or life threatening injuries occur in the age group from birth to three years, with decreasing frequency as children become older, although abuse may occur at any age up to eighteen years. All children under the age of three years presenting with a serious injury or burn should therefore be considered possible victims of child abuse.

A careful history should be taken and the likelihood of the given cause weighed against the extent and form of the injury. Older children, who fear their parents or caretakers, may confirm the history given by the adult even though it is obviously unacceptable. The author has experienced a situation where children have obviously been rehearsed in the history to be given and turn to their parents for confirmation of how the injury was allegedly acquired. Some even ask if they are telling the story correctly. It is preferable, therefore, to obtain the history of the injury from the older child while he or she is alone. If one does not suspect child abuse it will not be recognized. If more than one adult accompanies an injured child, taking the history from each adult separately may reveal discrepancies which invalidate the given cause of the injury. An example of this occurred when an infant presented with a head injury allegedly caused when he fell off the back seat of a car because his father braked suddenly. When asked separately, the parents gave different reasons for the sudden application of the brakes. One said a cat ran across the road, the other, that another car failed to stop at a stop sign.

Sex

There is no evidence of a significant difference in the incidence of physical abuse based on the sex of the child.

Ordinal position in the family

First-born children are more frequently the victims of child abuse than subsequent children. When later-born children are the only victims there is often a predisposing factor, for example, prematurity or abnormality of the child. In some families several children may be victims of abuse, and in others subsequent children become victims after the death or removal of an abused sibling.

Attitude of the child

Abused children often cling to their parents or are passively submissive. A fixed frozen stare on the face of the child may alert the examiner to the possibility of abuse which is as much emotional as physical. Failure to thrive and irritability may be indications of child abuse. Such indicators may be non-specific or specific to deliberate malnutrition or head injuries as described later on in this chapter.

Older children often present with problems at school. Their injuries may be covered by clothing and the child who is inappropriately over-dressed or reluctant to change for sports events may be hiding bruises or weals.

Changes in a child's school performance, truancy, and non-specific illnesses, such as headaches and abdominal pain, should alert a teacher to the possibility that a child is being abused. The child who is always seeking attention also warrants investigation. Teachers and crêche personnel should seek the assistance of a social worker in such instances.

SPECIFIC INJURIES INFLICTED
Specific injuries

1.   Bruising is easily recognized whether it be caused by a blow, pinching, or prolonged pressure, for example, by fingers on the arm (see Fig. 7.1; Figs. 7.1 to 7.11 can be found on pages 197 to 202).

The pattern and position of the bruises should alert the examiner to the likelihood of the aetiology being abuse. Most toddlers have bruises on their legs and even their heads from bumping into furniture and falling, but these are usually discrete. The distinct pattern of the sole of a shoe can be evidence of an adult having stood on a child. Bruises resulting from repeated injury can be judged by the variation in colour.

Under 24 hours a bruise is violaceous or red with sharp edges, becoming blue to black within 36 to 48 hours. The margins of a bruise become indistinct from about 48 hours onwards and the bruise itself turns yellow between 48 and 72 hours, gradually fading over three to seven days. Bruises must be distinguished from normally occurring Mongolian spots which are commonly found in infants with a dark complexion. Mongolian spots are blue, and flush with the skin. They are not tender and they may be discrete or extensive.

2.   Human bites leave a distinct elliptical pattern. The size of the mark would indicate that it was caused by adult teeth and forensic dentists can identify the perpetrator.

3.   Injuries to the mouth of a child may cause tearing of the frenulum of the upper lip (see Fig. 7.2). This bleeds excessively if torn and should be looked for in a child who is anaemic. Screwing a bottle into an infant's mouth can cause this injury.

4.   Figure 7.3 shows weals caused by a sjambok, stick, or belt which left a distinctive pattern.

5.   Burns caused by the deliberate action of an adult can usually be distinguished from those caused by accident.

   □   Cigarette burns are often found in the centre of the palm of the hand as shown in Figure 7.4, or on the sole of a foot, both very unlikely sites for an accidental burn.

   □   'Dunking' burns of the hands, feet, and buttocks have a clearly demarcated edge. An example of these, the 'glove' burn (shown in Fig. 7.5), depicts how the whole hand is evenly damaged. Accidental burns are unlikely to result in damage to the entire extremity alone. To have produced a burn of that extent, the whole hand must have been held in hot water to the line of demarcation.

☐ A burn caused by a steam iron applied to a child's thigh is illustrated in Figure 7.6.

☐ Chemical burns are unlikely to have caused damage to the entire penis as shown in Figure 7.7, without affecting any of the surrounding skin. In this instance battery acid allegedly 'fell accidentally' on this little boy.

Internal injuries

1. Fractures of limbs are not uncommon in older children who climb trees and who ride bicycles and skateboards, but infants and toddlers rarely suffer accidental fractures of long bones. A complete fracture through the middle of the shaft of a femur (thigh bone) in a young infant requires leverage by two adult hands or leverage against the bar of a cot. If caused by a direct blow with a blunt object, superficial bruising will show. Radiological surveys of children suspected of being abused often reveal healing fractures of long bones which may be detected up to three months after the event (see Fig. 7.9). Abuse should be suspected when a limb fracture is found in a child too young to tell the examiner how the fracture occurred.

2. Subperiosteal haematoma is a hallmark of child abuse. This occurs when the periosteal covering of a long bone is sheared off the bone by an adult holding the child's limb tightly. The periosteum is torn from the bone by rotation of either the abuser's hand or the struggling child's limb, resulting in bleeding between the periosteum and the surface of the bone. The child presents with a swollen, painful limb which may or may not show external bruising. X-rays of the limb taken in the acute stage do not show damage of the bone, but after four to five days calcification of the blood clot occurs and surrounds the shaft of the bone, as shown in Figure 7.8 (a). This condition, known as Caffey's Syndrome, is often found when radiological surveys are made of children in whom abuse is suspected.

3. Chip fractures near joints also occur in children whose limbs are rotated. Some, like the tiny fragment seen near the ankle in Figure 7.8 (b), are the result of sudden contraction of muscles due to pain, which causes the tendon attachment to pull away from the bone.

4. Rib fractures are caused by compression of the chest and should always cause suspicion when found in infants and toddlers. Often the fractures occur on both sides of the chest and sometimes they are only discovered when a radiological survey is done several weeks after the event. Such fractures cause severe painful embarrassment of the child's breathing and the fact that medical attention was not sought at the time of the injury is confirmatory evidence of child abuse.

5. Injuries to and rupture of abdominal viscera may occur alone or in combination with other injuries. Organs which are damaged, usually by a blow or compression, are the liver, the spleen, the urinary bladder, and even the bowel, which can be compressed against the spine, causing either rupture or damage to its blood supply and consequent gangrene.

6. Head injuries are common and while small children frequently bump their heads or fall onto their heads accidentally, severe injuries are uncommon except in motor-vehicle accidents.

   ☐ Fractures of the skull may be caused by striking the child's head with an object, or against a solid structure, or by compression. Accidental fractures are usually simple, linear, and confined to one skull bone. Inflicted injuries are usually more severe and may result in multiple fractures (see Fig. 7.10). Fractures of the jaw, nose, and facial bones result from direct blows.

   ☐ Haemorrhage into or around the brain may complicate a skull fracture or occur in the absence of a fracture. Such cases may present with loss of consciousness, convulsive seizures, or non-specific signs such as vomiting and irritability from pressure on the brain.
   The commonest site for haemorrhage is between the brain and its covering membranes, known as subdural haemorrhage. Haemorrhage may also occur within the substance of the brain and this may be large, due to a blow, or small, due to violent shaking. A small child's neck muscles are weak and if it is shaken repeatedly the brain moves within the oscillating head, tearing small blood vessels. Opthalmoscopic examination of the retina of the eye reveals this type of haemorrhage, and should be undertaken in any child who presents with unexplained irritability, failure to thrive, and vomiting. The availability of computerized tomography (CT scan) has made the identification of intracranial haemorrhage possible.

7.   The insertion of needles into various parts of the body is an unusual form of inflicted injury, evidently seen only in African children. These invariably become septic and present as multiple abscesses. In the case illustrated in Figure 7.11, needles had been inserted into the child's neck, flank, thigh, and abdomen. The child presented with urinary obstruction caused by a stone which had formed around a needle which had penetrated the bladder.

The administration of harmful substances

1.   Poisoning must always be considered in cases of unexplained sudden infant death.

2.   Von Munchhausen by Proxy Syndrome is a name given to the symptoms displayed by children who are deliberately made ill by a parent or caretaker. These children present repeatedly with episodes of vomiting, caused by the parent or caretaker giving salt solutions or syrup of Ipecacuanha, or with diarrhoea, caused by the child being given inappropriate food or laxatives. Another form of this syndrome presents itself as a complaint from the parent or caretaker that there is blood on the child's nappy, which is confirmed by the production of a blood-stained nappy. On testing, the blood is usually found to be that of an adult from the same blood group as the mother. This type of abuse is invariably an indication of a disturbed parent requiring both social and psychological treatment.

3.   The administration of alcohol or sedative drugs must always be suspected in children who present with loss of consciousness or bizarre neurological signs or behaviour.

4.   Among African children severe diarrhoea and even damage to the lining of the bowel is caused by the administration of toxic substances by enema. The customary use of enemas in children has been complicated by the availability of the rubber bulb with which substances such as Dettol, Jeyes Fluid, and soap solutions, as well as herbal mixtures are given. While many of these cases can be attributed to the ignorance of the parent, some are deliberate.

Suffocation

Children who survive suffocation may present as unconscious and suffocation must always be considered in cases of unexplained sudden infant death. Often tiny petechial haemorrhages are present on the eyelids of children who have been suffocated.

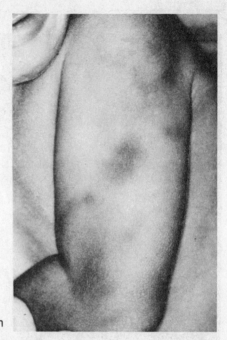

Figure 7.1: Bruises on upper arm

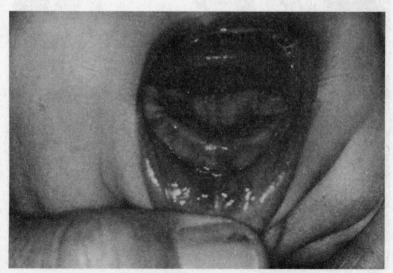

Figure 7.2: Avulsion of the upper lip frenulum

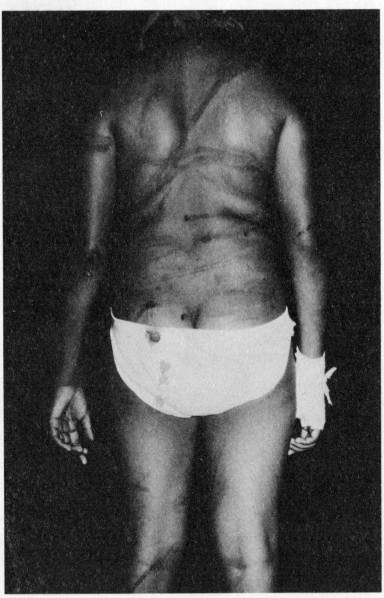

Figure 7.3: Multiple weals

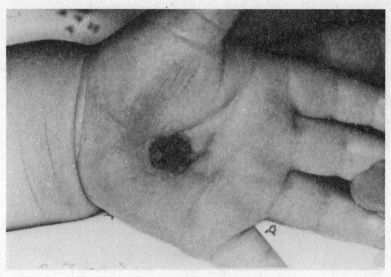

Figure 7.4: Cigarette burn

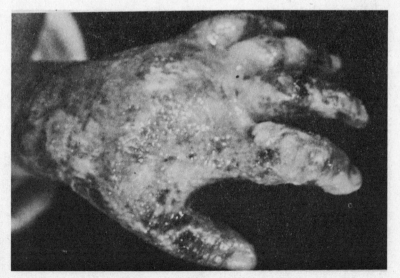

Figure 7.5: 'Dunking' glove burn

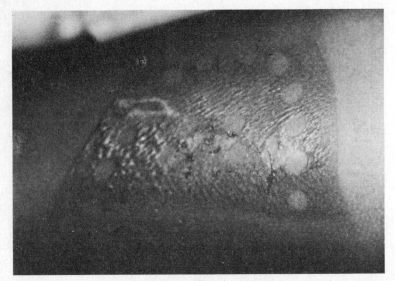

Figure 7.6: Imprint of a steam iron

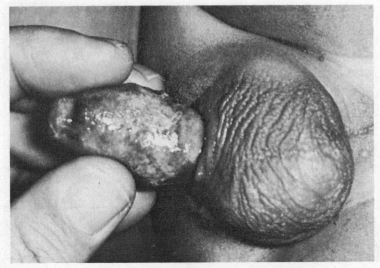

Figure 7.7: Chemical burn of the entire penis

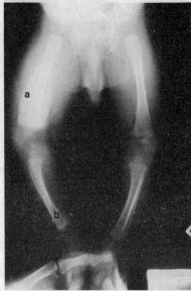

Figure 7.8: (a) Calcifying subperiosteal haematoma of the right thigh and (b) chip fracture close to ankle

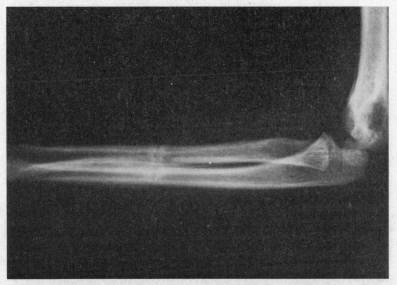

Figure 7.9: Healing fracture of the bones of the forearm

Figure 7.10: Multiple fractures of the skull

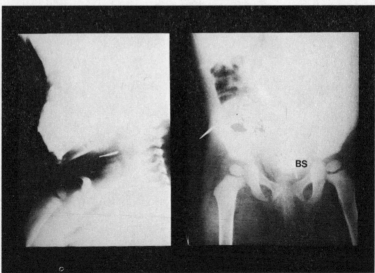

Figure 7.11: Needles embedded in various sites

Abandonment

Hundreds of babies are abandoned every year in South African cities. Most of these are African babies born to teenage mothers, while some are the product of cross-racial relationships.

CAUSATIVE FACTORS

Family violence

Many children are injured in the turmoil of violence occurring among family members. This occurs most frequently in the most deprived orders of society and is often associated with alcoholism and drug abuse.

Aggressive discipline is practised in many families in all sectors of South African society. Parents who have grown up experiencing harsh physical punishment for even slight misdemeanours apply the same methods of punishment to their children, often with serious consequences. Such parents give hidings to children under the age of three for disobedience or natural inquisitiveness, long before the children are able to reason or understand the connection between their actions and the physical trauma to which they are subjected. Particularly dangerous for the child's physical and emotional well-being is delayed punishment when the father is ordered to beat the small child for a misdemeanour which occurred earlier in the day. By the time the father comes home from work the child has forgotten about the incident and greets the father happily. The punishment carried out in cold blood is invariably excessive and is totally misunderstood by the child.

Aggressive discipline will continue to be used in South African society as long as corporal punishment is an accepted practice. Aggression breeds aggression and parental attitudes are in some cases derived from their experiences at school. Cases of excessive corporal punishment administered in schools and institutions can be considered physical abuse. This issue is discussed further in Chapter 12.

Marital stability

Many abused children come from broken or unstable marriages. Statistics in Durban show that 72 per cent of the mothers of abused children were under twenty years of age when they conceived their first baby. Most were unmarried at the time of this conception. At the time when the abuse occurred, less than half of the mothers were married for the first time and 40 per cent were single   parents, divorced, separated, or never married. The child's mother was the abuser in 55 per cent of the cases, while the other 45 per cent of abusers were almost equally divided between fathers, stepfathers, and mothers' boyfriends. In a few cases foster parents were the abusers.

Non-abusing mothers were in most instances passive accomplices.

While marital instability was a major causative factor, in almost every instance, whether married or single, a lack of preparation for parenthood and ignorance of both the needs of the child and the normal progression of childhood development were prominent features. Most abusing parents have expectations of their children which are far in advance of their children's developmental status. Such parents, faced with a niggly or colicky child, become disappointed with the child's behaviour and become punitive to even tiny infants. If the abuse is undiscovered, these children invariably become difficult later in life, presenting with be-havioural disorders, usually with anti-social characteristics, including deceitfulness and violence. It is not uncommon to obtain a history of a colicky, difficult, or even 'naughty' infant when investigating the history of patients of school-going age with behavioural problems

Social circumstances

Violence, and in particular the physical abuse of children, is common among socially deprived families. Children often become involved in adult quarrels and are injured incidentally during the general turmoil. However, the physical abuse of children is not confined to such families, and in South Africa cases have been recorded at every social level of society. In the experience of the author, company executives, university lecturers, and a variety of professional people have been found to have repeatedly physically abused their children. In some instances young couples from privileged social circumstances have been precipitated into parenthood through unplanned pregnancies. Such parents continue to indulge in a self-centred way of life with which their infants interfere. If these children do not receive satisfactory alternative care they become the victims of child abuse. Well into the first half of the twentieth century, the extended family consisting of several generations who lived in proximity to one another was the norm in all population groups in South Africa. Today such extended families are rare as rapid urbanization has led to nuclear units living separately from family members. The increased mobility of people and the need for employers to move their staff from one centre to another, as well as the movement of young people from centre to centre in search of employment, are important factors in breaking up extended families. In the higher earning groups there has also been a reduction in the size of families. As they grow up in these smaller families children do not have the experience of living with younger siblings and cousins. As young adults they are unprepared for the responsibilities of parenthood, and in particular for the care of infants and young children. Their own memories rarely extend beyond their earliest school days, by which time their lives had become formalized and disciplined. It is therefore not surprising that young parents have difficulty in coping with the stresses which a young infant generates and that some of them resort to physical abuse.

Precipitants of abuse

Many cases of serious physical abuse are one-off incidents. The precipitating factor is often the isolation of a mother who finds herself unable to cope with her child's needs, demands, or behaviour. An example of a young mother whose husband or boyfriend has deserted her may fall into this category. She often, through her relationship with the father of the child, alienates herself from her parents and family, or becomes stranded in an unfamiliar environment in which she has neither family nor friends. Resentful of her isolation and virtual imprisonment by the needs of her child, the child's demands may provoke a violent reaction from the mother, resulting in serious injury to the child.

A further example in this category of physical abuse is when the father has been transferred at short notice by his employers to another centre without consideration of the needs of the employee's wife and infant child, who may, in consequence, be left isolated in an unfamiliar environment. Such mothers invariably seek medical attention for their injured children but do not immediately reveal the true history of the cause of the physical abuse nor the factors which precipitated it. Parents in this category require different management from those who cause repetitive and malicious damage to their children.

The 'vulnerable' child

While first-born children are more vulnerable to abuse than their siblings, those most at risk are children born with handicaps.

For many years the medical and nursing professions misguidedly believed that prematurely born infants were at risk of infection from their parents. As a result the parents of such a child were not only excluded from the care of their infant but were kept at a distance, only being allowed to view their child through a window in the door of the ward where the child was nursed. This mismanagement denied parents the normal bonding process with their child for weeks and even months after the child's birth. By the time the prematurely born infant, still frail and difficult to feed and handle, was discharged to the care of the parents, the natural parenting instincts were blunted or obliterated by the enforced separation. In the case of first-born premature infants the parents had often returned to a way of life which existed prior to the infant's birth, and the intrusion of the infant contributed a disturbance and could and did in many instances provoke a punitive and abusive situation.

Today neonatal units are not only aware of the dangers of separating parents form their tiny infants, but actively encourage the parents to participate in the care of their children even when they are on life support systems. Mothers and fathers can be instructed in the basic hygienic precautions required to protect their infants from infection.

This involvement, including regular physical contact with the infant, is essential for securing the normal bonding process and protecting the child from later abuse. Similarly, children born with physical and mental defects are at increased risk of physical abuse if those managing such children do not ensure that the parents not only understand the child's handicap, but also become involved in the daily management and care of the child. Parents who do not understand the long-term implications of the child's defect can become frustrated by the child's failure to progress, and some resort to physical punishment in a misguided and irrational attempt to make the child conform to their expectations. Parents of handicapped children often feel guilty and many deny the reality of the handicap. Some abuse these children as they prefer to consider them lazy rather than handicapped. An example of such a case known to the author was a child born partially deaf, blind, and mentally retarded because the mother had rubella during the pregnancy. This child, seen in Figure 7.12, suffered fractures to both her arms, before presenting, at the age of three years, with a third-degree burn on her hand and numerous bruises and pinch marks all over her face and body. Her fractures had been treated by different orthopaedic surgeons without any consideration of how they had occurred or of the general state of the child.

Some children are particularly prone to injury and among these are many with physical and neurological handicaps. The possibility of abuse must, however, always be considered and carefully excluded before accepting that the child's injuries are accidentally acquired.

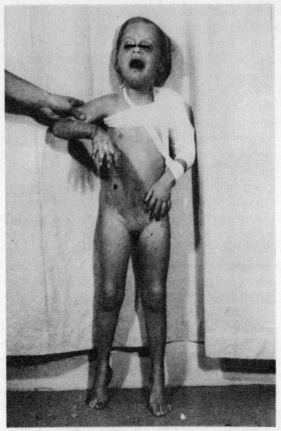

Figure 7.12: A child with rubella syndrome who suffered multiple
fractures, a burned right hand and numerous bruises

INTERVENTION
Immediate action

When the physical abuse of a child is suspected, great care must be taken
to confirm the suspicion before it is voiced to the parents.

Doctors are advised to obtain confirmatory evidence, for example by
undertaking blood tests to exclude bleeding dyscrasias and by obtaining
X-ray skeletal surveys where indicated to detect other evidence of abuse.

The doctor must carefully note all injuries and if possible have photographs taken for use as evidence. Parents should never be confronted at the first meeting. If a doctor is doubtful about the safety of a child a hospital admission for further investigation should be arranged. It should be noted that in terms of Section 42 of the Child Care Act 74 of 1983, doctors, dentists, and nurses are obliged by law to report all suspected cases of child abuse to the relevant Regional Director of Health and Welfare. Failure to do so is a criminal act.

A social worker should immediately be called upon to investigate the family circumstances of the child and the circumstances under which the child became injured. Depending on the local organization of services the investigation may, in the first instance, be initiated by the State Department of Health and Welfare or by a hospital social worker. It is imperative that the parents understand that such an investigation is in the interests of the child and is not primarily aimed at removal of the child from their care. If the parents are unwilling to co-operate and if the doctor considers it warranted, the social worker can apply for a detention order in terms of which the child can be kept in hospital or a place of safety for forty-eight hours while the necessary medical and social investigations are carried out and interpreted.

Where there is no doubt that the child has been physically abused in a manner which constitutes a criminal act, or when the parents adopt a belligerent attitude, the police should be involved from the beginning. In most large centres there are specialized Child Protection Units within the police force which deal specifically with child abuse. In cases where doubt exists, or where there is difficulty in obtaining information, a police investigation is advisable.

A case conference between the primary investigators, that is the doctor, the social worker, and the police, should be held as soon as possible to collate the evidence and plan appropriate action. Depending on the circumstances, a Children's Court inquiry or a criminal investigation may be decided upon. The emphasis is on the protection of the child and doctors initiating any of the above investigations are protected against litigation by the parents in terms of the Child Care Act of 1983, and by virtue of the fact that they are acting 'in the best interests' of the patient, who is the child, not the parents.

It is not, however, in the best interest of an abused child to institute criminal proceedings against the perpetrator unless there is substantial factual evidence and preferably witnesses to the act which caused the injury. The controversial subject of the child as a witness has still to be resolved. Under the present adversary system of justice, the child not only has to face the alleged abuser, but is also subject to cross-examination. This can be a terrifying experience for the child, often long after the event took place, and it is hardly surprising that the court, in most cases, finds the child's evidence inconsistent or that the child is unable to give the evidence in a satisfactory manner. It is therefore rarely advisable to subject the child to criminal court proceedings in cases of physical abuse.

Medical evidence is considered circumstantial evidence by the courts. For, regardless of how certain the doctor may be that the child could not have acquired the injuries accidentally, the doctor did not witness the event which caused them and can only postulate on how they occurred. The courts will not find an individual guilty without factual evidence or an admission of guilt, and should the court bring in a verdict of 'not guilty' on the basis of inadequate evidence, the child will be returned to the 'care' of the abuser. It is better in such circumstances to rely on a Children's Court inquiry when the appropriate provisions of the Child Care Act of 1983 can be invoked to protect the child and to render social services to the family. Only 13 per cent of the cases dealt with by the Child Abuse Unit at Addington Hospital have been submitted to criminal proceedings. Problem cases at this unit are referred to the Child Protection Co-ordinating Committee which is comprised of representatives of the various Departments of Health and Welfare; the child and family welfare agencies in the area; social workers, nurses and doctors from the local hospitals; educationists; the Child Protection Unit of the South African Police; and court personnel.

Long-term management of the abused child and the family requires the combined attention of all the parties involved. Regular follow-up reports on the medical and social aspects of the cases are discussed by the multidisciplinary team together with plans for the treatment and rehabilitation of the family. It is important in cases where an abuser has been found guilty of a crime in a court that those responsible for the treatment of the family should be aware of, and abide by, the rulings of the court. For example, the abuser may have been forbidden access to the child and an attempt to promote reconciliation by a well-meaning psychologist or social worker would be in contempt of court. This could result in a charge of contempt being brought against the psychologist or social worker. Access to a child by an alleged abuser may be forbidden by the court as a condition of bail before a case is heard, in which case any attempt to bring them together would be an offence.

Preventive action

The most important means of eradicating physical abuse of children is through education. A balance should be established in the education system between subject education and education for living. Parenthood is a most responsible task and children should be thoroughly prepared for it by learning from primary school level onwards that parenthood is a commitment involving the physical and emotional nurturing of children. Responsible parenthood also requires an understanding of the developmental stages through which every child progresses, and the financial and sociological commitments associated with maturation. Coping skills should be taught to both boys and girls at high school level.

Sex education should form part of a programme of education for living in perspective with the other aspects of responsibility.

The identification of abused children and their subsequent care and management is also important in the prevention of child abuse in the next generation. The majority of parents who abuse their children physically were themselves abused as children. It is therefore imperative that children who have been abused, and in terms of the Child Care Act of 1983 removed from their parents, should not be exposed to further abuse when placed in residential or foster care (see Chapter 13). Abused children are invariably disturbed children and are given to behavioural misconduct likely to provoke those caring for them. They are distrustful and insecure, often displaying 'victim' behaviour. It requires informed and sensitive care to overcome the effects of the abusive experiences to which such children have been subjected.

It must be remembered, as discussed earlier in Chapter 6, that the first five years of life are the most vital in the development of self-image and relationships with other people. The earlier an abusive situation is detected, the better the prognosis is for the child to develop a positive self-image and normal relationships with peers and older people.

The identification of child abuse is the first step in a long process, involving all the relevant disciplines, aimed at correcting the psychosocial dynamics of the family, thereby ensuring that the victim can grow up to be a satisfactory member of society.

REFERENCES

Kempe, C. H. *et al.* (1962) 'The Battered Child Syndrome', *Journal of the American Medical Association,* 181, 17–24.
Krugman, R. D. (1985) 'Editorial Comment', *Child Abuse and Neglect,* 9, 141.

8 Violence against children: sexual abuse

H. S. Sandler and N. L. Sepel

INTRODUCTION

Child sexual abuse is emerging as one of the most common forms of child abuse. As recently as a decade ago it was a problem that may have existed but went relatively unreported. A general liberalization of society, for example, the rise of feminism and other liberation movements, created a climate in the seventies for researchers to delve into what was up to then a fairly restricted field of study. New vistas were opened and society at large was exposed to the reality and extent of the problem.

Long-term studies have revealed that ten years ago there were many more unreported cases of child sexual abuse than were believed to have existed at the time. It is only now that those victims of child abuse are disclosing what happened to them when they were young. Grant Robertson, former Head of the Police Child Protection Unit in South Africa, brought to light American figures which demonstrate this. He stated on a radio programme that in the United States in 1978, one million cases of child sexual abuse were reported country-wide, and the estimate for unreported cases was also one million. In 1988 two-and-a-half million cases were reported. Therefore, it seems that there has not been a significant increase in the incidence of sexual abuse, but rather a significant increase in its exposure.

The South African pattern is very similar to that of the United States. Even five years ago, child sexual abuse would not have been a subject of discussion on television, radio, and in the newspapers. Today there are frequent programmes in the media which highlight the extent of the problem, and society's efforts to remedy it.

There are cross-cultural variants to what is considered child sexual abuse. Some societies do not consider certain forms of incest or certain sexual practices to be abuse. For example, in some communities cousin marriages are very common, while in others surgical removal of a young female's clitoris to prevent sexual pleasure is condoned.

Historically there is also evidence of this difference in attitude. In early Greek and Roman society child prostitution, castration of young boys, and anal intercourse between pupils and teachers were common practice and not condemned.

The recognition of child sexual abuse has evolved slowly in our society in more or less recognizable stages (Golding, 1988: 107):

1. The denial that child abuse existed at all.

2. Child abuse was considered to be an extension of psychiatric illness, and alcohol or drug abuse.

3. The recognition of child physical abuse.

4. The acceptance of the concept of emotional abuse.

5. The acknowledgement of the existence of sexual abuse.

6. The recognition of the rights of each child to loving care and a protected period of childhood.

In this chapter the authors propose to discuss child sexual abuse and its application to the South African situation. Although child sexual abuse is examined from a broad perspective, the focus is mainly on incest, thus favouring a psychodynamic stance.

DEFINING CHILD SEXUAL ABUSE

Defining child sexual abuse is fraught with difficulties. Most definitions are based on values and belief systems which are often bound by culture and time. There is a need to caution professionals not to apply definitions rigidly, but rather to consider the cultural context in which the abuse is occurring. Definitions are also usually limited because they do not include the wide spectrum of sexual encounters that may occur between the child victim and the offender.

Definitions range from:

> ... a rather vague statement about child sexual abuse as the involvement of dependent, developmentally immature children and adolescents in sexual activities they do not fully comprehend,

> to which they are unable to give informed consent or that violate
> the social taboos or family roles (Kempe & Kempe, 1974: 9),

to a more restricted type of definition, such as a legal one.

An example of a legal definition is 'sexual intercourse between persons so closely related that they are forbidden to marry by law' (Rist, 1979: 681).

In their most recent book, Mrazek and Kempe (1987: 12) have defined child sexual abuse as the 'exploitation of a child for the sexual gratification of an adult'. As forceful as this may sound, it still does not present a satisfactory working definition, because it excludes sibling sexual abuse, or the fact that the sexual act is not necessarily sexually gratifying for the adult, but may be the expression of aggression, the need for power, or inadequacy.

Working in the field of sexual abuse has led the authors to develop a definition that is more comprehensive than any of the above definitions, and which would include all the cases that they have dealt with to date:

> Child sexual abuse is any sexual activity, whether it be ongoing or a single occurrence, ranging from sexual overtones to sexual intercourse, between a sexually maturing or mature person and an unconsenting or consenting child who is cognitively and developmentally immature. This pertains whether or not the perpetrator has himself/herself committed the sexual act or has permitted or encouraged the child to indulge in any sexual activity, for example child prostitution.

CATEGORIES OF SEXUAL ABUSE

Child sexual abuse can be divided into two broad categories:

1. sexual assault by a non-family perpetrator; and
2. incest.

Sexual assault by non-family perpetrators

Sexual assault by non-family perpetrators has recently received wide publicity and is being recognized more and more as a major problem

Extra-familial abuse may be limited to an isolated episode or consist of repeated assaults. There may be a single victim or several children from the same family or different families may be involved, either individually or as a group. Russel (1983) found in her study that 31 per cent of the respondents reported extra-familial sexual abuse by the age of eighteen years. In her survey of 930 women in San Francisco who had suffered child abuse only 15 per cent of the perpetrators were strangers to the victim; 42 per cent were acquaintances and 41 per cent were more intimately involved with the victim. There are many different forms of non-family sexual abuse.

Child sex rings

This type of sexual abuse has been described by Burgess *et al.* (1978), who have worked extensively with this problem in the United States, and as Robertson (1989) points out, the situation in South Africa may be very similar to that described overseas.

Child sex rings may be characterized by repeated abuse of multiple victims from more than one family. Wild (1989) defines a child sex ring as comprising an adult perpetrator or perpetrators, and several children who are simultaneously involved in sexual activity and aware of each other's participation.

The true scale of the problem of sex rings is unknown, because thorough investigation has been difficult and accurate statistics are thus unavailable. Wild (1989) investigated a population of 710 000 in Leeds, England. Thirty-one child sex rings were identified during a two-year period. A total of 47 male perpetrators aged sixteen to eighty-two years old and 334 children aged four to fifteen years old were involved. During this two-year period the child sex rings made up 4,6 per cent of all the child sexual abuse cases reported.

Criteria for risk factors include dysfunctional family backgrounds and poor social circumstances. Victims involved are often from disadvantaged homes and are inadequately supervised. Furthermore, they are regular truants and have mothers who are unavailable to them due to the fact that they are working or emotionally unattached. These children are often being sexually abused in their own homes. Many times, the heads of these sex rings are well-known personalities or people who are directly working with children in the community, for example drama teachers, sports masters, or school teachers. The perpetrators may depend on bribery to coerce victims to participate.

Recently the newly established Police Child Protection Units, which were especially formed to deal with child-related problems of which child abuse is a major part, have uncovered sex rings and the perpetrators have been prosecuted. One of the consequences of the uncovering of these rings has been the suicide attempts of the perpetrators and the concomitant guilt and remorse of the victims. As Wild (1988) points out, the disclosure of sexual abuse causes profound emotional upheaval for the victim, the perpetrator, and the families.

Child prostitution

While both child prostitution and child pornography often occur with the active consent of the parent(s)/guardian, who directly benefit financially from the activities, in many cases runaway children and adolescents find life at home intolerable and look for an easier and a more rewarding existence. The family life they experienced offered them very little affection or attention and as a result the children have a very low self-esteem and a need for attention and approval. As these children have not achieved at school, they have no means by which to support themselves, and they see their sexual potential as their only value. Frequently children run away because they are sexually abused in their homes, and they fall into the trap of prostitution rings which promise support, security, and affection. A significant number of both young male and female prostitutes have suffered forcible sexual acts from either within or outside the family. They have learnt that there is a direct relationship between sex and material rewards. Some children involved in prostitution do so while living at home. In a recent example in a Child Abuse Clinic in Johannesburg, a group of black adolescent girls from the ages of twelve to fifteen years, were coerced by a white middle-aged man to 'work for him' as prostitutes for which they would receive a small percentage of the takings. As these girls were from deprived backgrounds and in need of material possessions, they were easily coerced into this activity. A few of these girls fell pregnant during the period of prostitution and underwent termination of pregnancies. The prostitution ring was broken by the Child Protection Unit and the girls were placed in substitute care.

Child pornography

Child pornography as a form of child sexual abuse is rarely based on any real relationship with the offender. Pornography, where children are forced to perform sexual acts, is usually filmed for a commercial market. These sexual acts could be with one or many different partners. Occasionally the offender may persuade the child to allow the photographing of the sexual act as part of an ongoing relationship. Children may be asked to perform unusual sexual behaviours that are erotic and deviant for photographing, such as group sex, sadomasochistic rituals, or bestiality. These victims are recruited by means of persuasion, by promises of money or gifts, or by seduction. Some children may be given alcohol or drugs to make them willing and perhaps unaware of their actions.

There is a close connection between pornography and prostitution. The child's involvement in one makes it difficult to resist involvement in the other. In a recent case exposed by the Child Protection Unit in Johannesburg, a sex ring led by a member of a well-known 'service club' was disclosed. A group of adolescents between the ages of twelve and fourteen years were enticed into believing that they were attending service club activities. When they reached the venue, they were made to consume alcohol and whilst under the influence of the alcohol were made to perform seductive and vulgar acts in front of a video camera.

Sexual abuse in children's homes

Helping professionals working within children's homes have an ethical responsibility to appropriately assess, diagnose, and treat the children placed within their care. However, sometimes a professional abuses a child, either physically or sexually. While obvious care is taken in the selection of staff, particularly house parents, potential abusers are difficult to identify. Hence, as Duncan (1989: 7) points out, children should be given 'clear and unambiguous structured guidelines' to follow should they have reason to be concerned about molestation. A clear and definite procedural statement regarding sexual molestation should be compiled by management and written into the service contract for staff. The phenomenon should also feature as part of education programmes for all staff, management, and children. The abuse of children in residential care is discussed in detail in Chapter 13.

Incest

Some theoreticians have been vague and non-specific in their definitions of incest. For example, Rist (1979: 681) describes incest as 'sexual intercourse between persons so closely related that they are forbidden to marry by law'. This definition has two major deficiencies. Firstly, is sexual intercourse a necessary criterion for incest, or can it involve any sexual activity from genitalia exposure to rape? Secondly, marriage laws differ from culture to culture, there necessarily providing a different criterion for incest. It must be kept in mind, however, that in most societies incestuous sex outside marriage may be prosecuted as a form of indecent assault or statutory rape.

Perhaps a better definition would be that of Herman and Hirschman (1981: 967) who describe incest as 'any form of physical contact between a father and daughter that has to be kept a secret'. However, we know from research on the subject that incest does not only pertain to a father-daughter sexual relationship.

Van der May and Neff (1982: 718) define incest more specifically as 'all forms of sexual contact, sexual exploitation and sexual overtures, initiated by an adult who is related to a child by family ties, or through surrogate ties'. The examples they give are a stepfather or an uncle. Although this definition includes any sexual contact, and also takes into account surrogate kinship roles, it fails to account for incest that may occur between siblings. Therefore, in reading the literature, the authors regard a combination of the following two definitions to be the most accurate and culture-fair. McIntyre (1981: 462) defines incest as 'any manual, oral or genital sexual behaviour that an adult family member or older sibling imposes on a child'. Sgroi *et al.* (1982: 10) use a psychosexual definition to define incest:

> Incestuous child sexual abuse encompasses any form of sexual activity between a child and a parent or step-parent or extended family member (e.g. grandparent, aunt or uncle) or surrogate parent figure (e.g. common law spouse or foster parent).

The authors would, therefore, define incest as:

> Any sexual encounter between a child and an older family member (parent, step-parent, or sibling), extended family member (uncle or grandparent), or surrogate parent figure (common-law spouse or foster parent), which exploits the child's vulnerability.

Types of incest

1. Father-daughter incest:

This is the most common form of incest. It seems to be the best understood as most research has been conducted in this area. For this reason the family dynamics of this type of incest have been selected for more detailed analysis in this chapter.

It must be noted that 'father' in this instance refers to any male that occupies the father role in the family, including a stepfather, the mother's boyfriend, or a foster father.

2. Mother-son incest:

This is a very rare type of incestuous relationship. It presents as a pathological relationship, often resulting from the loss of a father figure in the family and the subsequent overt seduction of the child by the mother. The family itself appears to have lost control of much of its functioning. Such mothers often suffer from a severe form of a mental illness, such as schizophrenia or depression.

3. Brother-sister incest:

This type of incest appears to be the least damaging to the victim. This could be normal peer experimentation that does at times occur in childhood, even in normally functioning families.

4. Homosexual incest:

This occurs between mother and daughter or father and son. This type of incest is viewed as having a severe pathological diagnosis and is rarely reported.

5. Grandfather-granddaughter incest:

According to Goodwin *et al.* (1983: 163) this accounts for 9 to 11 per cent of all incest cases. The grandfathers may have paedophile symptomatology or histories of childhood sodomy. Cases of this type of incest often show these men to have abused their own daughters as children.

6. Incest amongst other relatives:

Other types of incest may include sexual relationships between more distant family members such as uncles, aunts, and close cousins.

7. Multiple incest:

Multiple incest refers to incestuous relationships between different family members within the same family. Meiselman, in Mrazek and Kempe (1987: 104), reported that nearly 30 per cent of her psychotherapy sample had either been sexually involved with more than one family member, or knew of other incestuous affairs within their families.

DYNAMICS OF INCESTUOUS FAMILIES

Theories of incest

Many theories have been postulated as to the dynamics of the sexually abusing family.

The literature mainly focuses on three theories:

☐   a psychoanalytic view;

☐   a feminist view; and

☐   a psychodynamic view.

A psychoanalytic view of incest

Father-daughter rape was the foundation stone of the interrelated theories about sexuality which Sigmund Freud developed. The basis of this theory is male supremacy. Freud showed considerable empathy for the abused child. His audience at that time did not, however, show the same empathy. As Ward (1984: 104) points out, they linked 'sexual shock' with hysteria. Dr Alice Miller (1986), one of the world's foremost psychoanalysts, believes that 'the child is always innocent'. Freudian psychoanalytic thought would argue that all affectional family ties have sexual origins. For example, caressing young infants would be seen as a manifestation of this. This intimate relationship is, in fact, the dynamic mechanism that nurtures the child within the 'holding environment', and which allows the child to develop resources to form other close relationships. If, however, over-stimulation occurs, especially during adolescence, it may result in neurotic conflict and an inability in the victim to separate from the family; restricting too their ability to form and maintain lasting other relationships. Rist (1979: 685) points out that 'the incest taboo is a complex mechanism which encourages diffuse enactments of incestuous desires for proper development but prohibits specific sexual activities that might bind harmful dependency needs'.

The feminist viewpoint

The patriarchal society 'romanticises, spiritualises, emotionalises and pathologises the right of men to own women and children' (McIntyre, 1981: 463). This underlying sanction gives men the power to do what they will with their 'possessions' and this message is clearly channelled to the women and children in our society who condone it and live by it. Children in malfunctioning families have been reported to have perceived father as 'powerful' and mother as 'powerless', and by this conception the child duly learns that the father's love is given conditionally to those who are compliant. Therefore, if love is coupled with violent acting-out or exploitation of their genitalia, then the victim complies.

McIntyre (1981) examines sexist assumptions about the roles of family members by describing the mother, instead of the victim, as the one being blamed for the sexual assault. Many theoreticians provide the framework for blaming the mother by viewing the family in which incest occurs as disturbed and pathological. McIntyre (1981), on the other hand, presents an analysis of incest where the victim of male violence is empowered. Looking at sexual abuse from a feminist perspective, he regards the mother as a victim in the family, rather than an offender herself. According to him, mothers do not contribute to incest because of psychoanalytically or psychodynamically formulated personality characteristics, or because they cannot or do not fulfil their traditional roles of wife and mother. Although the family systems may be dysfunctional, the blame for the assault falls on the perpetrator and no one else. The reason a woman may not disclose the incest, once aware of it, is that she finds herself in a double bind whereby whatever decision she may make she loses. She therefore tends to initially protect the child, and sometimes reverses her position to support the father. Feminist analysis of incest links the sexual abuse of children by fathers to social and cultural values, and to behaviour and institutions that support them. Butler, in McIntyre (1981: 464), has indicated that incestuous assault must be seen:

> ... as part of an established social structure. This social structure perpetuates whether it be in myth or fact, in thought or action, the reality that one of the places where men can exert their power and dominance is in the home.

Authors such as Justice and Justice (1979), Forward and Buck (1978), and Meiselman (1978) have looked at incest and the role of the mother through examining patriarchy.

Thus, patriarchal culture and male dominance set the stage for incest to occur. Within this structure mothers as women have been taught several things. Firstly, that their roles have been defined purely by the needs, desires, and accomplishments of the men in their lives. Secondly, that when they cannot fulfil their roles, for whatever reasons, they must accept blame. Thirdly, that the mother is expected to satisfy not only the needs of the father, but also the needs of her offspring. Her needs come last. Thus when the incestuous assault occurs, many mothers faced with the option of protecting their daughters or protecting the security of their home life opt for the latter.

The psychodynamic perspective

From this viewpoint, there are two types of incestuous families:

☐   the multi-problem incest family; and

☐   the classic incest family.

1. The multi-problem family:

In this type of incestuous family many problems exist, for example, financial difficulties, alcoholism, and unemployment. Incest forms only one aspect of the total family disorganization. These families usually have contact with at least one or more social agencies on issues other than incest.

2. The classic incest family:

Incest between father or stepfather and daughter is a form of incest which is both common and harmful. This pattern accounts for three-quarters of reported incest. Therefore, a great deal is known about it. Each case of father-daughter incest is unique. However, there are enough common basic characteristics that exist for a classic pattern to be identified.

The most interesting aspect of this family is the fact that there is a façade of role competence and stability, and on a superficial level the family appears to be coping sufficiently. The pathology is primarily confined to the family and home, and the problems are well concealed. The phenomenon that holds this family together is that of secrecy. Each family member has an innate fear of family disintegration and thus does not disclose the incest.

In families where father-daughter incest occurs there is usually a poor marital relationship between the parents. The marital relationship has ceased to be both emotionally and sexually satisfying to either one or both parties. The mother often condones the incest as she prefers to keep her husband's infidelity within the home.

The family is usually patriarchal, whereby the father is the most dominant member and occupies a position of power. Other family members respect and acknowledge this and do not question his overriding authority. This is a multi-generational pattern which has been modelled to one or both parents in their families of origin. A very prominent feature of these families is the role reversal between mother and daughter. The mother is usually absent in the family, either physically or emotionally. This occurs because she is suffering from some disabling condition, such as depression or physical infirmity. Due to family dynamics the father is dominant and powerful and keeps his wife in a dependent and helpless role, which often suits her personality type, which is withdrawn, introverted, and accompanied with feelings of inadequacy. The daughter, who is most often the eldest daughter, then occupies a special and favourite position in the family, playing a parental role and taking on responsibilities such as caring for the other siblings and housekeeping. Included in this is having sexual relationships with her father.

Personality dynamics of the family members directly concerned

The personality dynamics of the three members of the family directly concerned in father-daughter incest, namely the father, the mother, and the daughter will be examined from a psychodynamic perspective, the viewpoint selected by the authors for this purpose.

The father (perpetrator)

Three types of personalities in the sexually abusive offender have been documented:

☐ the introversive personality;

☐ the psychopathic personality; and

☐ the psychosexually immature personality.

1. The introversive personality:
Most offenders fall within this personality type. The father in this category has feelings of masculine and sexual inadequacy and the incest compensates for feelings of insecurity. He has a weak and poor self-concept and is emotionally immature. He tends to justify and rationalize the incest, which in reality is serving his own unmet needs.

He cannot meet his needs in a non-sexual way. He is socially isolated and feels inadequate in interpersonal relationships, especially ones of a sexual nature. He is far more competent and self-assured in relating to a child. Often these feelings of inadequacy stem from his own childhood, which lacked adequate nurturing and mothering. This has contributed to his feelings of low self-worth and disabled him from developing a felicitous perception of appropriate parenting. Rist (1979) portrays the introversive personality as intelligent and educated. He is the patriarch of the family. He is the most dominant member of the family and carries all the decision-making power. He expects to have his will obeyed. He is inflexible to changes in the family and resistant to democratic decision-making. He is over-invested in his family and seeks to control their lives.

2. Psychopathic personality:
This type of offender is indiscriminately promiscuous. Not only does he have sexual relationships outside the family with other adults and children, but he also sexually abuses his own children. This personality type is severely emotionally disturbed. He is identifiable by loss of ethical

and moral standards, and he has no guilt or remorse for his offensive actions.

3. Psychosexually immature personality:

The psychosexually immature personality could be described as a 'paedophile'. According to Kempe and Kempe (1984: 11), a 'paedophile denotes the preference of an adult for prepubertal children as a means of achieving sexual excitement'. It is generally thought that many offenders may themselves have been victims in childhood. One characteristic of paedophiles seems to be the need to control a child sexually in order to convince themselves that their own past personal experience can be rendered harmless and can be idealized through repetition.

The mother (non-offender)

In writing about the California Sexual Abuse Treatment Programme, Giarretto (1982) recorded that 50 per cent of the mothers in the incestuous families knew about the sexual abuse and colluded with the offender, whereas the rest did not.

Non-offenders who collude do so for a number of reasons. The mother is usually physically, emotionally, and/or economically dependent on the offender, and by exposing the abuse she would sacrifice their family life and stability. She usually presents as infantile and has a poor self-esteem. She colludes with the incest in order to maintain the status quo in the family, which serves to protect her from major responsibilities and decision-making. Dietz and Craft (1980: 603) describe these mothers as 'passive, dependent and submissive, often chronically depressed, overburdened and unable to protect their daughters or exert a restraining influence on their husbands'. These women find it impossible to maintain an adult sexual role and sometimes frustrate their husbands sexually. The non-offender mother has unconsciously reversed the role of mother and daughter. As she has often come from a family where her own mother was cold and rejecting, she assumes a relationship with her daughter which she would have liked to have had with her own mother. Unfortunately, she is unsuccessful in achieving this, as she does not possess the necessary skills needed to establish this intimacy with her own daughter. Justice and Justice (1979) have formulated a list of six characteristics of non-offending mothers. They:

☐ want to reverse roles with their daughters;

☐ may be frigid;

☐ keep themselves tired or worn out;

☐   are weak and submissive;

☐   attempt to 'mother' their spouses; and

☐   are indifferent, absent, or promiscuous.

The mothers who do not know of the abuse suffer from shock, disbelief, and sometimes denial on learning about it. They also suffer guilt, feel humiliated, and blame themselves.

For all non-offending mothers, disclosure means destruction of their 'self'. They are challenged on three fronts — on their role as a mother, as a wife, and as a person.

The child (victim)

The majority of research on the subject of incest has focused on the victim of father-daughter incest. Usually the daughter is the eldest child in the family. The age range can vary. Selby and Calhourn (1980) report that the age can range between three and thirty years old. Their own study confirmed that most victims were between thirteen and eighteen years old. The incestuous relationship usually begins four years prior to puberty.

The personality profile shows an emotionally immature child, likeable, yet submissive. Despite this, she acts in a very mature way. She occupies a special and favoured position in the family. She plays a parental role and takes on responsibilities such as household tasks and caring for the other siblings. This is the classic role reversal found in child sexual abuse. According to Summit (1983), the child is given the power to destroy the family and the responsibility to keep it together. The child, not the parent, must ensure the survival of the other family members. The child must therefore secretly and without the necessary skills take on many of the role functions ordinarily assigned to the mother.

Moral values become split, and 'maintaining a lie to keep the secret is the ultimate virtue, while telling the truth would be the greatest sin' (Summit, 1983: 183).

Due to the mother's unavailability, the daughter is deprived of maternal nurturing. Although she is initially not sexually provocative, the secondary gains, such as satisfaction of her need for physical affection and closeness, are met by her incestuous relationship with her father. She may become over-eroticized and exhibit precocious or sexually acting-out behaviour in order to invite further encounters, especially with the father. Therefore, a sexually abused child is at severe risk of further sexual abuse by other males in her environment.

The daughter is usually poorly adjusted socially. That is, she struggles in relationships both with the same and opposite sex. She finds it difficult to establish and sustain relationships. She thus finds herself socially isolated, especially from her peer group.

During adolescence she remains caught between the need for true autonomy and independence, and the psychological and material gains in her special position. The victim of abuse is faced with intense anger and resentment towards both parents; towards the father for exploiting and betraying her, and towards the mother for not protecting her.

The Child Sexual Abuse Accommodation Syndrome

Summit (1983) has described what he calls 'The Child Sexual Abuse Accommodation Syndrome'. He defines this as a:

> … typical behaviour pattern or syndrome of mutually dependent variables which allows for the immediate survival of the child within the family, but which tends to isolate the child from eventual acceptance, creditability or empathy within the larger society (Summit, 1983: 179).

Clinical awareness of the Child Sexual Abuse Accommodation Syndrome is essential in understanding the behaviour of the victim. The pattern indicates how easily a child can become trapped in incest or other continuing abuse.

The following five stages are common to this syndrome:

- ☐ secrecy;

- ☐ helplessness;

- ☐ entrapment and accommodation;

- ☐ delayed, conflicted, and unconvincing disclosure; and

- ☐ retraction.

1. Secrecy:

Break-up of the family, the child's removal, imprisonment of the father, the parents' divorce, or being physically harmed are fears of the victim, and moreover are commonly used as threats by the perpetrator. As the perpetrator is the well-respected and adored father, who commands obedience and power in the family, the child will obey, and believe and trust his explanations of the events of the abuse. Intimidation makes it clear to the child that breaking the silence is something bad and dangerous. Thus the secret becomes, ironically, both the source of fear and the promise of safety.

2. Helplessness:

Victims are left to confront their own helplessness as they can see no way out of their situation. They are easily ashamed and intimidated both by their helplessness and their inability to communicate their feelings to other adults.

3. Entrapment and accommodation:

Generally, sexual abuse of children is not a one-off occurrence, but is ongoing. The adult may have guilt, fear, and make resolutions to stop, but the ease of the accomplishment as well as the forbidden quality of the experience seems to invite repetitions. This pattern continues until either the victim achieves autonomy in adolescence or the abuse is disclosed and prohibited in some way.

If no protective intervention is provided, the child has to learn to accept the situation and survive. She does this by learning to accommodate to the reality of the sexual abuse. The challenge of accommodating is not only to cope with the increasing sexual demands, but also to cope with the realization of betrayal by a parent who is idealized as protective, altruistic, and loving. The child cannot conceptualize the parent as bad; she believes that she has provoked the situation, and that through compliance she can earn love and acceptance. This is the trap in which she finds herself.

4. Delayed, conflicted, and unconvincing disclosure:

Most ongoing sexual abuse is never disclosed, at least not outside the nuclear family. Treated, reported, or investigated cases are the exception, not the norm. Disclosure may occur as a result of family conflict, accidental discovery, or professional intervention. If disclosure occurs due to family conflict, it is usually after years of continual sexual abuse, and disclosure follows the eventual breakdown of the accommodation mechanisms.

The victim of incest tends to remain silent until she enters adolescence, where she starts to challenge the authority of the parents. During adolescence, the father becomes more jealous and controlling because the daughter develops outside heterosexual interests which threaten his special relationship with her and his control over her. He then begins to warn her of the dangers of outside peer involvement. The child may become rebellious, try to abscond, abuse drugs, become promiscuous, or demonstrate delinquent behaviour. In fact, it is these behaviours that often expose the secret. What the daughter seeks is understanding and intervention at the very time that she is least likely to find it. Authorities faced with this pattern of behaviour tend to view her as a rebellious teenager and sympathize with the parents. They assume that the complaint of sexual abuse bears no truth and that the daughter is falsely incriminating her father. The daughter thus faces an unbelieving audience.

5. Retraction:
Often after disclosure, the victim is likely to retract her story. Even during the disclosure she remains ambivalent and wants to continue preserving her family. The child discovers that the threats made by the father during their sexual encounters have become a reality. A repercussion of disclosure is family fragmentation, either emotional or physical. The victim is blamed and feels responsible for the breakdown of the family. Therefore the child is punished for something for which she was not responsible. Unless special support for the child is provided and immediate intervention takes place, the victim will retract her complaint and the pattern will continue.

INCIDENCE OF SEXUAL ABUSE

Despite increased public and professional attention in South Africa over the past decade to the sexual victimization of children by family members and non-members, little South African research has been done, and most epidemiological data comes from the United States, Canada, and Britain. Reasons for inadequate South African material revolve mainly around the fact that a large proportion of the incidence of local sexual abuse remains officially unreported.

In South Africa, where Calvinistic attitudes prevail, the subject of sexual abuse provokes overwhelming feelings of fear, repulsion, and terror. These attitudes are prevalent not only in the community, but among professionals as well. This may be an underlying unconscious reason for a dearth of literature and research. Van der Mey (1988) confirms these research problems. He also discusses the problem of researchers making use of convenience samples, and analysing poor *post factum* victim reports. He reiterates that research is primarily or exclusively focused on the victimization of females only and not on the victimization of males also. Finally, there is a lack of replication and confirmation of completed research.

The authors will attempt to present a survey of available incidence statistics from the United States and will compare these to recent research statistics kept at hospital-based clinics in South Africa. It must be stressed that no official South African statistics on child sexual abuse are available.

This in itself presents serious problems for professionals working in the field, as well as for government bodies vested with the responsibility of accurately planning and budgeting to combat this social phenomenon.

General incidence

In estimating the incidence of incest in the United States, Selby and Calhourn (1980) suggest that it varies between 2,4 per cent and 6,3 per cent of the total population. They suggest that these figures are perhaps conservative due to a very poor rate of reporting and disclosure. According to the Child Abuse Prevention Foundation, Inc., Washington DC, one out of every four females in America is sexually abused before the age of eighteen years. This amounts to 22 per cent of all Americans, totalling thirty-eight million people, who were abused as children.

While child sexual abuse statistics are not shown for the general population in south Africa, some statistics are available from various hospitals and clinics. During 1985, 232 cases of child abuse were seen at the Red Cross War Memorial Children's Hospital in Cape Town. Out of these, 88 per cent were cases of suspected sexual abuse of children. At the Transvaal Memorial Institute for Child Health and Development (TMI) Child Abuse Clinic in Johannesburg, from May 1988 to May 1989, sexual abuse of children was the presenting problem in 90 per cent of the 227 cases seen.

The statistics presented are a reflection of a very small percentage of all child sexual abuse cases in South Africa. The statistics quoted are only a 'tip of the iceberg', as it is known that hundreds of cases go unreported. This is especially true in the case of African and 'coloured' families, as reflected in the fact that only 100 sexual abuse cases (ninety-eight females and two males) were seen by medical staff at Baragwanath Hospital and other clinics in Soweto during 1989. At Coronation Hospital, a hospital in Johannesburg for Indian and 'coloured' persons, for the period October 1988 to September 1989, only eighty-nine cases of child abuse were seen with 56 per cent of these found to be sexual abuse. The remaining 44 per cent were classified as physical abuse. At the Alexandra Health Clinic in Alexandra Township, Johannesburg, only sixty-four cases of sexual abuse were seen in the fourteen-month period ending in August 1989.

Statistics specific to perpetrators and victims

In South Africa very few statistics are available with regard to the perpetrators and victims. The authors will therefore make use of relevant

American statistics and where possible compare them to what is available in South Africa.

Child sexual abuse occurs among all *socio-economic classes*, at all *educational levels*, and among all *race groups, cultures*, and *religious groups* (Van der Mey & Neff, 1982; Herman & Hirschmen, 1981; Rist, 1979).

However, there is a tendency to assume that incest occurs only in the more deprived socio-economic classes. Rosenfeld, in Van der Mey and Neff (1982), suggests that incest is not correlated with social class. He suggests that it is a myth that it is more prevalent in the more deprived socio-economic groups. A reason for the higher statistics may be the fact that proportionately, a higher incidence of *reported* offences are from the more deprived economic classes, due to the fact that such cases will be dependent on state-funded resources and will thus become known to the authorities.

The educational level of the perpetrator varies. Van der Mey and Neff's (1982) study supports this. They found that the perpetrator's education varied from little education and poor success in school and college with poor income to adequate success in school and average income. The perpetrators' occupations may reflect their educational levels. Herman and Hirschman (1981) found that the perpetrators' jobs ranged from salesmen to middle-level executives and professionals. The findings at the Child Abuse Clinic in Johannesburg support these findings as perpetrators' occupations varied widely.

At the Thomas Jefferson Hospital in Philadelphia, De Jong *et al.* (1983) found that 81,8 per cent of all victims were *female*, while 18,2 per cent were *male*. At the Red Cross War Memorial Children's Hospital, 90 per cent of the cases presented in 1985 were female (Jaffe & Roux, 1988). At the TMI Child Abuse Clinic, De Villiers (1989) found similar figures, where females comprised 80 per cent.

World-wide, the most common *age* of victims of child sexual abuse is ten years old. However, the victims' ages may range from as young as three months to eighteen years. At the Red Cross War Memorial Children's Hospital the victims ranged from ten months to thirteen years of age. At the TMI Child Abuse Clinic, the largest number of children presented were under the age of ten (see Fig. 8.1).

In most child sexual abuse cases, the perpetrators are known to the victim either within the nuclear family or within close proximity. Russel (1983) has studied intra-familial as well as extra-familial sexual abuse. She interviewed 930 women in the general population. Out of these women, 152 (16 per cent) reported at least one incident of intra-familial

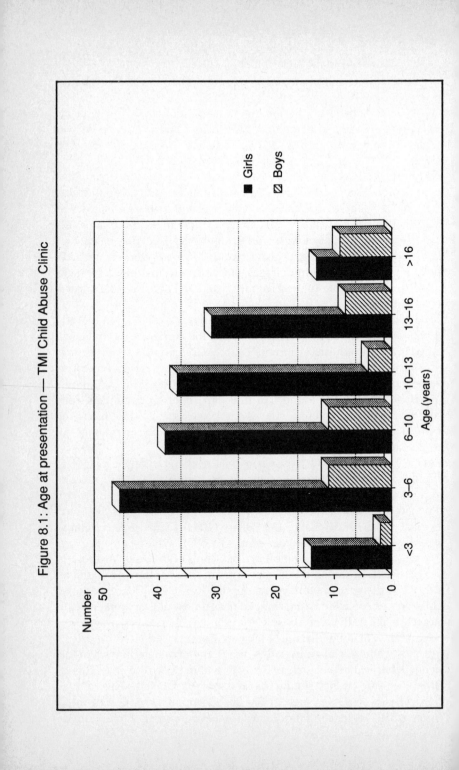

Figure 8.1: Age at presentation — TMI Child Abuse Clinic

sexual abuse before the age of eighteen. These women reported a total of 186 experiences with different perpetrators, as shown in Figure 8.2.

Thirty-one per cent of the total sample reported at least one experience of sexual abuse by a non-relative. Of these perpetrators, 85 per cent were known to the child, while only 15 per cent were strangers (see Fig. 8.3).

According to statistics for 1985 kept by the Red Cross War Memorial Children's Hospital, most victims (50 per cent or 58 per cent of all victims) could identify the perpetrator, either definitely or with strong suspicion. The confirmed or suspected perpetrators are reflected in Table 8.1.

Table 8.1: Identified perpetrators of sexual abuse

Perpetrator	Confirmed	Suspected	Total
Neighbour	12	4	16
Father	9	5	14
Other relative	4	4	8
Friend	4	3	7
Other non-relative	1	1	2
Stepfather	1	0	1
Sibling	1	0	1
Gang	0	1	1
Total	32	18	50

Source: Jaffe and Roux, 1985.

The severity of child sexual abuse

Russel (1983) has divided the severity of the abuse into three categories.

Firstly, she described 'very serious sexual abuse' as including completed and attempted vaginal, oral, or anal intercourse, cunnilingus and anilingus, forced and unforced. The term 'force' includes physical force, threat of physical force, or inability to consent because of being unconscious, drugged, asleep, or in some other way totally helpless. Secondly, 'serious sexual abuse' refers to completed and attempted genital fondling, simulated intercourse, and digital penetration, forced and unforced. Thirdly, 'less serious sexual abuse' refers to completed and attempted acts of intentional sexual touching of buttocks, thigh, leg, or other body part, clothed breasts or genitals, and kissing, forced or unforced.

It needs to be noted that less serious types of sexual abuse of children, such as genital exposure, masturbation in front of children, and other non-verbal sexual overtones have not been included in Table 8.2, which

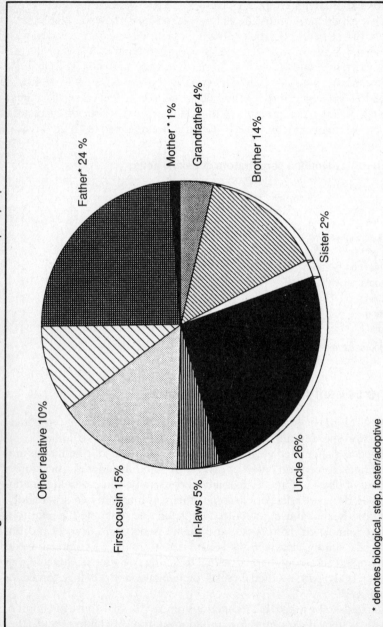

Figure 8.2: Intra-familial sexual abuse — relationship of perpetrator to victim

Mother * 1%

Grandfather 4%

Father* 24 %

Brother 14%

Sister 2%

Other relative 10%

Uncle 26%

First cousin 15%

In-laws 5%

* denotes biological, step, foster/adoptive

Adapted from Russell (1983)

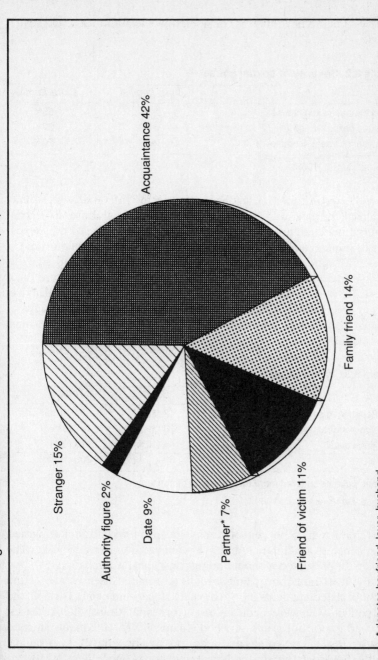

Acquaintance 42%

Family friend 14%

Stranger 15%

Authority figure 2%

Date 9%

Partner* 7%

Friend of victim 11%

* denotes boyfriend, lover, husband

Adapted from Russell (1983)

follows, but are nevertheless considered by the authors as child sexual abuse.

Table 8.2: Severity of sexual abuse

	Intra-familial	Extra-familial
Very serious sexual abuse	23%	53%
Serious sexual abuse	41%	27%
Less serious sexual abuse	36%	20%

Source: Russel, 1983.

As reflected in Table 8.3, in Johannesburg at the TMI Child Abuse Clinic, about half the patients suffered non-penetrative sexual abuse, 40 per cent suffered penetrative sexual abuse, and 9 per cent suffered non-sexual abuse. Some patients (10 per cent) suffered from more than one type of abuse. A higher proportion of boys, almost one third, had signs of chronic anal abuse, whereas only 5 per cent of the girls had suffered anal abuse. Fifty-five per cent of the girls had signs of chronic vaginal abuse, 10 per cent had signs of acute abuse, and for the remainder, signs of vaginal abuse were uncertain or absent. For the majority of victims, sexual abuse was proven by medical examination.

Table 8.3: Types of sexual abuse*

	Girls	Boys	Total
A Penetrative sexual	72 (43%)	12 (32%)	84 (40%)
B Non-penetrative sexual	84 (49%)	23 (59%)	107 (51%)
C Non-sexual	14 (8%)	4 (10%)	18 (9%)
Total	170	39	209 (100%)

* Some patients suffered more than one type of abuse.

Source: De Villiers *et al.*, 1989.

In Cape Town, 45 per cent of the cases seen in 1985 had genital injuries, 5 per cent had anal injuries, and 7 per cent had non-genital injuries. The remainder presented without findings on clinical examination.

At the TMI Child Abuse Clinic sexually transmitted diseases were found in about sixteen patients (approximately 10 per cent of all cases). Of the 152 patients who were medically tested for sexually transmitted diseases, two had gonorrhoea, and one had chlamydia. Three patients showed positive results for syphilis and six of positive hepatitis B. Two vaginal swabs showed garnerella, and one trichomonas (De Villiers, 1989).

Also in Johannesburg, 40 per cent of child sexual abuse patients at Coronation Hospital had sexually transmitted diseases, while the figure at Alexandra Health Clinic totalled 47 per cent.

In Cape Town, however, in 1985 only 19 per cent of child sexual abuse patients had sexually transmitted diseases (10 per cent had gonorrhoea, and 9 per cent syphilis). The discrepancy between figures from the Cape Town Red Cross War Memorial Children's Hospital and the Johannesburg figures from the Johannesburg Hospital and Coronation Hospital, and Alexandra Clinic, may perhaps be a reflection of the type of communities from which patients come. For example, at Coronation Hospital, statistics relating to child sexual abuse patients show that 50 per cent came from disrupted homes marked by single parents and poverty, and that 27 per cent of instances of abuse appeared to be alcohol-related.

It is clear from the above discussion that there is a serious shortage of available current statistics of child sexual abuse in South Africa. The government has only recently made efforts to set up a task force to identify the prevalence of child abuse in South Africa, which therefore means that at present South Africa is in the dark as to the severity of the problem. Only once statistics have been collected in every part of the country may appropriate efforts begin to combat the problem on both a preventive and a curative level.

EFFECTS OF SEXUAL ABUSE

The effects of sexual abuse on individuals

There are differing views as to the effects of sexual abuse on children. Some theorists believe that children suffer no profound effects from sexual abuse. Others believe that child victims are only affected as adults. Still others believe that all children who are victims of any form of child sexual abuse whatever will suffer some emotional damage. Tsai *et al*. (cited in Hancock & Mains, 1987: 19) point out that there is overwhelming evidence that a childhood sexual experience with an older person is negative and damaging, and has 'long-term effects on the quality of personal adjustments and interpersonal relationships'. Moreover, an editorial of the *Journal of Paediatric and Perinatal Epidemiology* (1988) points out that children who are sexually abused suffer from physical pain and trauma, the risk of sexually transmitted diseases, and inappropriate knowledge of sexual acts.

The extent of the effects of sexual abuse depends on four factors:

☐ the child's emotional state prior to the abuse;

☐ the ongoing nature of the abuse;

☐ the familiarity of the offender; and

☐ the family's way of coping with the abuse.

In other words, a child who is fairly stable from a well-adjusted family who is abused once by a stranger may not suffer from irreparable damage. However, a child who is emotionally insecure from a mal-functioning family and who is abused over many years by a close family member will most likely be left with severe emotional scarring. The abuse by the family member is not only abuse of the child's body, but abuse of the relationship of trust.

Short-term effects

There are short-term effects and symptoms that are commonly evident in the sexually abused child; nevertheless it should be underscored that not every child displaying these symptoms has been sexually abused. However, the behavioural indicators listed below help to alert profes-sionals to the possibility of abuse.

Common symptoms which the sexually abused child may display include:

☐ *Self destructiveness:* a child may show destructive behaviours on himself/herself, such as pulling out hair or biting himself/herself.

☐ *Withdrawal or depression:* a child may show signs of sadness and social withdrawal which is unlike his/her personality.

☐ *Hallucinations:* although rare, a child may begin to see, hear, or feel sensations that are not occurring in reality.

☐ *Aggression:* a child may display aggressive, acting-out behaviour such as hitting, punching, or pushing other children at school.

☐ *Sex related complaints:* a child may complain of recurring urinary tract infections or ongoing vaginal infections, or may masturbate excessively, or may display inappropriate sexual behaviours.

☐ *Running away:* a child may frequently run away from home, school, or substitute care.

☐ *School problems:* a child may show concentration problems at school and difficulty in applying himself/herself to school work he/she could previously manage.

☐   *Oppositional behaviour:* a child may become rebellious and protest to discipline that he/she would otherwise adhere to.

☐   *Anxiety, psychosomatic, and sleep disorders:* a child may show severe anxiety, restlessness, and an inability to sleep.

☐   *Attempted suicide:* a very large percentage of suicide attempts in adolescence result from incest.

☐   *Physical problems:* a child may experience eating and sleeping disturbances as well as suffer from enureses and encopresis.

☐   *Gynaecological disturbances:* adolescent girls may suffer from dysmenorrhoea (painful menstrual periods) or amenorrhoea (absence of periods). Vulvar lacerations and abrasions in the genital area and occasionally venereal and other sexually transmitted diseases may also occur.

☐   *Pregnancy:* adolescent girls may give birth or have abortions.

Long-term effects on individuals

Incest does not only have severe immediate effects but also has long-term ramifications. Faria and Belohlavek (1984) propose that while the incidence of incest itself suggests that more attention be paid to adults who are victims of childhood incest, there is another reason why this population should not be ignored, namely that the experience of incest is not innocuous.

Several of the long-term effects are discussed below.

1. Indiscriminate sexual activity:
The adult victim of incest has difficulty in differentiating sexual contact from affection. Therefore she/he indiscriminately uses sexual relationships to try and meet her/his affectional need. This is what Gordy (1983) describes as a 'splitting phenomenon'.

2. Prostitution:
Due to the reason described under 'Indiscriminate sexual activity' above, many victims become prostitutes in adulthood.

3. Sexual inadequacy:
The trauma of sexual abuse is likely to distort the victims' development of normal association of pleasure with sexual activity. In adulthood normal sexual relationships to some degree become delayed, altered, inhibited, or perverted. Common sexual disorders range from frigidity to vaginismus, nymphomania, promiscuity, or orgasmic dysfunction.

4. Confusion about sexual preferences:

Child molestation may lead to homosexuality. Finkelhor (1984) found in his study that boys victimized by older men were over four times more likely to be currently engaged in homosexual activity than were non-victims. Current literature on adult homosexual behaviour suggests that in many cases homosexuality has its roots in early childhood. Many men who currently identify themselves as homosexuals report being aware of sexual interest from an early age. It may then be possible that some boys who have been sexually abused by a man in early childhood could later remain attracted to the same sex.

5. Other long-term effects:

These include:

☐ Feelings of helplessness, low self-esteem and self-worth.

☐ Lack of confidence.

☐ A sense of isolation.

☐ An inability to form healthy heterosexual relations.

☐ Feelings of guilt, depression, and suicidal ideation.

☐ Self-destructive behaviour such as cutting, burning, or scratching oneself which is sometimes used to provide a physical outlet for the mental anguish the adult may feel. Anorexia nervosa or self-starvation is another form of self-destructive behaviour displayed by incest survivors. This behaviour may also result from feelings of low self-esteem, poor body image, and feelings of being asexual.

☐ Parenting problems, which can manifest as over-protectiveness of their own children, or an inability to show affection.

Effects of sexual abuse on the family

Sexual abuse has implications for each family member as well as the family as a whole. Intra-familial sexual abuse is synonymous with family dysfunction. The family members are enmeshed and family roles are not performed in an appropriate manner. Once the incest is revealed, the family is drastically affected as one or more of its members may be lost, and the family may in consequence be without a means of support. The family may also be ostracized by the community. Sexual abuse by a stranger, while not having the same sequelae as intra-familial abuse, still has an effect on the family. Commonly, family members become over-protective of the victim, or they may become over-fearful, or develop a need for revenge.

Effects of sexual abuse on society

One of the most outstanding features of the 1987 Cleveland case is the demonstration of the effects sexual abuse can have on society and particularly helping professionals. The Cleveland case represented an explosion of the issue of child sexual abuse. During the first half of 1987, suspected sexual abuse was diagnosed in a total of 121 boys and girls by paediatricians at Middlesborough General Hospital in England. After many months of bitter challenge in the courts, twenty-six of these children from twelve families were deemed by the judges to have been wrongly diagnosed. Most of the children were diagnosed by the paediatricians concerned after routine medical examinations as having been sexually abused. The symptom was anal dilatation. The diagnosis became the contested issue in the public debate generated by the Cleveland crisis.

The events of Cleveland showed most graphically many of the problems present in the current official response to child sexual abuse. For instance, concerned professionals, doctors, police officers, nurses, and social workers, who should have been working together for the benefit of the children, were not communicating effectively. Cleveland highlighted the dangers of acting too quickly and also the necessity for professionals to act in concert.

Another effect of sexual abuse on society is the hysteria which results from the media oversensationalizing such abuse. This occurs in response to a current case that is being prosecuted, or perhaps a sex-ring being exposed by the police. During such periods, society is led to believe that sexual abuse has increased dramatically, and the reaction is one of horror and disgust. As the media hysteria diminishes, so does the societal response.

Society is also faced with the dilemma of how to deal with the offender. Is he/she a criminal, to be treated as such, or is he/she a victim of circumstances in need of psychiatric intervention?

INTERVENTION IN CHILD SEXUAL ABUSE

In recent years there has been an increasing awareness of the need to prevent child maltreatment. However, in South Africa resources to combat this problem are limited and scarce.

Prevention at an early stage is known to enhance family functioning, which could be more effective than curative intervention after maltreatment has occurred. Because of this philosophy, as well as the fact that prevention is an attractive way of reducing the financial and human costs associated with maltreatment, a wide array of preventive programmes have developed in the United States. In South Africa, there is a move to develop similar programmes.

Prevention is commonly categorized as primary, secondary, or tertiary. Primary prevention addresses a sample of the general population, for example, a programme administered to all students in a school district on how to prevent sexual abuse. Secondary prevention focuses on specific sub-sets of the population who are thought to be at high risk from sexual abuse. Typically these efforts can be directed at single mothers who are poor, or families with a new infant. Tertiary prevention or treatment addresses situations in which child sexual abuse has already occurred and the goal is to decrease recidivism and to counteract the harmful effects of child sexual abuse. Helfer (1982) evaluated what was known about the prevention of child maltreatment and found that little scientific evaluation of intervention had been conducted. Dubowitz (1989) critically evaluated preventive programmes through literature surveys and agency reports. He found that although many programmes had been implemented, relatively few had been assessed, and those that had been, suffered from many serious methodological flaws.

Existing interventive programmes

Primary prevention

In South Africa most welfare services only become available after child sexual abuse has occurred and little primary prevention exists. Conte *et al.* (1988) and Finkelhor *et al.* (1984) have summarized the key components of efforts to prevent child sexual abuse, how to recognize abuse situations and how to respond assertively. These programmes often utilize audiovisual material as well as anatomically-correct dolls. They can be administered by both professionals and lay people who have been specifically trained to do so. In South Africa such programmes have just begun to be administered by organizations such as SASPCAN (South

African Society for the Prevention of Child Abuse and Neglect) in conjunction with a Child Welfare Society, as well as by dramatic associations. At present these programmes are being offered at nursery schools, day-care centres, community centres, and private schools. The difficulty lies in obtaining permission for preventive programmes of this nature to be offered to all children in government schools. Thus some children who are 'at risk' or have been abused are unlikely to be exposed to the programmes. Furthermore, these programmes are more prevalent in white urban areas. Attempts are being made to increase their input in 'coloured', Indian, and African communities. Rural areas are totally devoid of any such programmes.

Evaluation of these programmes in the United States has revealed mixed results. Some studies have demonstrated an increase in the knowledge of safety rules. Other studies have found that pre-school children have limited retention of the information. There has also been evidence that these programmes make children hyper-aware of people in their environment, to the extent that they become fearful and inappropriately critical of adults' behaviours.

Secondary prevention

While most interventions aimed at preventing child abuse occur in the category of secondary prevention, secondary prevention of sexual abuse is more difficult, as it is problematic to identify families 'at risk'. In most cases, intervention only becomes possible once sexual abuse has been disclosed. In some cases, secondary intervention is possible based on knowledge and assumptions concerning risk factors for sexual abuse and the target groups considered to be 'high risk'.

Secondary prevention most commonly takes the form of support groups and crisis services.

Support groups are a key ingredient in many programmes. Such groups offer an opportunity for people in similar situations to share experiences and information, thereby facilitating friendships and social networks. In South Africa at present, support groups are being offered to adults who were incest victims as children, providing them with an opportunity to work through their feelings together with other incest victims. The aim is to provide support as well as to prevent the repetition of the cycle of abuse in their own families. It must be emphasized that victims of sexual abuse will not necessarily abuse their own children. Siblings of children who have been sexually abused may be considered as another popula-

tion 'at risk' and support groups for them and programmes teaching them
to prevent abuse also resort under secondary prevention.

In addition to therapeutic groups led by professionals, there are self-
help groups such as 'Parents Anonymous' and similar groups for
children. Whereas many of the participants join after having maltreated
their children, some who recognize their propensity for abuse use the
group for preventive purposes. For example, mothers who suspect that
their husbands may be abusing their children may join such a group to
gain support in seeking help to change the situation, or fathers who are
already abusing their children may join such groups to help prevent them
from further abusing their children, or from abusing other children. In
South Africa, groups of this nature are not readily available. Attempts
have, however, been made in certain centres to establish such groups,
and in Cape Town they have been very successful. The need exists for
more support groups, especially in the more deprived socio-economic
areas where families lack other resources to deal with the problem.

Increasing numbers of cities and towns have *crisis services* available on
a 24-hour basis to handle crisis situations. Such services generally consist
of a telephone hotline such as 'Childline', offering comfort and guidance
to desperate parents of children. These services also present as reporting
and referral sources for the concerned public or professionals. Their
success can be measured by the fact that the Johannesburg Childline,
which was established in July 1988, received over 2 200 calls in its first
year of operation, of which 35 per cent were related to sexual abuse —
by far the largest category of types of calls received. Childline can be
seen as a preventive service in that it aims to break the cycle of abuse.
Other crisis services are available through various crisis centres, and
through Life Line, an organization which also renders assistance to
families at risk. Crisis services, when necessary, generally refer clients to
resources that offer long-term treatment.

Tertiary prevention

Tertiary prevention refers to those interventions that aim to decrease the
likelihood of further maltreatment after the problem has already been
identified. Interventive strategies can include monitoring, support,
therapy, restriction, or punishment. Several of the interventions
described in secondary prevention also present under treatment and
rehabilitative measures. With adults, the goal of tertiary prevention
programmes would be to enhance healthy functioning and thereby
decrease the propensity for future maltreatment. In children, treatment

aims to ameliorate the psychological trauma associated with abuse, and to foster health, growth, and development, thereby diminishing the risk that they will in turn maltreat their own children. A number of treatment programmes resort under tertiary prevention.

Casework in *child and family welfare services* programmes involves regular monitoring of abusive families in an effort to enhance family functioning through counselling and referral to local resources. Child welfare organizations have the statutory power to remove children from their families in instances of serious injury or risk and place them in substitute care.

Substitute care refers to care not provided by the biological family. It can take the form of foster care or residential care on a temporary or permanent basis. Such services are used when the family is unable to provide the child with an adequately safe environment. Services are rendered to the family and to the child. Recently, organizations such as the National Association of Child Care Workers (NACCW) and Child Welfare Societies have devised programmes which provide group therapy for children in residential care who have been sexually abused. While the child is in substitute care, 'permanency plans' are made for the child, and if reunification with the family is not feasible after reasonable efforts have been made in treating the family, the child may become eligible for adoption.

At present, there is a world-wide move to provide residential care for the offenders, or for the family as a whole. Based on Australian and American models, centres such as 'Safeline' in Cape Town are providing supportive and therapeutic services for the perpetrator and for families of abuse, which include residential treatment. While residential family care is successful in the treatment of physically abusing families, sexually abusing families do not respond favourably to this form of treatment. In the majority of cases the perpetrator himself needs to be removed and placed in treatment. Moreover, the perpetrator and victim need to be separated for successful treatment to take place, and individual therapy is necessary for all family members. The perpetrator can either enter into treatment facilities on a full-time basis, where he continues his employment and thus continues to provide for his family, or he can be admitted for weekend treatment. In Australia and the United State moves are being made to legislate for the removal of the perpetrator from the home and to make treatment mandatory. South Africa is beginning to follow this line of thought, although to date no legislation has been made in this regard. This philosophy is a very controversial one, as the psychiatric fraternity are opposed to forced treatment, and postulate a low success rate in compulsory treatment. However, in the United States Giaretto (1982) has shown that 30 to 50 per cent of the perpetrators taken into mandatory treatment in the Child Sexual Abuse Treatment Programme (CSATP) have recovered. The remaining perpetrators who drop out of the programme are placed in prison, with a high rate of subsequent re-offence. This programme has provided therapy to over 4 000 children and their families over the last ten years. About 90 per cent of the children have been reunited with their families, and the recidivism rate in families who have completed the programme is less than one per cent.

Psychotherapy and *counselling* are frequently major components of treatment programmes and can be offered to adults and children on either an individual, couple, family, or group therapy basis. Maltreatment may be prevented by providing the parents of children with psychiatric disturbances with an understanding of and an approach to their children's behaviour problems.

The CSATP uses *self-help groups* as a large component of its rehabilitation. 'Parents United' and its adjunct 'Daughters and Sons United' constitute the self-help component of the CSATP. These groups primarily provide group treatment for parents, offenders, victims, and siblings of abuse. These groups do not involve professional facilitation and are very intensive, providing up to twenty hours per week of support over a crisis period.

Family support services, such as parent aides, home health visitors, and support groups are interventions that are also used in treatment programmes. The goal is to enhance family functioning and thereby reduce recidivism by addressing the contributory aetiological factors of maltreatment.

Assessment and diagnostic services are provided as part of the major hospital services in all major centres in South Africa. They aim to provide medical and psychosocial assessment of the abused child and her family. Treatment services at these clinics are being increased, but the clinics serve primarily as a source of diagnosis. The Child Abuse Clinic in Johannesburg saw approximately 300 cases in its first year, of which 95 per cent comprised sexually abused children.

Although severe forms of child sexual abuse have long been considered crimes, there has been a trend in recent years to further *criminalize the problem* of child sexual abuse. The recently formed Police Child Protection Units (CPUs) deal with this criminal aspect of child abuse and their major goal is to punish the perpetrator of the crime of child maltreatment, thereby demonstrating that child maltreatment will not be tolerated by society. This punitive philosophy often clashes with the

therapeutic and rehabilitative stance of welfare agencies, but with training staff, the units are beginning to recognize the necessity of merging
the legal and therapeutic stance with the rehabilitative one.

According to the Child Care Act 74 of 1983, which came into operation
in 1987, only doctors, dentists, and nurses are legally obliged to *report
cases* of child abuse, either suspected or proven. This of course does not
include social workers, teacher, child-care workers, and others most
likely to encounter cases of child abuse. The Act needs to be adjusted to
include any person who is likely to encounter child abuse. Mandatory
reporters have to report cases to the Regional Director of Health and
Welfare, but the procedure which follows on reporting is unclear. An
obvious deficiency in the present system of reporting cases is that the
register is run on a local, racial basis. Various hospitals, state departments, private welfare organizations, the police, and voluntary organizations such as Childline also keep their own registers. Each register serves
a different purpose and collects different information. These registers
provide an important function in helping these resources to continue
their work. They also stand as symbols of the disunity and fragmentation
which exist among the service providers. It is clear that a joint non-racial
and national register is needed.

In the present legal system abused children are subpoenaed to court
as *witnesses* and often are required to give evidence in the presence of
the perpetrator. Because this is traumatic for the child, it in itself leads to
further abuse. Recommendations have been made by the organization
Lawyers for Human Rights to the Minister of Justice to minimize the
trauma of court appearances for children who have allegedly been
sexually abused. The use of videos, audio-tapes, as well as conducting
the interview with the child in the presence of a social worker behind a
one-way mirror have been recommended. A ministerial inquiry into the
matter has begun. In the opinion of Giles (1989) it is advantageous for
court proceedings to take place. Among the advantages for the child is
that a court appearance helps to identify the child as the plaintiff and
reinforces for the child that he/she is not in the wrong. It also enables
the responsibility of dealing with the problem to be placed with adults.
As far as the offender is concerned, the court hearing is an authoritative
procedure whereby he can be punished for his wrong-doing. For the
family the court provides integrative professional intervention and helps
to identify 'hidden victims'. Giles does, however, point out that not all
children make good witnesses and therefore not every case should go
to court. He highlights a number of practice implications, co-ordinated
intervention between services being one. He further recommends that

children should have more legal rights which should be written into the constitution, and that the courts themselves should change to be more appropriate venues for defending such rights.

In the present system parents convicted of child abuse in the criminal court or who have to appear in the Children's Court under the provisions of the Child Care Act of 1983 are entitled to legal representation by a lawyer. Although the police or the social worker present the facts of the case to the court, the presentation is unbiased and not on behalf of either party. No one is legally representing the child. Thus what is needed is a system of *child advocacy*, whereby the child is represented by a lawyer. Family courts could also help to alleviate this problem.

The Department of Health and Welfare, House Of Assembly, has launched a national survey to determine what issues need to be confronted in the prevention of child abuse. Recommendations to the Minister of Health and Welfare concerned have been made. The recommendations for the Johannesburg area include a non-racial programme for child abuse, educating children in the prevention of child abuse, improving treatment facilities for abused children and their families, the extension of mandatory reporting, the subsidization of specialized child abuse programmes, and the improvement of child-care facilities. The *government* has begun acting on some of these recommendations such as the creation of a *24-hour toll-free child abuse hotline.*

It would appear that this facility is staffed by members of the Child Protection Unit and social workers from agencies dealing with child abuse. This service offers both counselling facilities and a service to investigate alleged child abuse cases. While this service can be commended, its implementation was hasty, without consultation with experts in the field and without taking into consideration existing services of this nature, such as Childline, thereby once again duplicating services. Furthermore, as the service was implemented by the Department of Health and Welfare, House of Assembly, it will only be for the use of white consumers. Because it has been implemented by a state department, the community may prove to be reluctant to use it, being unsure of what the authorities will do with reported cases.

In conclusion, while facilities for abused children and their families are being improved upon, there still remains a great need for increased preventive treatment and statutory services for all children in South Africa who suffer sexual abuse. While the government fails to provide adequate funding for social work in programmes and posts and the working conditions for social workers remain unfavourable, the existing agencies will remain understaffed and the services they provide unsatisfactory.

The public and private sectors, in concert, must take responsibility for combating the sexual abuse of children. While education and public awareness are important in the prevention of child sexual abuse, they increase the demand for services and the provision of facilities to cater for the sexually abused child and his/her family.

REFERENCES

Bannister, A. (1988) 'Conclusions from Cleveland', *Social Work Today*, September 1988, 16–17.

Briere, J. & Runtz M. (1988) 'Symptomatology Associates with Childhood Sexual Victimization in a Non-Clinical Adult Sample,' *Child Abuse and Neglect*, 12, 51–9.

Burgess, A. W. *et al.* (1978) *Sexual Assault of Children and Adolescents*, Lexington: Lexington M.A.

Campbell, B. (1988) *Unofficial Secrets — Child Sexual Abuse — The Cleveland Case*, London: Virago Press Ltd.

Child Abuse Prevention Foundation Inc., Washington DC, unpublished pamphlet.

Conte, J. R. *et al.* (1988) 'An Analysis of Programs to Prevent Sexual Victimization of Children', *Journal of Primary Prevention*, in press.

De Jong, A. R. *et al.* (1983) 'Epidemiologic Variations in Childhood Sexual Abuse', *Child Abuse and Neglect*, 7, 155–62.

De Villiers, F. P. R. (1989) 'An Analysis of Patients Presenting to a Newly Established Child Abuse Clinic, unpublished paper.

Dietz, C. A. & Craft, J. L. (1980) 'Family Dynamics of Incest — A New Perspective', *Social Casework*, 61, 602–9.

Dubowitz, H. (1989) 'Prevention of Child Maltreatment — What is Known', *Pediatrics*, 83(4), 570–7.

Duncan, B. R. (1989) 'Child Abuse in the Children's Home', *The Child Care Worker*, 7(4), 7–8.

Elwell, M. E. (1979) 'Sexually Assaulted Children and their Families', *Social Casework: The Journal of Contemporary Social Work*, 4, 227–35.

Faller, K. C. (1984) 'Is the Child Victim of Sexual Abuse Telling the Truth?' *Child Abuse and Neglect*, 8, 473–81.

Faria, G. & Belohlavek, N. (1984) 'Treating Female Adult Survivors of Childhood Incest', *Social Casework: The Journal of Contemporary Social Work*, 10, 465–71.

Finkelhor, D. (ed.) (1986) *A Source Book on Child Sexual Abuse*, Beverly Hills: Sage Publications, Inc.

Finkelhor, D. (1984) *Child Sexual Abuse — New Theory and Research*, New York: The Free Press.

Finkelhor, D. (1979) *Sexually Victimized Children*, New York: The Free Press.

Finkelhor. D. & Hotaling, G. T. (1984) 'Sexual Abuse in the National Incidence Study of Child Abuse and Neglect: An Appraisal', *Child Abuse and Neglect,* 8, 23–33.

Forward, S. & Buck, C. (1978) *Betrayal of Innocence: Incest and its Devastation*; New York: Penguin Books.

Giaretto, H. A. (1982) 'A Comprehensive Child Sexual Abuse Program', *Child Abuse and Neglect,* 6, 263–78.

Gilder, S. S. B (1986) 'The Sexual Abuse of Children', *South African Medical Journal,* 70, 648.

Giles, C. (1989) 'The Child as Witness', *Child Care Worker,* 7(5), 5–7.

Glaser, D. & Frosh, S. (1988) *Child Sexual Abuse,* London: Macmillan Education Ltd.

Glaser, R. R. & Winship, W. S. (eds.) (1984) 'Child Abuse — A Southern African Problem', Proceedings of the 1984 National Conference.

Golding, J. (1988) 'Editorial', *Paediatric and Perinatal Epidemiology,* 2, 107–15.

Goodwin J. *et al.* (1983) 'Grandfather/Granddaughter Incest: A Trigenerational View', *Child Abuse and Neglect,* 7, 163–70.

Gordon, L. & O'Keefe, P. (1984) 'Incest as a Form of Family Violence. Evidence from Historical Case Records', *Journal of Marriage and the Family,* 2, 27–34.

Gordy, P. (1983) 'Group Work that Supports Adult Victims of Childhood Incest', *Social Casework: The Journal of Contemporary Social Work,* 4, 300–7.

Hancock, M. & Mains, K. B. (1987) *Child Sexual Abuse: A Hope for Healing,* Great Britain: Highland Books.

Helfer, R. (1982) 'A Review of the Literature on the Prevention of Child Abuse and Neglect', *Child Abuse and Neglect,* 6, 251–61.

Herman, J. & Hirschman, L. (1981) 'Families at Risk for Father-Daughter Incest', *American Journal of Psychiatry,* 138, 967–70.

Jaffe, A. M. & Roux, R. (1988) 'Sexual Abuse of Children — A Hospital Based Study', *South African Medical Journal,* 74, 65–7.

James, B. & Nasjleti, M. (1983) *Treating Sexually Abused Children,* Palo Alto: Consulting Psychologist Press, Inc.

Justice, R. & Justice R. (1979) *The Broken Taboo: Sex in The Family,* New York: Human Sciences Press.

Kempe, R. S. & Kempe C. H. (1984) *Sexual Abuse of Children and Adolescents,* New York: W. H. Freeman & Co.

Labuschagne, I. (1984) *Shadow of Menace,* Pretoria: Haum.

Lee, N. C. (1988) 'Suffer the Little Children', *South African Medical Journal,* 74, 49.

Levett, A. (1989) 'Child Sexual Abuse: The Damaging Effects of Popular Ideas', *Die Kinderversorger,* 7(6), 9–11.

McIntyre, K. (1981) 'Role of Mothers in Father-Daughter Incest — A Feminist Analysis' *Social Work,* 26(6), 462–6.

Meiselman, K. (1978) *Incest: A Psychological Study of Causes and Effects with Treatment Recommendations,* San Francisco: Jossey-Bass.

Miller, A. (1986) *Thou Shalt Not be Aware: Society's Betrayal of the Child,* New York: Penguin, Inc.

Mrazek, P. & Kempe. C. (1987) Sexually Abused Children and their Families, Oxford: Pergamon Press.

Mrazek, P. & Lynch, M. A. (1983) 'Sexual Abuse of Children in the United Kingdom', *Child Abuse and Neglect,* 7, 147–53.

Pats, K. (ed.) (1982) *Child Abuse, a Major Concern of our Times,* USA: Citadel Press.

Porter, R. (ed.) (1984) *Child Sexual Abuse Within The Family,* Great Britain: University Press.

Renvoize, J. (1982) *Incest: A Family Pattern,* London: Routledge & Kegan Paul.

Rist, K. (1979) 'Incest: Theoretical and Clinical View', *American Journal of Orthopsychiatry,* 49, 480–691.

Robertson, G. (1989) *Sexual Abuse of Children In South Africa — Understanding and Dealing with the Problem,* Hammanskraal: Unibooks.

Rosenfeld, A. *et al.* (1986) 'Determining Incestuous Contact between Parent and Child: Frequency of Touching Parents' Genitals in a Non-Clinical Population', *Journal of American Academy of Child Psychiatry,* 25(4), 481–4.

Russell, D. E. H. (1983) 'The Incidence of Prevalence of Intrafamilial and Extrafamilial Sexual Abuse of Female Children', *Child Abuse and Neglect,* 7, 133–46.

Search, G. (1988) *The Last Taboo — Sexual Abuse of Children,* London: Penguin Books.

Selby, J. W. & Calhourn, L. G. (1980) 'Families of Incest — A Collation of Clinical Impressions', *International Journal of Society Psychiatry,* 1, 7–16.

Sgroi, S. M. (ed.) (1982) *Handbook of Clinical Intervention in Child Sexual Abuse,* Lexington: D. C. Heath & Co.

Sgroi, S. M. *et al.* (1982) 'A Conceptual Framework for Child Sexual Abuse'. In *Handbook of Clinical Intervention in Child Sexual Abuse,* edited by S. M. Sgroi, Lexington: D. C. Heath & Co.

Sharma, A. & Sutherland, R. (1988) 'Incidence of Child Abuse: Depends who you Ask', *Paediatric and Perinatal Epidemiology,* 2, 158–60.

Summit, R. C. (1983) 'Child Sexual Abuse Accommodation Syndrome', *Child Abuse and Neglect,* 7, 177–93.

Tyler, A. H. & Brassard M. R. (1984) 'Abuse in the Investigations and Treatments of Intrafamilial Child Sexual Abuse', *Child Abuse and Neglect,* 8, 47–53.

Van der Mey, B. J. (1988) 'The Sexual Victimization of Male Children: A Review of Previous Research', *Child Abuse and Neglect,* 12, 61–72.

Van der Mey, B. J. & Neff, R. L. (1982) 'Adult/Child Incest: A Review of Research and Treatment', *Adolescence,* 17, 717–35.

Ward, E. (1984) *Father/Daughter Rape,* London: The Women's Press Ltd.

Wild, N. J. (1989) 'Prevalence of Child Sex Rings', *Pediatrics*, 83(4), 553–8.

Wild, N. J. (1988) 'Suicide of Perpetrators after Disclosure of Child Sexual Abuse', *Child Abuse and Neglect*, 11, 483–95.

Wurtele, S. K. (1987) 'School-Based Sexual Abuse Prevention Programs: A Review', *Child Abuse and Neglect*, 11, 483–95.

9 Family violence: wife abuse[1]

T. Segel and D. Labe[2]

INTRODUCTION

This chapter is concerned with the abuse that women suffer at the hands of male partners in intimate relationships. At the time of writing there is growing concern in South Africa with various forms of family violence. There has been extensive coverage in the South African press of topics such as child abuse and family murders. Despite the prevalence of the abuse of women by their male partners in this country, this subject has not received the media coverage afforded to other forms of family violence. Moreover there has been little systematic attention paid to the development of an indigenous theoretical formulation of this problem. There is also a dearth of adequate and appropriate social, legal, and psychological services to meet the needs of battered women. This relative silence on the topic is difficult to condone.

The abuse of women by their male partners is a feature of patriarchal gender relations under conditions of broader societal violence. Research has demonstrated a link between broader societal violence and violence in the family. Available evidence shows that the family is not randomly violent (Schechter, 1982). Certain members experience more abuse than others. The overwhelming majority of victims of adult family violence are women. Wife abuse in South Africa, as in many other countries world-wide, is a pervasive social problem.

Wife battery is a multi-determined phenomenon which can perhaps be best understood within the broad ideological and socio-political context in which it occurs. In this chapter wife abuse is seen as one of the many forms of violence which women suffer by virtue of their vulnerability and relative disadvantage within a broad social structure. The abuse that women experience in the home provides a lens through which women's subordination to men comes into focus. Binney (1981) has argued that women cannot achieve equality in public life without a radical reappraisal of their subordinate position in the family.

The authors hope to locate the issue of wife abuse within the South African context. In the course of this text an explanatory framework is proposed. The sections on the aetiological considerations of wife abuse and the effects of wife abuse combine to explain the total context of battery and its implications. It is argued that the socio-political context of abuse may be explored in conjunction with an exploration of the dynamics of violent interactions and individual features associated with the male batterer, to explain the origins of wife abuse. The effects and implication of abuse for the victim, children, and the extended family are also considered. The intervention strategies proposed in this chapter flow from the manner in which the problem of wife abuse is conceptualized. The primary, secondary, and tertiary levels of intervention involve the total context of battering. It is proposed that intervention strategies need to address the socio-political context which engenders and facilitates wife abuse; to provide for the material and psychological needs of battered women; and to treat the problems and pathology of men who batter.

The term 'abuse' is difficult to define and is open to subjective interpretation on the part of batterers, battered partners, researchers, and professionals in the field. Physical violence has been the accepted research standard in the area of wife abuse. Physical abuse includes a continuum of behaviours from pushing and slapping, to beatings and coerced sex, to assaults with deadly weapons. The difficulty in operationalizing and researching psychological and emotional abuse has resulted in these areas being inadequately studied. Emotional and psychological abuse is often experienced as being as traumatic and damaging as physical abuse. Walker (1979) argues that psychological abuse accompanies physical abuse and states that 'they cannot be separated, despite the difficulty in documentation' (Walker 1979: xiv–v). Emotional abuse, however, may occur without the direct use of physical force.

In this chapter, abuse is recognized as involving physical, sexual, and/or psychological force, coercion, emotional humiliation, degradation or torment, verbal assault, and economic deprivation or exploitation. The terms 'abuse', 'battery', and 'violence' are used interchangeably throughout the text.

Violence between intimate partners may occur regardless of whether the couple is legally married or not. In this text, we use the terms 'wife' or 'woman' to denote the female partner, and 'husband' or 'man' to denote the male partner.

INCIDENCE

The absence of statistics in South Africa makes it difficult to provide a definitive statement on the prevalence of either husband abuse or wife abuse in this country. To date, no large-scale national prevalence study has been undertaken in this country. Statistics concerning the incidence of spouse abuse which come from police records, hospitals, or social service organizations may be inaccurate because partner abuse is often not reported: in fact it has been suggested that it is more underreported than rape, and if documented at all, this may be done under generic categories of 'assault', 'disturbing the peace', or 'relationship problems'.

It has been estimated that in the United States as many as 50 per cent of all women will be victims of battering at some point in their lives (Walker, 1979). A more conservative estimate is given by Pagelow (1984), who states that between 25 and 35 per cent of all women in the United States are beaten at least once during the course of an intimate relationship.

Spouse abuse, which occurs across all socio-economic and racial groups, is widespread in South Africa. Welch (1987) reports that its incidence or its reported incidence is rising significantly. In his opinion South Africa conforms to a general Western trend regarding the seriousness of the consequences of spouse abuse.

A recent national survey by Life Line reported a 31 per cent increase in the incidence of calls relating to wife battering (*The Citizen*, 9 June, 1989). Whether this sharp increase indicates an escalation in actual violence, or an increased willingness to report violence is unclear at present. The apparently high incidence suggests that what is being confronted is not a problem of individual pathology but a severe social disorder.

AETIOLOGICAL CONSIDERATIONS OF WIFE ABUSE
The socio-political context of battery

Levels of violence in society directly affect the prevalence of wife abuse and the extent to which wife abuse is sanctioned (Sonkin *et al.*, 1985). At present South African society is notoriously violent. Harsh disrespect for human well-being is embedded in the very structure of laws and practices which govern human relations in this country. The brutality of the apartheid system cannot be overemphasized. The implications of apartheid in terms of poverty, hardship, ill health and divided families are well-documented across a range of literature. A comprehensive discussion of these circumstances is beyond the scope of this chapter except to say that these are conditions under which violence flourishes. Increasingly, conditions of structural violence and oppression give rise to multiple forms of reactive violence and resistance and these in turn produce responses of repressive violence, so that the spiral of violence intensifies.

The intensity of this spiral of violence in the South African context is highlighted by some statistics. In South Africa as a whole, including the reserves, the proportion of the total population living below the minimum living level in 1980 was estimated to be 50 per cent. No less than 81 per cent of households in the reserves were living in dire poverty (Wilson & Ramphele, 1989: 17). At the same time, 'South Africa's Gini coefficient (the statistic which measures the width of inequality between rich and poor) was the highest of the fifty-seven countries in the world for which data are available' (Wilson & Ramphele, 1989: 18).

Crime rates also provide a useful index of people's feelings of entrapment and despair. Cape Town has the highest crime rate of any large city in the Western world. More than twice as many people were murdered in the Cape Peninsula in 1986 than were murdered in the whole of the United Kingdom that year. The levels of distribution of crime are similar in most South African cities (Wilson & Ramphele, 1989: 153).

The widespread practice of detention without trial, illustrated by an estimated 33 000 people held in the period 1986–9; the escalating use of assassination to silence opposition; the repeated renewals of states of emergency; as well as the burgeoning state security infrastructures are all examples of the ways in which institutional violence has taken root in this country.

Violence in the home, like crime on the street, is a product of the sense of entrapment and insecurity that results from high levels of structural and institutional violence. This thesis is supported by empirical research carried out in the United States. There, two groups are isolated as being 'high risk' in terms of wife abuse. They are the prison population and the military. It is argued that both these groups are subjected to a highly regimented, rigidly hierarchical set of social relationships which set the stage for a sense of frustration and despair. In both these population groups levels of violence are high. Violence is seen as the primary method of conflict resolution. Prisoners and soldiers are often brutalized by their respective experiences of jail and combat. This has implications for the way in which they conduct relationships in civilian life (Sonkin *et al.*, 1985).

South Africa has the highest ratio of prisoners to total population in the world, with 440 out of every 100 000 people in prison (*SA Barometer*, June 1989). Conscription of white men is universal in South Africa. There are limited opportunities for conscientious objection. The authors suggest that there is a need for empirical research to be conducted on the relationship between wife abuse and the high military and prison populations in this country.

In conditions in which violence is overwhelming, a culture of violence develops. By this is meant a situation in which violence becomes accepted as a norm rather than as an aberration. It becomes the primary means of conflict resolution, and its use is so widespread that acts of violence do not produce any sense of outrage. Furthermore, the use of violence is sanctioned by the society. An example of an expression of the culture of violence in this country is the ownership of firearms, legal or illegal, which has become a norm in South African society. By the end of February 1988, a total of 2 756 635 firearm licences had been issued in South Africa (*SA Barometer*, June 1989). That a correlation exists between firearm ownership and domestic violence has been recorded in the literature on wife abuse.

The spiral of violence which produces a culture of violence explains the broad context in which wife abuse occurs, but cannot explain why women are the primary and consistent targets of domestic abuse between adults. The phenomenon can, however, be explained in terms of the patriarchal structuring of gender relationships. The inequality between men and women is encoded in a variety of linguistic, legal, institutional, and economic practices. The material, legal, and educational disadvantages that women experience in relation to men is supported by a complex ideological framework in which ideas of masculinity and femininity are constructed. Within this ideological framework men are perceived to be rational, assertive, strong minded, and independent. Women, by contrast, are perceived as being emotional, passive, fickle, and dependent. Traditional stereotypes of masculinity are empowering of individuals. Traditional stereotypes of femininity reinforce women's sense of powerlessness and vulnerability. It is precisely their structural disadvantage in the society, the ideological construction of femininity, and women's perceived sense of powerlessness, which make women the obvious targets of domestic abuse. Women's disadvantaged position in the economic sphere makes them particularly vulnerable to the onslaught of poverty. Their disadvantage in the domestic setting sets the stage for their abuse in the home.

Women's relative powerlessness in the home is deeply entrenched across a variety of cultures and communities in South Africa. It is reinforced by the laws and rituals surrounding marriage. In customary tribal law, marriages are contracted around a system of lobola in which the husband pays a sum in cash or kind to the wife's family in exchange for her. The marriage contract functions as a system of exchange in which women and goods transfer ownership. An ethos of the women as the men's property prevails. The South African legal system upholds a similar ethos. All marriages contracted before 1985 without an antenuptial contract subjected a woman to her husband's marital power. Amendments to the laws of marriage abolished the marital power clause.

Nevertheless, women's subjugation in the home has not been redressed. South African law does not recognize marital rape as an offence. The law upholds the idea that sex is the man's conjugal right. It does not afford the woman the status of equal partner in the sexual relationship, and offers her no recourse to justice should she suffer sexual abuse by her husband. At best marital rape is seen to be an aggravating circumstance in cases where the husband is charged with another offence such as assault. This is one example of the way in which the law maintains the oppression of women in the home.

The practice of patriarchy depends in large measure on the division that is drawn between the public and private spheres of social life. The private sphere, the family, is presumed to be a peaceful haven that is secluded from the demands and violations that characterize public life. Evidence of widespread, often lethal violence in the domestic setting shatters this myth. Donzelot (1979) extends his critique of this distinction by revealing the ideological underpinnings of the very process of setting up an opposition between two spheres. He argues that the family cannot be viewed in isolation from other social processes. The family is 'queen and prisoner of the social sphere' (Donzelot, 1979: 9). However wrong or misdirected this division may be, it has definite implications with respect to wife abuse. The division between the 'public' and the 'private' hides wife abuse from the public eye. Wife abuse is regarded as a private encounter between husband and wife. It is not seen as a social problem and is not met with appropriate social sanction. The hidden nature of abuse — its definition as a private affair — serves tacitly to legitimate husbands' violence towards their wives. It also serves to deepen the sense of isolation and shame experienced by many battered women.

Some feminists have argued that if a home is a man's castle it often serves as the women's prison, from which she cannot escape (Russell, 1982).

Given the sexism of South African society, an interesting and controversial set of questions may be posed. The crisis that apartheid has produced in South African family life is widely documented across a range of literature. The migrant labour system, group areas legislation, and forced removals have all been linked with a breakdown in family functioning. However, the relationship between family breakdown and the erosion of traditional patriarchal power relations has not received systematic attention. It may be argued that apartheid has produced a crisis in patriarchy and that in a rigidly sexist society such as South Africa the ripple effects of this crisis may include an increase in wife abuse. Some examples of the effects of apartheid on family life may elucidate the concept of a crisis in patriarchy. In her research *Childhood in Crossroads*, Reynolds (1989) found that although traditional Xhosa kinship structures are patrilineal and patrilocal, the children in her sample were more likely to describe kinship in matrilineal, matrilocal terms. Similarly, Simkins (1980, cited by Burman & Reynolds, 1986: 13) estimated that in the South African homelands, up to 60 per cent of households are female-headed, single-parent families. The possibility exists that the emasculation of men by the joint forces of racism and capitalism is producing a sense of impotence and rage which is being expressed through violence against women. As men lose their power base in the family and in the broader society, they struggle to regain this lost esteem through the subjugation of women. Certainly the high levels of rape in this country would seem to suggest some process at work.

An example borrowed from a context far removed from the supposed warmth and intimacy of the domestic setting highlights the above dynamic. In South African prisons rape is widely practised to establish hierarchies of status and privilege amongst prisoners. Prisoners use rape to subjugate and enslave fellow inmates. In the aftermath of the violent rape a relationship is established between rapist and victim. The victorious rapist assumes the status of 'man'. The victim of the assault is assigned the status of 'wyfie' (little wife). Within the brutal and harsh environs of the prison, the practice of battering or violating the 'feminine' functions to afford some status to men who by virtue of their incarceration are wholly depowered.

The feature of devaluing the feminine through violence is crucial in the understanding of the dynamics of violent interactions in the domestic setting. It is the thread which patriarchy, sexism, and radical inequality in gender relations weave through all violent interactions between men and women in the home.

The dynamics of violent relationships

Wife abuse can be viewed as an interaction between two individuals in which the abusive partner uses violence to control the abused partner. Walker (1979) provided the first transactional account of wife abuse. She argued that wife abuse is a cyclical phenomenon. There are three stages in the 'cycle of violence'. There is a stage of tension building in which minor battering incidents occur. This is followed by a stage of acute battery and assault. In the third stage of the cycle the abusive partner demonstrates contrite loving behaviour. Walker (1979) suggests that the third stage of the cycle of violence intermittently reinforces the positive feelings the woman feels towards her husband and maintains the relationship. Walker's cycle of violence is based on social learning theory. It helps to explain how women become victimized by abuse and learn to become helpless in relation to the violence they suffer. Her theory is seminal in wife abuse literature and other authors have extended her insights.

Elbow (1982, cited by Bograd, 1984) postulates a psychodynamic, systemic formulation of the pattern of the externalization/internalization characteristic of violent relationships. The batterer rationalizes his violence to avoid self-recrimination and the battered woman accepts blame to avoid feeling helpless. In a later article, Elbow (1977) argues that abuse involves projection on the part of the batterer. The abused partner becomes symbolic of a significant other, usually an introjected parent, onto which the batterer displaces blame and pain. The pathological addition of the battered woman to the violent relationship is widely recognized. A factor that is often overlooked is that the abuser experiences a similar psychological dependence on his wife. However, the reasons for and origins of these two sets of dependence are different. Elbow (1977) argues that abusers experience the loss of the abusive relationship as fundamentally threatening to their sense of ego integration. Loss of the relationship implies the loss of a dimension of the self.

Loss and fear of loss are central in the aetiology and maintenance of the abusive relationship. This is suggested by two common features of abuse. The first is that many abusive men report that they are provoked to violence by their wives' actual or perceived infidelity. Infidelity implies the loss of intimacy which can be experienced as ego threatening. In the South African context the migrant labour system has implications for this psychological phenomenon. The situation in which husbands and wives are forced to live separately breeds distrust and the opportunity for actual or suspected infidelity to occur.

The second feature of abuse which suggests the importance of loss is the fact that many abused women report that abuse either began or escalated during the first pregnancy. During pregnancy, assaults are often directed at the woman's abdomen (Martin, 1976; Walker, 1979). It could be argued that the abuser is unconsciously trying to dislodge the foetus that is now diverting his wife's attention from him. An abuser may experience pregnancy as a threatened loss of his wife or the marital relationship.

Denzin (1984: 488) suggests that violence may be defined as the 'attempt to regain through the use of emotional and physical force, something that has been lost'. He claims that violence is used to recapture the ideal of intimacy in the relationship. However, the use of violence has the paradoxical effect of destroying the intimacy it hopes to regain. The process of projecting blame onto the other and denying the autonomy of the woman militates against intimacy. The violent transaction is governed by a quest for the impossible. It hopes to possess the otherness of the other which by definition eludes possession.

Bowlby (1984) lends a development perspective to the dynamics of violence. He argues that just as an infant experiences acute anxiety coupled with intense rage when his or her source of gratification, the mother, is absent, so in later life these infantile responses of anxiety and rage are recalled when the adult experiences loss or impairment in attachment formation. The adult's capacity to contain this anxiety and rage depends on the extent to which the experience of loss was integrated and resolved in earlier years.

Battered women experience loss at many levels. They have to mourn the loss of the ideal relationship, the loss of self-esteem, the loss of control and self-determination, as well as the loss of the actual relationship should they decide to leave their husbands. Adams (1988) notes a parallel experience amongst batterers who seek treatment. These men pass through a stage of denial, anger, bargaining, and depression as they struggle to relinquish their violent behaviour. The stage of depression involves the batterer acknowledging his own sense of loss, and recognizing the loss of esteem and control which leads him to batter. It would appear that the extent to which his mourning process is negotiated and the degree of acceptance achieved will dictate the success with which batterers renounce violence. The same is true of the ability of women to leave violent relationships. If mourning of loss is nor negotiated, the defences of denial and projection remain intact and the abuse continues.

Individual features of men who batter

Traditional theories of wife abuse focus on the personality factors of abused women. There has been a shift in emphasis in contemporary literature on domestic violence. Growing attention is being paid to the personality factors of abusive men. The available literature on the male batterer indicates that batterers often experience feelings of shame, self-hatred, and low self-worth. He experiences a sense of being out of control of his life, has a low frustration tolerance, and has difficulty with impulse control. Psychological testing using the MMPI reveals that many batterers are angry and deeply depressed (Sonkin *et al.*, 1985). Many profiles of batterers reveal that batterers use denial and intellectualization as common defence mechanisms. It is very common for men who batter to minimize the extent of their violence or the far-reaching implications that their violence has for the victims of their abuse and significant others. Batterers may also use hostility, withdrawal, or substance abuse as a defence against feelings of vulnerability. The use of the defence of projection by all batterers has already been discussed as being intrinsic to the violent transaction (Sonkin *et al.*, 1985).

Elbow (1977) provides a useful model for understanding the psychodynamic features of the male batterer. She asserts that through the act of battery the man is able to master a basic anxiety which he experiences. The source of this anxiety, she argues, is always an internalized injunction. The male batterer defends against his anxiety by projecting this internalized parental injunction onto his wife. Elbow's clinical experience has revealed that there are four common syndromes of abuse. In the first syndrome, the batterer projects his anxiety around the issue of control onto his wife who functions symbolically as an object to be controlled. The second abuse syndrome involves the abuser projecting his anxiety around protection versus harm onto his wife. He defends himself against his anxiety of being harmed by symbolically constituting his wife as an object to be alternately harmed and loved. In the third syndrome the central issue for the abuser is his loss of self-esteem. He projects his anxiety around this issue onto his wife who functions symbolically as an object to reinforce his sense of self-worth. In the final syndrome the abuser experiences profound ego disintegration. He is unable to individuate or to differentiate self from other. In this syndrome the wife functions symbolically as a part of the abuser's self. Elbow (1977) notes that this fourth syndrome is most likely to produce lethal violence and result in suicide or homicide.

There is a high correlation between wife abuse and early impairment in attachment formation of batterers. Roy (1982) found that over 80 per cent of abusive men were abused as children or witnessed their fathers beating their mothers. In these early childhood experiences the men internalized a sense of violence as a norm.

Research demonstrates that men who batter uphold rigid sex role stereotypes and have very traditional and rigid expectations of marriage (Walker, 1979; Elbow, 1977). Flyn (1977) reports that the male partners in his study of wife abuse were ill-prepared to change or compromise their expectations, but demanded that their wives changed to fit in with their ideals of marriage.

No aetiological account of abuse is complete without recognizing the fact that organic or biochemical factors may be at play in violent behaviour. The use of drugs, particularly alcohol, is frequently associated with marital violence. There is some debate in the literature as to the relationship between alcohol and marital violence (Sonkin *et al.*, 1985). It is generally accepted that the use of alcohol may lower impulse control. It is important, however, to distinguish between the problem of alcohol abuse and the problem of violence. They are different issues which must both be treated.

In rare cases in which a person's violence is generalized beyond the domestic setting, it may be useful to consider the possibility of an organic condition underlying the violent behaviour. Certain organic disturbances, such as temporal lobe epilepsy, predispose individuals to violent behaviour.

THE EFFECTS AND IMPLICATIONS OF WIFE ABUSE

A fundamental methodological difficulty in formulating an explanatory framework for wife abuse is the interrelatedness of cause and effect. In the previous section it was demonstrated that wife abuse has its roots in historical attitudes towards women, the institution of marriage, as well as in the social and economic structure of the broader society. These factors have definite implications for the ways in which women will respond to the violence they suffer in their homes. The patriarchal structuring of gender relationships interweaves with other structural and economic factors in the society to lay the pre-conditions of woman abuse. These same factors serve to maintain abuse. Woman are often trapped in violent marriages by material and ideological conditions beyond their control.

Women's economic dependence on their husbands is cited as a reason why they are trapped in violent relationships (Martin, 1976; Walker, 1979; Kalmuss & Straus, 1982). Women's educational disadvantage and discriminatory labour practices often militate against women's economic self-sufficiency. One implication of leaving a violent relationship may be that the woman faces economic hardship or even poverty. This is particularly applicable in South Africa, where there is limited provision of social security benefits.

Other factors may also serve to maintain women in violent relationships. In South Africa there are many laws which discriminate against women on the basis of both race and gender. Until very recently, an African woman's rights to her house in an urban area would be forfeited if she became divorced from her husband. The influx control legislation which governed this practice argued that many women's rights to be in the urban areas and to have access to housing in those areas was based on their husbands' rights to be there. Thus many women found themselves trapped in unsatisfactory, violent relationships (Wilson & Ramphele, 1989: 178).

Ideologies such as woman's duty to preserve the family at all costs, and the belief that abuse is a private affair which should be hidden from other people, also trap women. Women internalize these beliefs. Families and friends may reinforce them. They prevent women from reaching out for help. The web of ideologies and practices which render women powerless in relation to men make them vulnerable to abuse. The violence they suffer entrenches and reinforces their vulnerability, thus women are maintained in a vicious cycle of entrapment.

Violence qualitatively changes the nature of intimate relationships. It has implications for all concerned, the batterer, the victim, their children, their extended family, and their social network, as well as for the broader community whose levels of violence are raised and maintained by domestic abuse. In the following section, effects on the victim, children, and extended family are discussed. The implications of battery for the abuser were dealt with in the previous section.

Effects on the victim

There are a variety of clinical features associated with abused women. These include social isolation, depression, listlessness, anxiety, emotional lability, agitation and feelings of guilt, self-blame, and shame. Abused women also report somatic complaints such as headaches, backache, and gastro-intestinal complaints. The literature suggests that these psychological, somatic, and social features are responses to the violence that women suffer.

The factor that puzzles and frustrates many workers in the field is that despite the obvious harm that women suffer as a result of abuse, many women do not leave their husbands. The maternal and ideological factors of entrapment explain this phenomenon in part. However, the dependence that some women demonstrate on their violent husbands needs to be explored further. The difficulty which many women have in leaving violent marriages is a discernible feature of the wife abuser syndrome.

Traditional theories of wife abuse explain women's addiction to violent relationships in terms of their inherent masochism. There is no evidence to suggest that women derive any sort of perverse pleasure from being beaten. Contemporary literature suggests that women's dependence on violent relationships is contingent on the dynamics of battery and is an effect of the abuse they suffer.

Traumatic bonding of abused women to their husbands may be explained in terms of the cycle of violence. In the first two stages of the cycle, the husband is abusive, but he is unusually attentive and loving in the third stage. Abuse leaves women feeling hurt, drained, and in desperate need of human warmth and comfort. Women turn to their husbands for whatever warmth and comfort these men can offer. The men, who often feel guilty and remorseful after a battering incident, provide nurturing for a short while. Women use the defence of splitting to keep the abusive and affectionate aspects of their relationships separate. Painter (cited by Caplan, 1985: 143) argues that women bond to the warmer, affectionate sides of their husbands in order to meet their healthy need to be loved.

Some researchers have found similarities between the psychological reactions of battered women and those of holocaust survivors. Russell (1982) sees similarities between the effects of battery and the effects of torture. Kuzwayo, a prominent South African social worker, was at one time herself a battered woman. She writes: 'My image of married life was far removed from the torture I was exposed to. I went through both physical and mental suffering' (Kuzwayo, 1985: 124). The discussion which follows explores the material similarities between wife abuse and torture. It lends Kuzwayo's description of her marriage as torture, a dimension of reality beyond its metaphorical usage.

The Stockholm Syndrome is a model that has been developed to account for the paradoxical psychological responses of hostages to their captors during and after hostage dramas (Dutton & Painter, 1981; Finkelhor & Yllö, 1985; and Hilberman, 1980, all cited by Graham *et al.*, 1988). The application of this model demonstrates that the psychological characteristics observed in battered women are the result, not the cause, of the woman's involvement in a violent relationship. It shows how extreme power imbalances between an abusive husband and battered wife can lead to strong emotional bonding (Graham *et al.*, 1988).

There are four pre-conditions for the Stockholm Syndrome to develop; which are also characteristic of violent relationships:

1. The aggressor threatens to kill the victim and/or is perceived as being capable of doing so.

2. The victim cannot escape, so his or her survival depends on the threatening person.

3. The victim is isolated from external perspectives and supports and the only perspective available to him or her is that of the threatening person.

4. The threatening person is perceived as showing some degree of kindness to the victim.

In addition, female hostages experience the pervasive threat or occurrence of sexual violence against them.

Violence and threat of violence produce extreme distress in victims. Their ego integration is threatened and they regress to earlier, less organized stages of ego development. In this state of psychological infantilism strong dependency needs are evoked. These needs are pathologically transferred onto the aggressor who is unlikely to respond constructively to the victim's needs. The predominant psychological defence that characterizes the Stockholm Syndrome is identification with the aggressor. This is born of the recognition that the aggressor has the power of life or death over her. Coupled with this first recognition is the perception that the aggressor has allowed her to live. She feels this to be an act of benevolence. She comes to view the aggressor as 'basically good'. This requires that she denies the life endangering dimensions of the aggressor's personality and behaviour. She internalizes the aggressor's viewpoint as being valid and denies her own perceptions of reality as well as the rage she feels towards the aggressor.

There are of course obvious differences between the two situations:

1. Marriage is an intimate relationship which is entered into voluntarily; hostage situations usually take place between strangers on an involuntary basis.

2. Battery poses threats to the victim's safety for much longer periods than the average hostage drama.

3. Public opinion is very much more sympathetic to hostage victims than to battered women, who are often blamed rather than supported.

4. Hostage survivors are freed by outside sources whilst battered women need to rely on their own, often depleted resources to escape from violent marriages. In many instances outside resources in fact fail battered wives.

Graham *et al.* (1988) emphasize that the traumatic bonding that occurs both amongst hostage victims and battered wives is first and foremost a survival strategy which may later develop into a maladaptive defence mechanism. In order to survive the victim must suppress her rage at the aggressor, she must avoid a direct and honest reaction to destructive behaviour or risk being punished further for her anger or wilfulness. She must of necessity become more attuned to her aggressor's needs than her own as it is the aggressor's will that prevails in the relationship. She learns to internalize a sense of inferiority, to believe in the aggressor's world view. The price that the victim pays for this pathological transference is that she entirely foregoes her own self-determination.

If the traumatic bonding persists, these psychological mechanisms serve to prevent a woman from ever leaving the batterer. The battered woman may internalize the experience of battery so effectively that her potential to enter into healthier, non-destructive relationships may be impaired. She may use alcohol, illegal drugs, or prescribed medications to help her to cope with the experience of abuse. Dependence on substances may occur as a secondary problem. Another response amongst abused women is to use retaliatory violence. In some instances battered women resort to suicide.

Effects on the children

Violence within the family has negative effects on children. Research on intra-familial violence reveals striking correlations between spousal abuse and various forms of violence involving children. Although a batterer may beat only his wife and not his children, and although one or both parents may attempt to shield the children from the violence, children who witness inter-parental abuse suffer from the exposure to the violence (Goodman & Rosenberg, cited in Sonkin, 1987). Child witnesses to inter-parental conflict — even if not directly assaulted themselves — have an increased risk of developing behavioural and emotional problems. These may include, *inter alia*, depression, anxiety, the presence of fears and phobias, insomnia, and enuresis, as well as acting-out behaviour such as stealing, truancy, temper tantrums, and aggression. In addition to the trauma of witnessing spousal abuse, children may themselves become victims of assaults, either directly or indirectly. Children often try to protect the victimized parent and when they do, their risk of physical injury increases substantially (Barnett *et al.*, 1980, cited by Goodman & Rosenberg in Sonkin, 1987). They may also become targets of either parent's displaced anger, frustration, and helplessness. With the feelings engendered as a result of the violence inflicted upon her, the mother as traditional caretaker may lose her effectiveness in taking care of her children (Geller, 1982). Consequently, the children may be neglected. Bowker *et al.* (1988), however, report that children whose mothers had been battered were more likely to be physically abused and less likely to be 'neglected' than children whose mothers had not been battered.

The relationship between wife battery and child abuse is an area receiving increasing attention. There is evidence indicating that child abuse is correlated with the battering of women. In families where the wife is battered by the husband, there is often child abuse as well (Straus, 1978; Gelles, 1980, both cited in Bowker *et al.*, 1988). Stark and Flitcraft (1985) report that children whose mothers are abused are more than twice as likely to be physically abused than children whose mothers are not battered. Bowker *et al.*, (1988) support this by saying that children of battered wives are very likely to be battered by their fathers. On the basis of their research, these authors suggest that professionals working with battered wives and battering husbands should assume that child abuse will accompany wife abuse in approximately 70 per cent of the families in which children are present. They suggest that the link between wife battery and child abuse may be related to the power inequity between husband and wife as well as that between parents and children.

The literature suggests, however, that children of battered wives are more often beaten by their fathers than by their mothers, and that the father is the typical abuser of the child if the mother is battered (Bowker *et al.*, 1988; Stark & Flitcraft, 1985).

Further to this, Bowker *et al.* (1988) demonstrate that the more severe the wife abuse and the higher the degree of husband dominance in a violent marriage, the more severe the child abuse. Another finding, although not as strongly substantiated by their empirical data, was that the more extensive the father's experiences with violence in his family of origin, the more likely he is to move from wife abuse to child abuse. This raises the issue of 'inter-generational violence'. According to Straus (1983, cited by Bowker *et al.*, 1988) the idea that wife-beating husbands come from violent families is now widely accepted. Roy (1982) found that over 80 per cent of abusive partners have a positive history of childhood abuse or have witnessed abuse against their own mothers. While batterers frequently come from violent homes, battered women typically do not (Walker, 1979; Roy, 1982). Stark and Flitcraft (1985), while refuting the idea of an inter-generational cycle of violence, still argue that there is a relationship between wife battery and child abuse. Their findings show that current abuse by a male intimate, not past experience, is the single most important cause and context of child abuse. They state that helping professionals would do well to look towards advocacy and protection of battered mothers as the best available means to prevent child abuse.

Effects on the extended family

The extended family also suffers the reverberations of partner abuse. The extended family members are progressively alienated as the abuse escalates. They may be alienated by the battered woman herself who withdraws from her family and friends in an attempt to placate the batterer or in an attempt to conceal the violence. Extended family members may also withdraw from the battered woman because of their feelings of helplessness, frustration, and confusion and/or because of the batterer's threats, or acts of violence towards them. Cause and effect are difficult to distinguish here. Nonetheless, since the battered woman is isolated and without an adequate social support system, the vulnerability to attack is substantially increased.

INTERVENTION

The cause of violence in intimate relationships and in the home is complex, and is determined by the interaction of the multiple factors discussed above. Intervention strategies need to be comprehensive in terms of the scope, context, and dynamics of the problem of wife abuse. The ideological, socio-political, and psychological factors involved need to be addressed.

Geller (1982) states that work with battered women and their abusers can have a battering effect on the worker. The field is difficult and demanding to work in. The pervasiveness of the problem and the multitude of needs of battered women can be overwhelming and workers may experience a sense of not even knowing where to begin. Further, the lack of resources and the gaps in service provision imply a high level of frustration for workers trying to intervene appropriately and effectively. The complexity of the dynamics of violent relationships and the well-organized system of psychological defences which maintain women in abusive relationships require an ability on the part of the worker to contain powerful, sometimes conflicting feelings and ambivalence, as well as the ability to make a commitment to a process of change. Workers have to confront their unresolved conflicts around violence and may be forced to challenge their own ideological assumptions.

Intervention in the area of wife abuse involves the provision of both material and psychological services that are systematically planned and co-ordinated. Furthermore, work in the field demands specialist knowledge and, under optimum conditions, specialized resources. In this section, a range of interventions at the primary, secondary, and tertiary levels are discussed. Empowerment and protection of people and the enhancement of the quality of human relations underlie intervention strategies at each level.

Primary intervention

Primary intervention strategies to eliminate the conditions that lead to the occurrence and maintenance of wife abuse need to be developed. Long-term preventative approaches to effect certain structural changes and changes in the attitudes and values of individuals, communities, and social institutions are essential.

Solutions to the problem of wife abuse require political restructuring. Not wishing to belabour the point, the authors believe that the dismantling of apartheid, direct interventions to combat poverty, unemployment, and the housing crisis, as well as the establishment of adequate health, welfare, and education systems are priorities in intervening in wife abuse. However, it is simplistic to argue that solutions to apartheid alone will eliminate the problem of wife abuse. Challenges to the ideologies and structures which engender and facilitate wife battery need to be instituted. The general level of violence in society at large must be reduced and child-rearing practices need to be reassessed. Sexism, the underbelly of violence against women, needs to be eliminated. The unequal distribution of power between men and women needs to be redressed at all levels: social, legal, psychological, and economic. In addition, sexist values, attitudes and practices, including sex role stereotyping, have to be abandoned. These long-term solutions would ensure that women are no longer subjugated and that violence against them is no longer sanctioned. In order for these ideals to be realized, there is a need for a strong feminist movement to take root in this country. The women's movement currently active in South Africa needs to take up the issues of gender oppression, including domestic violence against women, more vociferously. Gender issues are as important in shaping the future of South Africa as are issues of national liberation.

The establishment of an adequate welfare system is crucial in intervening in the problem of wife abuse at the primary level. Such a system involves a viable partnership between the state and the voluntary sector in providing services and material resources. The provision of social security benefits that are universally available is fundamental. Under conditions in which there is adequate welfare provision at all levels, people involved in abusive relationships are accorded alternatives that empower them. Kalmuss and Straus (1982) found that it is economic dependence rather than psychological dependence which keeps women in severely abusive marriages. Furthermore, Gondolf and Fisher (1988: 95) found that battered women are inclined to leave their batterers if they are provided with the resources to do so. The allocation of resources is crucial in enabling women to leave violent relationships.

At present in South Africa there is a fragmented, residual welfare system characterized by a lack of resources. The residual welfare system in this country poses frustrations and restrictions on all professionals and consumers of social services. Even where assistance is available, bureaucratic delays occur. Moreover, this assistance is given at a minimum level as well as being distributed according to race. Another problem is that even where services exist, they are poorly co-ordinated. The negotiation of this fragmented, residual welfare system in fact demands a level of ego strength which battered women often do not have.

Professional interventions in the area of wife abuse do not take place in a vacuum. Social workers in South Africa operate within the ideological context of apartheid, patriarchy, and the residual welfare system. Social welfare policies are rooted in these ideologies, and they entrench and perpetuate them. This has bearing upon the practices of social service organizations and individual social workers, and determines the material and therapeutic interventions offered by them.

The view of social workers as agents of social control is not new. The reader will be aware of the proposition that social workers act as agents of social control by reinforcing the status quo through their interventions and practices. It has been suggested that mental-health professionals may function as agents of social control by constructing explanatory frameworks biased against women, supporting social structures oppressive to women, and by defining stereotypically feminine traits, such as passivity and nurturing, as ideals of female mental health (APA Task Force, 1975, in Bograd, 1984). These formulations are applicable to the area of wife abuse. Traditional psychological theories of wife battery, based on the notions of women's masochism, have been criticized for being victim-blaming and being biased against women. In addition, social workers tend to abide by the ethic of preserving marriages. This may, in fact, be counterindicated in the case of wife abuse. The value placed on the preservation of marriages derives from a deeply ingrained set of functional and moral values. This reflects the attitudes of a culture that often sacrifices the woman to protect the man as well as the image of the family (Martin, 1976). Furthermore, social workers may perform a conservative function by ignoring the total context of wife battery and primarily defining the problem in terms of individual pathology. In this way, social workers tend to see wife abuse as an individual issue rather than as a broad social problem.

A study conducted in Johannesburg found a 'conspicuous lack of acknowledgement of socio-political factors in social workers' analyses of the causes of marital violence' (Segel, 1985: 23). Moreover, it can be argued that by not ensuring adequate and appropriate welfare provision and services for battered women, social workers are allowing wife abuse to continue and are sometimes offering therapeutic efforts as a substitute for a form of material provision that will enable women to leave violent relationships. In these ways, it can be contended that social workers tend to reinforce prevailing ideological assumptions and maintain existing structures which facilitate wife abuse.

The conscientization of mental-health professionals and the challenge of existing social policies governing practice are important tasks in primary intervention. Agency policies, intervention approaches, and therapeutic models need to be scrutinized for biases which perpetuate the very problems they attempt to solve.

Secondary intervention

Intervention at the secondary level promotes conditions which, through the creation of social censure and the creation of structures for empower-ment of women who are battered, prevent abuse from becoming chronic. Interventions at this level include early case finding and crisis intervention, as well as public education and the establishment of legal recourse and shelters.

Public education and information distribution are of central importance in advocating the rights of battered women. Consciousness-raising and public education can be productively used to effect fundamental changes in attitudes, values, and social policies. The issue of domestic violence against women needs to be raised and maintained in public consciousness. Community education efforts provide alternatives and challenge dominant views about wife battery. Community education also plays an important outreach function to victims of abuse. Schechter (1988: 72) writes of the effect of outreach on battered women as follows:

> They heard the messages: 'You don't deserve to be beaten; it's not your fault; you are beaten because society sanctions his behaviour, not because of anything you do wrong; evidence suggests that no matter how many times you change your behaviour to respond to his criticisms, you will probably be beaten again, through the years violence grows more severe', and they have reacted by reaching out for help.

The processes of public education, information distribution, and outreach may also facilitate the reporting of abuse and early case finding. In this way, the possibility of early detection and intervention is increased. Roberts (1981: 162) states that early intervention is important with all types of clients, but it is especially crucial in wife-beating cases where the woman's life is in jeopardy when the violence goes unchecked.

Community education has to be accompanied by institutional changes. Reform of the criminal justice system is of particular importance. Workers concerned with wife battery need to work with related professionals and client constituencies to lobby for a system of criminal justice and forceful authority that genuinely protects battered women. Such a system would, *inter alia*, create specific sanctions for wife abuse as a crime, provide adequate police protection for battered women, establish a family court to deal with cases of domestic violence, and develop appropriate sentencing options for offenders.

At present in South Africa, a woman wishing to seek legal remedy for wife battering has the following options available to her:

1. She may seek criminal sanction by laying a charge of assault against her husband. It is a difficult and drastic decision for a battered woman to lay a charge of assault against her husband. She is often terrified of the beating she will receive in retribution. Although the police are legally obliged to follow through on all assault charges, they are often unhelpful in cases of violence in the home. Women are not offered protection by law from severely abusive behaviour.

In addition, where prosecutions occur, the sentences meted out for assault are usually light and rarely exceed a minimal fine.

2.　A battered woman may seek a peace order restraining her husband from assaulting her. Section 341 of the Criminal Procedure Act 51 of 1977, which deals with the 'Compounding of other minor offences' provides for the issue of peace orders. Peace orders, obtained from the magistrate's court, are generally ineffective. If the order is breached, the offender is fined a mere R50,00. In many cases the breach of a peace order is not followed through at all. The peace order is not specific to the area of wife abuse; it covers a range of activities in which the peace is disturbed. An important feature of the peace order is that, although it is theoretically open to anyone, it is not easily obtained by women who have not separated from their husbands. Women involved in abusive relationships may be *de facto* excluded from the minimum protection that the peace order does afford.

3.　A Supreme Court interdict restraining abusive husbands may be obtained. This procedure is extremely costly and beyond the financial means of many women. It is, however, more effective that a peace order in so far as the police regard the breach of a Supreme Court interdict more seriously and are more likely to respond.

4.　Battered women can legally separate from or divorce their husbands. However, even when a woman divorces her husband, she may not be free from his attacks. Bowker (1983: 11, citing Carlson, 1977) comments that many divorced women are actively sought out by their ex-husbands for continued abuse.

Increasingly, as is demonstrated in the literature, police are being involved as an essential part of domestic violence programmes abroad. There is also a trend towards training police officers in crisis intervention (Martin, 1976).

The issue of police protection for battered women is a difficult one in the South African context. In many South African communities, the South African Police lack credibility as a consequence of the extreme brutality they have demonstrated as agents of apartheid. Many battered women and professionals advocating for their rights may feel that to include police involvement in battered women's programmes is to betray the trust of the community.

Experience in the field has highlighted the experiences of women reporting interpersonal violence to the police as being predominantly negative. Police in general seem to abide by a policy of non-interference in 'domestic disputes', regard this as an issue of low priority, and have been reported as unhelpful, unsympathetic, dismissive and uncoopera-tive. Sometimes, police may not respond at all to the requests of battered women.

The police are operational twenty-four hours a day and are the only organization empowered to remove a violent offender. In many cir-cumstances the police are the only recourse a battered woman has at her disposal to protect herself from violence perpetrated by her husband.

The police are well situated to play a potentially valuable role in dealing with domestic violence. With fundamental changes in orientation, at-titude, and procedure, and with appropriate education and training, the police may be able to intervene effectively when called upon to do so.

It is evident from the above discussion that the South African criminal justice system as it operates at present — especially with regard to battered women — is inadequate. It does not afford battered women sufficient legal protection and recourse. It also fails in the provision of criminal sanction of wife abuse as such. Abusive men are not made socially accountable for their behaviour, and wife abuse is tacitly legitimized and permitted or allowed to continue.

On the secondary level of intervention, there is an urgent need to create new services and to strengthen existing ones for battered women. The establishment of emergency refuges, shelters, and support services for battered women is of prime importance.

International experience shows that the provision of shelter to battered women is a cornerstone in intervening effectively in the area of marital violence. By offering the battered woman accommodation in a suppor-tive environment removed from the immediate danger of further violence against her, one is offering her the opportunity to assess realistically her position in the relationship, to begin to break free from the traumatic bonding with the partner, and to decide on a future direction for her life. The refuge also provides an opportunity for the battered woman to restore her depleted resources and to overcome her severe isolation. Schechter (1982: 299) writes: 'Any theory of violence against women which fails to account for the extraordinary personal transformation that occurs in shelters would distort the truth about battered women.'

There are at present only two shelters specifically for battered women in South Africa. People Opposing Woman Abuse (POWA) runs a shelter in Johannesburg which accommodates up to seven women and their children. The other shelter is run by Cape Town Rape Crisis, and has space for ten to twelve women and their children. Both are non-emergency shelters which provide women with accommodation for up to three months, once they have decided to leave violent relationships.

Significantly, both shelters are run by non-professional organizations. POWA and Cape Town Rape Crisis are voluntary democratic organizations which align themselves with the broad progressive movement in this country. Both organizations have resisted professionalization and are guided by a feminist perspective on the question of wife abuse. Also, they are non-racial in approach and action. As a result, they are unfortunately regarded with some scepticism by mainstream professional organizations. Despite the antagonism they experience, it must be acknowledged that they have taken initiative where professional organizations in general have not. They have begun to establish resources and networks for battered women which are arguably the most appropriate available in South Africa at present. In addition to providing direct services, they run public education and training programmes on the issues of violence against women.

The chronic lack of emergency refuges and shelters in this country is a severe stumbling block for effective intervention. The need for shelter is far in excess of the opportunities available for it. Needless to say, the existing shelters are unable to accommodate all who seek refuge. The situation reflects the social blindness to the problems of wife abuse and represents a reluctance on the part of welfare authorities to recognize the scope, severity, and nature of the problem.

Tertiary intervention

Tertiary intervention aims to assist those whose lives have been affected by violence. The goal of services at this level is the provision of a comprehensive treatment approach to battered women and to batterers in order to prevent further abuse.

The therapies reported to be most successful in intervening at this level are crisis intervention, individual psychotherapy, group therapy, and, in a limited number of cases, marital therapy. Regardless of treatment modality employed or the response orientation of the worker, an appropriate therapeutic response is based on the knowledge that violence has discernible and pervasive effects on battered women, and that violence exerts a threatening and organizing influence on relationships. It involves addressing the issue of violence directly as a primary treatment issue, understanding the specific dynamics of violent relationships, appreciating that these relationships are characterized by often brutal violence, and placing priority on ensuring the safety of the wife/victim.

Traditional generic social work approaches do not adequately address the issue of violence in relationships. Practitioners frequently see domestic violence as a peripheral part of their work, and in some instances do not define it is a problem at all. Johnson (1985: 115) notes the marked inclination of social workers to re-define the problem of marital violence. The assumption often made is that by addressing the 'real' issues, such as fear of intimacy or poor communication, wife battery — the symptom of underlying dysfunction — will disappear. Practitioners may overcontextualize violence in relationships by regarding violence as one of the many problems characterizing a marriage, alongside those of substance abuse, multiple losses, or unemployment (Bograd, 1984). On the other hand, practitioners may decontextualize violence and fail to understand the processes, forms, and function of violence or to consider the relationship between the client, the family, and the broader social and political environment.

The tendency of practitioners not to address the violence at all, or only indirectly, serves to trivialize the problem, leaving unchallenged the legitimacy of male violence as a means of controlling women (Johnson, 1985), and unwittingly minimizing the emotional and physical threats to the battered woman (Bograd, 1984).

Another problem in working therapeutically with battered women is that practitioners may not fully understand the dynamics of violent relationships or the effects of violence. Continued exposure to violence has cumulative and devastating effects on battered women, and produces specific characteristics in them. These, already discussed, include the effects of trauma and the use of self-destructive coping responses. Professionals frequently fail to distinguish the symptoms of victims of violence from the symptoms of the sufferers of mental illness, or to understand their interplay (Rosewater, 1988). Professionals commonly err by misdiagnosing responses of battered women. Such responses are created by repeated experiences of violence, and may appear to be psychiatric symptoms. Alternatively, professionals diagnose the woman as having a character disorder, which is seen as a predisposition for the violence that occurs.

Therapeutic interventions based on the assumption that the pathology is primarily located in the battered woman, or the notion that she is somehow responsible for the violence directed against her, have been challenged and criticized for being victim-blaming. The issue of violence is ignored, its sequelae are not considered, and the woman herself is labelled the problem and only she is treated. Frequently, battered women are viewed as being neurotic, provocative, or masochistic or are diagnosed as 'dependent', 'passive aggressive', 'paranoid', 'hysteric', or 'borderline' (Walker, cited in Moore, 1979). Psychiatric labels, incorrectly applied to victims of violence, have the effect of further victimizing them (Rosewater, 1988).

It is not uncommon for battered women to incorporate the blame and to accept responsibility for causing the violence directed at them (Symonds, 1974, cited in Geller, 1982). A battered woman may rational-ize that perhaps she did deserve the abuse, she may deny her own anger at being hurt, she may trivialize the event, or even accept her husband's abusiveness as legitimately directed at her. When a practitioner focuses only on the battered woman's behaviour, he/she colludes with her, denies the reality and inevitability of the situation, and implies that she can control the batterer's actions and responses. On the contrary, what the battered woman needs to acknowledge, and may need help in acknowledging, is that her husband's behaviour is not something she can control.

Douglas (1987) states that it is essential that the battered woman reject personal responsibility for the violence. As long as she assumes respon-sibility for it, or even the anger that preceded it, she may continue to look to herself for the solution to the batterer's violence. Helping the battered woman deal with her sense of responsibility in 'causing' the violence directed against her requires sensitivity to her confusion and inadequate self-esteem (Elbow, 1977). Although the relinquishment of responsibility for the violence may bring a sense of relief and a liberation from the guilt she experiences, it is also potentially very painful for the battered woman in that she is forced to deal with her helplessness and to confront many of the losses already described. Acknowledging the loss of a significant emotional relationship and allowing a battered woman to mourn that loss is important in the letting-go process (Graham *et al.*, 1988).

Dutton and Painter (1981, cited by Graham *et al.*, 1988) report that the loss of the relationship produces distress in battered women which pulls them back into the relationship. Certainly, battered women frequently leave and return to violent relationships. Walker (1979) points out that this back-and-forth movement may occur three to five times before a woman is able to detach herself from the relationship permanently. Elbow (1977) writes that if there has been a history of leaving and returning, it is helpful to identify this pattern and acknowledge the woman's ambivalence and her difficulty in giving up hope for change.

Douglas (1987) writes that the decision to stay or leave the relationship is one for the battered woman to make. A means of helping a battered woman gain a sense of mastery over her life is to help her realize that remaining in the relationship is an option (Elbow, 1977). Elbow states that this is not to say that, is she chooses to stay, she is masochistic or likes being abused, but that she has made a decision and has assessed the advantages of staying or leaving, at least for the time being.

If a battered woman stays in or returns to an abusive relationship, it is important to explore the possibilities for avoiding further abuse and the ways in which she can ensure her safety. Douglas (in Sonkin, 1987) writes that in accepting responsibility for her safety, the battered woman begins to define her situation as one over which she has control. Practitioners must be careful not to imply that the battered woman is to blame for the violence (Elbow, 1977).

Effectiveness and comprehensive intervention with battered women may involve a long-term process. Therapeutic objectives in this context may include: individuation from the symbiotic bond that exists between the battered woman and the batterer, integration of negative and positive aspects of the batterer, overcoming isolation, understanding the dynamics of the violent relationship and the coping responses employed, reducing the traumatic effects of victimization, mastering feelings of terror to prevent intrusive ideation which is characteristic of post-traumatic stress syndrome, getting in touch with anger and rage, and establishing nurturing non-abusive relationships with others.

Professionals need to respect the battered woman's right to self-determination. Just as it is potentially damaging and dangerous for the practitioner to ignore, redefine, or indirectly address the problem of violence in relationships, it may be damaging and dangerous to attempt to rescue a battered woman and prematurely plan her escape. The timing and accessibility of services are critical (Ball, 1977) and professionals need to be aware of indicators of the battered woman's readiness to leave (Elbow, 1977). Douglas (1987: 52) writes:

> Efforts by the victim toward removing herself from the abusive situation are frequently aborted far short of completion ... It is at this point that all too many professionals abandon the battered woman without a continued commitment to her struggle. The challenge for the professional is to recognise the battered woman's progress toward a safer environment in however small steps she takes.

Relatively recent family systems theories have emerged as an alternative framework within which to understand violent marital relationships. Marital therapy and family therapy have been the treatment modalities which have developed on this basis. Although these theories and practices reflect important changes in clinical attitudes towards wife battering and reflect an attempt to broaden the therapeutic focus, they are not without their problems (Bograd, 1984).

The very structure of conjoint therapy takes the focus off the batterer and suggests that his battering is a problem of the couple. Further in the therapeutic context of marital therapy, the battered woman may not be able to explore her ambivalence or to obtain skills to lead her to economic and psychological self-sufficiency (Bograd, 1984). In addition, marital therapy may have a conservative function by employing interventions that support a return to traditional gender-based roles or by not addressing the greater power inequality of the marriage.

Another problem is that marital counselling is used indiscriminately. Segel (1985: 26) reports that the consistently preferred form of intervention in cases of marital violence is, for the overwhelming majority of practitioners, marital therapy. Yet, there is evidence to suggest that traditional marriage counselling techniques are not effective with battered women and abusive men (Walker, 1981; Watts & Courtois, 1981, both cited in Bograd 1984: 566). Further, it has been stated that the best treatment alternative for the battered woman is to leave the battering relationship (Martin, 1976).

Martin (1976: 47) asserts that if reconciliation is regarded as the only solution or goal, wife beating will only be perpetuated. Bograd (1984: 566) supports this by stating that 'conjoint therapy may compromise the goal of ending wife battering by virtue of its emphasis on strengthening the existing relationship'. It is reported that marital therapy is only successful in a limited number of cases (Walker 1979: 231). Bograd (1984: 566) writes that the therapist, in dealing with abusive men and battered women and specifically in prescribing 'structured separation', must 'feel comfortable with the possibility that the couple will not reunite'. Walker (1979: 230) goes so far as to say that 'in working with battered women, psychotherapists must encourage breaking the family apart'.

Thinking systemically does not preclude the position that the husband is solely accountable for the battery incident (Bograd, 1984; Cook & Frantz-Cook, cited in Bograd, 1984; Geller, 1982). Nor does thinking systemically about a couple mandate working with the spouses together (Bograd, 1984: 563).

In the opinion of Walker (1979: 231), marital therapy should only be used in cases where both parties insist on keeping the relationship together, or more importantly, if 'a battered woman chooses to remain in the marriage' (Geller, 1982: 201) and then 'only after the batterer has learnt to avoid violent behaviour' (Martin, 1976: 258). Conjoint therapy should not be started and cannot continue if the husband is actively violent (Coleman, 1980; Cook & Frantz-Cook, 1984; and Walker, 1978, all cited in Bograd, 1984).

It has been reported that marital therapy will not eliminate violence. At best it will reduce the incidence of violence (Martin, 1976). When the reduction of violence, and not its total absence, is regarded as the criterion of successful treatment, therapists are implying that physical force is tolerable within certain limits and are unwittingly sanctioning violence between spouses as normal and inevitable (Bograd, 1984). The primary treatment goal of clinical interventions with battered women and abusive men should be the complete cessation of violence (Coleman, 1980; Cooke & Frantz-Cook, 1984; Koval *et al.,* 1982; Watts & Courtois, 1981, all cited in Bograd, 1984).

To stop the battering requires the treatment not of the victim, nor of the relationship, but of the perpetrator. Indeed, there has been a definite trend abroad which has involved a shift in the focus of treatment away from the wife/victim, to the offender. This is evidenced by the proliferation of treatment programmes and intervention strategies for batterers in the United States over the last five years. Although as yet little attention has been devoted to testing the effectiveness of such services, their emergence is important and reflects a most significant shift in the orientation of practitioners (Edelson *et al.,* 1985).

Several authors note the need for specialized services for batterers. The services, provided by programmes for abusive partners, aim to eliminate violence in the home. In the opinion of Roberts (1981) the goal for most services is not only to stop or prevent wife abuse at a particular moment, but to provide education and treatment which has the potential to change the assailant's violent and destructive behaviour. He maintains that in general, existing programmes focus on teaching batterers anger control techniques, behavioural approaches to stress management, and alternative communication skills. The objectives of these programmes are to help the individual to understand the dynamics of his out-of-control behaviour and to take responsibility for his actions. It seems that most programmes for batterers use a combination of behavioural insight orientated and feminist approaches. Techniques include assertiveness training (Sonkin, 1987; Saunders, 1984), systematic desensitization, cognitive restructuring and progressive relaxation, exploring the roots of aggression (Saunders, 1984), and understanding the relationship between violence and sex role behaviour (Sonkin *et al.,* 1985).

Adams (1988: 176–99) identifies several approaches to working with abusive men — including the insight development, ventilation, interaction, and cognitive behavioural models. Adams emphasizes how each model's primary techniques and methodology reflect different assumptions about and explanations for the battering of women. By further applying a feminist analysis to each model, he shows how some of these approaches collude with batterers by using techniques that do not adequately address the violence or by adopting modalities that compromise the man's responsibility for change. He goes on to describe a pro-feminist model of treatment for batterers. In his model, power and control are seen to be fundamental issues, and therapeutic interventions directly challenge the abusive man's attempts to control his partner through the use of physical force, verbal and nonverbal intimidation, and psychological abuse. Though the pro-feminist model, like the psycho-educational model, recognizes the need to provide basic education to batterers about caretaking and communication skills, and because of the reported tendency for abusive men to replace physical violence with more subtle forms of abuse, the pro-feminist model sees it as just as essential to challenge the sexist expectations and controlling behaviours that often inhibit men's motivation to learn and apply such skills consistently in an uncontrolling manner (Adams, 1988). While the focus of early treatment here is on the identification and elimination of violent and controlling behaviour, later interventions focus on sexist expectations and attitudes.

Adams (1988: 192) reports that many pro-feminist batterers' programmes provide counselling groups for men in which initial interventions are devoted primarily to the protection of the battered women. Men are expected to make 'safety plans' that minimize the possibility of continued violence (Norberg, 1986, cited by Adams 1988). Safety plans include respecting the woman's fears and state limits about the relationship, fully complying with restraining orders, eliminating drug or alcohol use if it has accompanied violent behaviour, and ceasing any pressure or intimidation tactics intended to change his partner's plans or to deny her contact with others. Beyond safety planning, early interventions also include confronting the many ways that men attempt to deny or share responsibility for their violence,. These include minimizing the violence, projecting blame onto partners, claiming loss of control, blaming alcohol or drugs, or citing internal or external stress as causes of violence (Adams & Penn, 1981, cited in Adams, 1988).

The broadening of therapeutic focus to the treatment of batterers is not reflected in general social work and clinical practice in South Africa. To the author's knowledge there are no specialized services for batterers in South Africa. In addition to the pressing need to provide refuge, resources, information and appropriate counselling/therapy for battered women, there is an equally pressing and important need to establish and implement complimentary services for the men who are battering. Services for battered women and batterers should coexist and operate simultaneously. A total approach that provides assistance to the batterers and the victims can only lead to a marked reduction in the incidence of violence (Roy, 1982).

CONCLUSION

The authors have argued strongly that battery of women should be understood in relation to the broad ideological, social, and political context in which it occurs. It is this context which determines the dynamics of the battery relationship, the direction in which the violence flows and the response from the community and state to battery and all forms of violence against women. It is been postulated that intervention strategies need to address the issue of women abuse at the broad ideological, social, and political level as well as at the micro level of individual relationships or intra-psychic issues. Without addressing the ideological and social context which engenders and facilitates abusive attitudes and behaviour towards women, it is impossible to truly redress the wrongs suffered by women in the domestic setting. Similarly, the process of addressing the violence directed against women in the home is a key element in the elimination of sexism in the broader society. At the core of intervention in the field of wife abuse is the empowerment of women and the key element at all levels of intervention, namely primary, secondary, and tertiary, is the redressing of unequal distributions of power which facilitate battery.

Intervention strategies and responses to wife abuse are directly determined by theoretical formulations and causal assumptions of the problem. Social workers in South Africa tend to favour an individualist approach to wife abuse. Aside from initiatives by individual social workers and women's organizations, the general thrust has been to view wife abuse as a problem of individual pathology, which has resulted in an inadequate and ineffective response to wife battery.

This field is particularly under-theorized and poorly resourced in this country. There is no systematic, clearly formulated policy for the establishment of resources and services at either a local or national level. Responses to the problem of wife battery are fragmentary and under-developed at this stage. This criticism applies to most welfare services in this country. However, in the authors' belief, part of the lack of attention and the inadequate resources in the field of wife abuse stems from the inherent sexism in the welfare structure. The choice between generic and specific welfare services in a basically Third World country which is characterized by overwhelming welfare needs is not a simple one. However, the field of wife abuse is specific and demands specialized knowledge and resources.

The challenge to social workers and other mental-health workers in South Africa is to develop and sustain a comprehensive and co-ordinated response to the issue of wife battery and violence against women. Such a response will, through the provision of adequate material, legal, and psychological services, address the conditions which engender battery, promote and guarantee the rights and welfare of women in the social economic and legal spheres, and work towards the empowerment of women who have been battered. Such a comprehensive response regards women abuse as a social problem rather than as an issue of individual pathology. As such, interventions need to move beyond the confines of individual treatment. There is therefore a need to use methods other than casework in intervening in wife abuse. Groupwork as a method has proved particularly effective in treating batterers and mobilizing battered women. There is scope for community work at the levels of policy formulation, the development of resources, and the establishment of support networks for battered wives. As indicated in the body of the text, there is a growing initiative among individual social workers and various women's organizations to address the area of wife abuse, perhaps indicating a rudimentary beginning of a battered woman's movement in this country.

The field of wife abuse is notoriously difficult and demanding of workers who report rapid burn-out and a feeling of being battered themselves. The workers' experiences of immobilization, hopelessness, and frustration parallel the experiences of battered women. A broad focus on the issue of wife abuse may diminish feelings of powerlessness by allowing workers scope for creativity. By viewing the problem of wife abuse broadly, workers are provided with many sites of entry into the field with new possibilities for multiple forms of intervention. By bearing in mind the broad aim of empowering battered women, helpless workers become able to recognize strengths in the women they work with and to acknowledge these women's very survival of battery as success.

NOTES

1. Violence towards husbands or 'husband abuse' remains a controversial area in the study of domestic violence. Literature on the topic of husband

abuse is rather sparse. Gelles (1985: 80) states that 'there has been considerable rhetoric on the topic, but, unfortunately precious little scientific data'. Many of the findings and conclusions of research into husband abuse are contradictory and inconsistent. It is apparent from the information available (and from clinical impression) that the incidence, frequency, and severity of husband abuse is nowhere near the magnitude of the problem of wife abuse. Pagelow (1984: 272) reports that 'almost all writers who discuss the question of wife abuse versus husband abuse come to the conclusion that the proportions of male victims are minuscule compared to female victims'.

However, it is no doubt true that a percentage of men are battered by their wives and that many women are violent and can create an environment of real fear and danger for their husbands. As such, workers should be aware of the issue of husband abuse, of resources available, and intervention strategies for dealing with the problem.

A primary concern in this area is that husband abuse may be less visible than wife abuse as it is less likely to take the form of physical violence. For the most part the average man's superior size, weight, and muscular strength mitigates against his becoming a helpless victim of physical abuse. Research has demonstrated that when women do use physical violence against their spouses or cohabitants, it is primarily in self-defence or retaliation; often during an attack by their husbands.

Although there is no doubt that women do become physically violent towards their husbands, it is extraordinarily rare for women to persistently initiate severe attacks. Saunders (1988) argues that to label self-defence as 'husband abuse' serves to direct attention away from the victimization of women and the function of male dominance. From the above argument it can be concluded that few men experience direct physical abuse at the hands of their spouses. However, there is little research into the multiple forms of emotional abuse that men may suffer.

Interestingly, the available literature suggests that male victims' experience of domestic violence is qualitively different from the experience of abused women. Adler (1981, in Pagelow 1985: 274) reports that while wives tend to take their husbands' or their own violence seriously, many of the husbands saw their wives' violence as ineffective and/or non-threatening. Deschner *et al.* (1986: 49) write that 'men victims do not show the terrible fear that so characterizes women victims'. They argue that there are not the same social and economic forces that trap men in violent relationships. Men are freer than their female counterparts to leave a violent relationship: 'Even though the men are receiving injuries, they seem to know they can be the ultimate winners any time they choose. Therefore, not they, but their violent wives, walk about with terror as a daily companion, just like their sisters who receive instead of inflict injuries' (Deschner *et al.*, 1986: 49).

In general, men are not physically or economically as trapped in violent relationships as are women. Unlike their female counterparts, most men do not have primary responsibility for children and are as such not restrained by concerns for the children. Most importantly, society does not sanction women's violence against their husbands and as such men are freed to experience and express outrage at the abuse they suffer.

Ironically, the very factors mentioned above may in themselves prove problematic for abused men. Emotional abuse is more difficult to identify than physical abuse. Men may feel ashamed or foolish because their status as victim in the relationship does not conform to expected societal norms of masculinity. This makes reaching out for help more difficult and the abuse may remain hidden.

2.   Many friends participated in the production of this chapter. Our thanks to those who read and commented on it. Special gratitude to Phillipa Kruger for the information on the legal issues pertaining to wife abuse, and to Michelle Aarons, whose editorial expertise, combined with her skills and knowledge in the area of wife abuse, was of invaluable assistance.

REFERENCES

Adams, D. (1988) 'Treatment Models of Men who Batter: A Profeminist Analysis'. In *Feminist Perspectives on Wife Abuse*, edited by K. Yllö & M. Bograd, Newbury Park: Sage Publications, Inc.

Aguirre, B. E. (1985) 'Why Do They Return? Abused Wives in Shelters', *Social Work*, 30(4), 350–4.

Ball, M. (1977) 'Issues of Violence in Family Casework', *Social Casework*, 58, 3–12.

Barrett, M. & McIntosh, M. (1982) *The Anti-social Family*, London: Verso.

Barry, K. (1985) 'Social Etiology of Crimes Against Women,' *Victimology: An International Journal,* 10(1–4), 164–73.

Binney, V. (1981) 'Domestic Violence: Battered Women in Britain in the 1970's'. In *Women in Society Interdisciplinary Essays,* The Cambridge Women's Studies Group, London: Virago Press.

Bograd, M. (1984) 'Family Systems Approaches to Wife Battering: A Feminist Critique', *American Journal of Orthopsychiatry*, 54(4), 558–68.

Bowker, L. H. (1983) *Beating Wife-Beating*, Toronto: Lexington Books.

Bowker, L. H. *et al.* (1988) 'On the Relationship between Wife Beating and Child Abuse'. In *Feminist Perspectives on Wife Abuse*, edited by K. Yllö & M. Bograd, Newbury Press: Sage Publications, Inc., 11–26.

Bowlby, J. (1984) 'Violence in the Family as a Disorder of the Attachment and Caregiving Systems', *The American Journal of Psychoanalysis,* 44(1), 9–27.

Brownmiller, S. (1973) *Against Our Will: Men, Women and Rape*, Harmondsworth: Penguin Books.

Burman, S. & Reynolds, P. (1986) *Growing Up in a Divided Society: The Contexts of Childhood in South Africa*, Johannesburg: Ravan Press.

Cannon, J. B. & Sparks, J. S. (1989) 'Shelters — An Alternative to Violence: A Psychological Case Study,' *Journal of Community Psychology*, 17, 203–13.

Caplan, P. J. (1985) *The Myth of Women's Masochism*, Great Britain: Methuen.

Carew-Jones, M. & Watson, H. (1985) *Making the Break,* Harmondsworth: Penguin Books.

Carlson, B. E. (1984) 'Causes and Maintenance of Domestic Violence: An Ecological Analysis,' *Social Service Review*, 58(4), 569–87.

Compton. W. C. *et al.* (1989) 'Intentions for Postshelter Living in Battered Women', *Journal of Community Psychology*, 17, 126–8.

Denzin, N. K. (1984) 'Towards a Phenomenology of Domestic, Family Violence,' *American Journal of Sociology*, 90(3), 483–510.

Deschner, J. P. *et al.* (1986) ' A Treatment Model for Batterers,' *Social Casework*, 67(55), 55–60.

Donzelot, J. (1979) *The Policing of Families*, London: Tavistock Publications.

Douglas, M. A. (1987) 'The Battered Women Syndrome'. In *Domestic Violence on Trial: Psychological and Legal Dimensions of Family Violence*, edited by D. Sonkin, New York: Springer Publishing Company, 39–54.

Edleson, J. L. *et al.* (1985) 'Group Treatment for Men who Batter', *Social Work Research and Abstracts*, 21, 18–21.

Elbow, M. (1977) 'Theoretical Considerations of Violent Marriages' *Social Casework*, 58, 515–26.

Finkelhor, D. *et al.* (1983) *The Dark Side of Families: Current Family Violence Research*, Beverly Hills: Sage Publications, Inc.

Flynn, J. P. (1977) 'Recent Findings Related to Wife Abuse' *Social Casework*, 58(10), 12–20.

Geller, J. (1982) 'Conjoint Therapy: Staff Training and Treatment of the Abuser and the Abused'. In *The Abusive Partner. An Analysis of Domestic Battering*, edited by M. Roy, New York: Van Nostrand Reinhold Company.

Gelles, R. J. & Cornell, C. P. (1985) *Intimate Violence in Families*, Family Studies Text Series, Beverly Hills: Sage Publications, Inc.

Giles-Sims, J. (1983) *Wife Battering: A Systems Theory Approach*, New York: The Guilford Press.

Gondolf, E. W. (1985) 'Anger and Oppression in Men who Batter: Empiricist and Feminist Perspectives and their Implications for Research', *Victimology: An International Journal,* 10(1–4), 311–24.

Gondolf, E. W. & Fisher, E. R. (1988) *Battered Women as Survivors*, Massachusetts: Lexington Books.

Goodman G. & Rosenberg, M. (1987) 'The Child Witness to Family Violence: Clinical and Legal Considerations'. In *Domestic Violence on Trial: Psychological and Legal Dimensions of Family Violence*, edited by D. Sonkin, New York: Springer Publishing Company.

Gottlieb, N. (ed.) (1980) *Alternative Social Services for Women*, New York: Columbia University Press.

Graham, D. L. R. *et al.* (1988) 'Survivors of Terror: Battered Women, Hostages and the Stockholm Syndrome'. In *Feminist Perspectives on Wife Abuse*, edited by K. Ylló & M. Bograd, Newbury Park: Sage Publications, Inc.

Hendricks-Matthews, M. (1981) 'The Battered Woman: Is She Ready for Help?', *Social Casework*, 63(3), 131–7.

Johnson, N. (ed.) (1985) *Marital Violence*, London: Routledge & Kegan Paul.

Kalmuss, D. S. & Straus, M. A. (1982) 'Wife's Marital Dependency and Wife Abuse' *Journal of Marriage and the Family*, 44(2), 277–86.

Koslof, K. E. (1984) 'The Battered Woman: A Developmental Perspective', *Smith College Studies in Social Work*, 54(3), 181–203

Kuzwayo, E. (1985) *Call Me Woman*, Johannesburg: Ravan Press.

Lockhart, L. (1985) 'Methodological Issues in Comparative Racial Analyses: The Case of Wife Abuse,' *Social Work Research and Abstracts*, 21, 35–41.

Martin, D. (1976) *Battered Wives*, New York: Pocket Books.

Moore, D. (ed.) (1979) *Battered Women*, Beverly Hills: Sage Publications, Inc.

Pagelow, M. D. (1985) 'The Battered Husband Syndrome: Social Problem or Much Ado About Little?' In *Marital Violence*, edited by N. Johnson, London: Routledge & Kegan Paul.

Pagelow, M. D. (1984) *Family Violence*, New York: Praeger.

Pagelow, M. D. (1981) *Woman-Battering: Victims and their Experiences*, Beverly Hills: Sage Publications, Inc.

Pahl, J. (ed.) (1985) *Private Violence and Public Policy*, London: RK Publishers.

Pleck, E. (1979) 'Wife Beating in Nineteenth-Century America', *Victimology: An International Journal*, 4(1), 60–74.

Reynolds, P. (1989) *Childhood in Crossroads*, Cape Town: David Philip.

Roberts, A. R. (1981) *Sheltering Battered Women: A National Study and Service Guide*, New York: Springer Publishing Company.

Rosewater, L. B. (1988) 'Battered or Schizophrenic? Psychological Tests can't Tell'. In *Feminist Perspectives on Wife Abuse*, edited by K. Ylló & M. Bograd, Newbury Press: Sage Publications, Inc., 200–16.

Roy, M. (ed.) (1982) *The Abusive Partner: An Analysis of Domestic Battering*, New York: Van Nostrand Reinhold.

Russell, D. E. (1982) *Rape in Marriage*, New York: Collier Books.

Russell, G. W. (ed.) (1988) *Violence in Intimate Relationships*, New York: PMA Publishing Corp.

Saunders, D. G. (1988) 'Wife Abuse, Husband Abuse or Mutual Combat?', A Feminist Perspective on the Empirical Findings'. In *Feminist Perspectives on Wife Abuse*, edited by K. Ylló & M. Bograd, Newbury Park: Sage Publications, Inc.

Saunders, D. G. (1984) 'Helping Husbands who Batter', *Social Casework*, 65(6), 347–53.

Schechter, S. (1988) 'Building Bridges between Activists, Professionals and Researchers'. In *Feminist Perspectives on Wife Abuse*, edited by K. Yllö & M. Bograd, California: Sage Publications, Inc., 299–312.

Schechter, S. (1982) *Women and Male Violence: The Visions and Struggles of the Battered Women's Movement*, London: Pluto Press.

Segel, T. L. (1985) 'The Social Work View of Marital Violence', Honours dissertation, University of the Witwatersrand.

Sonkin, D. J. (ed.) (1987) *Domestic Violence on Trial: Psychological and Legal Dimensions of Family Violence*, New York: Springer Publishing Company.

Sonkin, D. J. *et al.* (1985) *The Male Batterer: A Treatment Approach*, New York: Springer Publishing Company.

Star, B. (1983) *Helping the Abuser: Intervening Effectively in Family Violence*, New York: Family Service Association of America.

Star, B. (1980) 'Patterns in Family Violence' *Social Casework*, 61(6), 339–46.

Stark, E. & Flitcraft, A. (1985) 'Women Battering, Child Abuse and Social Heredity: What is the Relationship? In *Marital Violence*, edited by N. Johnson. London: Routledge & Kegan Paul.

Steinmetz, S. K. (1977–8) 'The Battered Husband Syndrome', *Victimology*, 2(3–4), 499–509.

Symonds, M. (1984) 'Discussion of "Violence in the Family as a Disorder of the Attachment and Caregiving System"', *American Journal of Psychoanalysis*, 44(1), 29–31.

Symonds, M. (1975) 'Victims of Violence: Psychological Effects and Aftereffects', *American Journal of Psychoanalysis*, 35, 19–26.

Szechtman, S. (1985) 'Wife Abuse: Women's Duties — Men's Rights', *Victomology: An International Journal*, 10(1–4), 253–66.

Turner, S. & Shapiro, C. H. (1986) 'Battered Women: Mourning the Death of a Relationship', *Social Work*, 31(5), 372–6.

Truesdell, D. L. *et al.* (1986) 'Incidence of Wife Abuse in Incestuous Families,' *Social Work*, 31(2), 138–40.

Walker, L. E. (1983) 'Victomology and the Psychological Perspectives of Battered Women', *Victimology: An International Journal*, 8(1–2), 82–104.

Walker, L. E. (1979) *The Battered Woman*, New York: Harper & Row, Publishers, Inc.

Welch, G. J. (1987) 'Cognitive Behavioural Intervention for Spouse Abuse', *Social Work/Maatskaplike Werk*, 23(3), 154–9.

Wilson, E. (1983) *What is to be Done about Violence against Women? Crisis in the 80's*, Harmondsworth: Penguin Books.

Wilson, F. & Ramphele, M. (1989) *Uprooting Poverty: The South African Challenge*, Cape Town: David Philip.

Yllö, K. & Bograd, M. (1988) *Feminist Perspectives on Wife Abuse*, Newbury Park: Sage Publications, Inc.

10 Family violence: familicide

S. I. du Toit

A GROWING PHENOMENON?

Before 1980 familicide was a relatively unknown phenomenon in South Africa and elsewhere, as it still is in the rest of the world. Since then the incidence of familicide has gradually increased in this country. Until 1988, the Bureau for Statistics did not differentiate between familicide, suicide, and homicide. As a result, the incidence of familicide is uncertain for the preceding years, and the incidence of homicide and suicide is higher than usual because of the inclusion of familicide within these categories. With the figures for familicide available for 1988, a striking feature emerges, which is that while press reports for 1988 mention thirteen cases of familicide, the actual number proves to be forty. From this it is reasonable to conclude that the figure for the eighties could be higher than the figure deduced from press reports. This discrepancy gives rise to the possibility that familicide could occur even more frequently than suggested by the figures which have raised alarm over recent years.

DEFINING FAMILICIDE

The specific kind of familicide discussed in this chapter refers to circumstances in which the father or mother kills the rest of the family, and then commits suicide, or at least makes a serious attempt to do so. This type of familicide seldom occurs in the rest of the world. Violence in the form of wife or child battering does occur everywhere, perhaps even more frequently elsewhere than in South Africa. Such violence does develop into a family murder. In other parts of the world, most cases in which a family member murders the rest of the family can usually be attributed to a serious pathology or to escalating family violence. In contrast to this, a history of violence or pathology is usually absent in the specific brand of familicide found in South Africa.

DISTINCTIVE FEATURES OF FAMILICIDE

In addition to newspaper reports, a few articles written by psychiatrists, psychologists, social workers, and criminologists have revealed the following features of familicide:

1. Most familicides were committed by white South Africans. Interim statistics for 1988 mention twenty-seven white families, three 'coloured' families and twelve African families. Further details relating to these cases could not be ascertained. It appears from newspaper reports, however, that most of the whites were Afrikaans-speaking. It also appears that black people only commit familicide in the case of severe pathology, and/or as a result of mystic rituals. If this incidence of familicide among the white population, especially Afrikaans-speaking people, is compared with the incidence of homicide and suicide per 100 000 within the different races, it does not differ significantly (Erasmus, 1988).

2. The South African brand of familicide occurs very seldom in other Western countries. In an analysis completed by Erasmus (1988) it was found that the South African incidence of homicide and suicide per 100 000 of the population was comparable to that in other countries, while the peculiar form of familicide found in South Africa was virtually unknown elsewhere. Other causative factors, besides those usually associated with homicide or suicide, are identifiable in familicide. In the available literature on familicide the following explanations have been proposed:

    ☐ Uncontrollable aggression, unstable behaviour, and alcohol abuse (Shapiro, *The Star*, 17 November 1986).

    ☐ Uncontrollable jealousy, religious fanaticism, violent family relations, psychotic behaviour, poor sexual relations, and immaturity (Lang & Shepperd Smith, *Sunday Times*, 25 April 1982).

    ☐ Despair and emotional build-up concerning the loss of a loved one. Erasmus (1988) found the loss of a love-object to strongly prevail in most cases of familicide.

    ☐ The escalation of political unrest and violence in this country, which leads to desperation (Shapiro, *The Star*, 17 November 1986).

☐ The romanticizing of death by certain religious groups who seek solutions in the hereafter (Kruger, *Sarie Marais*, 22 May 1985).

☐ The political isolation and economic sanctions which create a feeling of helplessness and desperation (Schmidt, *Die Beeld*, 26 August 1987).

☐ An arrogance in which a parent takes his/her family with himself to the grave (De Klerk, 1986).

☐ Detected also was a lack of willingness to face life.

☐ A tendency to see the spouse and children as personal property, leading to a warped sense of responsibility (Luttig, 1985; Van Arkel, 1985; Pretorius, 1987).

☐ A major depression which was found to exist in individuals who survived after killing their families (Roos, 1988).

POSSIBLE CAUSATIVE FACTORS

The different features of familicide in South Africa cited above suggested four possible causative factors:

1. Familicide can be attributed to psychopathology, especially to depression.

2. A specific type or personality has emerged; that of the vulnerable, dependent individual who cannot bear a financial crisis or the loss of a love object.

3. A third line of thought seeks the explanation in the current violence in the South African society. This refers to structural violence and the resultant riots and atrocities, such as necklace executions and police intervention. The argument is that such violence overflows into brutalities such as family murders. In similar vein other writers suggest a connection between the political situation and familicide. Pressures from outside the country, such as sanctions, might precipitate desperate acts by individuals.

4. Other writers have postulated that facets of the Afrikaner 'national character', such as the supposed authoritarian approach in the patriarchal family and the tendency to expect more happiness in the hereafter, may predispose a father to assume the right to make fatal decisions for the whole family, and take them with him into eternity.

These proposed causative factors merit discussion:

☐ *That pathology, especially depression, also characteristic of suicide, results in familicide:* Against this assumption stands the fact that little pathology can be traced in the pre-traumatic histories of the perpetrators. Roos (1988) did find serious depression in the individuals who committed familicide and survived their own suicide attempts. However, the question remains as to what extent the depression was a result rather than a cause. Another unanswered question lies in why depression in these cases resulted in familicide, rather than suicide or some other form of self-directed violence. That depression could have played a role can be accepted, but why does depression run this course only in South Africa? Some other factors must play a role, even if depression has effected the course of the event.

☐ *That familicide presents as an overflow of the violence in the South African scene:* In this connection reference is often made to the incidence of homicide, suicide, and road accidents to confirm the violence in society, with familicide as yet another occurrence. This notion seems to be strengthened by the fact that familicide increased following the escalations of riots after 1980. However, while familicide has escalated over the past four years (since about 1986), rioting drastically decreased during the last few years of this decade.

Kleck (1987) made an extensive investigation into the theory that postulates connections between one form of violence and another. He compared all the available statistics on the incidence of homicide in the United States during the Second World War, the Korean War and the Vietnamese War, and found a decrease of homicide during the Second World War and the Korean involvement, but a slight increase during the Vietnamese War. He also found that the slight increase during the Vietnamese involvement could be attributed to factors not related to the war in Vietnam at all. He concluded that possibly it is only persons at high risk of doing violence, such as persons with a criminal record, who connect state and private violence.

In addition, it must be noted that official statistics do not bear out the claim of a high incidence of violent death in South Africa. Erasmus (1988) compared the incidence of homicide and suicide per 100 000 of the South African population from 1981 to 1985 to that in the United States and Canada. According to these statistics, South Africa ranks slightly lower than the United States and slightly higher than Canada. It must also be remembered that during those years incidence of familicide in South Africa was included in the calculations for the occurrence of homicide and suicide. It is apparent that evidence is lacking to support the hypothesis that the high intensity of political violence in South Africa has an overflow in these types of private violence.

In this connection it should also be borne in mind that the incidence of familicide in South Africa does not run parallel to escalating family violence. This is the first striking fact that arose from the investigation into familicide conducted by Erasmus (1988). An attempt to relate familicide to perceivable violence overlooks this important finding. Nevertheless, the fact remains that familicide portrays macabre violence. For this reason it is necessary to discuss the essential nature of violence, which will be done presently in this chapter.

☐ *That certain national characteristics of the white South African, especially the Afrikaans-speaking people, are responsible for this phenomenon:* This kind of assumption is illustrated by the following: 'Many Afrikaners feel discriminated against. Apprehensive, suspicious, inhibited. Quick to feel humiliated. Therefore self-centred and pitying themselves.' This is the profile of a potential family murderer (De Klerk, 1986: 68). However, this assumption is dubious.

Should, in the same vein, the recent soccer violence in England be attributed to the national characteristics of the English people, it would not only sound repulsive to many, but also unconvincing. Milgram (1974) started his well-known experiment with the hypothesis that German discipline and submission to authority led to the massacres of the Second World War. He did not move beyond the United States with his experiment because his hypothesis proved pertinent to America (Milgram, 1974). This underscored the adage that 'we are simply more human than otherwise'.

CHARACTERISTIC CIRCUMSTANCES IN FAMILICIDE

In the absence of well-documented psychological, social, or psychiatric case studies, the extensive newspaper coverage of family murders will be drawn on. Twenty-one cases of familicide in which the event and the circumstances were extensively described were selected from forty newspaper reports. These reports were supplemented by interviews with neighbours and next-of-kin. The observations outlined in the text that follows came to the fore.

The offender and his/her family

In ten of the cases, the offender was described by neighbours, friends and other family as quiet, agreeable, and apparently happily married. Although account must be taken of the tendency to speak well of deceased acquaintances, the ability of journalists to dig up everything sensational should at least have balanced out the description of the perpetrator.

In only two cases was evidence found to the effect that the husband sometimes ill-treated his wife. It is significant that in all these cases evidence of mutual attachment also came to the fore.

In one case the perpetrator had had a traumatic experience, in that both her legs had been amputated two years prior to committing the familicide.

One family had a child who was hard of hearing and unable to speak. The effect of this disability on the family could not be ascertained.

In three cases the parents were divorced before the event, and in two other cases marriage problems were mentioned.

In four cases evidence pointed to the possibility of depression.

It is notable that on the surface, no distinctive characteristics common to all these families were identifiable except that all were white South Africans, and that most of them were Afrikaans-speaking.

Factors which precipitated the deed

In three cases, preceding quarrels were reported, while in three others the perpetrators were unemployed and had financial problems.

In six cases, letters were left behind, or verbal reasons given as to why the deed was contemplated. The following reveals the nature of these communications:

'We love each other, all must go together.'
'It is for the better.'
'I want to save the children and take them with.'
'I am deeply concerned with my wife's suffering.'
In one case, love for his family was declared in the note left by a father.

Thus attachment and concern of some kind was expressed or suggested in statements prior to death.

It is difficult to arrive at anything conclusive from such meagre information. Even circumstantial evidence is unsatisfactory. Depression has been established in cases where the offender himself survived his own onslaught. The aggravating effect of the event, however, could well mar the clinical presentation. Only in one case was evidence of a disturbed personality found, although a formal diagnosis was not available. In only one case was previous treatment for depression mentioned.

In the majority of cases the offender and his family were described as amiable people with close family relationships.

The psychiatric, psychological, and environmental circumstances of twenty-one families could well represent the average family in an ordinary setting. For the messages left behind in writing or in previous communication very often pointed to attachment and agreeable relationships and an endeavour to do the best possible for the family members. Yet the fathers concerned were convinced that the eradication of the family would save it. They exercised a gruesome right to decide what would be good for their loved ones. This feeling of responsibility for the family seems to be the essential and characteristic feature of the South African family murderer. The offender wants to do the best for his/her family! That an exclamation mark should follow such a finding is appropriate in the face of such motivation and logic.

Familicide constitutes a seemingly senseless and macabre act. To find a noble motive in familicide asks for an excursion into the essence of aggression.

Aggression in the service of attachment

Kelly (1969), in an endeavour to describe the essence of aggression, related the myth of Prochrestos. This well-meaning innkeeper was always ready to go to any length to provide for the comfort of his guests. One of his specialities was to provide a bed of exact length for everyone. One night he was harassed by the thought that the bed he had allocated to a guest would be too short. His investigation confirmed his fear, and to rectify the 'terrible' mistake, he took his sword to shorten the length of the guest by chopping off his feet ... for his own benefit, in order for him to fit the bed. *This is violence with a noble motive— the other person must fit the bed.* A striking characteristic of such types of violence is that they are considered to be justifiable in the light of a good cause, very often the welfare of the victim. Thus, violence is rendered against the victim for his/her own good.

Motives behind the devastating religious wars, and for that matter behind every war, always propound lofty aspirations. The extent of such 'noble motives' in service of a 'good cause' makes frightening history. The number of lives sacrificed in the nine crusades in the twelfth and thirteenth centuries cannot be estimated. In the Thirty Years War, one third of the German population was annihilated for religious and other convictions. When Wallenstein revolted and went into a depression because of the senseless slaughter, he was killed and Tilley appointed in his place to continue the 'good fight'.

More than half a million Americans died in their Civil War in service of a cause — the emancipation of slaves. After that war, the president in office himself fell victim to violence. In the fifty years following the war more than 5 000 people were lynched, all in pursuit of the ideal of a pure white race on the one hand, and of human rights on the other hand (Toch, 1968).

Koestler (1967: 234) pointed out this characteristic of violence with noble insight:

> The crimes of violence committed for selfish personal motives are insignificant compared with those committed 'ad mojorem Dei' out of self-sacrificing devotion to a flag, a religious faith or political conviction.

In 1984 a group of students scrutinized reports on world events in available newspapers. They tried to establish the extent to which mortality could have been ascribed to action in service of 'good' motives such as law and order, human rights, or loyalty to religious beliefs. It happened to be a week wherein no significant combats took place in the war between Iran and Iraq nor other confrontations which could have loaded the findings. It was found that violence which could be ascribed to lower needs and drives, such as those attributable to the *id* of Freud, the *shadow* of Jung, the *learnt aggression* of Wertham, or those that could be explained in terms of the *territorial imperative* of Lorenz, or which could be classified as due to stimulation of the lateral hypothalamus or other organic disturbances, in other words everything categorized as 'disintegrating functions', constituted only 5 per cent of the causes of the death of victims in that week. (Du Toit, 1986).

The discussion thus far underscores the phenomenon of familicide as aggression in the service of attachment.

This thesis, worded in different terms, corresponds with the findings of Van Arkel (1985), Luttig (1985), Pretorius (1987), and De Klerk (1986). They found that the family murderer acts out a right of ownership of his/her family which results in an overdrawn, misplaced feeling of responsibility. This theme also creeps into letters left behind. More than once something was written to the effect that the family would be killed for their 'own good'. Freely translated, De Klerk (1988: 68) verbalizes it thus:

> The paternalism which leads the father or mother to decide that they are endowed with the authority to know what is good and

becoming … This godlike authority organizes, with absolute care, everyone's life … including the right to a familicide.

This perceived right to determine the lives and good of other people and the resulting overdrawn and warped sense of responsibility which is a factor in familicide, requires further consideration in the light of its significance in the history of South Africa.

A WARPED SENSE OF RESPONSIBILITY

The founders of South Africa did not massacre the indigenous population of the entire country in significant numbers, as was done in many other countries colonized by whites. It is postulated that they instead assumed guardianship over the local population. The essence of guardianship is to adopt the power to determine the conduct of those considered not yet to be of age. In accordance with the concept of guardianship, it was determined by whites where people of colour could live, the work they could do, and with whom they could have social connections. It is of course questionable whether the founders wanted to take the issue to these limits. Nevertheless, this tendency was affirmed under British rule due to the snobbishness of the English, who were reluctant to associate socially with uneducated people whom they considered to be inferior.

Subsequently in the early 1930s, a group of students who included Verwoerd, Diedericks, and Meyer, introduced the 'herrenvolk' idea from Germany. This input, together with the initial feeling of guardianship, cultivated a line of thought which culminated in the apartheid ideology. Guardianship preceded apartheid and directed its course. It was the assumed right of whites to determine the lives of other people — for everyone's good. Most white South Africans accepted this right to determine the life of people considered as 'not being of age' as natural, and even as the will of God.

Apartheid resulted in discrimination, whereby people in power decided the destiny of others. For those people for whom decisions are made, the practice is abhorrent, as expressed by a black home-help who posed the question: 'How can one nation "shift" another nation?' The serious issue in apartheid, which is the assumed right by those to determine the lives of others, is abhorrent.

It is, however, the further implication inherent in apartheid that takes the greater toll, namely the implication that guardianship creates responsibility. Whoever accepts guardianship inevitably takes on responsibility for the provision of facilities of every kind. It is interesting that Plato in his *Republic* proposed such an economic and civil situation, whereby the superior reigning class would control and provide for the well-being of everyone. Although brutalities have been committed through the ages, no government has ever before taken the risk to subject people to such control. It is realized that Nazism and communism approach such an extreme, but these ideologies are based on different philosophies.

The author ventures to suggest that authorities in the past shrank from that degree of control over the lives of people because of the all-encompassing responsibility it would create. South Africa was perhaps the first country to discard the wisdom of the ages by undertaking the right to determine the lives of other people with its consequent burden of responsibility. The exertion of extensive control over people, and the unmanageable responsibilities attached to this can lead to a feeling of hopelessness, an occurrence comparable with the situations reflected in the circumstances preceding familicide. The central feature of this preceding situation is that the parent, almost always the father, sees no future for his family because he feels inadequate as a provider. This predominant sense of responsibility for the total well-being of his family flows out of his commitment to take charge of their lives and well-being. Because he sees himself as the person who determines their lives, he feels he should be able to solve all their problems. By being the director of their lives he creates a situation wherein he feels that their lives depend on this responsibility.

This thesis links the uniqueness of the South African family murder; the uniqueness of guardianship and responsibility inherent in apartheid in the South African situation. It seems as though this right to determine the lives of people, which has been legitimated in the national life, has filtered through to the family life patterns of some families. In every familicide the responsible parent unnecessarily felt that 'the end of the world' had arrived. Yet his/her children no doubt would have been able to cope with what he/she considered as unbearable. What they were saved from would probably not have been catastrophic to them. It was the parent's exaggerated, misguided sense of responsibility that inflated the problem to desperate proportions.

The question posed is whether the 'warped' sense of responsibility felt by certain white South Africans on a national basis can filter down to the family. Also, whether the phenomenon of the extended suicide manifested at micro level could be manifested too at macro level, in the form of a national suicide. On such an issue anyone is bound to speak with discernment, but certain observations seem to be relevant. When the late Dr Verwoerd discussed independence for the Transkei, which he saw as a necessity but also as a risk, in his expression of determination to carry this through, he quoted the words of Esther: 'If I perish, I perish'.

Such a tendency is also revealed in the unrealistic set of values which have developed — 'If my child must go to school with a black child, that would be the end of the world', or 'Should I share a ward with a black patient in hospital my world would collapse'. The accidentals have become essentials for many, and should these accidental values be threatened, some may feel as though the essentials are 'at risk'. Socio-political developments indicate that the end of such self-made values are in sight, and it may well feel to some whites as if 'the end of the world' has arrived. This kind of reasoning could be detected in the trial of the 'Wit Wolf'[1]. It would be irresponsible to identify the white population as a whole with this atrocity, just as it would be irresponsible to typify the whole of the white population as potential family murders. Yet the evidence produced in this chapter recurrently points to a warped sense of responsibility amongst the white population in South Africa.

In this thesis on familicide, certain aspects remain difficult to explain. Why was it that the first settlers did not try to annihilate the indigenous tribes as their contemporaries did in other countries? Is it possible that a feeling of responsibility preceded the attempt to determine the life of these people? Is it possible that the well-known words of Jan van Riebeeck's prayer wherein he mentioned responsibility for the spiritual welfare of the black people were more than a ritual? Did they perhaps signify the roots of a tendency that grew in proportion, and developed into the unwanted interference into, and regulation of, the life of other groups of people?

If a transfer of this tendency towards misplaced responsibility from a national to a family level did occur, as proposed in this chapter, it would be difficult to explain the dynamics of this transfer. The analogy, however, is evident, although the operative mechanisms remain clouded.

Because of this inability to describe the linear cause-effect process, the reasoning and observations in this chapter could well be discredited. In this case, the need would remain to give another explanation for the statistical fact that familicide is almost always confined to the white and Afrikaans-speaking South African family. It should also be noted that the thesis advanced in this chapter is in essence a reformulation and extension of observations already recorded in connection with feelings of 'right of possession' and 'overdrawn responsibility' (De Klerk, 1986; Pretorius, 1987; Luttig, 1985; Van Arkel, 1985).

CONCLUSION

What then is the message incorporated in familicide? It would appear to the author that this abusive manifestation carries a message about something tolerated among some people in this country which is equally abusive, but not always recognized as such, namely the right claimed by white South Africans to determine the lives of black people, as incorporated in apartheid laws, namely the motivation of guardianship, which is acceptable to some. Its unacceptable nature and destructive effect is reflected in parents who, with equally noble motives, capitulate under the stress of a type of futile guardianship comparable to the guardianship held by whites for blacks.

NOTES

1. The 'Wit Wolwe' is an extreme right-wing minority group advocating the use of extreme violence to maintain white privilege. Barend Strydom (the 'Wit Wolf') was sentenced to death in May 1989 for the mass murder of eight black people in Pretoria.

REFERENCES

De Klerk, W. J. (1986) 'Gesinsmoord', *de Kat*, April 1986.
Du Toit, S. I. (1988) 'Die Aanvaarding van Beskikkingsreg as Faktor in Gesinsmoord', paper delivered at Psychiatric Conference on Familicide, Pretoria, July 1988.
Du Toit, S. I. (1986) *Aggressiwiteit*, Pretoria: Van Schaik.
Du Toit, S. I. (1986) 'Geweld in die Samelewing', inaugural lecture, University of Pretoria.
Ellul, J. (1969) *Violence*, London: Mowbrays.
Erasmus, J. A. K. (1988) 'Enkele Sielkundige Aspekte van Gesinsmoorde', paper delivered at Psychiatric Conference on Familicide, Pretoria, 1988.
Goldstein, A. P. *et al.*, (1983) *Prevention and Control of Aggression*, New York: Pergamon Press.
Kelly, G. A. (1969) *Clinical Psychology and Personality*, New York: John Wiley & Sons.
Kleck, G. (1987) 'America's Wars and the Legitimation of Domestic Violence', *Sociology Inquiry*, 57(3), 238–50.
Koestler, A. (1967) *The Ghost in the Machine*, London: Hutchinson.
Luttig, B. (1985) 'Gesinsmoord', paper delivered at 'Simposium oor Gesinsgeweld', Rand Afrikaans University, 21 March 1985.
Milgram, S. (1974) *Obedience to Authority*, New York: Harper & Row.

Pretorius, R. (1987) 'Gesinsmoord in die Republiek van SA — 'n Misplaaste Sin van Verantwoordelikheid', *SA Tydskrif van Strafreg en Kriminologie*, 135–41.

Roos, J. L. (1988) 'Psigiatriese Aspekte van Gesinsmoorde', paper delivered at Psychiatric Conference on Familicide, Pretoria, July 1988.

Toch, H. (1969) *Violent Men*, New York: Aldine.

Van Arkel, T. de J. (1985) 'Pastoraal-Teologiese Perspektief op Gesinsmoord', *SA Tydskrif vir Strafreg en Kriminologie*, 140–8.

Wertham, F. (1967) *A Sign for Kain*, New York: Macmillan Co.

11 Family violence: abuse of the elderly

S. C. A. Eckley

INTRODUCTION

Abuse, ill treatment, neglect, and victimization of older persons are growing phenomena which are demanding greater public attention and response as more persons live far beyond their economic productive years and become increasingly dependent on others. It is important to look closely at this occurrence in order to understand, present, and cure this problem.

The acknowledgement of elder abuse is new, although evidence of tension, conflict, and even violence in the family can be found in the history books and literary sources of many cultures over centuries. The increasing numbers of very old people in the population, changing patterns of family and community life, the success of the child abuse movement, the existence of 'protective services', and the public's openness to intervention can be cited as reasons for increased public and professional interest in an ancient problem.

The phenomenon was first described by Burston in 1975 in a letter to the editor of the *British Medical Journal* entitled 'Granny battering'. Thereafter violence against the elderly became the subject of several investigations in Great Britain in the late seventies. In 1978 at a United States congressional subcommittee hearing on family violence, reference was made in a statement to 'parent-battering'. This statement served as the catalyst for a series of hearings by the subcommittee which led to various studies, training seminars, legislation, and social and law enforcement programmes for the detection, assessment, and treatment of elder victims in that country. Canada, Australia, and other European countries soon followed suit (Wolf & Bergman, 1989: i–v).

In 1981 the South African National Council for the Aged brought the need for action against victimization and abuse of elderly persons to the attention of the government. Seminars were held country-wide during the early 1980s (Droskie, 1981: 9). However, the phenomenon of violence against the elderly has not up till now been fully researched in South Africa, and its exact nature and extent in this country has not been determined.

CLARIFICATION OF CONCEPTS

The literature does not contain clear definitions of what constitutes elder abuse, neglect, or victimization. The assumption seems to be that the theoretical definitions of the above terms are inherently understood. However, if one begins without a conceptualization, one has no foundation upon which to evaluate behaviours or decide whether a situation is abusive or neglectful or violent. For example, is strapping an elder to a chair violent behaviour? Clear conceptualization enhances the development of theory, diagnostic instruments, as well as preventive and treatment strategies. Thus the concepts of elder abuse, elder neglect, and elder victimization beg clarification.

Elder abuse

Terms such as 'granny-bashing' and 'granny battering' used by the media to describe 'non-accidental injury' to older persons are unsatisfactory on a number of accounts. 'Bashing' and 'battering' are suggestive of actions of thugs and criminals, rather than someone who could be a close relative or care-giver. The word 'granny' is also suggestive of sweet innocence on the part of the older person. There must be both acceptance and recognition of the fact that non-accidental injury to the elderly can occur in ordinary households.

O'Malley *et al.* (1979: 2) provide this conceptual definition of elder abuse:

> ... the wilful infliction of physical pain, injury or debilitating mental anguish, unreasonable confinement or deprivation by a caretaker of services which are necessary to the maintenance of mental and physical health.

Although useful, the definition gives a narrow description of elder abuse and does not take into account intentional harm inflicted by other individuals, nor the independent-living elderly who may fall victim to abuse. Eastman (1984: 23) defines elder abuse as 'the systematic maltreatment, physical, emotional or financial, of an elderly person by a care-giving relative'.

This definition emphasizes that abuse is processional and intentional and that it is limited to persons outside institutional care. However, abuse of an elderly person can also take place within an institutional setting.

It is important to make a distinction between activities that are deliberate abuse and those that represent neglect or unintentional harm. Hooyman and Lustbader (1985: 23) noted that:

> ... most instances of abuse are not intentional, but result from the accumulation of stress and limited resources for providing care. In many cases caregivers do not recognize their abusiveness: those who acknowledge it often are at a loss as to how to stop their harmful behaviour.

Taking the various definitions into account it is obvious that the term 'elderly abuse' is as yet not fully understood in terms of the type of harmful behaviours which result from abuse, nor the type of effects produced in the elderly.

Elder neglect

The term 'neglect', as against maltreatment, is typically used in the literature in conjunction with children and older persons. The implication is that persons in the early and late stages of life may be neglected because they are powerless and dependent, and thus unable to protect themselves. It is, however, erroneous to equate advanced chronological age with dependence and powerlessness.

In the literature 'elder neglect' is defined mainly through behavioural typologies. Hageboek and Brand (1981: 3) define it as 'the deprivation of food, medicine, treatment, physical exercise, personal care or lack of supervision'. This definition refers to a deliberate or unintentional withholding of food, and personal and medical care, and the failure to provide adequate shelter and supervision. Behaviours which are also closely linked to neglect are isolation, lack of attention, or the deprivation of rights. It is obvious that neglect and abuse are closely related, although unique in certain respects.

It is also necessary to distinguish between passive and active neglect. According to Douglass (1983: 398), in passive neglect, the elderly dependant is ignored, left alone, or not supplied with essential foods, clothing, and medications, because of the ineptness or inability of the care-giver. In active neglect the elderly dependant is deprived intentionally of social contact, goods, and services. From the above definition it is obvious that neglect refers to behaviour of a frequent nature by a care-giver to a dependent elder.

It is also necessary to distinguish between neglect and self-neglect. Self-neglect refers to the failure of a person to provide for himself/herself the necessary goods and services to maintain an adequate quality of life, thereby avoiding physical harm, mental anguish, or mental illness.

The definition of neglect offers two common themes, namely the omission and the careless or indifferent performance of a duty, thereby the failure to exercise the care that the circumstances demand (Hudson, 1986: 151).

Elder victimization

Victimization refers directly to acts of crime such as assault, rape, robbery, purse snatching, swindle, theft, housebreaking, and fraud, to name a few. Victimization of an elderly person differs very little from any other person who may be a victim of crime. Studies undertaken in South Africa and in overseas countries have found that of all victims, the effect of such crimes on older people is more serious, physically, emotionally, and financially. McMurray (1985: 4) in a study of criminal victimization of the elderly defined the term as follows:

> A specific criminal act as it affects a single victim. In criminal acts against persons, the number of victimizations is determined by the number of victims of such acts. A victimization can be either household or personal.

AETIOLOGY OF ELDER ABUSE

The increasing evidence and growing public awareness of abuse, neglect, and victimization of elderly persons have caused speculation about why it happens. A review of research and other literature indicates that no single explanation for mistreatment of elderly persons predominates. Hickey and Douglas (1981: 501–76), in a study based on case experiences and responses by professionals, found that problems of elder abuse can be attributed to multiple causes, overlapping in many respects. In an attempt to describe as clearly as possible the aetiology of the problems, a number of theoretical approaches to elder abuse will be addressed, namely the *pathological, developmental,* and *environmental.* Certain ethical issues also bear discussion.

Theoretical approaches to elder abuse

Pathological behaviour

A pathological framework explains mistreatment of the elderly in terms of personal problems inherent in the abuser. Elderly persons become vulnerable to abuse or neglect or victimization because of their proximity and visibility, and their dependency on people who may present with pathological behaviour problems. For example, a person with criminal tendencies performing tasks in a home for elderly persons may view that person as an 'easy' target.

A study by Steuer and Austin (1980: 372–6) found that in 25 per cent of such cases studied, the abuser was an alcoholic. These findings correspond with other studies which also revealed that the abuser was experiencing some form of stress, one such stress being that of alcoholism. Bristowe and Collins (1989: 57–61) studied a sample of sixty-three abused elderly persons. In 51,7 per cent of these cases, the abusers used alcohol before acts of violence.

The same researchers identified a high incidence of depression among both the victims and the perpetrators, namely 80 per cent of the former, and 9 per cent of the latter.

Developmental approach

Also referred to as the life-cycle approach, this view regards abusive behaviour as a recurring phenomenon within the family. It is suggested that children of dysfunctional parents are themselves unlikely to develop integrated relationships. Abuse of elders may be a recurring pattern of violence in the family's history over several generations (Shell 1982: 9).

Although a lack of consensus regarding the aetiology of family violence is evident in the literature, research is consistent in revealing that abusive adults were themselves more likely than not to have been the victims of such behaviour as children. Thus destructive behaviour learned as a child is likely to be manifested under stressful circumstances and/or when dependency roles are reversed. Eastman (1984: 42–51), referring to past research, states that abuse of elders is more likely to happen when the abuser and abused come from families with a history of violence and/or families that were poorly integrated. Thus, the study of the family histories of abusers may shed light on the behaviour of abusing individuals.

Environmental approach

Irrational reactions to life crises and negative environmental conditions can play an important role in causing elder abuse, neglect, and victimization. However, because individuals react differently to situational conditions and conflicts, environmental factors *per se* are insufficient predictors of elder mistreatment. Eastman (1984: 42) views the problem as multi-faceted. Pratt *et al.* (1983: 147), referring to studies undertaken on the aetiology and nature of elder abuse, state that consistent themes in these studies were the perception of both the abused and the abuser as being victims of situational and emotional stresses. Stresses such as parental dependence, a family history of violence, inadequate resources, and social norms that legitimize violence were viewed as interacting to produce the neglect, physical abuse, and psychological abuse of the elderly.

Hickey and Douglas (1981: 501–76) found in their research that the sudden and unwanted dependency of a parent, coupled with the autonomy and private nature of the family, provided an environment for mistreatment and were key factors in understanding neglect and abuse. The dependent elderly person can be a source of emotional, physical, and financial stress to adult family members who may be unprepared or unable to assume these responsibilities. These researchers concluded that the most critical factors associated with abuse were the care-giver's inability or disinterest in responding to the needs of vulnerable family members, and the demands of the dependency relationship of an older adult. Anderson (1981: 79) reports research findings which show that the health of the elderly person and care-giver, and attitudes towards ageing, are significant correlates of the quality of the relationship.

Many care-givers may themselves be elderly. Anderson (1981: 78) discusses a study of persons who were principal care-givers for elderly people. The majority of these were themselves over fifty years of age and nearly one-fifth of the sample were over seventy years of age. From this evidence it seems that the increasing strain placed on care-givers who are themselves elderly, with possible increased health and financial problems, may provide a situation conducive to potential abuse.

Research findings on elder abuse among different ethnic groups are largely unavailable. Eastman (1984: 44) reports that although American blacks may experience higher rates of family violence due to cultural, economical, or socio-political factors, the incidence of elder abuse may be lower because older persons are normally highly respected and honoured. However, the general observation within the South African society tends to indicate that due to the dismantling of traditional family life, black elders are just as prone to abuse as elders in other race groups.

Victimization of the elderly is influenced by socio-economic and environmental factors. The following factors could influence the increase of criminal violence against the elderly:

☐ Isolation—older persons living alone or in circumstances where they have little social contact are more easily targets of criminals (Van der Merwe, 1988: 11).

☐ Predictable living routine — elderly persons tend to follow the same routine at home and when moving around in the community (Hahn, 1976: 75).

☐ Inadequate security precautions both at home and when on the street (McMurray, 1985: 22–4).

☐ High-density areas, which tend to produce higher crime rates (McMurray, 1985: 37).

☐ High unemployment, which correlates with an increase in crime against the elderly (McMurray, 1985: 38).

Ethical issues

The concepts of autonomy, dependency, and paternalism need closer examination in order to understand the ethics of respectful caring in comparison to those of respect, or caring.

The central idea that underlies the concept of *autonomy* is indicated by the etymology of the term —'autos' (self) and 'nomos' (rule) (Pelaez, 1989: 3). Autonomy refers to the capacity of persons to define their 'self', give meaning and coherence to their lives, and take responsibility for the kind of persons they are. If recognition is given to others as equal persons, weight must also be given to the way they define and value their world, decide on their actions, and exercise their right to self-determination. There is often conflict between a wish to protect a person and to provide appropriate care, and an individual's right to refuse protection and deny interference. In some cases of elder abuse it has been found that care-givers tended to disregard the older person's right to choice and forced their decisions onto them, resulting in abuse or neglect.

Dependency is closely related to the need for support, subjection, and subordination. Within the concept of old age, Eastman (1984: 14–15) describes a dependant as 'an individual who is reliant on some form of personal assistance to maintain him or her in everyday life'.

The role of a dependant will be affected not only by his or her own psychological make-up, but also by the way the dependency is perceived by those around him/her. Intimate relationships, particularly in the family or group, are maintained on a tightrope of control and power. Dependency can be used as a method of controlling the one on whom one is dependent. The physical and emotional demands by elder dependants on care-givers can cause extraordinary tensions and feelings of bewilderment, frustration, despair, and even helplessness.

Closely related to the concepts of autonomy and dependency is *paternalism.* Pelaez (1989: 4–5) found that professional and private care-givers have a strong tendency towards paternalism. Care-givers hardly ever question whether they are violating the basic human rights that they accord to any other member of society, when serving an older person. In the process, a basic conflict is created between the ethic of caring and the ethic of respect.

The two values that should guide the actions of care-givers are:

☐ promotion of the older adult's well-being; and

☐ respect for individual self-determination.

Decisions to intervene in the life of an elderly person can thus only be taken on the basis of shared decision-making (Pelaez, 1989: 5–6). Shared decision-making requires that a care-giver seek not only to understand the person's needs and develop reasonable alternatives to meet those needs, but also to present the alternatives in a way that enables the older person to choose the preferred one. In cases of diminished competency, the principle of 'substituted judgement' is recommended, based on the foundations of the capacity to decide, the ability to process information, and freedom from coercion.

Most cases of elder abuse reflect a total disregard for the ethical values of autonomy and the right to self-determination of elderly persons, who are viewed as being dependent, lonely, helpless, and senile.

Nature of violence

A description of the profiles of the victim, the abuser, and the symptoms of violence should further increase the understanding that care-givers, professionals, and elderly persons have of abuse, neglect, and victimization.

Profile of the victim

Bristowe and Collins (1989: 53–6) compared the characteristics of elderly care recipients who were victims of abuse against those who enjoyed appropriate care, and found the two groups notably similar except with regard to depression and incontinence, which was higher with the abused group. Eastman (1984: 35–8) conducted an evaluative study on the abused elderly. The findings of these two studies concur with the following description of the victim:

☐ *Average age:* between seventy and eighty years.

☐ *Sex:* seven females to one male.

☐ *Mental stage:* depressed, confused or demented, and/or demanding.

☐ *Physical state:* chronically ill, immobile, incontinent, and/or aphasic.

☐ *Social factors:* limited financial resources, social interaction, and living space, and previous experience of family violence.

☐ *Care needs:* constant supervision, assistance with daily living requirements, and night care.

From the above it is clear that elderly abuse victims demand a great deal of care and attention and are highly dependent on their care-givers. However, it must be appreciated that persons in appropriate alternative care may be equally demanding.

Profile of the abuser

Eastman (1984: 57–8) identifies four factors which place a care-giver 'at risk' of becoming an abuser. These are:

☐ responsibility for more than one dependant;

☐ friction between family members;

☐ lack of professional help; and

☐ lack of outside support.

Bristowe and Collins (1989: 55–8) contrasted the care-giver in abusive situations with care-givers who provided appropriate care. It was found that abusive care-givers drank excessively, suffered from depression, and were more likely to experience uncertainty and confusion.

If the research findings of Bristowe and Collins are combined with those of Eastman (1984: 42–56), the following profile of the abuser can be drawn:

☐ *Average age:* between fifty-five and fifty-seven years.

☐ *Sex:* 53 per cent of abusers were female and 46 per cent males.

☐ *Relationship to the victim:* 86 per cent of abusers were related to the victim. Of these 34 per cent were daughters; 26 per cent sons; 17 per cent spouses; 12 per cent in-laws; 7 per cent grandchildren; and 4 per cent other relatives.

☐ *Psychological factors:* feelings of loss of control, depression, confusion, frustration, low self-esteem, resentment, helplessness, and guilt, and lack of acknowledgement and positive support.

☐ *Social factors:* constant negative and aggressive communication, accompanied by punishment through hurtful criticism or withdrawal; poor interrelationships; isolation and lack of social interaction; financial stresses; inadequate housing; lack of appropriate caring skills; no knowledge and understanding of needs, nor how to respond to them; and no knowledge of other resources.

☐ *Physical factors:* physical strain, tiredness, and self-neglect.

One cannot help but realize that the care of older and especially frail persons within a family setting places great demands and responsibilities on carers. Eastman (1984: 47), in referring to the changes that come through taking on the care of an elderly dependant, refers to the carer becoming an inhabitant of a strange and unreal world — a 'world of changed responses. Small things take on the proportions of major events and major events become small ripples'.

Forms of abuse

It is now an established fact that the place where people are most likely to be victimized is the family home. The ability to identify the signs of abuse can have a profound effect on preventing and solving the problem.

Dolon and Hendricks (1989: 76–8) and Eastman (1984: 58–68) have identified the following as forms of abuse, and have studied them in order to identify the critical factors involved:

1. *Sexual abuse:* Although few cases are reported, it is known that infirmity of age is regarded by some as sexually provocative, lending itself to sexual perversion. The incidence of rape outside and inside homes by criminals and younger family members, is, according to police observation, on the increase.

2. *Misuse of medication:* In such cases, care-givers can either over-medicate or withhold medicine from the elderly person. This may occur as a form of punishment or be an attempt to hospitalize the elder person in order to provide some respite for the abusing care-giver.

3. *Recurring or unexplained injuries:* Repeated hospitalization for 'falls' or injuries that cannot be logically explained should be viewed with suspicion. Injuries which require investigation are: bruises to the face and arms, welts, lacerations, punctures, fractures, or burns.

4. *Physical constraints:* The physical constraint, or bondage, of an elderly person frequently occurs in spouse abuse. Most forms of constraint, however, are used to prevent falling or wandering.

5. *Malnutrition:* Unless the victim has become obviously mal-nourished it is quite difficult for a lay observer to identify this as a factor of abuse. For the elderly dependant may either not be in a position to remember whether he/she has eaten or else may make false allegations of starvation. One useful indicator is where the care-giver is also neglecting himself/herself, stating that he/she cannot be bothered to eat, or that he/she may not even want to eat.

6. *Lack of personal care:* Personal neglect of an elderly person can be an indicator of abuse. It should not be mistaken for self-neglect. In many instances the personal neglect of a care-giver is an indication of possible elder neglect.

7. *Financial exploitation:* Elderly persons are at times financially exploited by means of criminal theft or through being forced to cede property by threats, deception, or battering.

The following secondary factors must also be taken into account:

1. *Physical and/or emotional vulnerability:* The elderly dependant may be physically and/or emotionally vulnerable, thus becoming a scapegoat and hence a target for conflict with the care-giver and the family.

2. *Lack of support networks:* Other persons may withdraw from the primary care-giver, or the care-giver may receive inadequate support from the community. Isolation places both the elderly person and the care-giver 'at risk'.

3. *Poverty:* Poverty can be a significant predisposing factor towards abuse, although care-givers without financial problems may still be at risk of abusing.

4. *Inadequate accommodation:* Accommodation should be adequately spacious and lend itself to adaptations should these prove necessary in the care of an infirm person. Inadequate living arrangements can trigger abusive situations or behaviours.

5. *Unemployment:* The loss of identity, self-esteem, and income due to unemployment, are factors which can increase the risk of abuse and even victimization.

6. *Limited options:* There are very few options open to elderly people should they expose their abusers. The fear of not knowing where to go if they 'inform' on the abuser and the possibility of rejection by close relatives causes a reluctance to act. In a sense, abused elderly usually find themselves trapped in circumstances over which they have limited control.

THE EXTENT OF ELDER ABUSE
Victimization in family homes and homes for aged persons

Professionals and researchers regard violence against the elderly in the family, the community, and institutional settings as one of the best kept secrets. The reasons cited for this family secrecy is the reluctance of elderly persons to report cases of violence, their lack of mobility, and their increasing isolation which keeps them, especially those who are frail, out of the sight of members of the public or of professionals. Child abuse, on the other hand, may be more visible because children normally come into contact with others outside the family (Matlaw & Mayer, 1986: 85–6).

The extent of elder abuse is difficult to measure, describe, and assess due to a lack of empirical data, and also because it encompasses a wide variety of behaviours, conditions, and circumstance.

The media, world-wide, has in the past created the impression that the problem is extensive, and in response the public have demanded a solution. Estimates have been drawn from very small samples and projected nationally (Callahan, 1988: 453–5). After close scrutiny by Callahan of research in the United States, it was concluded that it is a problem affecting relatively small numbers. This has been confirmed by research findings in Great Britain, Denmark, Sweden, and Israel.

Research findings indicate that between one and six per cent of persons over sixty-five years of age may be victims of abuse. However, figures on the extent of neglect seem to be much higher — between 25 and 65 per cent. No research findings on the extent of the problem in South Africa are available. A survey completed in 1985 by the South African National Council for the Aged, in order to identify the number of cases known to welfare organizations, was inconclusive. Reasons cited for this were the unwillingness of older persons to report abuse or neglect, and the lack of awareness of the problem on the part of professionals. The lack of awareness and knowledge of elder abuse by professionals has been found by Callahan (1988: 455) to be a world-wide trend; this also highlights the limitations of agency-based research as an epidemiological tool.

In an attempt to determine the extent of the problem, Tornstam (1989: 37) tried to pinpoint which types of elderly person were most likely to be victims of violence. The findings correspond well with other studies overseas and observations in South Africa. The elderly who are 'at risk' are normally female; older than seventy-five years of age; in failing health; with increased dependency on help with tasks of daily living, and with limited mobility; living alone or with a spouse, children, relatives or other persons in a dwelling with limited living space; and living on a low income. If these criteria are applied to the South African situation, between 15 and 30 per cent of elderly persons of all population groups are at risk.

Tornstam (1989: 43) also identified frail persons in institutions, and such persons receiving home-care services, as being 'at risk' to abuse, neglect, and victimization.

Callahan (1988: 456–7) concluded that the extent of the problem of elder mistreatment cannot be measured accurately through a study of the dependency needs of the elderly alone, but must also incorporate assessment of the ability of care-givers to provide the appropriate care. Perhaps care-giving is taken for granted, without it being appreciated that care-givers themselves need a great deal of support and 'care'.

Criminal victimization

Over the past two years, intensive media coverage has been given to the growing extent of criminal victimization of the elderly. According to police sources, the number of incidents has increased markedly since 1986. Van der Merwe (1988: 83–9) researched forty victims in the Cape Peninsula. He found that elderly victims of crime were particularly vulnerable in view of failing health, immobility, lack of security consciousness, isolation, and low income status. Females between the ages of sixty and seventy years who lived alone with little social interaction were prime targets. Criminal victimization took place more frequently during the day.

The types of crime more often committed were robbery, theft, bag snatching, fraud, assault and battering, and rape. Street crimes totally outnumbered crimes committed at home. An interesting finding was that 51 per cent of victims involved in the research had had previous encounters with criminals. This was similar to the finding of Goldsmith (1976: 19) who found in a study in the United States that 33 per cent of elderly crime victims had been victimized before. The reasons for this phenomenon are still largely unknown, except for speculations that it could be attributed to the victims living in areas with high crime and unemployment rates, and the inability of elder persons to change riskful habits or lifestyles.

The typical criminal who victimizes an elderly person is an unemployed young person between the ages of eighteen and twenty-three years of age (Butler 1976: 304). In cases of physical assault or robbery, two or more criminals will often carry out the victimization. This fact emphasizes the seriousness of physical crime against the elderly.

EFFECTS OF ELDER ABUSE, NEGLECT, AND CRIMINAL VICTIMIZATION ON INDIVIDUALS, FAMILIES, AND COMMUNITY

The effects of elder abuse and neglect are not well researched and documented. However, the effects of elder victimization have been thoroughly researched and provide useful information. The main reason for this can be found in the fact that elder abuse and neglect within family and institutional settings is not as 'visible' as is criminal victimization.

The effects of abuse and neglect

Pillemer and Prescott (1989: 65–72) researched the effects of elder abuse and found that little information existed regarding its consequences. Nevertheless, certain psychological and social effects on the victim, his/her family, and the community can be described.

Psychological effects

Researchers have borrowed a great deal from research on child and wife abuse in an attempt to assess the psychological impact of elder abuse. Depression, self-destructive behaviour, anxiety, feelings of isolation, poor self-esteem, tendency towards re-abuse and substance abuse disturbed eating and sleeping patterns, and helplessness also featured in elder abuse (Pillemer & Prescott, 1989: 66).

Pillemer and Prescott (1989) researched specifically the psychological effects of physical abuse, neglect, and chronic verbal aggression. The most striking finding was that abuse and neglect emerged as the strongest predictors of serious depression, which led in turn to a range of negative reactions like deterioration of health and eating habits, feelings of helplessness and loneliness, and withdrawal. The most important implication for dealing with elder abuse is that depression among victims may prevent them from seeking help and alternatives to their current situations, which could lead to further abuse.

Within a family setting the psychological effects on the elder victim, especially depression, could have an extremely negative impact on the whole family, which could lead to the manifestation of destructive behaviour, low self-esteem, and anxiety, thereby creating a vicious circle of violence and mental illness.

Eastman (1984: 39) refers to American research which found that abuse of an elderly family member created an atmosphere of psychological violence which led to other members also becoming victims of abuse. This could have far-reaching implications stretching into future generations.

The negative psychological effects of elder abuse can also rub off on the wider community. Already there is a growing popular belief that three generations cannot live under the same roof. The negative experiences of families in caring for older family members can result in a reluctance and/or a refusal to accept responsibility to care for their older members.

Social effects

The social effects of abuse and neglect on the individual were studied by Podnieks (1989: 121–9). Elder abuse and neglect was found to be closely related to the appropriateness of family structure and the quality of relationships. If a family cannot appropriately deal with the demands for care of an older member, an explosive situation develops which could erupt in elder abuse, thereby destabilizing and disrupting the basic functions of the family.

Podnieks (1989) identified a number of social consequences. As far as the elder individual is concerned, the following was found: self-neglect, lack of personal care, isolation, disinterest, alienation, refusal of help or increased demands, spiritual distress, and destructive behaviour. The effects on the family could be: social isolation, increased tension and violence, marital breakdown, behavioural problems, disintegrated family relationships, alienation, disrupted role behaviour, and financial problems.

In assessing the effects of abuse on the family, it must be understood that the identified effects can in most instances also be viewed as causes. This is because families with internal structural and role deficiencies and a family history of integrated relationships and violence will often not be able to provide appropriate care for an elderly member. Taking in an elderly person with care demands could release family violence and disruption.

The social effects of elder abuse on the wider community have been a concern in many countries, especially as regards social policy and service delivery. In North America, there is a strong movement towards a solution to the abuse and neglect of the elderly in the form of legislation. In eleven American states legislation has been enacted which gives authority to a court to order a public social services agency to provide protection services, protective placement, or emergency service to victims. Attempts are now underway for a mandatory reporting law as in the case of child abuse.

Media exposure of elder abuse has created the need for specialist social services to deal with the problem. Podnieks (1989: 123) points out that elder abuse increases the pressure for more protected housing communities and institutional care for aged persons. This tendency not only affects the provision of social services but can create the impression that families are not appropriate settings to care for older people. Within the South African context it is important to recognize that increased institutionalized care would be very costly.

The effects of criminal victimization

Physical effects

Elderly persons are very vulnerable to assault and battering. Cook (1976: 645) found that elderly crime victims 'were more likely to suffer from internal injuries or become unconscious or receive bruises, cuts, scratches and black eyes'. Elderly persons do not normally physically resist their attacker. In cases of strong physical resistance the extent of injuries can be more severe. As was confirmed by Van der Merwe (1988: 109) in his study of criminal victimization in South Africa, injuries to an elderly person can result in accelerated frailty.

Material effects

Elderly persons normally live on fixed incomes and the majority of victims, 78 per cent, tend not to have insurance cover (Katz-Shiban, 1989: 85). The loss of money or property is not easily replaced, which has a negative effect on the victim's life-style and standard of living.

Social effects

Katz-Shiban (1989: 84–5) found that 79 per cent of victims changed their life-styles in reaction to their experience. Changes related to *protection* (installing burglar alarms, gates, locks); *prevention* (change of habits, going out in pairs, carrying a cane); and *avoidance* (44 per cent isolating themselves at home or moving away, usually to a housing scheme or institution). Female victims preferred avoidance behaviour, while men tended to lean towards protective actions. Older victims, those in the seventy to eighty age range, were less inclined to change their life-styles than the younger group. Low-income victims were more likely to adopt avoidance behaviour, while higher-income victims took protective and preventive actions.

Van der Merwe (1988: 119) found that in South Africa, 13 per cent of victims withdrew themselves socially, resulting in loneliness and isolation.

Psychological effects

The psychological effects of victimization of the elderly do not substantially differ from those suffered by other victims (Van der Merwe, 1988: 115). These reactions are normally shock, anger, tension, fear, grievance, and upset. Goldsmith (1976: 19) described the predominant emotional reactions of elderly victims as fear and uncertainty — fear of the criminal and future victimization, and uncertainty about future consequences.

McMurray (1985: 35–6) found that 46 per cent of the elderly persons in his study did not report criminal victimization which they had experienced. Reasons given for this phenomenon were a belief that nothing would be done (79 per cent) and a fear of retaliation by the criminal (25 per cent). Van der Merwe (1988) confirmed the above trends, but also pointed out that elderly victims tended to withdraw charges because of the fear of retaliation and an uncertainty about police and court procedures.

Van der Merwe (1988: 116) also identified the victims' physical and emotional responses to their fear and uncertainty. Twenty per cent of the research group indicated that they suffered from sleeplessness and lack of appetite, which could be an indication of depression.

PREVENTION AND INTERVENTION

That elder abuse is a significant social problem has been established. The challenge now is not so much to document its incidence, but to consider establishing methods of reducing its prevalence and of offering support to carers and their elderly dependants (Eastman, 1984: 69).

In South Africa, the welfare and public sectors have been slow to recognize the extent and significance of elder abuse. In consequence, both the legal tools to deal with the problem and community-based services have remained rather limited. The lack of well-documented research and public awareness of the problem are stumbling blocks in developing appropriate preventative and curative action.

The family, the community, and social welfare services each have a role to play in the prevention of elder abuse and victimization, and in the treatment of victims.

The role and tasks of the family

The care of an elder within a family setting can be both demanding and risky but also rewarding and meaningful. Because the overall majority of African, 'coloured', and Indian aged, and a substantial number of white old people in South Africa stay with family and friends, every effort should be made to promote appropriate private care-giving. It must also be recognized that private care-givers need support, assistance, and encouragement to ensure meaningful family care.

Kosberg (1988: 43–8) studied the possibilities of preventive and curative actions by families, and concluded that care-givers should be made aware of and become knowledgeable about the risks involved in caring for the elderly, and be helped to acquire the necessary care-giving tools. Such a preventive approach was advocated because the problem of elder abuse is virtually invisible, occurring within the confines of private dwellings, and because the elder person is reluctant to report the abuse, and professionals fail to recognize it.

Preventing high-risk placements

High-risk placements can only be prevented when the elderly person, the care-giver, and the family system are compatible with one another and can be integrated into a care system. It is necessary for all parties to understand the critical factors that may produce elder abuse before a placement is considered. Critical factors relate to the elderly, the care-giver, and the family.

Critical factors relating to the elderly

No elderly person is immune to the possibility of abusive behaviour. Based on research findings and professional observations, the following characteristics of some elderly persons appear to make them especially vulnerable to elder abuse:

☐ *Gender:* Older women are less likely to resist abusive behaviour and are more vulnerable to sexual molestation.

☐ *Advanced age:* The older the person, the higher the risk of abuse due to physical and mental impairments.

☐ *Dependent:* Economic and physical dependency can provoke hostility by a care-giver.

☐ *Problem drinker:* An alcoholic or problem-drinker is susceptible to abusive behaviour.

☐ *Inter-generational conflict:* Problems between a parent and child do not decrease with the passage of time, indeed they may become intensified by increasing dependency of the older person.

☐ *Internalizes blame:* An older person who engages in self-blame may be especially vulnerable to abuse through self-deprecating behaviour.

☐ *Excessive loyalty:* A person with a strong sense of loyalty to an abusive care-giver will probably not seek 'outside' help in times of crisis.

☐ *Past abuse:* Persons who have been subjected to abusive behaviour by others in the past are candidates for similar treatment.

☐ *Stoicism:* Some persons tend to accept their troubles without seeking help.

☐ *Social isolation:* Persons with limited interaction become increasingly dependent, and are vulnerable to abuse, which may be difficult to detect.

☐ *Impairment:* Physical or mental impairment may induce abusive behaviour by care-givers. Depression is cited as a high-risk factor.

☐ *Provocative behaviour:* Overly-demanding, ungrateful, ingratiating, and unpleasant reactions can provoke abusive behaviour.

Critical factors relating to the care-giver

Key characteristics of individuals who may become abusive care-givers must be assessed before a placement is considered:

☐ *Problem drinkers,* who may tend to act out negative feelings.

☐ *Drug abusers,* who may be unaware of the consequences of poor care, or who may have distorted judgements resulting from substance abuse.

☐ *Senile dementia or confusion* in the care-giver which would impair individual judgement of appropriate care, or the consequences of poor care.

☐ *Poor care-giving experiences in childhood* may influence the care-giving role.

☐ *Economically troubled* persons may view the elderly member as a financial burden.

☐ *Adults abused as children* are potential elder abusers.

☐ Individuals who face *emotional and social stresses* may become depressed and frustrated in the care-giving role.

☐ A care-giver with *limited contacts outside the home,* who may feel isolated and unsupported.

☐ An individual who tends *to blame others* for problems related to pressures or burdens may well direct anger toward the older person.

☐ *Unrealistic expectations* regarding the care of older persons and their prognosis can lead to disillusionment, anger, or frustration.

☐ *Economic dependence on the elderly person* may lead to negative behaviour resulting from greed or resentment.

☐ *Hypercritical persons* can become impatient and abuse.

☐ *Lack of support:* If care-givers have no other relatives/friends available to assist in care-giving or provide periodic respite, the care burden may become too great.

☐ *Care-giver reluctance:* If a care-giver is reluctant or hesitant to provide care, poor results can be predicted.

Critical factors relating to the family

The following characteristics of 'high risk' families need assessment before a decision is taken on the family providing care for an elderly person:

☐ *Overcrowding:* It is riskful to place an elderly person in a family dwelling if it is already overcrowded. Lack of privacy is known to lead to intra-family conflict and violence.

☐ *Isolation:* A family which is isolated from others places a vulnerable older person in an invisible position, and abusive behaviour may go undetected.

☐ *Marital conflict:* Placement of an elder person in a family undergoing marital difficulties should be avoided.

☐ *Inter-family problems:* Families already overburdened with unemployment and alcoholism must not be considered for placement, as it may increase family stress and conflict.

☐ *Economic pressures* can lead to resentment in caring for older dependants.

☐ *Desire for institutionalization:* Any family which seeks institutionalization for an elderly relative should be considered carefully. Persons must not be forced to care for an elderly person. Ideally the correct motivation of a family to care for an elder should be based on a genuine commitment, and the care should be provided voluntarily.

☐ *Disharmony in shared responsibility* between family care-givers can exacerbate the stress on the primary care-giver. All family members must accept part of the responsibility in caring for an elder.

From the above it is clear that not all families are suitably equipped to accept responsibility for the full-time care of a dependent elder. However, the assessment of all the critical factors as a preventive measure is not enough. The internal functioning of the family needs to be carefully structured and organized in such a way that elder abuse can be prevented and/or dealt with when it may occur.

Guidelines to families in the care of the elderly

Eckley (1983: 329–39) compiled the following guidelines for families to whom the care of elder dependants may be entrusted.

1. *Decision-making:* In view of the wide range of implications for all persons involved, it is necessary that the decision to care for an elder dependant be taken both individually and jointly. The tendency to force the decision on the elderly person or on other family members must be avoided at all times.

2. *Contracting:* In view of the unpredictability of human behaviour and changing circumstances and expectations, all parties concerned must negotiate an agreement on matters such as finance, roles and tasks, privacy, and living arrangements. The agreement must be evaluated from time to time, and adjusted when necessary. Alternative arrangements need to be identified beforehand.

3. *Independence:* It is important to respect and maintain the independence of all persons in the family. This means respect for privacy, association, activities, and decision-making.

4. *Social interaction:* Social interaction both within the family and outside should be furthered and maintained. The elder's social contacts with persons outside can provide both personal fulfilment and at the same time prevent loneliness and tension within the family. Other family members also need to continue with their normal social life outside. Social interaction within the family must be planned and organized both informally and formally.

5. *Shared tasks:* Ordinary tasks in the family need to be shared by all, including the elder. If specific tasks are assigned to the elder he/she will experience this as meaningful and feel a valued part of the family. The tasks in caring for a frail person need to be shared between family members.

6. *Full day of activities:* The daily routine of the elderly person depends on the person's state of health, but should provide for maximum and constructive mental, social, and physical involvement and participation. Lack of stimulation and purposeful activities can lead to frustration and isolation.

7. *Relationship-building:* As in the case of any family, intra-family relationships need continuous strengthening. Opportunities should be created for 'building bridges', especially between the elderly and younger family members.

8. *Outside support:* In caring for a frail elderly person it is necessary to know where and how outside support can be recruited. The support services normally needed are nursing, day or respite care, consultation, and visiting. Short-term alternative care should also be available when required.

The family should be aware of the following pitfalls and know how to deal with them:

☐ *Seeking acknowledgement and love from outsiders:* At times aged persons may give the impression to outsiders that they receive little attention from their own family members and they may over-react to the attention given by others. This should be seen as an attempt to involve others and be ignored by the family.

☐ *Anger:* The elderly person and the carer may at times react angrily towards one another. This may be a sign that the carer needs respite from care, or the aged person needs to be placed in other care for a period of time. It is best to openly explore and discuss the reasons for the anger.

☐ *Anti-social attitudes:* These may occur with the increase of dependency and/or heavy care demands. If they occur, it is necessary to seek outside support or consider respite care or alternative placement.

☐ *Reversal to parental role:* At times the elderly person may tend to regard the carer as a child, with subsequent attempts to dominate. This must be accepted as a normal phenomenon due to the elderly experiencing a lack of independence. By the carer not over-reacting emotionally, and reconfirming the agreement, this tendency may disappear.

☐ *Emotional 'blackmail':* This is a cruel and disrupting behaviour pattern. It occurs when the aged person demands continuous attention and even threatens the carer that he/she will die if, for example, he/she is left alone or is unable to get medical help. Outside help must be summoned and a replacement considered.

☐ *Exhaustion, feelings of guilt or frustration:* Such feelings in the carer result from demanding care-giving or an inability or unwillingness to share its tasks. When this occurs the contract must be renegotiated and alternative placement considered.

The role and tasks of the social services

In comparison to most Western countries, South Africa still lacks specific programmes for preventing and intervening in elderly abuse, neglect, and criminal victimization. This can be attributed to the relative lack of identification of the problem, and the lack of empirical research on aspects of the phenomenon. Practitioners speculate that this may be due to the large number of elderly people living with families, their degree of dependency, the extent of the poverty they experience, and the nature of their living circumstances.

Formal interventive measures and programmes can be divided into those which are preventive in nature, and those which are curative.

Preventive intervention

1. Legal protective mechanisms:

Protective services are traditionally described as 'a system of preventive, supportive and surrogate services for adults living in the community to enable them to maintain independent living and avoid abuse and exploitation' (Shell, 1982: 11). Protective services programmes are generally characterized by two features, the co-ordinated regulation of services to persons 'at risk' and the authority to provide substitute decision-making.

The service component may consist of various health, housing, and social services which in South Africa are regulated by welfare legislation and specifically the Aged Persons Act 81 of 1967. The authority to intervene directly involves the legal system and, as a general rule, this requires not merely a presumption of harm to the individual and the benefit to be derived from intervention, but also requires evidence of the aged person's inability to protect himself/herself or a diminished capacity to make decisions. This aspect of protective services includes such legal mechanisms as the power of attorney and an order of supervision. Legal mechanisms in respect of the elderly in South Africa do not make a clear distinction between financial management and the supervision of a person in order to monitor or control protective problems in all spheres.

Furthermore, when legal provisions are used as a means of extending help to older persons, issues such as the invasion of privacy versus the preservation of rights surface.

Frail elderly people living independently in the community, and who are vulnerable but not mentally disordered, and/or who have neither friends nor family to properly assist them, do not currently have access to protection. The services required by such persons can range from information, consultation, referral, home-help, escort services, attendance at out-patient programmes, and consultation and assessment by a multi-disciplinary team. This multi-disciplinary approach is necessary for the successful identification and management of situations of abuse and involves at least three major services systems, namely medical, legal, and social.

In recent years a number of Western countries have introduced legislation to enforce the statutory reporting of elder abuse (Salend *et al.*, 1984: 62). In evaluating such statutes in eleven states in the United States it is evident that the definitions contained in the acts concerned are unstandardized and vague, and the reporting procedures confusing. They also fail to mandate the establishment of a central registry.

Nevertheless, early detection of elder abuse is of vital importance in combating the problem and to provide much needed help. Callahan (1988: 458) argues that legal enforcement of the detection and reporting of elder abuse is extremely limited in view of the status of elderly adults, their needs, and the circumstances under which abuse takes place. Callahan recommends a five-point strategic plan which is comprehensive and sensitive to the uniqueness of the problem.

Firstly, problems of abuse should be considered as falling within the domain of the social service system. By providing this system with more resources it will be enabled to initiate and provide special abuse programmes. Secondly, where criminal laws have been violated they should be enforced. Thirdly, more information about the needs of older persons should be made available to the helping professions, care-givers, and older persons themselves. Fourthly, policy must recognize that the greatest abuse that can beset older persons is the failure to provide them with the economic means for a decent life and the opportunities to exercise their own choices. The economic health of older persons can go a long way in alleviating situations of abuse and neglect. Fifthly, legal protective mechanisms in preventing and combating elder abuse can be helpful, but should not be viewed in isolation from the social service system.

2. Risk reduction strategies:
The literature reports a number of risk reduction strategies and programmes which are in operation in some countries, such as care-giver support groups, victim support groups, and a central register. None of the above strategies are actively in operation in South Africa.

3. Care-giver support groups:
These groups have developed spontaneously in some countries over the past eight years as a method to cope with the special circumstances and problems inherent in the care-giving role. They are settings for learning, sharing, and getting help from other persons in similar situations. The target population consists of persons who are directly involved in care-giving — spouses, private persons, children, siblings, nieces, nephews, or grandchildren. Support groups are not encounter or therapy groups for people with deep-seated emotional problems. The small size of these groups — five to ten persons — is especially conducive to peer support.

In countries like Great Britain and the United States national associations co-ordinate and promote this concept. However, care-giver support groups operate at local level with little interference from welfare organizations or professionals, who act merely as referral resources or facilitators, or who foster the development of peer support in groups.

There are two basic types of care-giver groups, the self-help type and those which are professionally led. These two types are not mutually exclusive in that self-help groups often consult professionals, and professionally-led groups often consult non-professional care-givers. Because care-giver support groups usually process shared experiences and information it is important that they also process specialized knowledge on rendering services to the elderly. Typical topics for a care-giver support programme can include:

☐ the physical and psychological aspects of ageing;

☐ communication with elderly persons;

☐ self-care;

☐ coping with stress and burn-out;

☐ drug interactions;

☐ legal issues;

☐ dealing with guilt and anger;

☐ locating and using community resources;

☐ alternative living arrangements; and

☐ the identification and handling of elder abuse.

A care-giver support group can be a valuable and effective instrument in dealing with elder abuse at both the preventive and interventive levels.

4. Respite care:

A simple definition of respite care is 'time off' or relief for the regular care-giver or dependent elderly person. According to Crossman (1985: 33–9), a respite care programme is a must if elder abuse in the family is to be effectively prevented.

Respite care usually operates both formally and informally, and is organized by welfare services, or by care-giver support groups, or among relatives, friends, and neighbours. Basically respite care is not a service, but a function or outcome of a number of formal and informal services. From the literature it is evident that informal respite care activities may develop into fully-fledged service programmes as the need for respite support grows.

As a by-product of social services, respite care is provided through *home-care services*, such as nursing services, meals-on-wheels, and cleaning services, and through *adult day care* which offers supervision, socialization, and personal and professional care to the aged.

When this serendipitous respite is not enough, programmes may be designed with respite as the primary function. Programmes will vary according to the amount of time off afforded to the care-giver, and the type and amount of care required by the care recipient.

The respite programme will therefore be designed to meet a specific need or range of needs, falling into the categories of:

☐ *Short-term respite*, which offers care-givers a few hours off on a regular, or 'by request' basis.

☐ *All-day respite*, which is usually provided through senior centres or adult day-care centres, and which allows the care-giver to maintain regular employment or other activities which do not permit the full-time care of the frail, older person.

☐ *Overnight and weekend respite*, which gives the care-giver time for a brief vacation or time to participate in other activities which extend beyond one day.

☐ *Longer-term respite* of a few days to several weeks, which enables the care-giver to take a longer vacation. This type of respite is usually offered by institutions.

In South Africa respite care still needs to be recognized as a valuable method in furthering informal care-giving and preventing elder abuse and neglect. If linked to a volunteer programme, respite care can become a viable service component to benefit both care-giver and elderly person.

5. Central registry:

One approach to abuse risk-reduction is the establishment and maintenance of a central registry of information on cases of abuse and neglect. It could provide valuable research data, which is much needed in understanding the problem. It could also be useful in creating an awareness of the extent of the problem, as well as in identifying any previous incidents of abuse recorded and alerting protective services programmes to take appropriate action.

Shell (1982: 18), in evaluating the central register in Manitoba, Canada, found it to be an important tool in identifying the elderly who are 'at risk' and in initiating and directing preventive and rehabilitative services. In South Africa such a register has as yet not been established.

6. Education and training:

Education as a preventive measure disseminates knowledge concerning ageing and elder needs and care requirements. Shell (1982: 19), in a study of care-givers, identified a need for more information counselling, and for more training in dealing with problems such as incontinence, dementia, stress, anger, and burn-out.

Education of care-givers in high-risk situations could be carried out by carefully selected and well-trained volunteers who would serve as adjuncts to professionals. Volunteers, as well as providing information and referral services, could visit families and help care-givers with day-to-day problems.

Crime prevention programmes in most Western countries fulfil an important role in combating crime against the elderly. Most of these programmes are educational, and seek to remove unwarranted anxieties and to encourage sensible precautions.

The South African National Council for the Aged, in co-operation with the South African Police and the private sector, has compiled guidelines for crime prevention, and conducts educational seminars on subjects such as security at home, on the street, and during travel.

Curative intervention

Interventive strategies have been hampered by a number of factors. The lack of a universally accepted definition of elderly abuse has divided professionals and laypersons alike in their efforts to agree upon the nature and extent of the problem. In South Africa, government, the welfare sector, and the general public have been slow in recognizing the significance of the problem and in consequence, legal tools and supports and community-based services have remained limited in many communities.

In the view of Bookin and Dunkle (1985: 3) the 'lack of adequate community support has placed a heavy burden upon practitioners who are assigned to cases of elder abuse'. For the individual practitioner, intervention in cases of elder abuse presents specific problems and challenges for which the limited knowledge of elder abuse provides few answers. Workers also experience difficulties related not only to the nature of the problem, but also to their own personal feelings, biases, and attitudes about violence and ageing.

In evaluating curative intervention programmes run by social workers both in overseas countries and in South Africa, the following strategies can be identified as appropriate in various stages of the intervention process.

1. Stage one — problem identification:

The lack of scientifically sound data on the aetiology, extent, and impact of elderly abuse, and the absence of insight into personal and cultural biases, pose the biggest obstacles for practitioners. In general the abused elder person is relatively invisible to professional human services in the community. Bookin and Dunkle (1985: 6), in referring to research on the identification of elder abuse, found that 'differential exposure to different forms of elder abuse can make some professionals more expert at recognising some symptoms and forms of elder abuse than others'. This can cause practitioners in different disciplines to develop their own personal 'profile' of the abused elder. It is therefore necessary to adopt a multi-disciplinary strategy in identifying the abused elder.

The second obstacle to overcome concerns cultural biases. The norms, values, and cultural influences of all those involved in the identification process, namely the abused elder, his or her family, the worker, and significant others, come into play at the time when the investigation of possible maltreatment begins.

Violence has become a common feature of family life in South Africa with a high baseline tolerance of violence. The norms of many societies legitimize and support the use of violence in the family as a means of punishment, control, and resolution of conflict. While not all families accept violence and the use of force in either the same manner or degree, the important ramification is that all individuals, through socialization in the family, adopt some attitudes about the appropriateness and legitimacy of violence and control. Such attitudes in turn affect the individual's perceptions about the phenomena he or she will experience or observe. The professional attempting to intervene in a case of elder abuse is confronted with a situation in which perceptions of the maltreatment by all relevant parties may vary significantly.

Professionals and abusive families providing care to elders differ significantly in their perceptions of the role that stress plays in the functioning of the family. Bookin and Dunkle (1985: 8) found that caseworkers tended to perceive family care-givers as experiencing a higher level of stress than did the care-givers themselves. Such a discrepancy can impede a practitioner's efforts to intervene by focusing attention on the wrong facet.

2. Stage two — gathering information:

Specific information concerning the variables relevant to causation of abuse are necessary for assessment purposes. Bookin and Dunkle

(1985: 8) and Eastman (1984: 73–4) agree on the type of information required, which includes the:

☐ *Family value system:* attitudes, level of vulnerability and dependency, and evidence of exploitation and violation of rights.

☐ *Past history of coping with problems:* methods of resolving conflict, and sources of and responses to stress.

☐ *Care needs of the elder:* extent of needs and generalized stress/demand.

☐ *State of family support:* its financial situation, living arrangements, environment, relationships, social networks, possible sources of support, and availability of community services.

☐ *Pathological symptoms:* evidence of pathological behaviour such as mental illness, alcoholism, or crime, and type of abuse, whether psychological, social, or physical.

3. Stage three — case conference:
The case conference can offer a method of gathering and evaluating information, and of deciding on intervention strategies and the means by which to evaluate progress. The multi-professional structure of the case conference provides a comprehensive approach to the plan of intervention.

4. Stage four — intervention:
Elder abuse generally occurs within the context of a family system. The worker is therefore dealing not only with the problems of the elderly client but also with those of the family in which such behaviour exists. Intervention is thus directed at the whole family.

Bookin and Dunkle (1985: 9) came to the conclusion that intervention in problems of elder abuse is particularly demanding on the practitioner due to factors in the family such as the:

☐ complex system of relationships;

☐ high level of stress and tension;

☐ resistance by the elder and the family;

☐ powerlessness and feelings of worthlessness of the elderly person;

☐ inaccessibility of the elderly person;

☐ level of physical and mental frailty of the aged person;

☐   feelings of inadequacy in dealing with violence; and

☐   ineffectiveness of professional skills with older persons.

Research by Pratt *et al.* (1983) on the effective use of curative interventive strategies, identified the following as key points of reference:

☐   focus on the family and not only on the abused;

☐   communicate directly and sensitively with the abused and the family members;

☐   maintain a flexible therapeutic relationship, with emphasis on education;

☐   utilize a multi-disciplinary approach; and

☐   plan comprehensive intervention through the co-ordinated efforts of a number of social service agencies.

From the above and other literature sources it is suggested that appropriate interventions should be based on:

1.   the preparation of social and health professionals to respond to the special needs of the abused elderly and their families;

2.   the development of skills for sensitive interaction with the abused and the abuser;

3.   the development of procedures for assessing the needs of the victim, identifying community services to meet these needs, and providing timely interventions;

4.   the clarification of the legal definition of abuse and the appropriate role of the police in cases of abuse; and

5.   the development of a system for review and co-ordination of the linkages between services.

Furthermore, it is critical to reach beyond the ageing services network, as a wide range of professionals, physicians, clergymen, attorneys, and other persons are likely to encounter elder abuse.

Special intervention programmes

Special crisis intervention programmes are in operation in most Western countries. These programmes vary from 24-hour telephone services and special referral units, to victim support schemes.

CLOSING REMARKS

Elder abuse, neglect, and victimization need to be addressed on both the macro and micro levels. On a macro level, attitudes which result in the maltreatment of the elderly can be influenced through increased efforts in the area of community education. Greater awareness, and thus more accurate identification of the problem of elderly victims, can lead to the re-shaping of attitudes and the broadening of knowledge about abuse and the services required. Social workers, who of all the helping professions are presently in the widest range of settings serving the elderly, are in a unique position to assume leadership in an effort to further community awareness and action. Finding a working definition for elder abuse appropriate to the South African society is a priority, if the problem is to be successfully addressed.

On the micro level, successful preventive and curative intervention requires professionals and laypersons to acquire adequate knowledge of this phenomenon, knowledge of the self, knowledge of the dynamics of ageing, knowledge of abuse within and outside of the family, knowledge of cultural and societal influences, and knowledge of appropriate helping strategies and the skills to implement these.

REFERENCES

Anderson, C. (1981) 'Abuse and Neglect among the Elderly', *Journal of Gerontological Nursing*, 10(2), 77–85.

Bookin, D. & Dunkle, R. E. (1985) 'Elder Abuse: Issues for the Practitioner', *Social Casework — The Journal of Contemporary Social Work*, 3–12.

Bristowe, E. & Collins, J. B. (1989) 'Family Mediated Abuse of Non-Institutionalized Frail Elderly Men and Women Living in British Columbia', *Elder Abuse and Neglect*, 1(1), 45–64.

Butler, R. N. (1976) *Why Survive? Being Old in America*, New York: Harper & Row.

Callahan, J. J. (1988)'Elder Abuse: Some Questions for Policy-Makers', *The Gerontologist*, 28(4), 453–68.

Cook, F. L. (1976) 'Evaluating the Rhetoric of Crisis: A Case Study of Criminal Victimization of the Elderly', *Social Services Review*, 632–46.

Crossman, L. (1985) 'Respite', paper presented at a symposium on support for family caregivers, National Council on the Aging, Washington.

Dolon, R. & Hendricks, J. E. (1989) 'An Exploratory Study Comparing Attitudes and Practices of Police Officers and Social Service Providers in Elder Abuse and Neglect Cases', *Elder Abuse and Neglect*, 1(1), 75–90.

Douglass, R. L. (1983) 'Domestic Neglect and Abuse of the Elderly: Implications for Research and Service', *Family Relations*, 395–402.

Droskie, Z. M. (1981) *Annual Report of the SA National Council for the Aged*, SA National Council for the Aged, Cape Town.

Eastman, M. (1984) *Old Age Abuse*, London: Age Concern.

Eckley, S. C. A. (1983) 'Die Versorging van die Bejaarde' In *Venster op die Gesin*, edited by J. Kroeze, Potchefstroom: Potchefstroomse Universiteit vir CHO, 329–39.

Goldsmith, J. (1976) 'Police and the Older Victims: Keys to a Changing Perspective', *Police Chief*, 43, 19–23.

Hageboek, H. & Brandt, K. (1981) 'Characteristics of Elderly Abuse', unpublished paper, Iowa: University of Iowa Gerontology Centre.

Hahn, P. H. (1976) *Crimes Against the Elderly: A Study in Victimology*, Santa Cruz, California: Davis.

Hickey, T. & Douglas, I. (1981) 'Mistreatment of the Elderly in the Domestic Setting: An Exploratory Study', *American Journal of Public Health*, (71) 5, 500–7.

Hooyman, N. R. & Lustbader, W. (1985) *Taking Care*, New York: The Free Press.

Hudson, M. F. (1989) 'Analyses of the Concepts of Elder Mistreatment: Abuse and Neglect', *Elder Abuse and Neglect*, 1(1), 5–26.

Hudson, M. (1986) 'Elder Mistreatment: Current Research'. In *Elder Abuse; Conflict in the Family*, edited by K. Pillemer & R. Wolf, Dover: Auburn House.

Katz-Shiban, B. (1989) 'The Impact of Victimization on the Elderly in Israel: Acquisition of the Victim Role in Three Profiles of Elderly Victims'. In *Stress, Conflict and Abuse of the Elderly*, edited by R. S. Wolf & S. Bergman, Jerusalem: JDC Brookdale Institute, 79–92.

Kosberg, J. I. (1988) 'Preventing Elder Abuse: Identification of High Risk Factors prior to Placement Decisions', *The Gerontologist*, 28(1), 43–50.

Matlaw, J. R. & Mayer, J. B. (1986) 'Elder abuse: Ethical and Practical Dilemmas for Social Work', *Health and Social Work*, 85–94.

McMurray, H. L. (1985) 'The Criminal Victimization of the Elderly', Occasional Paper No. 22, Washington: Institute for Urban Affairs and Research, Howard University.

O'Malley, H. S. *et al.* (1979) 'Elder Abuse in Massachusetts: A Survey of Professionals and Paraprofessionals', Massachusetts: Department of Legal Research and Services for the Elderly Organization of Massachusetts.

Pelaez, M. (1989) 'Ethical Issues in Protective Services for the Elderly'. In *Stress, Conflict and Abuse of the Elderly*, edited by R. S. Wolf & S. Bergman, Jerusalem: JDC Brookdale Institute, 3–10.

Pillemer, K. & Prescott, D. (1989) 'Psychological Effects of Elder Abuse: A Research Note', *Elder Abuse and Neglect*, 1(1), 65–74.

Podnieks, E. (1989) 'Elder Abuse: A Canadian Perspective'. In *Stress, Conflict and Abuse of the Elderly*, edited by R. S. Wolf & S. Bergman, Jerusalem: JDC Brookdale Institute, 111–40.

Pratt, C. C. *et al.* (1983) 'Service Workers' Responses to Abuse of the Elderly', *Social Casework*, 147–53.

Salend, E. *et al.* (1984) 'Elder Abuse Reporting: Limitations of Statutes', *The Gerontologist*, 24(1), 61–7.

Shell, D. (1982) 'Protection of the Elderly', unpublished paper, Winnipeg: Manitoba Council on Aging.

Steuer, J. & Austin, E. (1980) 'Family Abuse of the Elderly', *Journal of the American Geriatrics Society*, (28)8, 370–6.

Tornstam, L. (1989) 'Abuse of the Elderly in Denmark and Sweden: Results from a Population Study'. *Elder Abuse and Neglect*, 1(1), 35–44.

Van der Merwe, J. P. (1988) 'Die Viktimisasie van Blanke Bejaardes in die Kaapse Skiereiland', unpublished MA (Social Work) Dissertation, University of Stellenbosch.

R. S. Wolf & Bergman, S. (eds.) (1989) *Stress, Conflict and Abuse of the Elderly*, Jerusalem: JDC Brookdale Institute.

Part 4

Violence in institutions

Introduction

When people are required by the state to attend, be resident, or be detained in institutions, standards of care in these places should be humane: if law or regulation forces people to be part of an institution, the state has the responsibility to ensure that care is adequate.

This is often not the case. Part 4 of this book examines violence in some institutional contexts which people have no choice about entering: schools, which children of specified ages are required to attend; residential children's homes, to which children are committed on court order; and places of detention, where adults and children are held in terms of South Africa's security and/or emergency legislation.

Involuntary participation in an institution renders people particularly vulnerable, since they are in the control of those who operate the institution, be it a school, children's home, police station, or prison. Moreover, when they are in the institution by compulsion, they are isolated from sources of redress should their rights be violated.

The parents of a child at school have little say over the school's operation, and should their child receive corporal punishment, there is little that they can do about it. Even when the corporal punishment exceeds that which is legally permissible, public prosecutors have often declined to proceed with charges that have appeared to be clearly illegal instances of physical violence, and besides, parents fear victimization of their child if they complain. In children's homes, there is no built-in checking system that permits children to report abuse to an independent authority — even state inspections of these homes rely upon the information given by the care-giver, not the feedback of the child. Still more starkly, in the case of adults and children who are detained in terms of the country's security and emergency legislation, the law itself isolates them, for in terms of the Public Safety Act 3 of 1953 there is restriction on information relating to detainees, resulting in what Thomas terms in Chapter 15, 'the detained person being at the mercy of security forces to whom almost complete immunity has been granted'. Those detained under the Internal Security Act 74 of 1982, as amended, are similarly disadvantaged, since they have no access to family, lawyers, or their own doctors and spiritual advisers, unless special permission is granted.

Five themes run through the institutional situations described in Part 4. Some of these themes will be familiar from earlier parts of this book, but in the context of people forced to be part of violent institutions, they assume special meaning: persons in control of institutions do not openly and willingly recognize that when some people have, legally, near total control over the lives of others, abuse is not only possible, but likely; the law in practice protects the person in control, not the person being cared for; violence and abuse is counter-productive to the institution's ostensible aims; violence in institutions produces a bitter harvest of more violence; and feasible ways exist, although presently unused, to reduce and control violence in institutional settings.

The fact that people in control of others in institutions do not readily concede that abuse can occur is demonstrated in a number of ways, of which the absence of statistical records and the lack of adequate investigative systems for allegations of abuse are two good examples. Systematic public records detailing violence in institutions are rare: although school principals are required to record every instance of corporal punishment, composite figures are not made available; there are no South African figures whatsoever on violence to children in group care; and in the case of detainees, regulations governing the state of emergency effectively curb press reporting and restrict disclosure of information. Indeed, the state has had to be pressurized to disclose statistics on the number of adults and children detained, and even though the figures have been reluctantly issued, they are incomplete — people detained in the so-called independent homelands are not taken into account, and often in the case of children, those of sixteen years of age or over are not included.

The lack of adequate investigative systems for allegations of abuse in institutions reflects complacency, and perhaps also defensiveness. A critical requirement for fair and unbiased inquiry is a neutral investigator of alleged abuse, who is located outside the institution. However, the practice within schools, children's homes, the police, and the prison service is to investigate allegations of violence and abuse internally. In such circumstances, investigators have a vested interest in denying or minimizing the allegations made. In theory, when there is illegal use of corporal punishment in schools, or when children are abused in group care, there is recourse to the courts, but with many detainee situations, such recourse is absent. For example, adults and children detained in terms of the Internal Security Act 74 of 1982, as amended, have no assured access to family or lawyers, and courts have no jurisdiction over the act of detention of people detained 'preventively', or for interrogation, or as possible witnesses. The absence of an external investigatory body acts to promote the possibility of abuse.

A second theme of the chapters in Part 4 is that the effect of the law is to protect persons in control of institutions, not the persons being cared for. In schools, corporal punishment is legally sanctioned for boys at the subjective discretion of the principal; in the case of children's homes, there is an extraordinary immunity for failures in their care-giving, compared with abusive parents; and secrecy and legal prohibition act to hide detainers' possible abuse of detainees, as for example in the instance of the Public Safety Act 3 of 1953, which makes it an offence to publish the 'circumstances of or treatment in detention of a person who is or was detained under regulation 3 of the Security Emergency Regulations'.

A third theme running through the chapters is that violence and abuse in institutions are harmful and counter-productive to the institutions' ostensible goals. Schools, for instance, exist to prepare, socialize, and educate youth to be productive, contributing members of society, and correctly, a sense of discipline in pupils is a key requirement. Yet 'discipline' is not an externally-imposed set of do's and don'ts reinforced by punishment, so that obedience is ensured by fear; it refers to behaviour directed voluntarily from within, and the exercise of a sense of will independent of the commands of authority. Physical punishment does not develop this real personal discipline, and indeed breeds violence and aggression in the learner, as well as seriously impairing his or her learning.

In similar vein, a child is placed in alternative care when his or her home circumstances are so harmful to his or her interests that this extreme step is necessary. Yet children's homes sometimes have standards of care that violate the child's basic rights, and moreover, often train children to survive in the institution, rather than for the stated goal of developing the skills and attitudes that they will need for successful community living.

The negative consequence of violence and abuse to people in detention is perhaps the most paradoxical of all. If people, young or old, commit crimes, South Africa has a conventional legal system whereby they may be charged and dealt with through the courts. Detention without trial, whether in terms of security or emergency legislation, is an act of violence aimed at upholding a political system with which most people do not agree. The inadequate standards of detainee care, and the harassment and violence to which some detainees are subjected, is highly unlikely to reduce their personal opposition to injustice, and will probably increase it.

The paradox of an institution's use of violence contradicting its stated goals can be clarified in terms of two concepts. The first is that institutions, over time, develop a life and set of values of their own, shaped largely by those who wield power within the institution. Hence, some teachers within schools may move to practices which make their own lives more comfortable and less demanding, such as resorting to violent punishment, rather than the more taxing alternative of developing human communication skills, open discussion, and shared decision-making. Similarly, care-givers in children's homes, who are frequently overworked and universally under-paid, may choose options which favour the smooth, 'trouble-free' and ordered running of the institution over options which involve time-consuming and sometimes emotionally-draining responses to the needs of individual children. A second concept that is useful in understanding the identified paradox is that of socially-acceptable justification. In terms of this notion, an institution may give out as its primary aim a function that is socially acceptable, for example preventively detaining a person deemed to be a threat to peace and good order in the community. This helps to validate the detention in terms of a widely held community value. However, a more or equally important — but covert — goal might be to use the detention to dehumanize, demoralize, and destabilize the person, so that he or she becomes alienated from others, including family, peer group, community, and the organizations of which he or she has been a part. While these possibilities may help to explain the apparent paradox of violence in some institutions, they heighten rather than reduce the culpability of 'care-givers' who use violence: violence in such institutions is especially harmful, short-sighted, and counter-productive, and instead of reducing or smothering problems, usually compounds them.

A fourth theme of this section is that violence produces a bitter harvest of more violence. This fact is one of the most consistently supported findings in the entire scientific research literature on human behaviour. People repeat behaviours to which they have been exposed — if violence has been used to try to control and shape their own behaviour, they will in all probability try to use violence to influence the behaviour of others. Hence, corporal punishment in schools can be expected to create future parents who will rely on violence to impose their will on their own children; violation of the rights of children in group care is likely to produce damaged human beings who will be unable to bond adequately with others, and whose children will be especially at risk; and violence to detainees who oppose a flagrantly unjust political system may increase their and their community's anger and opposition, and may well contribute to uncontrollable aggression in the future.

A final common theme that permeates the chapters constituting this section is that when the means of reducing violence in institutions are explored, in every case clear, simple, and logical strategies can be identified to prevent its occurrence, and to ameliorate its effects upon people if it has occurred. All violence is obscene, but it is particularly gross when it is done to people who are vulnerable because they have been forced into a situation of dependency. Hence, the means of reducing violence suggested by the authors of the chapters in this section merit special consideration.

12 Violence in schools: discipline

T. L. Holdstock

INTRODUCTION

The teacher is part of the world of the student, either as a model or as an arranger of reinforcing consequences. Historically, the consequences have been almost always punitive: if not the birch rod or cane, then criticism or failure. The three classical by-products of punishment follow: escape (truancy), counterattack (vandalism), and stubborn inaction (Skinner, 1986: 572).

Discipline, in schools and at home, is undoubtedly of the greatest importance in determining the future well-being, not only of the individual, but of society at large. Yet, few issues in education are as misunderstood, receive as little attention, and are as poorly handled as discipline. Thus, instead of facilitating the resolution of conflict and violence, the approach to discipline in our schools contributes to the epidemic proportions that violence has reached in the country.

Education in South Africa is stuck in its approach to discipline. The model which is adhered to is one based on externally imposed do's and don'ts, which are enforced by the power of punishment, physical or otherwise. Teaching is the only profession in which a person in authority is permitted to physically hurt a subordinate. Indeed, the use of physical force and other forms of punishment to 'motivate' children, or to 'teach' and 'maintain discipline' in school, is truly frightening. The blindness of our society to the legalized child abuse which occurs daily in white and black schools in every community, in every part of the country, is one of the saddest indictments of the moral tenor of our society.

We attempt, in various ways, to minimize and negate the violence involved in legally permissible physical punishment. Terms such as 'corporal punishment' are used to soften the violent nature of the action, while we rigidly hold on to the completely unfounded notion that corporal punishment instils and maintains discipline. We furthermore absolve ourselves from moral responsibility by the fact that corporal punishment is legally permissible. None of these arguments counter the fact that hitting someone else, especially someone younger, smaller, and utterly defenceless, constitutes a violent act. This is true even in those instances where people claim that they cane 'in love'.

We can call corporal punishment by a thousand names and find a thousand justifications for its use, but it nevertheless remains child abuse. The abuse is many-faceted. Not only does it cause physical pain and emotional turmoil, it also invades the personal space and violates the human rights of the child. Justifying the abuse in moral, legal, and educational terms as we do is even more reprehensible than the child abuse which occurs amongst the general public. A society and educational system which provides legal and moral protection for itself while abusing its children is indeed a sick and misguided society. Unfortunately, this is the situation in South Africa today.

AETIOLOGY

The poor management of discipline in educational institutions and its resultant effect on the overall level of violence in the country can be attributed to several causes. To start with, the use of physical force at school is sanctioned by law (see Olmesdahl, 1984, for a detailed list of relevant Ordinances). Secondly, the law is based on the belief that there is no better way to maintain discipline than through the use of punishment. Thirdly, the necessity of punishment derives from prevailing beliefs about the innate nature of humankind. Fourthly, the reliance on violence has developed a psychological denial of its deleterious effects. And lastly, caning pupils provides a short-cut to career advancement.

Regulations exist which permit children to be caned

Although the various education departments in the country do not have a uniform set of rules for the administration of corporal punishment, the following regulations apply fairly generally. Caning of boys is allowed in the principal's office, by the principal, or someone delegated by the principal. All regulations limit corporal punishment to the buttocks, and it is to be carried out with a cane not exceeding certain dimensions. The punishment is not to be 'cruelly administered', and has to be recorded in a punishment book. Under existing regulations, the offences justifying corporal punishment are usually the following: bullying, indecency, gross insubordination, lying, continued or grave neglect of work, and truancy and other grave breaches of discipline.

In terms of Cape Ordinance 20 of 1956, section 231, the Cape Director of Education is given authority to frame rules with respect to corporal punishment. In the case of schools for 'coloured' children, the offences are not spelt out, but corporal punishment may be inflicted only 'as a last resort in cases of serious misconduct'. Only in the Transvaal are children in kindergarten specifically excluded from being beaten. With respect to African and Indian scholars, the regulations expressly stipulate that the number of strokes administered during a single day should not exceed four (see Olmesdahl, 1984).

Apart from the legal administration of corporal punishment, surveys done (Davis, 1985; Rakitzis, 1987; Rice, 1986; Weiss, 1985), and correspondence and telephone calls received by the author during the past decade, make it abundantly clear that many aspects of the law are vague and open to subjective interpretation, thereby making possible the indiscriminate administration of corporal punishment. However, it is not only indiscriminate use of corporal punishment, but its very administration in an educational context, which models and fosters the resolution of conflict through violent means.

Belief in the importance of corporal punishment

In his classic work on the structure of scientific revolutions, Kuhn (1962) provided perspectives which can throw light on the continued adherence of education in South Africa to an outmoded approach to discipline. Kuhn proposed that science functions under the control of paradigms. Paradigms are implicit sets of assumptions which are seldom thought about or questioned. One such implicit assumption which dictates educational policy is the belief that corporal punishment is essential for instilling or maintaining discipline. It is difficult to imagine the origins of this assumption, for, in reality, nothing can be further from the truth. Discipline does not require punishment. Discipline refers to behaviour directed from within and not to compliance with demands made by others. It also does not refer to behaviour motivated by fear. Punishment, especially physical punishment, generates fear.

Discipline does not refer to the regimentation associated with most school procedures: lining-up, sitting in straight rows, speaking only when spoken to by the teacher, and a host of other rigid measures of control. Unfortunately, the greater the control that is exercised and the greater the subservience to that control, the better the 'discipline' at a school is considered to be. However, discipline has little to do with the imposition of rigid regulations. Teachers are there to teach, not to act as police.

Despite the extensive research literature indicating the mutual exclusivity of corporal punishment and discipline (see Holdstock 1987a), the mass of accumulated evidence is insufficient to break the stranglehold of the original belief that discipline is instilled by corporal punishment. As Kuhn (1962) pointed out, anomalies that do not fit a paradigm are usually ignored, minimized, or evaded. This seems to be what has happened with research findings concerning corporal punishment and discipline, since the evasion of relevant data is astounding. The author never ceases to be amazed how such a vast body of research as that related to the adverse effects of corporal punishment and the conditions necessary for the establishment of discipline can be avoided so assiduously.

Belief that the innate nature of humankind is not trustworthy

Another implicit assumption which dictates educational policy generally and which also determines attitudes towards corporal punishment is the belief that the basic nature of the person is not trustworthy. The individual is not regarded as having the potential to develop self-discipline unless he or she is forced to behave appropriately. Perhaps this mistrust is an expression of the attitude adults have about themselves and of the externally enforced discipline to which they have been exposed as children. Trusting neither their own potential and innate goodness nor that of others, teachers and parents rely on power and force to instil discipline in their pupils and children. A vicious cycle of violence becomes established. We know, as the subject has been the basis of numerous studies (see Holdstock, 1978a), that people replicate behaviour they have been exposed to. The use of force and power to control behaviour thus becomes a self-perpetuating mode of behaving. Few facts in psychology are as well substantiated as the finding that aggression breeds aggression, and that violence leads to violence.

Moral atrophy

In searching for a psychological explanation for the widespread reliance on corporal punishment, other factors which come to mind are authorization, routinization, and dehumanization. Because there is a law condoning corporal punishment, we no longer have to question our actions in this regard: 'People learn to look to official definitions of actions rather than to their human consequences in assessing their legitimacy' (Kelman, 1973: 54). What is more, many educators claim biblical sanction for caning children.

In such circumstances, individual moral principles no longer apply, and the individual is absolved of the responsibility to make personal moral choices. 'Authorization processes create a situation in which the person becomes involved in an action without really making a decision' (Kelman, 1973: 46).

The legal authorization of corporal punishment makes it easy to slip into caning as a matter of routine. When this happens, the opportunity never arises to question the moral efficacy of the punishment. Inevitably, the net result is a dehumanized approach to discipline in the school.

The dehumanization affects the total educational process. The psychic numbing and sense of detachment which becomes part of the personality make-up of the educator, prevents him or her from developing a sense of community, from caring, and from having compassion for the pupils. This, the author believes, is why so many educators can maintain that they 'cane with love'. 'As he gradually discards personal responsibility and human empathy, he loses his capacity to act as a moral being' (Kelman, 1973: 52).

The moral atrophy evident in our schools was again brought home to the author while he was working on this chapter. His son, who had been caned over his wet swimming costume within his first week at a local high school during a compulsory swimming practice, told him that he recently met one of the teachers who had taught at the school at the time. She told him how much they had laughed in the staffroom about his father's complaints to the principal. And the author's son described her as one of the 'nice' teachers.

This moral atrophy extends far beyond the school. The psychological denial of the damage that is caused, not only by educators, but also by some medical and social welfare personnel and particularly by law enforcement and judicial authorities, is an unhappy reality. In an alarming number of instances during the past few years, public prosecutors have declined to proceed with charges laid concerning what appeared to be clearly illegal instances of corporal punishment. Hence there seems to be collusion to protect the educational system from being held responsible for its actions.

Caning and career advancement

To be able to 'maintain good discipline' is a primary requisite for a teacher to get ahead in our educational system. Aspiring teachers and principals therefore have the maintenance of discipline high on the list of their priorities. Unfortunately, the perception of 'good discipline' is almost unfailingly regarded as quiet subservience to those in authority, and the way to achieve such obedience is through power and through instilling fear by the use of physical punishment.

It is clear, as Kuhn (1962) has pointed out, that a change in belief systems rather than in objective evidence alone is required for a paradigm shift to occur in our thinking about the role of punishment in discipline. Perhaps the escalating incidence of violence in all sectors of the South African community may facilitate a change in the prevailing belief that punishment, and especially corporal punishment, is beneficial for teaching and maintaining discipline.

INCIDENCE OF CORPORAL PUNISHMENT AT SCHOOLS

Although no one will ever admit it, fear has become the cornerstone on which our school education is based. The use of force to 'motivate' children to learn and resolve interpersonal conflicts is widespread. The extent to which it forms an integral part of the educational repertoire and belief systems of so many principals, teachers, and parents is frightening. As one principal said, 'Corporal punishment is one weapon that the teacher does have to strengthen his role. Without it his discipline is whittled away and the impact of his teaching is lost'. These words unfortunately represent the opinion of many school principals in South Africa. And it is not only the use of physical force, but also verbal abuse and the general abuse of power that are equally misguided ways utilized to 'motivate' students.

In a survey done by Rakitzis (1987) amongst male and female first-year students at the University of the Witwatersrand, the Rand Afrikaans University, and Vista University, 267 of 300 respondents (89 per cent) reported that they had been physically punished at some stage or another during their school career. Moreover, while it is supposedly illegal to hurt girls, 163 of 193 females (84,5 per cent) reported that they had been subjected to physical punishment in some form or another.

Although the percentage of illegal punishments of boys was not calculated, it was likely to constitute the majority of beatings. It was evident from the respondents' replies that the law was broken by school authorities on numerous occasions and in numerous ways. For instance, the law was broken with respect to the following: the location where punishment was administered — the majority of beatings occurred in the classroom; the place on the body where pain was inflicted — the hands and parts of the body other than the bottom were favoured; the instruments used — the regulation cane existed almost only in theory; the severity and manner in which the assault took place — damage ranged from broken skins and jaws to concussion and even the reported death of a fellow scholar; and numerous unjustifiable reasons for administering punishment. Table 12.1 indicates that the reported incidence of physical punishment is significantly higher in schools for white Afrikaans-speaking and black children than in schools for white English-speaking children, while Table 12.2 indicates that black pupils get hit most often.

Table 12.1: Incidence of corporal punishment, ethnic group and gender

	Afrikaans/white	Black	English/white	Total
Female	97,1% (68)	100,0% (55)	58,8% (40)	84,5% (163)
Male	96,7% (29)	97,8% (44)	96,9% (31)	97,2% (104)
Total	97,0%	99,0%	71,0%	89,0%

Source: Rakitzis, 1987: 23.

Thirty per cent of the black students reported being hit on a daily basis. The frequent occurrence of physical punishment to black children is substantiated by a study conducted in Bophuthatswana, where 50 per cent of children reported being beaten on a daily basis at primary school, and where one respondent commented, 'They beat me like a donkey' (Weiss, 1985: 8).

The high incidence and severity of physical punishment in black schools is of interest in view of the fact that in Rakitzis' study, black pupils reported much lower physical punishment at home. Compared to 8,4 per cent Afrikaans-speaking and 30,4 per cent English-speaking white students, 41,2 per cent of black students reported not being physically punished at home. Where then does the practice of beating pupils come from? Emulating the use of force by white educationists is certainly a major contributing factor. Another, in all probability, is displaced

Table 12.2: Frequency of corporal punishment and ethnic group

	Afrikaans/white	Black	English/white	Total
Once a day	2,1%	30,3%	1,4%	12,4%
Once a week	19,6%	22,2%	7,1%	17,3%
Once a month	22,7%	13,1%	18,6%	18,0%
Once a quarter	32,0%	8,1%	21,4%	20,3%
Once a year	15,5%	5,1%	12,9%	10,9%
Once an entire school career	2,1%	2,0%	27,1%	8,6%

Source: Rakitzis, 1987: 29.

aggression as a result of the great deal of frustration experienced by black males. Since upward social mobility is directly linked to aggression (Eron, 1980), the high incidence of corporal punishment at black schools can also be due to the emergence of a black bourgeoisie in the townships. The same may be true of the high incidence of corporal punishment among the Afrikaans-speaking community.

From the surveys done by Rakitzis (1987) and others during the past few years on the Witwatersrand and in Bophuthatswana (Davis, 1985; Rice, 1986; Weiss, 1985), it is clear that caning and other forms of physical abuse occur quite indiscriminately in black and white schools throughout the country. Principals and teachers know that they function within a society that condones and relies on violent means to resolve conflict, and as such they are confident of having the backing of their community. They also know that most parents are ignorant of the law and legal procedures. Besides, legal fees are notoriously high and cannot be afforded by most people.

OFFENCES FOR WHICH PUPILS GET CANED

Children have been caned 'legally' and otherwise for any number of offences. The variety is so great that offences can actually be sorted into a number of categories. To start with there is a scholastic category. Failure to perform in any number of subjects has on innumerable occasions been cause for caning. Among the ones reported have been: not reaching the standard that has been set for the pupil; not writing down homework; not doing homework; mistakes in composition; not attending afternoon study; leaving books at home; not doing memoranda of old examination papers; not submitting the correct book; not writing tests; being late for class or school; and so the list goes on.

'Offences' related to sport are even more intriguing. Boys have been caned for being offside in a soccer match; for losing a rugby match; for not attending rugby practice; for not batting properly in a cricket match; to build up team spirit; for not clapping during a match; and for talking during the start of a swimming event.

There also seems to be something about music which brings out aggression in teachers. Children have been caned for playing with the fluff of the carpet during a music lesson. Girls have been thrashed for not singing during assembly. Other 'offences' include being late for band practice, not being able to sing in tune, missing a cue in a play, and 'goofing-off' during the rehearsal of a musical.

Another category of 'misdemeanours' for which children are caned with regular frequency is that pertaining to personal appearance. Long hair on a boy is one of the most frequently punished 'crimes' in school. A few years ago, when the author's two older sons were at a local high school, all the boys whose hair was longer than the allowable minimum were caned — the number amounted to several hundred. Hair that curled was straightened out to see whether it reached over the collar and ears! Stepping the hair, or cutting it in too fashionable a style, is another sure way to get caned. Undoubtedly the most insensitive instances of caning for hair that is too long have occurred at a South African school for deaf children, where boys wear their hair long to cover their hearing aids. Wearing trousers not made of flannel fabric or unpolished shoes, not wearing the correct uniform, or leaving the shirt hanging out of the pants have all been reason enough to warrant corporal punishment. If girls wear nail-polish, they are asking for trouble. Girls have had their skirts lifted by female prefects to reveal whether they were wearing regulation panties.

Behaviour for which children have been beaten ranges from swearing to not replying to the teacher. Behaviours that draw physical punishment include snickering, fighting on the playground, being cheeky, flicking papers over the shoulder, rocking the chair the pupil sits on, making a noise outside or inside the classroom, smoking, and running in the corridor. The son of a friend of the author was caned for sitting on the grass during break with his girl-friend's head on his lap. She was compelled to witness the caning in the principal's office.

A final category of behaviour for which children are often caned can be labelled 'miscellaneous'. Under this category fall such offences as not having the regulation satchel, or simply being a member of a class in which someone or something had evoked the displeasure of the teacher.

Where and how pain is inflicted

The site chosen for inflicting the pain ranges from the ears, the face, the side and back of the head to the chest, legs, the backs of knees, calves, thighs, the back, hands, knuckles, and even feet. Legally, the buttocks have been sanctioned as the target site. The case of a pupil having to strip naked before being beaten brutally at least reached the courts (Olmesdahl, 1984), as did the use of flowered pants that had to be worn for caning at an industrial school for girls in the Eastern Transvaal (*Rapport*, 18 & 25 August, 1985).

The weapons used to inflict pain include leather straps, riding crops, planks, sticks, quince canes, open hands, balled fists, fan belts, ordinary belts, sjamboks, rulers, chalkboard dusters, window openers, leather thongs, aerials, hosepipes, strips of tyres, and water-pipes. Even a bucket has been used! Perhaps the use of a cricket bat to notch up a high score takes the batting prize. Hockey sticks have also found their niche in discipline. An alternative use for pencils in the area of pain infliction has been discovered as well. In this instance the pupil is instructed to place the palms of his or her hands together with fingers outspread. The pencils are then placed between the joints of the fingers and the ends pressed together.

Pinching and hair pulling occur frequently, as do ear pulling and ear boxing. Being kicked, slapped, and punched have also been reported, as have being flung against the wall, being made to do exhausting physical exercises (frog jumping, crouching on the heels with the arms stretched out in front, holding stones above the head) and being verbally abused (for example, being called a slut). A teacher in the northern suburbs of Johannesburg readily admitted to Rice (1986) that he disregarded the regulations openly, and regularly beat boys with a plank measuring three inches by fifteen inches. He used the pallor of the child to estimate when to stop the beating.

It is not often that teachers admit to flagrantly violating the law. However, even principals have acknowledged being unable to curb the use of corporal punishment in their schools. The regional director of the Department of Education in Pretoria, Mr P. J. Felstead, conceded: 'I'm not going to say the allegations aren't true. We can't control corporal punishment properly' (*Rand Daily Mail*, 26 April, 1984).

Isolating girls for unspecified periods of time, up to fourteen days in a room with only a mattress, blankets, and toilet bucket, is a regular form of punishment in industrial schools for girls. Often the isolation is in addition to being caned 'not more than six strokes at a time'. Effectively, that number often exceeds twelve strokes. For example, the principal of the industrial school which received so much publicity during 1985 said in court that he continued with the caning unless the victim showed sufficient repentance during the discussion which followed after the initial series of hits. Smoking, being cheeky, and running away from school were most often the reasons for the punishment (*Rapport*, 18 & 25 August, 1985).

There is an inverse relationship between the frequency with which boys and girls are beaten in primary and high school. The surveys conducted indicate that while boys are beaten more as they continue their schooling, girls experience less physical abuse. However, the decrease in physical abuse of girls is countered by an increase in verbal abuse during the high school years. Being called slut, hussy, or bitch is unfortunately not a once-only event. Regrettably, there is no reduction in the verbal abuse of boys with the increase in physical assault. Seventy-six per cent of the male respondents in the survey by Rice (1986) reported that they had experienced verbal abuse regularly at school.

Deaf, blind, and spastic children comprise minority groups which are not protected at all against physical assault. A seventeen-year-old deaf boy had his glasses knocked off his face. A few years ago a deaf girl was hit so hard on the side of her head that her hearing aid cracked, and reports have been received about deaf children bleeding from the ear after being hit. In one case a deaf and spastic seventeen-year-old boy was caned by the female principal of the school for 'snickering' during break.

Unfortunately, it is not possible to determine the exact frequency of legal corporal punishment in our schools. Such figures are available though, for principals are required by law to record every incident, including the name and age of the pupil concerned, the reason for the punishment, the number of strokes inflicted, the date, and the name of the person by whom the punishment was administered. To obtain such data is a virtual impossibility, however. While this may mean that the responsible authorities are ashamed of revealing the extent to which corporal punishment is administered, it could also mean that they are insufficiently concerned to regard the compilation of overall figures as important.

EFFECTS OF CORPORAL PUNISHMENT

The effects of corporal punishment are vast and penetrating in their extent. Obviously some children are more susceptible than others, and those who are sensitive, deprived, or experiencing problems in living are the ones most vulnerable. They are the ones who are already living under stress and who are in greater need of understanding and guidance, not violent rejection.

People who have been subjected to physical injury at school often· claim that it has done them no harm, or even that it has done them the world of good. It is quite likely that many people will be able to overcome and interpret the abuse constructively, for the human organism is capable of tremendous resilience in the face of adversity. We adapt to the greatest upheavals in our lives, even to the death of beloved ones.

However, it can be said with certainty that although we are able to overcome abuse, we are never quite the same afterwards. We will, in our own particular way, manifest the effect of being beaten, or of being unwilling witnesses to the abuse of our peers. Furthermore, extensive research evidence indicates the deleterious effects of corporal punishment in schools.

Physical injury

The extent of our adaptation to the abuse of our children is such that weals left on the buttock for days after the caning are not really considered to constitute a physical injury. While it is newsworthy when a teacher breaks a pupil's jaw in several places (*Rand Daily Mail*, 5 May, 1984), some violent teachers only make the newspapers after their third or fourth attempt. What stopped one teacher from continuing his jaw-busting campaign at a private school in Johannesburg was that he nearly got his own jaw broken (Personal Communication). There might be justification in the use of violence to curb violence after all.

Besides broken jaws, broken teeth and head injuries have also been reported, as have cracked ribs and fractured wrists (*Rand Daily Mail*, 5 May, 1984). Rice (1985) reported that a nine-year-old girl was flung against the blackboard with such force that she sustained a leg fracture. Bald patches have been left where hair has been pulled out, and purple bruises bear silent testimony to being pinched or hit. Bleeding from the nose and ears has also resulted from being hit in the face.

According to a survey conducted by the Health Workers' Association, nine children are treated daily in Soweto clinics for injuries suffered as a result of corporal punishment (*Rand Daily Mail*, 5 May, 1984). A 21-year-old schoolgirl in Soweto lost consciousness and had to be taken in a serious condition to hospital (*Rand Daily Mail*, 20 October, 1982). She was held to a table by six pupils and flogged on her buttocks and back by a teacher until she lost consciousness. Others have paid an even heavier price. A few years ago, Koos Seakgoe, eighteen, fainted at his desk minutes after having been caned, and later died in hospital (*The Star*, 22 September, 1980). Even younger pupils have been reported to have died following severe beatings (*Rand Daily Mail*, 27 March, 1985).

Educational impairment

In a decade-long study of 2 700 primary schools in Britain, Rutter and his colleagues (1979) found that rigid discipline, punishment, and teachers who were negative models tended to produce depressed achievement scores, regardless of student potential at entry. Not only was scholastic performance impaired, but fear of school, fear of teachers, and aversion to educationally related matters were generated. The long-term educational harm which was done was unquestionable.

Hentoff (1973) concluded that punishment caused a deterioration in the learning process and led to the inhibition of learning rather than the acquisition of skills. Punishment creates fear, and as John Holt (1967) surmised, we stop learning dead in its tracks when we make children afraid.

Educational impairment is manifested through the many undesirable side-effects and the unfortunate and unforeseen consequences of punishment (Green, 1982; Risley, 1968). Since the aversion is directed towards everything concerning the school, the student withdraws wherever possible from the punishing situation. Tardiness, truancy, dropping out of school, and poor student-teacher relationships are the result (Azrin & Holz, 1966; Azrin *et al.*, 1965; Bongiovanni & Hyman, 1978; Borin & Coleman, 1970; Dubanoski *et al.*, 1983; Hutchinson, 1977; Meacham & Wiesen, 1969; Skinner, 1986). Continued use of punishment maintains the undesirable behaviour (Azrin & Holz, 1966; Skinner, 1953). The extensive research conducted by Aspey and Roebuck (1974) in the United States, and by Reinhard and Anne-Marie Tausch in Germany (see Rogers, 1983) supports the above findings. These two groups found that students who were taught by teachers who received low ratings on empathy, congruence, and positive regard learned less, were absent more, were less creative, were less capable of problem-solving, and behaved poorly. Physical pain was not even a factor and yet the scholastic impairment was obvious.

When placed under competitive stress, children with learning disabilities often attempt to compensate for their feelings of frustration in ways that disrupt others. The probable effect of punishment for such conduct is to compound the stress of the children and reduce the likelihood that the true nature of their difficulty will be detected. For these children in particular, physical punishment adds a new problem to the serious one they already have.

Violence breeds violence

Perhaps there is no greater consensus among clinical observations and research literature anywhere than that relating to the finding that aggression breeds aggression, and that violence is a learned response. In dozens of books and hundreds of articles this fact has been documented again and again. The words of John H. Meier, Director of the Research Division of Childhelp USA/International and Past Chief of the US Children's Bureau, capture succinctly the essence of all the research studies: 'The roots of much family violence and even much international violence are traceable to violent child-rearing and punitive pedagogic procedures' (in Suzukawa & Riak, 1984: 19–20).

'Aggression is a behaviour that is learned very early in life and is learned very well — the pay-off is tremendous', concluded Eron (1980: 244) after twenty-five years of research which included laboratory experiments, field studies, and longitudinal investigations. Thomas Gordon, internationally famous workshop leader and author of books on teacher and parent effectiveness training, concluded similarly:

> Research studies consistently show that punishment doesn't prevent aggressive behaviour of children, but it actually causes aggressive behaviour. Nearly 100% of children whose parents use physical punishment commit violent acts against other children as opposed to only 20% of children whose parents have not used physical punishment … (in Suzukawa & Riak, 1984: Preface).

The child who has experienced the use of physical punishment will tend to become, as an adult, someone who uses force to solve problems, including family problems. A report to the United States Congress in 1978, on violent and safe schools, found a high correlation between physical punishment and violent behaviour in pupils (*Violent Schools*, 1978). The work of Bandura and his colleagues clearly demonstrates how the teacher who strikes a student provides a model of aggressive behaviour to be copied by the student (see Bandura, 1973 & 1977).

Aggression becomes justified as a teacher-sanctioned method of problem-solving. Hyman (1981), for instance, found that teachers who had been caned by their parents tended to use corporal punishment in the classroom.

McCandless (1967), a foremost developmental psychologist, wrote that children imitate or model upon aggressive adults. The conclusion can therefore be drawn that arbitrary and unreasonable methods of control and high levels of punishment will be associated with aggressive child behaviour. Eron (1980) and his associates initially anticipated that punishing aggression would lead to inhibition of aggression. What they found was the opposite: punishment routinely increased aggression.

A near perfect correlation exists between the amount and severity of physical punishment endured by a child from two to twelve years of age and the amount and severity of antisocial aggressiveness that the child displays during adolescence (Button, 1973; Welsh, 1974), and mothers who severely punish aggressive behaviour in their children have more aggressive children than mothers who lightly punish aggressiveness.

Counter-aggression is a logical consequence of being beaten. It comes to expression in multiple-forms such as resentment and retaliation against persons — teachers, classmates — and property (Dubanoski *et al.*, 1983; Wright, 1982).

Bandura (1965) and Wright (1982) have pointed out additional ways in which physical punishment becomes self-perpetuating. As a result of the attention which a punished student receives from his or her peers he or she can actually end up courting punishment. As Rice (1985: 25) says '… rampant masochism triumphs over common sense!' Physical punishment of a child may have the effect of temporarily suppressing conduct which is troublesome to the teacher, thus creating the illusion that the problem has been corrected. In this way, inner conflicts which might otherwise be resolved are repressed. At a later time, however, these same conflicts are apt to reappear, sometimes in violent form. Numerous controlled studies conducted in America and Europe have confirmed that, with few exceptions, child-beaters and persons convicted of violent crimes, including rape, were beaten or otherwise abused when they were children.

It is often claimed that physical punishment is used as a 'last resort'. However, there is abundant evidence to show that in schools where children are hit, such treatment, or the threat of it, often represents a first line of approach. As long as violent options are available, they will be used; and the least competent of teachers will rely most heavily on their use.

The relationship between teachers and children will be undermined by fear, resentment, hostility, and suspicion. It is most unlikely that such an environment, devoid of trust, can contribute anything to the development of responsible adulthood.

The following brief, but dramatic, personal account sent to the author clearly demonstrates the progression from being on the receiving end of violence to utilizing it 'legally' and illegally:

> Your article on corporal punishment recalled thirty years of conflict; the highlights being my mother destroying me into submission with a horse-riding whip and all the teachers at College, two of whom were Springbok rugby players, giving me cuts on such a frequent basis that I started a game of cricket amongst all the college boys. Each cut represented a run. On one day I received more than a dozen cuts. I was unaware of the psychological abuse until I stood before a Supreme Court Judge as a first offender and received a thirty year sentence. During my incarceration the psychologists showed how the violence I was subjected to in turn became the violence that I used as a vehicle to success, as a policeman, and later as a criminal.

It is therefore not surprising that O'Leary and O'Leary (1977), in discussing the use of punishment procedures in classroom management, suggested that physical punishment should be avoided at all possible costs.

Psychological harm

Apart from breeding violence, numerous studies have documented scores of psychologically damaging effects of corporal punishment. 'The damaged individual tends to have lowered self-esteem, possesses weakened negotiation and communication skills and is burdened by the experience of submission to abusive treatment by authorities', concluded Parents and Teachers Against Violence in Education in a statement submitted to the US Attorney-General's Task Force on Family Violence (in Suzukawa & Riak, 1984: 1).

Lowered self-esteem, emotional abuse, and feelings of rejection and depression as a result of caning in schools have also been reported in many other studies (for example, Dubanoski *et al.*, 1983; Green, 1982; Strickland & Campbell, 1982; Walters & Grusec, 1977). Educational psychologists agree that self-respect and a healthy self-concept are not only necessary in order to be able to respect others, but are directly related to academic achievement.

On the virtually endless list of undesirable behavioural patterns which have been documented as a result of corporal punishment, are low courage in adulthood (Adler, 1970); a lack of self-direction and immaturity in childhood (Smith *et al.*, 1979); more dependence and inhibition, less co-operation, less friendliness towards others, and less spontaneity (Gordon *et al.*, 1979); a weakly developed sense of conscience (Solheim, 1982); a diminished belief in free will and a strong belief in determinism (Viney *et al.*, 1982); low student achievement (Lambeth, 1978; Rosenshein & Furst, 1971); rigidity, fixation, regression, displacement, primitivization, and resignation (Yates, 1962); more personal problems, heightened anxiety, and depression (Maier, 1974; Walters & Grusec, 1977); and more negative social interaction, a greater number of problems with addiction, and a greater likelihood of describing achievements as below average (Bryan & Freed, 1982). The detrimental effect of corporal punishment is long-lasting (Maurer, 1974). Various forms of psychopathy in children are found to correlate positively with the degree of physical punishment received (Feshbach & Feshbach, 1973). Even neurotic, psychosomatic, and psychotic symptoms have been reported as a result of punishment (Brady, 1958; Gantt, 1944; Masserman, 1943).

Psychosomatic effects which have been noted are skin problems, insomnia, nightmares, headaches, muscle tension, ulcers, various other stomach upsets, general fatigue, and accident-proneness. Suicidal tendencies and even suicide have been reported.

Sociological effects

Corporal punishment acts as an incitement to rebellion and general criminal behaviour. Welsh (1974) maintained that he had never interviewed a juvenile delinquent who had not been beaten by his parents, while Glueck and Glueck (1950) found that physical punishment was the favoured disciplinary method of both fathers and mothers of delinquent boys: 'Violent adults endured violence when they were young' (Curtis, 1963: 386).

There is a direct relationship between the frequency and severity of corporal punishment and student violence. After the Inner London Education Authority abolished corporal punishment, attacks on teachers dropped from an average of sixty to sixty-three per year to an average of two to three. Counter-aggression is frequently manifested in the vandalizing of school property (Azrin *et al.*, 1964; Ulrich & Azrin, 1962). The idea has often been expressed that vandalism is a retaliation for punishment and humiliations suffered in school (Kvaraceus, 1945; Maurer, 1974; Welsh, 1974). Glasser (1978) wrote that corporal punishment should be abolished for many reasons, but the most important reason is that it causes more problems of vandalism and violence than it solves. A study of Oregon schools by Maurer (1974), found a strong correlation between the frequency and severity of physical punishment and school vandalism costs per pupil. After studying thirty schools over a three-year period, Clegg and Megson (1968) found that those not using the cane had less delinquency than cane-using schools.

Corporal punishment is a major contributing factor in substance abuse, lying, and running away from home and school. Caning boys for smoking actually increased their cigarette consumption, during a period when smoking amongst children was generally in decline (Palmer, 1965). Even though girls at industrial schools are afraid of the risks involved in hitch-hiking to their home town, they nevertheless take the risk repeatedly, in order to escape the caning they are subjected to at school. It is one way in which they can exert some measure of control over the abhorrent conditions threatening their young lives. Smoking is another attempt to manifest some control.

Sexual deviations

Substantial evidence exists which points towards sexual deviation as one of the side-effects of corporal punishment. In *The English Vice*, Ian Gibson (1978) cites the observations of numerous pre-modern writers regarding the connection between corporal punishment and sexual perversion. He refers to the classic study of sexual deviance, *Psychopathia Sexualis* by Krafft-Ebing, which cautions that spanking should be avoided at all costs because of its potential for activating deviant tendencies.

More recently a task force of the British Psychological Association (1980) concluded that corporal punishment was a significant factor in the autogenesis of sexual perversion (in Suzukawa & Riak, 1984). The existence of such erotic magazines as the *Joy of Spanking*, *Art of Caning*, and *Sting*, which are exclusively devoted to corporal punishment, demonstrates an unwholesome interest in corporal punishment. In order to make a profit the magazines must have a wide circulation.

'Trauma in childhood, including corporal punishment, may be associated with an interruption of normal sexual development and lead to numerous other forms of disorder' (Alexander & Ross, 1961: 104). Bakan (1971), Livingstone (1975), and Morris (1967) concur that corporal punishment in childhood can lead to sexual deviation.

Confessions about the sexual excitement and even orgasm experienced during the process of beating a child exist in the literature (Anthony, 1969), while instances of sexual excitement being experienced while being beaten at school have been reported in local radio phone-in programmes.

The author often wonders at the symbolic significance of choosing the buttocks as an area where caning can be executed officially. Why, for instance, not the shoulder blades? Could it be that, due to the proximity of the buttocks to the sexual organs, we are expressing our sentiments about sexuality in an unconscious way?

Moral atrophy

The violation of body space and the invasion of children's privacy which occurs during corporal punishment convey to them the message that adults have special authority over their bodies, including the right to inflict pain. Apart from denying children the right to the dignity of their bodies, it dis-empowers them and prepares the ground for them to become victims, as in the many cases of sexual abuse.

Moral helplessness also comes about indirectly. By merely being a helpless witness to psychological bullying and violent classroom management, children learn to negate their inner experiences. Eventually they become passive and psychologically numb, losing much of their empathic ability. Several workers attribute the alienation from, and indifference to, others in society to be a direct result of the moral helplessness children experienced in school. The internalization of social morality is retarded. Corporal punishment produces personalities which lack a sense of will independent of the commands of authority (Stensrud & Stensrud, 1981).

It is not only the victimized, but the victimizer who becomes dehumanized. Dehumanization of the victimizer is a gradual process that develops out of the act of victimization itself (Kelman, 1978).

Conditioning of the autonomic nervous system

During physical hurt and psychological abuse, functions of the autonomic nervous system (such as heart rate, blood pressure, skin resistance, gastric secretions, blood vessel dilation, hormonal secretions) are thrown into turmoil. Since autonomic functions condition extremely rapidly, they become immediately associated with the conditions — teacher, subject matter, school, and education in general — which caused their arousal. Once such an association has been formed between the autonomic function and the school situation, it is virtually impossible to extinguish it. Thus, the effects of a single act of caning can result in a long-term association between aspects of schooling and hyperactive autonomic functioning. We also know that we see and hear less sharply when, for instance, the heart-rate increases too much above resting levels. Thus, caning impairs perceptual functioning, not only in the short term but the long term as well. Optimal learning occurs when we are relaxed. And being relaxed means more than just appearing relaxed. It requires a state of physiological activation which does not become hyperactive when confronted with the school situation and education-ally-related matters.

Damage to interpersonal relationships

Punishment drives out the love, trust, and intimacy from adult-child relationships in the home and in the classroom. It does not prepare children to become co-operative productive and self-motivated adults. School is to prepare the child for adulthood. The teacher is likely to be the first important authority figure outside the family whom the child meets, and the classroom the first formal social situation. The school experience is important, not only in the acquisition of knowledge and skills, but also in determining long-term ethical values and behavioural traits. In employing corporal punishment and verbal abuse within our educational system, we perpetuate the ills in our society that we would like to eradicate.

Classrooms are essentially small-scale societies, with a wide variety of human interaction. What better place is there to learn interpersonal skills, intra-personal awareness, and personal responsibility than in the class-room, where natural human comforts and discomforts bring about close interpersonal relations, as well as conflicts, not only between children, but also between children and adults? The way in which these conflicts can be resolved is one of the most important lessons children can learn. If the behaviour that is modelled by those in authority is based on power and punishment, as is the case at present, we have no chance of lessening the excessive amount of violence in our society. We have abundant evidence that children who are abused by authority, when they them-selves rise to positions of authority, tend to have difficulties in relating to their subordinates.

Interpersonal relationships based on power rather than communica-tion have far-reaching detrimental effects on establishing and maintain-ing intimate and loving relationships. Psychoanalytically-oriented mental-health workers regard punitive behaviour by adults as a form of delayed revenge-taking.

Though being hit may not always damage every child thus treated, it does damage every 'hitting teacher'. It is virtually impossible for one human being to hit another without being in an aggressive state of mind and the teacher who hits must either be one whose aggressive emotions run out of control, or one who deliberately generates feelings of aggression in order to hit. The alternative is an emotionally atrophied person. In either case, whether the teacher indulges violent feelings or encourages them, the result is the same. The 'hitting teacher' eventually assumes a habitual response to children in general — one of profound dislike; and, being surrounded by them, is in a state of constant readiness for aggressive action. Obviously, the essential skills of a good teacher — patience, understanding, respect, the ability to generate enthusiasm for learning in all kinds of children — have little opportunity to develop in such circumstances. The aggressive teacher moves in the opposite direction, teaching less and intimidating more. Abolition of physical punishment will benefit the entire teaching profession because it will seal off this one route to professional disillusionment and failure which currently claims so many unhappy individuals.

Powerlessness of parents

Over the years the author has not only received numerous letters from children expressing their resentment against corporal punishment at school, but even more parents have expressed their anger and hurt over the pain inflicted on their children. The author, too, has spent sleepless nights about the senseless caning of two of his sons (Holdstock, 1987a). In his struggle to have his children treated with respect while they were at primary and secondary school, it became abundantly clear that parents have no rights when it comes to the education of their children (Holdstock, 1987b). The power with which the educational system functions is truly frightening.

Of the many letters received by the author, the comments have ranged from mild to extreme concern. One mother wrote:

> I worry about having to send my sons to school where a minor act of forgetfulness or a genuine mistake is punishable with physical violence and I think my husband worries too, but he seems to think that if we don't hear about it, it won't be happening. I feel powerless in a situation which should not even exist in a civilized country.

Another mother wrote:

> Yesterday my child woke up and cried softly into the pillow. He would not tell me a thing. He stalled and dawdled getting dressed.

More tears fell into his breakfast. I asked what was upsetting him. "Everything — just everything — I can't take school any more. I just want to die. I don't want to live any more". "Who is upsetting you?" I asked. "No one in particular, just everyone and everything about school. I hate it. I just can't go on".

One of the saddest aspects about the communications that the author has received from parents is that so many of them have asked to remain anonymous for fear of victimization: 'I apologize for remaining anonymous but HAVE to, as I have children in school at present'.

Parents on the platteland (country areas) have expressed an additional concern of not having an alternative school to which they could send their children. Parents of disabled children shared the same concern. Even in the cities, there is usually only one school for a specific disability.

Whether the threat of victimization is real or not, the important thing is that the fear of their children being victimized is very real. Parents have come to live in fear of fear. They therefore do not dare to question the behaviour of teachers or principals.

INTERVENTION
Abolishing corporal punishment

Without question the most important task awaiting education is the abolishment of laws and regulations which legitimate corporal punishment in schools.

In no other country in the world is there such total condonation of corporal punishment. Even in the few countries where there is not a total ban on corporal punishment, as in the United States and Australia, one state after another is passing legislation outlawing the use of corporal punishment in schools. There is a universal call from professional organizations against the use of corporal punishment, and for the passing of legislation to bind all education authorities who have not already done so to a code of positive human rights to all youngsters. Among organizations active in this respect are the American Academy of Pediatrics, the Task Force of the National Education Association in the United States, the American Medical Association, the American Psychological Association, the Austrian Teachers Union, the Child Guidance Services of the Dutch Ministry of Education, the Western Australia Council of State School Organizations, and numerous others (Holdstock, 1987a).

World famous scientists and scholars have voiced a similar plea. Among these can be counted Albert Einstein, B. F. Skinner, Carl Rogers, Linus Pauling, Karl Menninger, and hundreds of others. In fact, documented concern about corporal punishment dates back to the first century AD. In his *Institutio Oratoria*, Quintillian, teacher of rhetoric, wrote:

> ... I am entirely against the practice of corporal punishment in education, although it is widespread, and even Chrysippus does not condemn it. In the first place, it is a disgusting and slavish treatment which would certainly be regarded as an insult if it were inflicted on adults. Further, the pupil whose mind is too coarse to be improved by censure will become as indifferent to blows as the worst slaves. Finally, these chastisements would be entirely un-necessary if the teachers were patient and helpful. But nowadays teachers seem to be so slack that the boys are not induced to do what is right, but are punished for not doing it. And consider how shameful, how dangerous to modesty are the effects produced by the pain or fear of the victims. This feeling of shame cripples and maims the spirit, making it flee from and detest the light of day. And if we do not take more care to choose teachers and instructors of good character, I blush to think how shamefully such con-temptible fellows will misuse their rights. But I will spend no longer time on this matter — we know enough of it already ...

Revision of basic values

Psychologists are in agreement that aggression is learned behaviour. In order to reduce the level of aggression in society it is essential that we intervene early in the socialization of children so that they learn alterna-tive ways of solving problems and do not have to rely on aggressive techniques to gain their objective. Boys should be exposed to the same training that girls traditionally receive in our society, and should be encouraged to develop similar kinds of socially positive, tender, co-operative, nurturing, and sensitive qualities, which are antithetical to aggressive behaviour. Unfortunately, such an approach is contrary to the 'might makes right' attitude that is pervasive throughout the Western world.

In the final analysis, one cannot help but wonder at the extent to which education is a reflection of the overall authoritarian structure of Western society, its trust in power and force, its lack of open communication, and its disrespect for the dignity and potential of others, be they of different skin colour or age. It seems equally obvious that there is nothing in our present educational approach that will provide the present generation of young people with the skills necessary to equip them to solve the interpersonal problems of the country.

We need to rethink our firm conviction that education is something done by those in the know to those who are ignorant. This may require a total overhaul of some of the holy cows of Western civilization. Our emphasis on dynamism and action needs to be blended with the principles operative in other cultures. And perhaps no greater step can be taken in education today than to realize the ancient wisdom of Lao-tse:

> He who imposes himself has the small manifest might; he who does not impose himself has the great secret might ... The perfected man does not interfere in the life of beings, he does not impose himself on them, but he helps all beings to their freedom.

The philosophy of Krishnamurti is equally powerful and perhaps it could do us the world of good to develop attitudes in accordance with his statement that 'The wise wield no authority, and those in authority are not wise'.

Courses in interpersonal relations

What is going on in our educational system? How is it possible that principals, vice-principals, and teachers do not know of alternatives to motivate children and to maintain discipline, especially in this day and age, when there is such widespread exploration of holistic and person-centred approaches to education? Should some of the educational budget not be set aside to provide opportunities for teachers to attend courses on the human dimensions of their profession? And, if such courses do not exist, they should be created.

In the light of the knowledge and methods available to us in education today, it is sad that the law legalizing the use of violence in the principal's office should still be on the statute books. There is absolutely no reason whatsoever why any violence, on the part of the principal or any teacher, should be necessary and be tolerated.

It is the negation of the essential humanness of children, and the disregard for the importance of the interpersonal aspect of the pupil-teacher relationship, where education fails so miserably. Undoubtedly, the most important thing lacking in our educational system revolves around the issue of the child as person and not the child as pupil. Education claims to have the whole person at heart, but that claim is often nothing more than empty rhetoric. Respect for the child is absent. Understanding, care, and empathy are lacking, as well as honesty.

The European way

Since European schools do not sanction the use of corporal punishment, the Society for Teachers Opposed to Physical Punishment (STOPP) in England has been interested in determining the nature of teacher-pupil relationships on the Continent. Several independent studies such as *Europe at School* by Norman Newcombe (1977), and *Lessons from Europe* by Max Wilkinson (1977) have also been conducted. The general consensus is that European teachers have very pleasant and easy relations with their pupils.

An observation by a Dutch teacher about English schools also holds for South African schools. She remarked that the difference between British and Dutch schools was pronounced. In British schools there was an enormous gap between teachers and pupils. This was something that her exchange students remarked upon each year. There were much better relations between children and teachers in Dutch schools. Pupils were able to come and talk out problems, and it was much easier to work in this relaxed atmosphere.

One of the main reasons why teacher-pupil relationships tend to be much friendlier and more relaxed on the Continent than in Britain is that petty and unnecessary rules and regimentation are virtually unknown there. Pupils in Europe often have more freedom in such matters as dress, coming and going, smoking, and personal appearance. Thus, disciplinary problems can be reduced by relaxing our attitude toward non-essential matters. STOPP notes (Occasional paper, undated) that where only necessary and sensible rules are made, they are much more readily accepted by pupils: the resentment, bred by petty restrictions, which often leads to so much trouble in British schools, is consequently absent. European teachers tend to assume that children are responsible people, unless the children prove themselves not to be: the general effect of this is to make the children more co-operative.

Of course, even with an atmosphere generally more conducive to good behaviour, problems will arise, but there are many procedures and techniques used regularly by European teachers — and by good teachers everywhere — which help to ameliorate such difficulties. In the first place, European teachers believe much more strongly in the importance of consulting about their children. In contrast, South African teachers can beat children without informing, let alone consulting parents. In fact, children are beaten in defiance of parental wishes. As already stated, parents in South Africa effectively have no rights as far as the education of their children is concerned.

European teachers also realize that persistent behavioural problems are often outward manifestations of deeper conflict. If effective and long-lasting improvement in behaviour is to be achieved, it is necessary to understand the root causes of 'misbehaviour'. For instance, in Norway the Basic School Act lays down that the schools must determine whether misconduct has been caused by the teaching methods, class situation, or home environment; by teacher-pupil, home-school, or pupil-pupil relationships; or by the mental or physical health of the pupil.

Every European country emphasizes the importance of consulting parents who, after all, will normally know their children better than even the most conscientious teacher. STOPP concluded that parents in West Germany are probably consulted to the greatest extent (Occasional paper, undated). They are frequently involved not only in disciplinary committees, but also in conferences discussing other aspects of school life. Of course, the right to be consulted carries with it a corollary to accept greater responsibility for the behaviour of their children. Parental involvement of this nature is vastly more extensive than the conceptualization of parent-teacher associations in South Africa. Here parent-teacher associations are little more than fund-raising bodies and are powerless as far as basic educational issues are concerned. This is true even of the governing bodies of the different schools.

In some European countries, notably France and Germany, pupils are represented on various disciplinary and other committees connected with school life. Although the spectre of 'pupil power' might worry some teachers, the participation of children in at least some of the decision-making processes of the school tends to improve the atmosphere of the school community, since it breaks down feelings of 'them' and 'us' and increases the commitment of pupils to their school. If children are given more responsibility and feel that their opinions count, they tend to behave in a more concerned and responsible way.

Disciplinary committees, often involving pupils, teachers, and parents, ensure that arbitrary decisions are not taken by an individual teacher in the heat of the moment, but allow time for reflection and consideration of all the relevant factors by a variety of people.

Tricks of the trade

The reviews of European schools by STOPP (Occasional paper, undated), Newcombe (1977), and Wilkinson (1977) are in full agreement with the research carried out in Germany by Tausch (in Rogers, 1983), in England by Rutter (1979) and in the United States by Aspey and

Roebuck (in Rogers, 1983): it is the attitude of the teacher and the quality of the interpersonal relationship with the pupils which are the prime determinants of the quality of discipline and academic standards. However, due to the 'intangible' nature of these two variables, our materialistic and technological orientation makes it difficult to conceive of them as concrete techniques to be utilized in maintaining discipline. In fact, the attitudes of the teacher and the nature of the interpersonal relationship do more than simply maintain discipline, they are strategies for instilling discipline (see Holdstock, 1987a).

The author has often had the feedback, during talks on discipline in which he discussed the attitude of the teacher and the nature of the relationship with the pupils, that he (the author) failed to say anything about how discipline can be kept in the classroom. Advising people how to be, rather than telling them what to do, is not considered concrete and tangible enough to allow people to feel that they have techniques at their disposal which can be employed to maintain discipline and facilitate learning.

In counselling parents about the problems they experience with their children, the author's advice to them is to work on themselves, to stay with their own consciousness. By doing that they provide the best possible model for their children. It is the best and the most helpful thing that can be done; it is also the best and the most helpful thing for any teacher to do.

We have to move away from being resentful of the poor behaviour of students and of their low grades, and from being reluctant to spend time and trouble dealing with behavioural problems, to a willingness to use the conflict as an educational opportunity.

This requires a willingness to view behavioural problems from the pupil's point of view; a willingness to be empathic, which often means spending a lot of time and energy on one behavioural problem; a willingness to be open and to be a real human being; and also a willingness to involve parents fully in the process. The attitude change required is a move away from an attitude of 'power over' to one based on person-centred values.

All the authorities on disciplinary methods agree that situations in which the teacher is the sole decision-maker in setting up behavioural guidelines should be avoided. The collective wisdom of all the persons in the classroom should be utilized to the common good of all. The teacher is an important member of the classroom community and has his or her rights and needs which must be respected. But the same goes for every other member. The more the students are actively involved in creating an orderly climate for learning, the more likely they are to preserve that climate.

In addition, there are strategies which the teacher can employ with good effect to control disruptive behaviour. 'Time-out' is one. It gives the student and teacher the chance to regain self-control; the message is not punitive; and the exiled student is not criticized. It is important to avoid stigmatizing pupils. 'Time-out' is utilized differently in various parts of the world. In Europe, children who are not behaving are sent to another class, preferably one in which the same subject is taught, or to the teacher in whose class they were the previous year. In serious instances of misconduct they are sent to time-out rooms where they can work under supervision. The latter is a form of punishment regularly encountered in South African schools for relatively minor offences.

Reinforcing positive and ignoring negative behaviour is a very important and effective means of shaping the conduct of pupils in the classroom. However, it is easier said than done. It requires considerable patience and self-control to persistently ignore disruptive behaviour, although the long-term effects are rewarding.

Consulting with the child after the class period, or after school, is also to be recommended. In addition, many disciplinary problems can be avoided by introducing innovative teaching methods. For instance, it is much more effective to whisper in the ear of the student who does not behave than to shout at him or her. Another 'trick of the trade' is to have as much direct eye contact with the pupils as possible. In essence, though, this technique, like all the other ones which are most effective in maintaining discipline, depends upon the quality of the interpersonal relationship and the basic humanness of the teacher and the educational situation. However, research on this approach needs to be done in rural African communities where eye contact has other cultural connotations.

So-called disciplinary methods are only necessary where the interpersonal relationship between teacher and students has broken down. The most important task awaiting education is to prepare teachers not only academically, but in a personal sense. Our focus has to shift toward recognizing the value of human relations as of prime importance. If it does not start at the top, we cannot expect it to come about. Time, money, and energy have to be devoted to educating teachers in the skills of interpersonal communication along the lines of person-centred principles.

There are undoubtedly thousands of teachers who have the best possible relations with their pupils. They are the ones who model the values that facilitate actualization of the potential of the children in our schools. Unfortunately, their task is made so much more difficult by the prevailing focus on content acquisition and the good they do can easily be undone by the actions of overzealous colleagues.

CONCLUSION

To summarize, general agreement exists among informed professionals that punishment in any form, and corporal punishment specifically, is to be avoided at all costs, due to the deleterious effects it has on scholastic performance and behaviour as well as on personality growth. Not only will the quality of our education improve if we abolish punishment, but by doing so, we will help to reverse the trend of family, social, and political violence in our society. It is imperative that the South African teaching profession be persuaded to set an example of how conflict can be resolved without resorting to violent means. The way things are, the teaching profession and all others concerned in education, stand indicted of irresponsibility by their disregard of the facts concerning corporal punishment. Our country can ill afford such irresponsibility. The saving in the cost of remedial services, and the financial advantage of improved educational skills, are likely to run into tens of millions of rands.

REFERENCES

Adler, A. (1970) *The Education of Children*, Chicago: Gateway.

Alexander, F. & Ross, H. (1961) *The Impact of Freudian Psychiatry*, Chicago: University of Chicago Press.

Anthony, E. J. (1969) 'It Hurts Me More than it Hurts You — An Approach to Discipline as a Two-Way Process'. In *From Learning for Love to Love of Learning: Essays on Psychoanalysis and Education*, edited by R. Ekstein & R. J. Motto, New York: Brunner/Mazel.

Aspey, D. N. & Roebuck, F. N. (1974) 'From Humane Ideas to Humane Technology and Back Again Many Times', *Education*, 95, 163–71.

Azrin, N. H. *et al.* (1965) 'Motivational Aspects of Escape from Punishment', *Journal of the Experimental Analysis of Behaviour*, 8, 31–44.

Azrin, N. H. *et al.* (1964) 'Pain Aggression towards Inanimate Objects', *Journal of the Experimental Analysis of Behaviour*, 7, 223–8.

Azrin, N. H. & Holz, W. C. (1966) 'Punishment'. In *Operant Behaviour* edited by W. K. Honing, New York: Appleton Century Crofts.

Bakan, D. (1971) 'The Effects of Corporal Punishment in School', *Journal of the Ontario Association of Children's Aid Societies*, November, 1–13.

Bandura, A. (1977) *Social Learning Theory*, Englewood Cliffs: Prentice-Hall, Inc.

Bandura, A. (1973) *Aggression: A Social Learning Analysis*, Englewood Cliffs: Prentice-Hall, Inc.

Bandura, A. (1965) 'Behaviour Modification through Modeling Procedures'. In *Research in Behaviour Modification*, edited by L. Kramer & L. P. Ullman, New York: Holt, Rinehart & Winston.

Bongiavanni, A. F. & Hyman, I. (1978) 'Levitan is Wrong on the Use of Corporal Punishment', *Psychology in Schools*, 15, 290–1.

Boren, J. J. & Coleman, A. D. (1970) 'Some Experiments on Reinforcement Principles within a Psychiatric Ward for Delinquent Soldiers', *Journal of Applied Behavioural Analysis*, 3, 29–37.

Brady, J. V. (1958) 'Ulcers in "Executive Monkeys"', *Scientific American*, 199, 95–103.

Bryan, J. W. & Freed, F. W. (1982) 'Corporal Punishment: Normative Data and Sociological and Psychological Correlates in a Community College Population', *Journal of Youth and Adolescence*, 11, 77–87.

Button, A. de W. (1973) 'Some Antecedents of Felonious and Delinquent Behavior', *Journal of Child Clinical Psychology*, 2, 35–7.

Clegg, A. & Megson, B. (1968) *Children in Distress*, Harmondsworth: Penguin Books.

Curtis, G. C. (1963) 'Violence Breeds Violence', *American Journal of Psychiatry*, 120, 386–7.

Davis, M. (1985) 'Legal Aspects of Corporal Punishment', unpublished undergraduate project, School of Law, University of the Witwatersrand.

Dubanoski, R. A. *et al.* (1983) 'Corporal Punishment in Schools: Myths, Problems and Alternatives', *Child Abuse and Neglect*, 7, 271–8.

Eron, L. D. (1980) 'Prescription for Reduction of Aggression', *American Psychologist*, 35, 244–52.

Feshbach, S. & Feshbach, N. (1973) 'Alternatives to Corporal Punishment', *Journal of Child Clinical Psychology*, 2, 46–9.

Gantt, W. H. (1944) *Experimental Basis for Neurotic Behavior*, New York: Hoeber.

Gibson, I. (1978) *The English Vice*, London; Duckworth.

Glasser, W. (1978) 'Disorders in our Schools: Causes and Remedies', *Phi Delta Kappan*, 59, 331–3.

Gluek, E. & Gluek, S. (1950)*Unraveling Juvenile Delinquency*, Cambridge, Mass.: Harvard University Press.

Gordon, D. A. *et al.* (1979) 'A Measure of Intensity of Parental Punishment', *Journal of Personality Assessment*, 43, 458–95.

Green, R. T. (1982) 'Does Punishment Work with Children?, *School Psychology International*, 3, 169–74.

Hentoff, N. (1973) 'A Parent-Teacher View of Corporal Punishment', *Today's Education*, 62, 18–21.

Holdstock, T. L. (1987a) 'Discipline', in *Education for a New Nation*, Johannesburg: Africa Transpersonal Association, 159–99.

Holdstock, T. L. (1987b) 'Wettesloosheid in die Klaskamer', *Die Suid-Afrikaan*, 31–3.

Holt, J. *How Children Learn*, New York: Pitman.

Hutchinson, R. R. (1977) 'By-Products of Aversive Control'. In *Handbook of Operant Behavior*, edited by W. K. Honig & J. E. R. Staddon, Englewood Cliffs: Prentice-Hall, Inc.

Hyman, I. A. (1981) 'Research'. In *The Last Resort: Newsletter of the Committee to End Violence against the Next Generation*, edited by A. Maurer.

Kelman, H. C. (1978)'Violence without Moral Restraint: Reflections on the Dehumanization of Victims and Victimizers', *Journal of Social Issues*, 29, 25–61.

Kuhn, T. (1962) *The Structure of Scientific Revolutions*, Chicago: University of Chicago Press.

Kvaraceus, W. C. (1945) *Juvenile Delinquency and the School*, New York: World Books.

Lambeth, R. (1978) 'The Effects of Punitiveness on Academic Achievement: A Review of Recent Literature', paper presented to the Department of School Psychology, Temple University.

Livingstone, S. (1975) 'Implications of Corporal Punishment', *New Behaviour*, 490–2.

Maier, N. R. F. (1974) *Frustration — The Study of Behavior without a Goal*, New York: McGraw-Hill.

Masserman, J. M. (1943) *Behavior and Neurosis*, Chicago: University of Chicago Press.

Maurer, A. (1974) 'Corporal Punishment', *American Psychoanalyst*, 29, 614–26.

McCandless, B. R. (1967) *Behavior and Development*, New York: Holt, Rinehart & Winston.

Meacham, M. L. & Wiesen, A. E. (1969)*Changing Classroom Behavior: A Manual for Precision Teaching*, Scranton, Pa.: International Textbook Co.

Morris, D. (1967) *The Naked Ape*, New York: McGraw-Hill.

Newcombe, N. (1977) *Europe at School*, London: Methuen.

O'Leary, K. D. & O'Leary, S. G. (1977) *Classroom Management: The Successful Use of Behavior Modification*, New York: Pergamon Press.

Olmesdahl, M. C. J. (1984) 'Corporal Punishment in Schools', *The South African Law Journal*, 101, 527–44.

Palmer, J. W. (1965)'Smoking, Caning and Delinquency in a Secondary Modern School', *British Journal of Preventive Social Medicine*, 19, 18–23.

Rakitzis, A. (1987) 'A Cross-Cultural Study of the Educative Use of Corporal Punishment', unpublished BA Hons dissertation, University of the Witwatersrand.

Rice, J. (1985) 'A Study of Punishment and its Effects on Learning', unpublished BA Hons dissertation, University of the Witwatersrand.

Risley, T. R. (1968) 'The Effects and Side Effects of Punishing the Autistic Behaviors of a Deviant Child', *Journal of Applied Behavior Analysis*, 1, 21–34.

Rogers, C. R. (1983) *Freedom to Learn for the 80s*, Columbus; Charles E. Merrill.

Rosenshein, B. & Furst, N. (1971) 'Research in Teacher Performance Criteria'. In *Research in Teacher Education*, edited by B. O. Smith, Englewood Cliffs: Prentice-Hall, Inc.

Rutter, M. *et al.* (1979) *Fifteen Thousand Hours. Secondary Schools and the Effects on Children*, Cambridge, Mass.: Harvard University Press.

Skinner, B. F. (1986) 'What is Wrong with Daily Life in the Western World?', *American Psychologist*, 41, 568–74.

Skinner, B. F. (1953) *Science and Human Behavior*, New York: MacMillan.

Smith, J. D. *et al.* (1979) 'Corporal Punishment and its Effects for Exceptional Children', *Exceptional Children*, 264–8.

Solheim, J. S. (1982) 'A Cross-Cultural Examination of the use of Corporal Punishment on Children: A Focus on Sweden and the United States', *Child Abuse and Neglect*, 6, 147–54.

Stensrud, R. & Stensrud, K. (1981)'Discipline: An Attitude not an Outcome', *The Educational Forum*, 161–7.

STOPP (undated) Occasional paper.

Strickland, E. V. & Campbell, K. C. (1982) 'End the Other Abuse — Damaged Self-Concepts', *Childhood Education*, 9–12.

Suzukawa, D. F. & Riak, J. (1984) 'The Case for Immediate Abolition of Corporal Punishment in American Schools', unpublished paper presented to the Attorney-General's Task Force on Family Violence, Washington.

Ulrich, R. E. & Azrin, N. H. (1962) 'Reflexive Fighting in Response to Aversive Stimulation', *Journal of the Experimental Analysis of Behavior*, 5, 511–20.

Viney, W. *et al.* (1982) 'Attitudes towards Punishment in Relation to Beliefs in Free Will and Determinism', *Human Relations*, 35, 939–50.

Walters, G. C. & Grusec, J. E. (1977) *Punishment*, San Francisco: W. H. Freeman.

Weiss, A. (1985) 'A Survey of Corporal Punishment in Schools in Bophuthatswana', unpublished paper, 1985.

Welsh, R. S. (1974) 'Severe Parental Punishment and Delinquency: A Developmental Theory', *Journal of Child Clinical Psychology*, 5, 17–21.

Wilkinson, M. (1977) *Lessons from Europe*, London: Centre for Policy Studies.

Wright, L. S. (1982) 'The Use of Logical Consequences in Counseling Children', *The School Counselor*, 37–49.

Yates, A. J. (1962) *Frustration and Conflict*, New York: John Wiley & Sons.

13 Violence in group care

C. Giles

INTRODUCTION

This chapter is written primarily for practitioners in the field of child care. Its value resides very much in the degree to which it contributes to the strengthening of existing processes which aim to reduce the range and severity of violence to which those in group care are presently subjected.

It must be said at the outset that when the conditions under which residential child care is rendered in South Africa are borne in mind, we must marvel not that so many children are abused in group care, but that not more are. What follows is presented in the belief that the examination of what is at present deficient in group-care work can point the way to better practice. That in turn means a better start for children in group care, and a greater chance that their own children will escape the institutional-care cycle.

This chapter will confine itself to children who are in group care. It will be further restricted to children who have been placed in residential group care in children's homes in terms of the Child Care Act (Act 74 of 1983), which provides for children to be placed in the custody of their own parents, in children's homes, in foster care, or in schools of industry (section 15).

The reasons for these delimitations are:

1. Children in children's homes form the largest group of children in group care. In 1987 there were a total of 14 233 children in children's homes, places of safety, or schools of industry. In comparison, there were 8 843 resident children in 'care dependent' institutions for the mentally handicapped, and 5 634 places in schools for children with cerebral palsy, by no means all of which were residential (Dept of National Health & Population Development, 1987: 112).

2. Children's homes are the aspect of group care of which the author has the most experience and knowledge. Foster children are excluded because they are not in group care. The Child Care Act clearly differentiates between foster care and group residential care, and considers only a residence for six children or more to be an institution.

3. While there is very little local research on violence or abuse in group care, there is at least some. It appears from correspondence with other providers of group care to children (and adults) and from searches of listed research that there is not elsewhere a larger body of coherent data or planned research.

4. It is reasonable to suppose that many of the issues apply to all in care regardless of their age or why they are in care (Line, 1980). Children placed in terms of the Child Care Act 74 of 1983 are a diverse group with heterogeneous needs, but arguments can nevertheless be made with reference to them that are not vulnerable to dismissal on the grounds of severely limited applicability.

5. There exists a national South African organization (The Institute for Child Care, under the auspices of the National Association of Child Care Workers — NACCW) which is committed to identifying, and then to encouraging adherence to, certain minimum standards for children in care. This chapter is principally dedicated to the work of this group, and to the children who are damaged by the inadequacies of our present practice.

Definitions

Children are said to be in *group care* when they are legally removed from their parents or guardians and placed at an institution recognized by the Child Care Act (1983) as a place of safety, a children's home, or a school of industry.

The violence that occurs to children in group care is generally referred to in the literature as *institutional abuse*. This type of abuse occurs at three levels according to Gil (1982: 9), who also provides a general definition:

> Institutional abuse is any system, programme policy, procedure, or individual interaction with a child in placement that abuses, neglects or is detrimental to the child's health, safety or emotional and physical well-being or in any way exploits or violates the child's basic rights.

According to Gil, this abuse of children in out-of-home care is of three types: physical and sexual abuse, programme abuse, and system abuse. In this chapter various terms are used for each of three levels: at the first level, abuse is referred to as 'abuse by an individual care-giver', or 'abuse within an institution'; at the second level, programme abuse, terms used are 'abuse by an institution' and 'institutional abuse'; at the most general level, the terms 'system abuse' or 'institutionalized abuse' are used. There is little uniformity in the literature and these various terms, within each level, are used interchangeably.

AETIOLOGY OF INSTITUTIONAL ABUSE

Overview

The perpetration of violence on children in group care must be seen in the context of child abuse in general.

Children have always been abused, and indeed the abuse of children is the historical norm. Exploration of the history of childhood shows that 'the further back in history one goes the more bizarre are the attitudes to children' (De Mause, 1974: 7). What are now seen as disturbed and unacceptable attitudes or behaviours towards children were once quite normal and unexceptionable. Children were once sacrificed, abandoned, sold, or killed with little or no concern. The notion that children have *inalienable* rights and special needs from infancy onwards is one that has only relatively recently gained widespread acceptability. Child abuse or neglect emerges as a possibility only once the notion of children's rights is accepted. Efforts to reduce child abuse are therefore campaigns to identify and defend the rights of children. This chapter is an attempt to articulate a defence of some of the rights of a particularly vulnerable sub-group of children.

Why have children been so abused? An explanation offered by De Mause (1974) in his psychodynamic exploration of the history of childhood is that until recently, in historical terms, adults have been psychically immature to the point where sustained identification with, and empathy for, children was impossible. The argument is made that the earlier the historical period is that is examined, the greater this immaturity was. The more widespread and pronounced the immaturity was, and the more common it was for adults to fear for their survival, the more they resented the demands children made of them, and therefore the more they used children as defences against an anxiety they felt to be overwhelming. This entailed that children might normally be sacrificed, quite literally, in order to keep adult fears, anxieties, and frustrations within tolerable limits.

Over time, adults have coped more and more adequately with this anxiety as they have gained maturity.

> The history of childhood is a series of closer approaches between adult and child, with each closing of psychic distance producing fresh anxiety. The reduction of this anxiety is the main source of child-rearing practices at each age (De Mause, 1974: 3).

Child-care institutions are an expression of our culture's determination that all children are entitled to freedom from grossly inadequate or psychically primitive parenting. These institutions are our best attempt to care more adequately for those children of our time whose parents cannot cope with the emotional stresses of childrearing, and whose inadequate attempts to do so have damaged their children.

Where child abuse occurs within the family, it may be argued that the emotional and political economy of that family has regressed for a variety of reasons to that typical of a much earlier stage of human development. The pressures leading to the abuse of such a child may be found on each of the three levels identified by Gil (1982) — in individual dynamics, family dynamics, and broader socio-political dynamics. The level of dynamic that is identified as primary will differ from situation to situation. For example, at the one extreme, in an affluent, stable culture and in an extended family, individual dynamics will probably play a primary role in explaining and ending abuse. At the other extreme, it is quite inappropriate to assume parental or familial incompetence or psychopathology when child abuse is detected within a context of the absence of basic necessities, such as food, shelter, and safety (Cockburn *et al.*, 1988: 103). It is important for service providers to appreciate that the notion of 'child abuse' is a relative one in a country such as ours. Wilson and Ramphele (1989) state that South Africa has one of the world's highest Gini co-efficients (a comparative measure of material disparities), and hence both of the extremes noted above are everyday realities here. It is vital to develop and sustain an idea of what child abuse is, but it is equally important to consider which factors lead to and maintain particular instances of it.

An understanding of the abuse of children within an institutional context requires a similar starting point. The standards of care that might be expected are in some cases only very rarely met, and the reasons for this are structural rather than the outcome of any individual's shortcomings. On the other hand, there are some more affluent and stable institutions where such standards are generally met, and where incidents of abuse are appropriately seen as the responsibility of individual care-givers.

In the pursuit of a more equitable society, it is appropriate to set basic standards which operationalize and allow the defence of children's rights. For precisely the same reason, it is essential in each case to attribute accountability to, and to expect remedial action in terms of, the relevant dynamic level or levels concerned in the abuse of these rights.

Individual dynamics

Within a context of group care for children, various studies have ex-amined these different dynamic levels. At the level of the individual, South African authors Wright *et al*. (1987) reported consternation on discovering that children were abusing each other within an institution run by their organization. They discovered that sexual exploitation amongst the children in their care was common. The authors understood this behaviour in terms of the children's previous history of having been molested and abused themselves. Once they discovered how prevalent this behaviour was they not only began an internal treatment programme, but also undertook to research the situation in other institu-tions in South Africa. At the time of writing the outcome of this survey was not yet available.

Some authors point to other features of children which it is argued lead to abuse. Hirschbach (1982: 104) writes that some children are abused because they are 'unreachable', and therefore frustrate beyond contain-ment those staff who suffer from the delusion that 'there is no such thing as an inaccessible child'. He argues that institutions would be less abusive if they identified those children whom they could neither restore to psychological health, nor help to live reasonably successfully with their burdens. These children should be cared for by adults who have less unrealistic expectations. The characteristics of these children are that they have suffered severe and prolonged early deprivation as infants, have established psychopathic personality traits, and have a history of multiple placement failures. Hirschbach says that they are the 'terminal patients' of child care, children whose 'most serious problem is their inability to tolerate treatment modalities that in any way attempt to control their impulsive behaviour'. 'Terminal' they may be; that they go on living makes looking after them such a difficult thing to do.

A study by Maurer (1982) has examined some features of adults which may lead to abuse within institutions caring for children. He found that having a fundamentalist belief system was a cause of violence to children within the context of group care. He reports further that fundamentalist care-givers showed attitudes and behaviours which were similar to those found in abusive parents in non-fundamentalist communities. As is usually the case, however, the association was far from absolute, and while such beliefs more frequently lead to unacceptably violent behaviour, this is not always so.

There are, therefore, a variety of authors who identify a range of individual experiences, attitudes, behaviours, and beliefs as being contributory to any violence which occurs within institutions. The same analysis can be made at the next level of dynamics.

Institution dynamics

An example of an examination of the second level of dynamic, what Gil (1982) termed 'programme abuse', is Berkman and Lippold's (1982) work in relation to the health needs of juveniles in care. They quote figures to show that the majority of medical problems which were identified when children were taken into care were not subsequently followed up. Furthermore, youngsters becoming ill during their period in care were not referred in any systematic way to a specialist or to a hospital. It was established that while the rate of medical problems was high amongst the population in question, there was no organized or adequate response from the institutions involved. Nevertheless, Rindfleisch and Baros-Van Hull (1982) have shown that not all institutions are equally likely to sustain abusive practices, and have identified features of institutions which tend to be associated with abusive practices. Such institutions are large, understaffed, isolated from those living around them, and are not often exposed to the public via the mass media. They are inadequately regulated by management and by licensing agencies, they work within a context where there is little imaginative thought given to alternative ways of coping with difficult behaviour, and a high level of unresolved resentment is felt by staff towards the more difficult children living in the institution.

Several studies have examined the interrelations of factors between these first two levels, that is, how the way an institution is run effects those within it (Durkin, 1982; Atten & Milner, 1987; Jaudes & Diamond, 1985). Findings were that the measured child abuse potential of workers in institutions decreased as workers had greater job clarity and more job satisfaction. Durkin (1982), who saw many similarities between the abuse of children in institutions and those of children in families, has argued that institutions themselves often behave like abusive parents towards their staff, or care for the children at the expense of the staff. Child-care staff are 'on call' twenty-four hours a day — but the institution does not provide 24-hour backup. In the 'therapeutic team' it suits the nine-to-five clinical staff to give generalized and often conflicting advice to the child-care staff — and then to go home. Those who do the work and take much of the strain and real responsibility get neither the pay nor the recognition nor the necessary support and rest. Child-care workers share with unhappy single parents several characteristics — youth, being isolated from their family and community, lack of a support system, and 'hanging on the ragged edge emotionally and financially' (Durkin, 1982: 17). There is a significant similarity between many features reported of abuse-prone parents, and the effects of burn-out induced by over-exposure to the insatiable demands of deprived children — hostility to the child and institution, apathy, lack of emotional involvement, negativism, inattentiveness, chronic illness, cynicism, and acceptance of low standards of care. The effects of the institution on children and staff may react with the prior histories and personalities of both, to induce and maintain violent and abusive relationships.

Institutionalized abuse

At the most general level, that of institutionalized or structural or system abuse, Thomas (1982: 146) initiates an analysis by suggesting that the term 'child abuse' is an:

> … oblique way of talking about adult needs and troubles. The child is a messenger. The sum of all the messages sent to a child welfare agency in the course of a year amounts to a catalogue of our national social problems and pressures including poverty, poor education, alcohol and drug abuse, crime, urban slums, inflation, and the deterioration of community life.

Thomas criticizes four aspects of the way in which child protection has become socially institutionalized, and therefore in his view inherently abusive.

He argues that the way in which services to children and their families are organized means that to achieve promotion, the once-good direct service worker must abandon her/his client-servicing skills and acquire organization-servicing skills. The fact that *institutions* offer services is in his view a major limitation on the quality of service available.

He next argues that access to and control over resources is so restricted and so bound by conditions that in pursuing and acquiring these resources, both worker and client are forced into a bureaucratic and dependence-inducing form of relationship. Families are irretrievably split up, so as to be eligible for resources. This makes of the alleged resource a real life impediment.

The capitation grant whereby institutions (and foster parents) survive financially when children enter and remain in their care:

> ... creates a condition conducive to systemic incarceration: children become trapped in a system that moves them from one home to another. The longer they remain in the system, the less likely is their return to their biological parents, the more they are damaged, and the more difficult they are to adopt (Thomas, 1982: 150).

Negative effects from having a legal mandate to protect children arise when, for example, in the passing of laws which require the notification of even suspected child abuse (Child Care Act, section 42), the child-care system inadvertently erodes and makes illegal previously existing and often highly effective informal responses to child abuse by concerned neighbours and lay helpers. In this way, the attempts to make the life of children safer and improve the quality of relationships within a community actually have the reverse or paradoxical effect of reducing and even of criminalizing caring and protective responses to children.

Thomas provides an extreme, but provocative view. In many instances the reverse of his points can be argued. For example, in providing staff promotion opportunities, an organization retains and makes the best use of its most able direct service workers. These workers can then 'work their magic' at another level in the service-delivery system — a system that needs therapy and change as much as the individual child does. Thomas' view, it can be argued, would deprive institutions of good quality management.

It is essential that institutions offering group care to children are aware of these issues, and of their place in this wider and highly conflicted service-delivery system. They must also themselves question how it is that they have what abusive families do not have — an extraordinary immunity from accountability for those failures in their care-giving which do occur. The number of children who have been in multiple placements is high (Giles, 1982) and would be higher still were it not for the largely unchallenged myth that six years in one children's home with four different child-care workers and a constantly changing group of peers, not to mention several failed host-parent relationships, constitutes a stable and single placement. This is harmful to children, but it is common. Yet nobody is held responsible. Parents who arranged as many care-givers for their own children would not escape so lightly.

The added effects upon children of a malignant and discriminatory government policy have been documented at a psychological level by Straker and Moosa (1988) who speak of children in a state of chronic traumatic stress, and at an economic level by Wilson and Ramphele (1989). Wilson and Ramphele chart in stark detail the inequities in the distribution of, and access to, resources in South Africa. Residential child care is no exception where distorted provision is concerned. Sixty-three per cent of all residential places available in South Africa in 1987 were for white children. There has, since then, been an increase in provision for African children. Even after recent increases in the capitation grant, for African children it is about half of that for all other children. On the positive side, however, previous financial discrimination between white, 'coloured', and Indian children has been ended.

Another sort of dislocation and inconsistency within the welfare service delivery system is rooted in its history (Potgieter, 1973). The present day outcome of the origins of welfare services which began with church patronage is that many service organizations are still sectarian-based. Thorny issues of language, religion, territory, and ideology often lie ill-concealed beneath thin veneers of professionalism. This leads to duplication, inconsistent policy and procedures, an unpredictable and patchy service, and a narrowing of referral options for clients.

The government insistence, despite repeated protest by many organizations, that welfare be a racially 'own affair' has meant that many supposedly therapeutic interventions also reinforce notions of racism and disparagement. This also means that the difficulty in achieving coherent and complete data of even the simplest kind has become almost overwhelming. The reason for this is that each Department of Health Services and Welfare has its own idea of what data should be collected. One of the most apparent things about South African welfare services is how little they are researched, and how little reliable systematic information is available. A great deal of time, energy, and money is devoted to co-ordinating what should never have been separated. The policy of privatizing welfare services has meant that the state is the funder of last resort, and that individuals are held primarily responsible for financing their own welfare. The result of this policy is an impoverished, fragmented, and often anti-therapeutic welfare system which is virtually unknowable and almost impossible to evaluate, or to plan sensibly for.

In its own way each of the three levels described above is violent, in that each has been designed to promote the interests and protect the well-being not of the client but of the ostensible service provider. This is violence because it is exploitative, harmful, and dishonest, even if it is almost invariably unintended. In order to reduce the violence endured by children in group care, action must be taken at each of these levels — the individual, the institution, and at the level of the service-delivery system.

INCIDENCE OF INSTITUTIONAL ABUSE

No South African data on the frequency of episodes of violence in group care were found. These figures are not available for the children discussed in this chapter, nor are they available for those children in psychiatric care, nor for the mentally handicapped. Although there is an attempt at present to identify categories of abuse (Wright *et al.*, 1987) there are not even any reliable national figures on the number of children abused within their own families. If our experience in this context is to be similar to that of other countries, we cannot expect reliable figures on institutional abuse until at least a decade after accurate data on intra-familial abuse are available. The proliferation of government departments involved, the several parallel but uncoordinated national registers being established at present, and the historical territoriality and parochialism of the private sector in welfare make the emergence of such statistics highly unlikely in the foreseeable future.

The literature that is available does not reliably distinguish between abusive incidents which occurred because of individual, institutional, or institutionalized dynamics. An overall incidence figure can, however, be estimated by extrapolating from data presented by Rindfleisch and Rabb (1984). In 1979 they surveyed 1 700 American institutions in which 69 271 children were resident. There were in that year 2 692 allegations of abuse or neglect reported. Their figures cover a range per 1 000 children per year of between a maximum of 55 and a low of 25, depending on the institutions under review. The average incidence was 39 per 1 000 children per year.

In South Africa there are approximately 14 000 children in institutional care as defined in this chapter. Using Rindfleisch and Rabb's (1984) figures it can be argued that there are in the region of 500 children per year who are abused or neglected within residential institutions in South Africa.

The same authors report that in their sample, 40 per cent of respondents denied that abuse ever occurred within their institutions. That this is more a failure of detection than a true lack of abuse is suggested from the average incidence figures quoted above, and from the commonly-made observation that a pre-condition for the perception of abuse is an admission of the possibility of its occurrence. Further evidence of this comes from Rindfleisch and Hicho (1987), who report a 48 per cent rise in detection and reporting rates by workers in child-care institutions once appropriate training and support was provided. Taken together, these considerations suggest that 500 incidents per year is likely to be a conservative estimate of the amount of child abuse within South African institutions.

This underestimation can be counterbalanced by the finding by the same authors that a minority (23 per cent) of reports are formally substantiated. Often this is because of a lack of clarity in investigation and substantiation procedures, rather than because reports are un-founded. A reasonable working assumption may however be that there are in the region of 500 incidents per year of violence to children in group care in South Africa and that these incidents are so severe that, if the process existed and if overseas norms were applicable, 500 cases of child abuse within institutions would be substantiated each year.

This 'incident counting' approach of course only addresses violence at the first level — that of the abuse of children by care-givers. Programme abuse or institutionalized abuse affects larger and larger groups of children and does damage on a much wider, if perhaps less easily detected scale. It is quite clear, however, that the abuse that in all probability takes place is of a scale sufficient to warrant immediate attention. There is no ethical defence of practice which removes children from a familiar but violent context, and places them in an unfamiliar and violent one.

EFFECTS OF INSTITUTIONAL ABUSE

The effects of violence in group care can be examined on each of the three levels of abuse identified at the beginning of this chapter.

Individual level

At the level of violence by individuals, the effects on children are much as they would be were the abuse to occur within a family setting (Durkin, 1982; McCord, 1983; Toro, 1982). These effects have been detailed in earlier chapters. It is sufficient to note here that while resilience factors make the routine prediction of measurable harm to a child inappropriate (Rutter, 1987), many authors have noted the damage done to children, the effects of which may be felt throughout the children's lives (Sgroi, 1982). It also will be apparent that in this context abusive individuals not only violate children who are vulnerable and often already damaged but that they also betray the trust put in them by those children, their families, and by society. The effects on children of being abused within a context in which they had every right to expect safety, can be devastating. Wright *et al.* (1988) provide a graphic description of these children's functioning and their inability to resolve their pain and anger.

Institutional level

There is evidence that children admitted to residential care often come from discordant, impoverished, psychiatrically disturbed, and disrupted families, and that such children have difficulty forming and sustaining relationships (Stricklin, 1972; Wolkind & Renton, 1979; Rutter, 1971). Children reared for long periods in institutions have been found to show not only excessive attachment behaviours such as clinging and following, but also to show little selective bonding and a poorly-developed ability to sustain deeper relationships with particular individuals (Tizard & Rees, 1975). Also, the bonding that does occur tends to be rather insecure, which leaves children vulnerable to distress on separation and less likely to explore novel situations fully and confidently (Stayton & Ainsworth, 1973). For these reasons and because children in institutional care are vulnerable to language delay and lower verbal intelligence, and to social disinhibition and indiscriminate friendliness (Wolkind, 1974), it is imperative that the daily care they receive is attentive, consistent, responsive, and creative. Kunkel (1983) has argued that children in group care are particularly vulnerable to violence at the level of programme abuse, by which he means the many minor daily incidents which remind the child that he/she does not have somebody who can be devoted just to him/her. Many of these incidents flow from the fact that frequently too few adults are caring for too many children. The result is a lack of fit between what the child experiences as his/her needs, particularly for attachment and comfort, and what the institution can offer. In this way the child is placed in an emotional environment which, while perhaps not as violent and unpredictable as the one at home, is still experienced as unresponsive and which is therefore less likely to promote his/her full development.

Kunkel (1983) charts the stages through which children who cannot find an adult with whom to connect go. These are the children who get 'lost' when an institution does not have the staffing levels and creative energy to go to the extraordinary lengths needed to reach what he calls 'alienated' children — those who feel 'separate, apart, not able to relate effectively with another, not belonging, and with an impaired ability to connect the inside world of feelings with the outside environment' (Kunkel, 1983: 479). These stages — defensiveness, anger, depression, apathy, and finally, self-isolation — will be familiar to residential staff who have watched a child slipping away. At the final stage the child is described by Hirschbach (1982) as being beyond reach.

As is so often the case in published work from overseas, Kunkel's solution of intensive interpersonal engagement is totally impossible in South Africa. His staff have the time to concentrate on children who are deeply disturbed — for example, they walked all afternoon with one child four afternoons a week for three months. This one minor example illustrates a level of financing and staffing inconceivable in South Africa, and supports the earlier argument that reasonable expectations of child-care staff must be relative.

Institutionalized abuse

At the third level — that of abuse by the service-delivery system itself, the negative effects on children are primarily those associated with institutionalization. As Gil (1982: 11) puts it, 'the greatest problem is that children in care tend to remain in care'. By institutionalization is meant the process whereby children in long-term residential care acquire new skills which enable them to cope with the demands of living within the institution — and at the same time lose or fail to develop other skills or attitudes which they will need after their discharge. Some even acquire skills and attitudes which impede their return to their community of origin. For example, most institutions often require children to learn how to use quite complicated systems whereby certain clothes are washed on certain days and then are available several days later, often in a different building. Very few of the children involved will have clothes washed for them after discharge. In this process they learn skills which will be of no use to them in the future — and at the same time acquire unrealistic expectations about cleanliness and the availability of replacement or repaired garments, expectations which create major problems for them when discharged from the institution.

Another aspect is the gradual rift which is opened between the child and his/her family. Most children coming into care are from im-poverished working-class families (Stricklin, 1972; Brown, 1948), yet the majority of residential institutions are in the more middle-class areas of cities, and are staffed, particularly at management level, by people with middle-class backgrounds, values, and training. It is common for families to 'dress up' when going to visit their children, and too frequently children talk of or act out shame at how their family dresses or copes with the china tea cups set out to welcome them. Mothers may be encouraged, for example, to care for and perhaps wash their children's hair, but often embarrass themselves and their children by not knowing how to work shower fixtures or how to regulate the temperature of running hot water. Children in care are inundated with charity parties, films, outings, and are indulged by host parents. Not surprisingly, they are sometimes reluctant to go home, and are demanding and dismissive when they get there. Democratic parenting techniques taught to child-care workers are put to use and lead the children to expect that they will have a say in family decisions and will be left to make their own decisions in many areas of their lives. These expectations clash with the paternalis-tic values still dominant in many working-class and perfectly functional families.

It is also quite possible for a child to be moved across the country to a residential institution, and while it is said that those involved plan to sustain contact between the child and his/her family, it is all too often quite impossible. There are also children from rural areas who are placed in towns, and vice-versa. This again leads to the acquisition of values, tastes, and skills which make re-integration a stated goal but an infre-quent reality.

The above negative effects are found primarily in children who have been in residential care for far longer than the maximum two-year period which the Child Care Act stipulates. There is now a tendency within the child-care field for older more disturbed children to be in care for shorter periods of time (Giles, 1982). It is not institutional care *per se* which damages children (Larsson *et al.*, 1986) nor is it separation *per se* (Rutter, 1971). Rather it is these longer-term processes which apart from anything else signal that the children involved are living in a form of limbo.

INTERVENTIONS

The goal of intervening in the situation so far described should be to develop an accepted set of standards for the group care of children, and to design a procedure for investigating and correcting deficiencies once they are detected.

To do this is it necessary first to establish the rights children in group care should enjoy. Secondly, an operational definition of institutional abuse at each of the three levels is needed. Thirdly, an adequate proce-dure for evaluating the routine functioning of children's homes is re-quired as well as a procedure for investigating alleged abuses. Finally, it is necessary to outline improved ways of reporting abuse once this is uncovered, so that corrective action is ensured.

The rights of children in group care

Admission to group care should be based on the conviction that children admitted to a children's home will experience an improved quality of life compared to what they would experience if they were to remain at home. In 1964, the Child Welfare League of America (CWLA) identified the following as being necessary conditions for residential care to be indicated for a particular child and to be a positive experience for him/her. The main issues can be grouped under themes of adequate institutional care, basic values concerning children, and appropriate standards.

Adequate institutional care

1. The institution must see itself as providing for the protection, the care, and the treatment of the child.

2. The institution must see work with the family as being an integral part of its work with the child

3. The institution must be committed to inter-agency, inter-professional, and community planning and co-operation.

4. The institution must either:
   (a) accept only those children who can benefit from the services it has to offer; or
   (b) modify and adapt its services to provide what is needed by children for whom they must accept responsibility; or
   (c) help develop appropriate forms of care and treatment for children they cannot serve (CWLA, 1964: 2–3).

5. The institution must strive for clarity and consensus on differential admission criteria which would identify those children who are best returned to parents, or best placed in foster care, in children's homes, in schools of industries, or in adopted homes.

6. The institution should offer care 'planned with a foreseeable termination. Prolonged or indefinite periods of institutional care resulting from a lack of adequate planning or lack of casework with parents are not considered acceptable practice' (CWLA, 1964: 14).

Basic values concerning children

☐ Any child regardless of age, sex, race, colour, creed, social circumstances, national or religious origin, sickness, or handicap has a right to be respected, and to have the best possible care in accordance with his/her needs.

☐ Every child needs the affection and security of a family of which he/she feels that he/she is a part.

☐ Living in a family within a community is the natural and desirable way of life.

☐ Any child who can live in a family and benefit from doing so should have the opportunity to do so.

☐ It is best for a child to be reared by his/her family of origin so long as it can meet his/her needs or be helped to do so.

☐ Children need and must have constant and age-appropriate experience of affection and loving care, of recognition and respect, of relationships with a variety of different people, of experiences that enrich and promote growth and development, of security, and of continuity and stability (CWLA, 1964: 12–14).

Appropriate standards

The CWLA has set goals for the main aspects of group care, including nutrition, treatment, control, visitation, education, health care, administration, building plant and so on.

In each case, what is considered most desirable is stated in terms of broad principles. Individual institutions are then expected to put these into practice in ways appropriate to their circumstances.

In the matter of setting standards, Thomas (1982: 27) goes somewhat further than this. He argues that:

> … when the state decides to assume responsibility for children for a period of time or more permanently, it implicitly asserts that it is more capable than the children's parents of child rearing. Thus the state assumes an obligation to assure the children's rights to achieve developmental goals.

For Thomas, this argument leads to the need for a very much higher set of standards. The reason for this is that while parents have the right not to develop some of the capacities evidenced by children in their custody, the state, Thomas (1982: 27) argues, cannot make this decision about children in its custody without doing '*de facto* harm to the children's rights to achieve consistent with their abilities'. His point is that to justify its intrusion into parenting seen as incompetent, the state must subsequently provide perfect parenting. While his conclusion is rejected, his notion that residential care must have as its goal the achievement of developmental goals consistent with individual goals is endorsed. This is joined with the CWLA's ultimate goal of returning every child to family life in the community, to constitute the two key elements of a mission statement for institutional child care. These two principles are also the essence of the rights of children in care in residential institutions.

Operational definition of institutional abuse

Arriving at a definition

Institutional abuse would, following the above scheme, be practices within institutions which do not respect or which impede the fullest possible enjoyment of children's rights to full personal development and permanent placement within a family context. There are various frameworks for operationalizing these rights. Rabb and Rindfleisch (1985) propose eight categories of behaviour which they suggest will be useful for the development of an operational definition of institutional abuse. It is important to develop operational definitions because only then can theoretical insights and knowledge be put to work practically for the benefit of all involved. The categories suggested by Rabb and Rindfleisch (1985) are:

☐ non-accidental injury;

☐ sexual abuse;

☐ failure to provide care;

☐ failure to supervise;

☐ emotional maltreatment;

☐ questionable moral behaviour (by staff);

☐ harmful restraint; and

☐ setting up (making failure or humiliation likely).

  While all the categories in Rabb and Rindfleisch's definition are related to the behaviour of the individual care-givers (that is, to abuse *within* an institution), they could with few exceptions be equally operationalized to refer to aspects of programme abuse (abuse by an institution), or abuse by a service-delivery system (institutionalized abuse). For example, 'failure to provide care' is defined by these authors as 'an adult care-giver's failure to provide a child with the food, clothing, shelter or medical care necessary …' (Rabb & Rindfleisch, 1985: 287). It could equally well apply to a failure on the part of the institution to detect or respond to the medical needs of children, as Berkman and Lippold (1982) have shown many indeed fail to do. Further, it could be applied to the failure on the part of government agencies, which do not identify inadequacy in service provision as a problem, and then act decisively to end this.

Similarly, the category of 'setting up' is defined as 'caregiver deception, gross inconsistency or unrealistic expectations which result in substantial provocation or predictable failure of a child' (Rabb & Rindfleisch, 1985: 287). This could be extended to include abuse by an institution. A common gross inconsistency is that families are said to be welcome and vital to the institution's work, but distance, class values, and unexplored conflicts over the child's loyalties are all too often allowed to erode and eventually to end any contacts. Similarly, children are told that they are being prepared to return home, but they learn values and experience styles of living which may be alien to their home environment.

The same category of abuse is found at the service-delivery level (institutionalized abuse) in the acceptance by the state of gross inconsistencies in service provision and in levels of subsidy, of which children are only too aware, and which has often led to anger and sometimes to their rejection of the status quo.

It is vital that functioning at all levels be examined; it is individuals on the staff of children's homes, as well as those who manage, support, or refer clients to welfare organizations, who need to understand and modify their behaviour. They need to do this every bit as much as the index client, the child. The abused child does not appear in a vacuum, and his/her family does not become unable to care for him/her in a vacuum. Moreover, all existing knowledge and research shows that organizations and cultures do not arise in isolation from the people who constitute them. Hence, in examining and treating only the child, or even only the family, we are trivializing our work and relegating it to the function of maintaining the status quo.

Putting the definition to work

A recent workshop run with about 200 child-care workers from all levels of management provides an example of how the process of examining child care at each level may begin. This group examined present South African child-care practice for abuse at all three levels. Approximately forty types of incidents or omissions were identified. These can be classified according to the matrix shown in Table 13.1. This matrix was developed by identifying the tasks at each level of the care-giving system at each of Maslow's levels of need, based on a table conceived by Ward

Table 13.1: Elements of adequate group care for children

1. Physiological needs

Direct care-giver	*Institution*	*Service system*
Provide for food, warmth, shelter, fresh air, personal space, bodily care and maintenance, sleep and rest, sexual needs.	Provide resources; ensure equitable and appropriate distribution; assess needs; monitor development.	Ensure equitable and appropriate distribution of resources between institutions; develop and apply standards of basic care, administration, plant, etc.

2. Safety needs

Direct care-giver	*Institution*	*Service system*
Protect from injury and ensure freedom from pain.	Apply criteria to check for abuse or neglect; provide medical care; set minimal restrictions consistent with safety; provide safe housing and play area.	Develop and apply standards; clarify and implement procedure to investigate allegations; act to reduce likelihood of recurrence.

3. Belongingness and love

Direct care-giver	*Institution*	*Service system*
Friendship, love, affection, contact, communication, relationships, participation, involvement.	Apply admission and discharge criteria; value and provide adult time for children; provide informal respectful atmosphere, individuation; promote significant adult-child relationships; involve child in treatment planning; provide supervision for staff.	Develop and apply appropriate standards for admission/discharge and for internal moves of a child; check adequacy of permanency planning; survey attitudes of service consumers; provide feedback.

4. Esteem

Direct care-giver	*Institution*	*Service system*
Promote individual identity and autonomy; acknowledge need for prestige and status; give a share in daily running of unit; provide a flexible negotiated routine, privacy needs	Encourage participation in running unit; create development opportunities for child and staff.	Develop and apply standards regarding staff selection and training; involve institution in developing mission statement and goals, to locate themselves within a spectrum of services.

5. Self-actualization

Direct care-giver	*Institution*	*Service system*
Provide new experiences; enable competent coping outside the institution; plan for permanency and a viable future.	Plan discharge; prepare child; support permanent placement; maintain permeable boundaries with 'outside world'.	Undertake follow-up and epidemiological research; help fund/create permanent placements.

(1980). In this way, the ideal functioning of the system as a whole can be portrayed. The tasks and functions at each level need to take place if each child's rights to develop fully and to live in a family setting are to be respected. Institutional abuse occurs when these rights are infringed at any level.

In the course of the workshops, abuses and omissions were identified at each of Maslow's levels, and in nearly every aspect of child care. Examples of abuse or neglect at the level of the child-care worker would be those outlined in the following sections.

Abuse in institutions

1. Not giving medication.

2. Sexual abuse going undetected because nobody is confident of the consequences of detection or of disclosure.

3. The misuse of confidential information in order to hurt a child or get revenge.

4. The failure to provide a child with a systematic account of what is happening in his/her family and of the choices which face them.

5. Any behaviour, activity, or omission which tends to make it harder for children and their parents to retain bonds that exist.

At the second level are abuses or omissions that are appropriately seen as due to organizational issues in the institution.

Abuse by institutions

1. A tendency to be reluctant to refer a child for needed specialist medical attention.

2. Internal controls being either lax or even non-existent, or, on the other hand, paying too much attention to the 'smooth running of the institution'.

3. Vague or unimplemented admission or discharge procedures and criteria.

4. The keeping on of apathetic, 'burned out' older staff members who frustrate newer members of staff and fill them with foreboding; yet not responding to the 'burned out' staff members' needs.

5. The practice of overprotecting children and of failing to apply constructive pressure on them to move out of the home at the earliest opportunity.

Abuses or omissions which were seen to follow from practices and conditions within the welfare system as a whole were identified as outlined below.

Institutionalized abuse

1. The removal of children being recommended in the absence of normative data about unfamiliar cultures, standards, or parenting practices.

2. While no example was given at the workshop of this, one possibility might be the failure on the part of the state to develop and implement any checks on the frequency of abuse within institutions.

3. An overloaded welfare system having to deal in a routinized and hasty way with families, and the fact that this often leads to hasty, unreliable judgements.

4. Failure on the part of the state to survey in its present evaluation system the attitudes and needs of the consumers of the service. Another example could be the child-care workers' perception of family reconstruction services as being ineffective — this has the result of making it much harder for children to settle back with their families, and of leaving them vulnerable on discharge.

Corrective measures

Those present at the workshop went on to identify some corrective measures. These will be briefly presented, and, as will be seen from comparison with the final section of the chapter, these suggestions are echoed in much of the literature addressed to decreasing the incidence of abuse to children in group care.

At the level of the child-care worker suggestions were as outlined below.

Decreasing abuse in institutions

1. There should be clear procedures to guide child-care workers when abuse is detected, so that they know exactly what to do next.

2. Child-care workers should visit other institutions in order to become clearer about practices that are unique to their institution and which therefore may well be highly creative and useful, or abusive and neglectful.

3. Each children's home should define very clearly for itself exactly what it understands the rights of residents and staff to be.

Corrective actions at the level of the organization were also identified, and are given below.

Ways of reducing institutional abuse

1. In-service training should be aimed specifically at educating staff about the incidence and causes of institutional abuse.

2. There should be pressure on middle-management staff to take clear decisions. They should state the criteria used in making the decision, what the decision is, what action should be taken, when and by whom.

3. Procedures within the organization should be committed to writing and should be followed.

4. There should be a permanency plan made for each child within a certain length of time after admission.

5. Each home should have, and should follow, clear admission and discharge criteria and procedures.

At the last level, that of the service-delivery system in general, suggestions included the following.

Ways of reducing institutionalized abuse

1. Systematic attempts should be made to identify and to discourage the often unintended cultural re-socialization of children, which means that they often do not return to the family and community from which they originated.

2. The funding departments of state should be pressurized to undertake epidemiological and follow-up research.

3. There should be an expectation that all referring and after-care agencies should meet regularly to discuss and co-ordinate their policies.

4. No direct residential child-care service should be allowed before the person concerned has had an orientation period of in-service training.

Evaluating the functioning of children's homes
Present procedures

There is provision in the Child Care Act (section 31) for the annual inspection of children's homes and these inspections are routinely carried out. They cover two main areas (according to the guidelines of Form WP215) — the physical aspect of the institution, and the care and treatment of the children. These areas are divided further into thirty categories, such as statistical particulars, buildings, administration, and food, clothing, vocation facilities, education, discipline and punishment, discharge and after care. The official outline inspection report is long and detailed. It asks, for example, what types of children are provided for, whether they are destitute or neglected, difficult or problematic, or physically handicapped. It also asks in relation to the extent and treatment of problems the following:

1. Do the following problems occur: neurotic behaviour problems, uncontrollability, child anxiety, nocturnal enuresis, absconding, vandalistic tendencies, sexual misconduct, theft, others?

2. What methods of treatment were used?

3. Were these methods efficient?

4. Number of children referred because of unmanageable behaviour problems?

Whilst between them these thirty categories cover most of the areas of potential abuse identified in Table 13.1, there are omissions, and the inspections could be more adequate if the changes outlined below were made.

Necessary improvements

1. There is no provision for the users of the services, that is the children and their parents, to state their views. The risk is high that service-provider issues will dominate and that even serious complaints from those who ostensibly are most important will not be heard.

2. The evaluation categories that are used are not designed to produce quantifiable responses, so that little of what information is gathered can be used to promote planning and direct staff training, or to exert control.

3. There is no process of negotiating specified standards either with each institution or within funding departments. It is felt that such a co-operative process of evaluation would be more fruitful than the present system of imposing departmental inspection norms on to passive organizations. If the process was to be jointly undertaken, additional benefits would be that all aspects of functioning could be evaluated. At present, many important areas are perforce examined only superficially due to lack of human resources and time. An

understandable desire to 'look good' in the face of an evaluation where standards have not been negotiated also means that weaknesses or omissions will not be openly examined. Finally, such a joint process is more likely to lead to evaluations which reflect developmental trends in, and differences between institutions — information vital to those responsible for placing children.

4. The mission statements, goals, and objectives of organizations are not expected or examined, nor are admission criteria and discharge criteria required to be specified. One inspection does not in practice set goals to be met by the next one. Each inspection therefore takes place in a strategic and temporal vacuum.

5. There is no expectation that even basic information on referrals not accepted, and on children after they have been discharged, should be kept. It is thus impossible to establish which children's homes are succeeding (or failing) to provide an effective service to children with particular needs.

6. Another major omission is the lack of an attempt to record infringements of children's rights while in care. Over the past decade there have been registers kept of parental infringements of their children's rights — but there has been no such check on the behaviour of those employed in residential child care, of whom even higher standards of behaviour can reasonably be expected. There is no record kept of how many changes of care-giver a child has endured, although continuity and stability are two of the primary justifications for residential care. There is also no record kept of associated service-providing organizations which do not deliver what was expected of them. A children's home is deeply dependent on schools, hospitals, the police, welfare organizations, service clubs, and others, and if these are unreliable, the child and his/her family will suffer the upset of separation without the benefit of the specially integrative and responsive environment which the removal was intended to obtain for the child.

While the present state-implemented inspection system has these major shortcomings, it is in theory comprehensive (although in practice many evaluations are cursory), and it has already been developed and used for a number of years. It is seen as capable of being developed into a genuinely useful instrument. For the present evaluation system to be effective, it needs to become a more goal-directed, systematized, quantified, and negotiated undertaking. It needs to focus on each of the levels at which abuse may occur, since it is at each of these levels that good service must be rendered.

Investigation of alleged abuse

There is consensus that the investigation of alleged abuse within a group-care setting is a specialized and difficult task (Thomas, 1982; CWLA, 1964; Wright *et al.*, 1987). There are a number of factors which contribute to its difficulty.

Different standards of care

Different criteria should be applied in the identification of child abuse or neglect, depending on whether a child is at home or in an institution (Thomas, 1982). Because parents have the presumptive right to raise their child as they see fit, in finding a parent to be abusive a court will want evidence that the behaviour in question has had negative consequences on the child. Where the alleged perpetrator is an agent of the state, however, less of this latitude remains, since the child should now be reared and treated in a much more closely defined and monitored way. Any unplanned omission of these prescriptions is technically abusive, regardless of the impact of this behaviour on the individual child. Similarly, while it would need to be shown that parentally-inflicted injuries to their children were non-accidental, any injury to a child in care is theoretically abusive. The reason for this is that the removal of the child from one abusive context was justified on the basis that the child would be placed in a relatively more hazard-free environment.

In a sense, the professional service provider is guilty until proven innocent, whereas the obverse rightly applies where concern arises about the child-rearing practices of a parent. Thomas (1982) advocates the adoption of a dual set of standards for making determinations of child abuse or neglect, one for the family or community environment, and one for residential placements:

> ... agents of the state are held to stricter standards and (investigators) have less margin for exercising the benefit of the doubt in the investigation process. More often than in the family or community context, proof of the occurrence of an event or omission will be sufficient to a finding of abuse or neglect in a residential placement (Thomas, 1982: 36).

No statutory care-giver has childrearing rights equivalent to those of birth parents, and therefore many extenuating circumstances such as personal values, lack of funds, or cultural belief are to a much greater extent irrelevant.

Who should investigate?

The CWLA (1964) is clear that all residential institutions should be required by law to meet certain specified standards and that there should be penalties for not doing so. As has been argued above, the present South African system does not comply with this because while there are inspections, there are, with a few exceptions, no standards laid down, and no penalties for non-compliance. It is recommended by the CWLA that investigators should be employed by state departments, and that the aspects of care examined and the standards set should be agreed by prior consultation. One difficulty with applying this recommendation in South Africa is that a state employee may be likely to overlook or not be free to comment on or investigate the abuses to children that arise from institutionalized discriminations or omissions. In South Africa, one major cause of institutionalized abuse, the fragmentation and lack of co-ordination of services for children (Nunno & Motz, 1988), would be a direct outcome of the policy of the state department employing the abuse investigator. Any effective investigator of institutional abuse must therefore have a demonstrable authority to examine practice at each of the three levels described in this chapter, and a mandate to require changes at any or all levels in accordance with a prior consensus reached as to the rights of children in care.

Investigation techniques

The investigative skills and powers of a social worker are seen as the best starting point for the development of adequate techniques in this area. In addition to the skills, knowledge, and attitudes of competent social work practice must be added a knowledge of existing state department inspection practice. Persons with these qualifications then need to learn to cope with the complexities of examining the causes of any identified abusive practice on each of the levels identified throughout this chapter. In addition to understanding how personal dynamics can lead to abuse, they must also understand organizational dynamics and the impact of the service delivery system as a whole on the individual institution.

It is also argued in the literature that a unique set of factors make the child who is abused within an institution extremely vulnerable. Nunno and Motz (1988), for example, state that most such investigations should assume high risk to the child and should be initiated on the sole basis of the report without any screening criteria. This implies that the investigator would need to develop a specialized set of criteria for assessing risk, and develop ways of providing immediate protection for the child involved.

In the investigation of child abuse at the family level, a crucial element in adequate inquiries is that a groundwork is laid for the successful resolution of the incident, and this applies equally to the investigation of alleged abuse in children's homes. A clear commitment is necessary to the principle that abuse, once identified, must stop. Commitment is also required to the notion that the offender (be it a person or an institution) has the right to be involved in any necessary changes, provided that the offender accepts that the unacceptable behaviour has been in violation of children's rights, and there is no likelihood of the abuse recurring. Any abusive person or organization has the right to an opportunity to change unacceptable behaviour.

When decisions do in the end need to be made, there are elements not found in familial abuse which need to be considered. These are not only whether or not the incident occurred (irrespective of circumstance, intent, or impact on child), but also precisely where and to what extent various levels of administration bear responsibility, and whether and how the problem may be administratively redressable. There is a small specialist literature on these issues, and on the techniques involved in this work (Ryan *et al.*, 1986; Cavara & Ogren, 1983). Kelleher (1982) adds one further point when she stresses that a post-evaluation strategy must routinely follow if the necessary changes to the ecology of the institution are to occur. This strategy may well be far-reaching and take years to implement, but its completion must be taken seriously and should be part of that institution's licensing conditions in subsequent annual evaluations. In the case of an individual being held responsible for abuse, the criteria for successful rehabilitation must be clearly identified.

Improved reporting of abuse

Barriers to reliable reporting

Rindfleisch and Rabb (1984) have shown that the number of reportable incidents that are in fact reported varies both in terms of the different institutions involved, and in terms of to whom the reports were made. This variance is in the order of five to one and is therefore a highly significant factor which must be allowed for. The main reasons Rindfleisch and Rabb give for this unreliable reporting are that incidents are viewed differently within different institutions, and reporters fear making reports to outside agencies whose response is typically unpredictable and often directed only at the individual level. Child-care workers know that if a colleague is fired, nothing will change. Rindfleisch and Bean (1988) identify further barriers to reporting. These include conflicts between residential staff and potential investigators over control of treatments used   and what counts as 'desirable practice'. Another factor is the pervasive and often untested assumption that alternative care will inevitably and intrinsically be better than conditions from which the child was removed. The authors showed that staff commitment to residents' rights increased their willingness to report, but that physical and sexual abuse were much more likely to be reported than were unacceptable control techniques, questionable moral behaviour by staff, and neglectful behaviour to residents. Also, reports were more likely to be made about more experienced staff — an important consideration when so many child-care workers do not remain in the field for long. Interestingly, support by the organization for reports to be made was only minimally influential in increasing the likelihood that reports were made.

Overcoming these barriers

These barriers cannot be rapidly overcome by the passing of laws requiring reporting, or by legislating for the availability of protection in all circumstances (Besharov, 1983). Among the steps recommended to decrease the incidence of institutional abuse and to increase the rate at which such events are reported is the strong plea that standards of care, procedures for reporting, and procedures for investigation should be negotiated between consumer bodies, service providers, and state departments, and then committed to writing (Mercer, 1982; Rindfleisch & Hicho, 1987). There are specific issues which need resolution before reporting can be expected to occur freely to investigative bodies who enjoy the confidence of both adult and child, provider and consumer in residential care. These are:

☐ Consensus must be reached as to who would employ, control, and authorize those examining for, and maintaining standards. Once this has been decided, those charged with this task should ensure the following:

  (a) A written set of standards for residential child care must be evolved. These should be used in judging whether child abuse or neglect has occurred within an institution.
  (b) The investigative procedures and powers of investigators must enjoy consensus support and must be committed to writing.

(c) Any institution caring for children should agree not to investigate complaints internally, and should be prohibited from doing so.

(d) The investigative team should receive all reports of alleged abuse or neglect.

(e) This investigative team should have the authority and the recognition to question staff and to require changes at any level in the service system.

(f) Specialized training for this team must be provided.

(g) Finally, this group should develop standards for the protection of alleged perpetrators during the investigation, and for rehabilitation or for continuing identification once a finding has been made.

CONCLUSION

As is the case with service provision to abusive families, the issue of the detection, reporting, and investigation of abuse within institutions is ultimately the issue of the recognition of children's rights and the increasingly appropriate use of power. The goal of achieving complete and accurate reporting, together with full and fair investigation and subsequent effective corrective action, is the goal of non-violent behaviour within a democratic system.

In all countries children removed from parental custody remain at risk of secondary abuse by their supposed protectors. In South Africa, inequitable distribution of resources, lack of coherence between government departments, a welfare policy that promotes racial discrimination, and a fragmented private welfare system all add to the pressures and difficulties experienced elsewhere and reflected in the literature surveyed. The central theme of this chapter has been that in the existence of institutional abuse — in the fact that violence is done to children in group care by individuals, by institutions themselves, and by a wider network of services which represent society at large — lies a fundamental challenge to those who see themselves as caring for children. This challenge is to examine our own behaviour as scrupulously and rigorously as we do that of these children's parents. The challenge is to free children from violence directed at them by individuals, by organizations, or by society. And we must not rest while any of us do violence to any child.

REFERENCES

Atten, D. W. & Milne, J. S. (1987) 'Child Abuse Potential and Work Satisfaction in Day Care Employees', *Child Abuse and Neglect*, 11(1), 117–23.

Berkman, D. J. & Lippold, R. W. (1982) 'In-Patient Treatment: Institutional Neglect of Juvenile Health Needs', *Child and Youth Services*, 4(1-2), 65–78.

Besharov, D. J. (1983) 'Protecting Abused and Neglected Children: Can Law Help Social Work', *Child Abuse and Neglect*, 7(4), 421–34.

Brown, M. H. (1948) 'Die Sosio-Ekonomiese Agtergrond van Sorgbehoewende Blanke Kinders in Inrigtings in die Westerlike Kaap Provinsie', MA Thesis, University of Stellenbosch.

Cavara, M. & Ogren, C. (1983) 'Protocol to Investigate Child Abuse in Foster Care', *Child Abuse and Neglect*, 7(3), 287–95.

Child Welfare League of America (CWLA), (1964) *Standards for Services of Child Welfare Institutions*, New York: CWLA Inc.

Cockburn, A. *et al.* (1988) 'Brazil' (a report on child protection services within a Third World context), internal publication, Child Welfare Society, Cape Town.

De Mause, L. (1974) 'The Evolution of Childhood'. In *The History of Childhood — the Evolution of Parent-Child Relationships as a Factor in History*, edited by L. de Mause, Norwich: Fletcher & Son, 1–75.

Dept. of National Health & Population Development (1987) 'Treatment'. In *Disability in the Republic of South Africa* Vol. 3, Pretoria: Government Printer.

Durkin, R. (1982) 'Institutional Child Abuse from a Family Systems Perspective: A Working Paper', *Child and Youth Services*, 4(1–2), 15–22.

Gil, E. (1982) 'Defining Institutional Abuse: Institutional Abuse of Children in Out-of-Home Care', *Child and Youth Services*, 4(1–2), 7–13.

Giles, C. (1982) 'Children Found to be in Need of Care: A Study of Current Management Practice', M.Sc. Thesis, University of Cape Town.

Hirschbach, E. (1982) 'Children Beyond Reach', *Child and Youth Services*, 4(1–2), 99–107.

Jaudes, P. K. & Diamond, L. J. (1985) 'The Handicapped Child and Child Abuse', *Child Abuse and Neglect*, 9(3), 341–7.

Kelleher, M. E. (1982) 'Investigating Institutional Abuse', *Child Welfare* LXVI(4), 343–51.

Kunkel, B. E. (1983) 'The Alienation Response of Children Abused in Out-of-Home Placement', *Child Abuse and Neglect*, 7(4), 479–84.

Larsson, G. *et al.* (1986) 'Prognosis of Children Admitted to Institutional Care during Infancy', *Child Abuse and Neglect*, 10(3), 361–8.

Line, B. F. (1980) 'Resident Participation. A Consumer View'. In *Residential Care: A Reader in Current Theory and Practice*, edited by R. G. Walton & D. Elliott, Oxford: Pergamon Press, 243–52.

Maurer, A. (1982) 'Religious Values and Child Abuse', *Child and Youth Services*, 4(1–2), 57–63.

Mercer, M. (1982) 'Closing the Barn Door: The Prevention of Institutional Abuse through Standards', *Child and Family Youth Services*, 4(1–2), 127–32.

McCord, J. (1983) 'A Forty Year Perspective on Effects of Child Abuse and Neglect', *Child Abuse and Neglect*, 7(3), 265–70.

Nunno, M. A. & Motz, J. K. (1988) 'The Development of an Effective Response to the Abuse of Children in Out-of-Home Care', *Child Abuse and Neglect*, 12(4), 521–8.

Potgieter, M. C. (1973) *Maatskaplike Sorg in Suid-Afrika*, Stellenbosch: Universiteitsuitgewers en Boekhandelaars.

Rabb, J. & Rindfleisch, N. (1985) 'A Study to Define and Assess Severity of Institutional Abuse or Neglect', *Child Abuse and Neglect*, 9(2), 285–94.

Rindfleisch, N. & Baros-Van Hull, J. (1982) 'Direct Care-Workers' Attitudes Toward Use of Physical Force with Children', *Child and Youth Services*, 4(1–2), 115–25.

Rindfleisch, N. & Bean, G. S. (1988) 'Willingness to Report Abuse and Neglect in Residential Facilities', *Child Abuse and Neglect*, 12(4), 509–20.

Rindfleisch, N. & Hicho, D. (1987) 'Institutional Child Protection: Issues in Programme Development and Implementation', *Child Welfare*, LXVI(4), 329–41.

Rindfleisch, N. & Rabb, J. (1984) 'How Much of a Problem is Resident Mistreatment in Child Welfare Institutions?', *Child Abuse and Neglect*, 8(1), 33–40.

Rutter, M. (1987) 'Psychosocial Resilience and Protective Mechanisms', *American Journal of Orthopsychiatry*, 57(3), 316–22.

Rutter, M. (1971) 'Parent-Child Separation: Psychological Effects on the Children', *Journal of Child Psychology and Psychiatry*, 12, 233–60.

Ryan, C. *et al.* (1986) *Draft Manual for Conducting Child Abuse Investigations in Residential Child Care*, New York: New York State Department of Social Services, Albany.

Sgroi, S. M.(1982) *Handbook on Clinical Intervention in Child Sexual Abuse*, Lexington: Lexington Books.

Straker, G. & Moosa, F. (1988) 'Post-traumatic Stress Disorder: A Reaction to State-Supported Child Abuse and Neglect', *Child Abuse and Neglect*, 12(3), 383–95.

Stayton, D. J. & Ainsworth, M. D. (1973) 'Individual Differences In Infant Responses to Brief, Everyday Separations as Related to Other Infant and Maternal Behaviours', *Developmental Psychology*, 9, 226–35.

Stricklin, A. B. (1972) 'A Psychological Study of Children Legally Removed from Their Parents', Ph.D. Thesis, University of Cape Town.

Thomas, B. R. (1982) 'Protecting Abused Children: Helping Till it Hurts', *Child and Youth Services*, 4(1–2).

Tizard, B. & Rees, J. (1975) 'The Effect of Early Institutional Rearing on the Behaviour Problems and Affectional Relationships of Four-Year-Old Children', *Journal of Child Psychology and Psychiatry*, 16, 61–74.

Toro, P. A. (1982) 'Developmental Effects of Child Abuse: A Review', *Child Abuse and Neglect*, 6(4), 423–31.

Ward, L. (1980) 'The Social Work Task in Residential Care'. In *Residential Care — A Reader in Current Theory and Practice,* edited by R. G. Walton & D. Elliott, Oxford: Pergamon Press, 25–37.

Wilson, F. & Ramphele, M. (1989) *'Uprooting Poverty: The South African Challenge: Report for the Second Carnegie Inquiry into Poverty and Development in South Africa'*, Cape Town: David Philip.

Wolkind, S. N. (1974) 'The Components of "Affectionless Psychopathy"'. In 'The Institutionalized Children', *Journal of Child Psychology and Psychiatry*, 15, 215–20.

Wolkind, S. & Renton, G. (1979) 'Psychiatric Disorders in Children in Long-term Residential Care: A Follow-up Study', *British Journal of Psychiatry*, 135, 129–36.

Wright, J. *et al.* (1988) 'Handling Sexual Abuse in Residential Care', *The Child Care Worker*, 5(2), 11–12.

Zigler, E. (1979) 'Controlling Child Abuse in America: An Effort Doomed to Failure?' In *Critical Perspectives on Child Abuse*, edited by R. Bourne & E. H. Newberger, Lexington: Lexington Books, 171–213.

14 Violence in detention

The Human Rights Commission

THE POLITICS OF VIOLENCE

At the outset it is necessary to distinguish the process of what we regard as detention from the process of arrest. In the context of this chapter, 'detention' is used to mean detention without trial. Although detainees may be subsequently charged and brought to trial, this is not the presumption of the law that sanctions their imprisonment. A person who is arrested may, under the Criminal Procedures Act 51 of 1977 be held for a maximum of forty-eight hours before being released or brought before a magistrate. A person who is detained is not under the jurisdiction of the courts (the provisions of the various sections of detention legislation will be described later), but is held for political reasons. A detainee may be held indefinitely, may have no automatic access to lawyers, and the fact of his or her detention is not necessarily even public information.

Detention is regarded in all human rights documents as a violation of human rights. Article 9 of the Universal Declaration of Human Rights, adopted by the United Nations in 1948, states that 'no one shall be subjected to arbitrary arrest, detention or exile'. Human rights documents are also unanimous in their prohibition of the violence associated with the use of detention. Article 5 of the Universal Declaration states that 'no one shall be subjected to torture or to cruel, inhuman or degrading treatment or punishment'.

A brief history

Detention was introduced in response to the concerted resistance which met the implementation of apartheid policy in the 1950s. However, repression of black resistance had always been a part of the colonial history of South Africa as was evidenced by 200 years of conquest and occupation.

Two forms of legislation have been used to empower the government to practice detention: security legislation, which has been in effect since 1963; and emergency legislation, which functions only when a state of emergency has been declared.

Development of security legislation

In 1963, the General Laws Amendment Act 37 was passed, section 17 of which provided for up to 90 days detention, in isolation, without access to the courts, for the purposes of interrogation (the '90-day clause'). It allowed for renewal at the end of the period. In 1965, the '180-day clause' was enacted. Under section 215 of the Criminal Procedure Amendment Act 96, a person could be held for up to 180 days under the same conditions as under the '90-day clause'. The stated purpose of this legislation was to isolate potential witnesses from any intimidation or interference.

The General Laws Amendment Act 62 came into effect in 1966. Section 22 provided for short-term 'preventive' detention for up to fourteen days, renewable. In 1967, the Terrorism Act 83 was introduced with the justification that it was necessary to combat terrorism in South West Africa (Namibia) — a response to SWAPO guerrilla action. Within a year it was put to use in charging South Africans. Section 6 provided for indefinite detention without trial for the purpose of interrogation in solitary confinement.

In 1976 the Internal Security Amendment Act 79 was introduced during the Soweto uprising for the purpose of withdrawing political activists from the political arena. Section 10(1)(a) *bis* provided for long-term 'preventive' detention of up to twelve months, renewable. Section 12B provided for up to six months detention of potential witnesses, in solitary confinement.

Then in 1982, the Internal Security Act 74 was introduced to streamline and supersede all previous security legislation. It is currently on the statute books. In this Act:

☐ Section 28 provides for long-term (12 months) 'preventive' detention.

☐ Section 29 provides for indefinite interrogatory detention.

☐ Section 31 provides for six months detention as a potential witness.

☐ Section 50 provides for short-term (14 days) 'preventive' detention.

In 1986, the Internal Security Amendment Act 66 was passed to add a further category of detention without trial. Section 50A provides for 180 days 'preventive' detention and overcomes court challenge problems experienced with section 28 of the 1982 Act.

Development of emergency legislation

In 1953, the Public Safety Act 3 was introduced in response to the 'Defiance Campaign', a campaign of passive resistance to discriminatory laws which was then being conducted by the African National Congress (ANC) (before it was banned) and other organizations. It empowers the Head of State to declare a state of emergency in certain circumstances, and to make regulations conferring a wide range of powers, including detention of persons without trial, for a period limited only to the duration of the state of emergency.

On 30 March 1960, a state of emergency was declared for the first time, nine days after the Sharpeville massacre in which sixty-seven people died, and two days after the banning of the ANC and the Pan African Congress (PAC). It was lifted 156 days later on 31 August 1960.

In spite of considerable unrest in 1976 relating to the Soweto uprising, a state of emergency was not declared, reliance being placed on security legislation to suppress this unrest. It was in 1985, on 21 July, that a state of emergency was declared for the second time, subsequent to ever-increasing and widespread political unrest arising out of the tricameral elections, Black Local Authorities Bills, and rent increases in the Vaal area. It was lifted seven and a half months later on 7 March 1986, having been operable in forty-four magisterial districts.

A national state of emergency was declared in all magisterial districts of South Africa (excluding the 'independent' homelands) on 12 June 1986, and massive levels of detention were experienced during the subsequent months. This state of emergency was subsequently renewed in 1987, 1988, and 1989.

Current legislation empowering detention

Security legislation

The Internal Security Act 74 of 1982, together with the Internal Security Amendment Act 66 of 1986, provides for detention without trial for three different stated purposes:

☐ detention for interrogation (section 29);

☐ preventive detention (sections 28, 50, and 50A);

☐   detention of a potential witness (section 31).

Detention for interrogation

Section 29 allows for a detainee to be held in solitary confinement without access to lawyers, family, friends, or anyone else other than state officials (interrogators, magistrates, district surgeons, etc.) for the purpose of interrogation. The period of detention is effectively unlimited — until 'all questions are satisfactorily answered', or 'no useful purpose will be served by further detention'. The jurisdiction of the courts over such detention is specifically excluded.

Preventive detention

Section 28 allows for the holding of a person in prison by ministerial order (as opposed to court sentence) if the Minister believes that that person is likely to commit a security offence. The period used has been six or twelve months, and is renewable. The courts have no jurisdiction, and access to the detainee is restricted to state officials. Although still on the statute books, this section of the Internal Security Act has fallen into disuse, perhaps because the wording requires the Minister to give reasons for the detention.

Section 50A is similar in effect to section 28, but does not require any reasons to be given for the detention. It is simply dependent upon the opinion of a police officer of the rank of lieutenant-colonel or above, and serves to remove the victim from society for up to 180 days, which can then be renewed. This section must be brought into effect by proclamation by the State President, which has not been necessary due to the continuing existence of a state of emergency under which powers of preventive detention are even wider.

Section 50 allows the holding of a person for a short period (up to fourteen days) and was very extensively used in the past either when no state of emergency was in existence, or during a partial state of emergency in magisterial districts not falling under the state of emergency. It would serve no purpose during a state of emergency, but remains on the statute books.

Witness detention

Section 31 allows the Attorney-General to order the detention of a person in solitary confinement, without any access to family members or to his/her own doctor or legal representative, beyond the jurisdiction of any court, if he/she believes that that person could be a material witness in a security trial. The time limit is six months, unless the trial starts before then. Almost invariably, section 31 detention is an extension of section 29 detention when, as a result of the interrogation process, it is decided that the detainee shall become a state witness.

'Homelands' legislation

The security legislation in force in the 'independent' homelands (Transkei, Bophuthatswana, Venda, Ciskei) mirrors the Internal Security Act very closely, particularly with regard to the detention clauses. The relevant acts are as follows:

☐ Venda Terrorism Act (same as Terrorism Act 83 of 1967).

☐ Transkei Public Security Act 30 of 1977.

☐ Bophuthatswana Internal Security Act 22 of 1979.

☐ Ciskei National Security Act 13 of 1982.

Emergency legislation

The Public Safety Act 3 of 1953 empowers the State President to:

1. Declare a state of emergency under section 2, with a time limit of 12 months, if, in his opinion, circumstances are such that the ordinary laws of the land are inadequate to maintain public order.

2. Proclaim Emergency Regulations under section 3, such as he deems necessary, including the summary arrest and detention of persons.

Under the Emergency Regulations, any member of the security forces (including the lowest-ranked members of the South African Police, Defence Force, and Prison Services) has the power to detain and interrogate. An emergency detainee has no automatic right of access to lawyers, family, or friends and may be held for the duration of the emergency. Since successive states of emergency can be, and are declared, this means that the time of detention is open-ended.

The wider context

Detention without trial in South Africa must be seen as a part of the political system which it is used to uphold. It is but one of many forms of legalized repression playing its part in the smothering of political opposition, the most basic one being denying the majority of people the right to vote for their government. Because the system of detention without trial has been internationally publicized and the anathema of the international community has been vociferously expressed, it has become an embarrassment to the state, and is now being replaced to some extent with the system of restriction under which a person's right to freedom of movement and association in daily life can be severely curtailed.

The violence of the system of detention which is described in this chapter should be seen as a form of violence tolerated in a society which also allows political assassinations and disappearances of political opponents to go unchecked, that permits right-wing attacks on opposition organizations, and that allows the operation of state-approved vigilante groups against groups who organize against the system of government in South Africa.

DETENTIONS: THE EXTENT AND SCOPE OF VIOLENCE

In recent years the outstanding images of violence in South Africa have been those of riot police armed with guns and sjamboks in hot-blooded pursuit of peaceful protesters and hapless bystanders; and side-by-side with this, the image of thousands upon thousands of detainees, activists, and ordinary citizens locked up in the country's jails and police stations, unseen, unheard, and untried. Each detention is not only in itself a violent denial of an individual's human rights authorized by the law of the land, but the law offers little or no protection against physical violence and psychological abuse of the detainee. This section gives an indication of the scale of detentions without trial and the incidence and nature of the violence inherent in the situation, and also that deliberately perpetrated.

Gathering accurate statistics on detentions has become increasingly difficult as the state has grown more secretive, no doubt as the world has grown more interested. However, it is significant that the state has seldom refuted the figures released by monitoring groups, apart from the figures of children in detention where the arguments have centred on the ages of the children and not on the fact that they were, or had been, in detention. This would indicate that the figures released by these groups tend to be conservative rather than inflationary. This is also likely in view of the fact that these groups rely on information from the families, communities and organizations of those detained, and there is every likelihood of some detentions not being reported to them. This is especially so where families have suffered intimidation, and where organizations have been disrupted by repression.

Detentions under security legislation from 1963 to 1989 compiled by the Human Rights Commission are shown in Table 14.1. These are conservatively calculated and the actual figures must be substantially higher. It is interesting to note that in the last five years there have been

Table 14.1: Detentions under security legislation

Years	Interrogation	Witness	Preventive	Sub-total	Homelands	Total
1963–6	1 095	247	—	1 342	472	1 814
1967–75	800	293	94	1 187	187	1 374
1976–7	2 500	504	350	3 354	120	3 474
1978–81	800	260	1 700	2 760	500	3 260
1982	107	100	3	210	83	293
1983	149	16	38	203	215	418
1984	339	47	191	577	532	1 109
1985	463	41	1 932	2 436	1 953	4 389
1986	477	143	3 512	4 132	520	4 652
1987	532	84	—	616	286	902
1988	315	13	—	328	556	884
1989 (6 months)	41	1	—	42	66	108
Totals	7 618	1 749	7 820	17 187	5 490	22 677

Source: Human Rights Commission records.

more detentions under security legislation than in the previous twenty years, in spite of the heavy incidence of detentions in the year following the Soweto uprising of June 1986. The figures illustrate a clear correlation between detentions and levels of political resistance in the increased detentions in the 1976–81 period and the 1985–6 period. However, they also reflect the change in state strategy following the hunger strikes of early 1989, which resulted in the release of hundreds of detainees and the wariness of government in the period before and after the election in 1989.

Details of detentions under the Emergency Regulations are given in Table 14.2. In total there have been in the region of 50 000 detentions thus far under the Emergency Regulations during the six states of emergency since 1960.

Table 14.2: Detentions under Emergency Regulations

Year	Detail	No. of detentions
1960	Partial state of emergency (29/3/60 to 31/8/60)	11 727 (official)
1985–6	Partial state of emergency (21/7/85 to 7/3/86)	7 996 (official)
1986–7	Total state of emergency (12/6/86 to 11/6/87)	25 000 (estimated)
1987–8	Total state of emergency (11/6/87 to 10/6/88)	5 000 (estimated)
1988–9	Total state of emergency (10/6/88 to 9/6/89)	2 547 (estimated)
1989–90	Total state of emergency (9/6/89 to early 1990)	300 +

Source: Human Rights Commission records.

Figure 14.1 shows the official figures and the figures estimated by detention monitoring groups during this period of secrecy. From the beginning of the first national state of emergency on 12 June 1986, the authorities have consistently refused to publish figures for all emergency detentions, but have only revealed the names of those persons detained for longer than thirty days, as required by section 4 of the Public Safety Act 3 of 1953.

Torture and assault in detention

Over the years and right up to the present time there has been a continuous stream of allegations of torture and assault in detention. Court proceedings abound with such allegations, and those reaching court can only be considered to be a small portion of the whole picture. Furthermore, the courts are not always seen to be fair-handed in these cases where the word of a single detainee is judged against the testimony of several security policemen. Criticizing the magistrate's findings in the

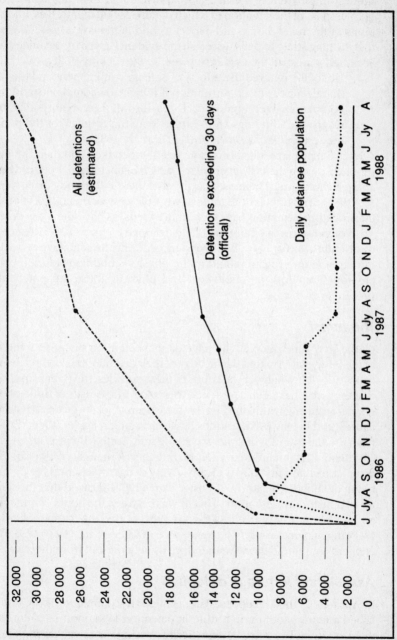

Figure 14.1: Emergency detentions, 12 June 1986 to 31 August 1988

All detentions (estimated)

Detentions exceeding 30 days (official)

Daily detainee population

32 000
30 000
28 000
26 000
24 000
22 000
20 000
18 000
16 000
14 000
12 000
10 000
8 000
6 000
4 000
2 000
0

J Jy A S O N
1986

D J F M A M J Jy A S O N D
1987

J F M A M J Jy A
1988

inquest of Dr Neil Aggett in 1983, Mrs Helen Suzman highlighted the helplessness of the situation in which detainees find themselves, and the limits of the relief they could expect to find in the law courts. She said that the magistrate had dismissed all the evidence given by detainees and accepted almost all the evidence given by the security police:

> He totally ignored the effects of solitary confinement and the fact that detainees faced retribution if they made complaints and that complaints were ignored. Does the Minister realise that the magistrate's findings went further than the counsel for the police requested? (*Rand Daily Mail*, 4 February 1983).

Several major investigations have been undertaken and their findings reported during the last seven years, which detail torture, both physical and psychological. The most important of these is the study by Foster *et al.* (1987). In particular the intensely hostile environment of section 29 interrogatory detention has come under focus, as have the mass detentions of the states of emergency. The detainee is exposed to violence in three main areas of his or her experience: during the actual arrest, whilst undergoing interrogation, and in the physical conditions of the prison environment. Both psychological and physical abuse are potentially present in each case.

The arrest

Of the sixty-nine people who have died in detention since 1963, fifteen of these have died within the first day of their detention, six of them being from 'suicide'. Whatever the cause of these suicides, the figures indicate that the arrest has been a violent experience. The causes of three of the deaths occurring within the first day have been officially given as 'natural' causes, and in May 1985, Andries Raditsela, a union leader, allegedly fell from the Casspir in which he was being transported after his arrest and sustained a fatal head injury (Human Rights Commission, 1989b). The actual arrest and first day is clearly a very dangerous period for people being detained. The study of Foster *et al.* (1987) showed that the most usual time for the detention to occur was between the hours of midnight and 6 a.m., and 70 per cent of the sample reported the manner of arrest as being violent, rough, or aggressive (Foster *et al.*, 1987: 95). The elements of intimidation are therefore usually present from the start.

Assault and torture in detention

In April 1982, the Detainees' Parents Support Committee (DPSC) published a memorandum on torture in detention to support its claim that the security police were systematically abusing detainees during interrogation. They reported the following forms of torture from the statements of seventy ex-detainees:

☐ sleep deprivation (20 cases);

☐ enforced standing for long periods and enforced physical exercise and exertion (28 cases);

☐ being kept naked during interrogation (25 cases);

☐ suspension in mid-air (11 cases);

☐ beating, slapping, kicking, etc. (54 cases);

☐ electric shocks (22 cases);

☐ attacks on the genitals (14 cases).

These were all noted again in the study of Foster *et al.* (1987), as well as the following methods of physical torture:

☐ hooding;

☐ food deprivation;

☐ strangulation;

☐ dousing in cold water;

☐ water deprivation;

☐ applications of lit cigarettes and chemicals onto the skin;

☐ bright light;

☐ being exposed to excessive cold and heat;

☐ being made to walk barefoot over glass, stones.

Eighty-three per cent of the sample of 175 detainees claimed some form of physical torture.

In a study by the National Medical and Dental Association (NAMDA) conducted on detainees seen by its members between December 1985 and June 1986, a very high level of physical abuse was also recorded, in this case 72 per cent of a sample of 131 detainees. The study went further in examining the detainees for injuries consistent with the alleged forms of assault and found that in 97 per cent of cases where injuries were present, the claims were substantiated by the nature of the injuries (Browde, 1987: 3–6). Considerable evidence of systematic torture of detainees also came to light in a supreme court application by Dr Wendy Orr, a district surgeon, and forty-three others in the Eastern Cape, to prevent the security police from assaulting detainees (*Orr v Minister of Law and Order*, 1985).

Women have not been exempt from violent treatment, although they have not suffered physical torture to the same extent as men. Theresa Ramashamola, who was on death row convicted of political violence, and who has subsequently been reprieved, was in solitary confinement under section 29 before coming to trial. During her trial, evidence was submitted that she had been subjected to electric shocks applied to her nipples (CIIR, 1988: 43).

Many charges have been laid against the police of assault and torture in detention, and between 1969 and 1983, R5 503 762 was paid out in settlements covering 717 cases. Table 14.3 shows the escalating cost of these settlements over this period.

Table 14.3: Settlements in respect of court actions by ex-detainees, 1969 to 1983

Year	Successful or settled actions	Total paid in settlement (R)
1969	14	5 845
1970	4	990
1971	14	10 500
1972	43	23 076
1976	39	33 667
1977	69	87 185
1978	78	178 725
1979	100	252 626
1982	190	418 914
1983	166	4 492 234

Source: The Star, *2 October 1986.*

Psychological abuse

All the ex-detainees in the Foster *et al.* (1987) study reported some form of psychological abuse. The study categorized these forms into four different types of techniques:

☐ Those involving communication techniques, which are the most common, and include verbal abuse, false accusations, bribery, and misinformation.

☐ 'Mentally weakening' devices, such as solitary confinement, prolonged interrogation, sham executions, and the administration of drugs.

☐ 'Psychological terror tactics', which are those designed to produce extreme degrees of fear, for instance, threats to the detainee her-self/himself or to her/his family, or being made to witness the torture of another detainee.

☐ Humiliation, which includes being kept naked, excremental abuse, and other situations which may cause the detainee extreme embar-rassment (Foster *et al.*, 1987: 106). Women are allegedly subjected to body searches and vaginal examinations for no reason other than harassment and humiliation (CIIR, 1988: 22).

Methods reported most consistently in the Foster *et al.* (1987: 106) study are:

☐ false accusations;

☐ solitary confinement;

☐ verbal abuse;

☐ good/bad interrogators;

☐ misleading information.

Solitary confinement

Writing in the *South African Medical Journal*, Marcus of the Centre for Applied Legal Studies at the University of the Witwatersrand stated that the solitary confinement of detainees — specifically authorized in terms of the Emergency Regulations — was, in medical terms, a form of torture. Contravention of the discipline imposed upon detainees and awaiting trial prisoners (even children in detention) could result in punishments including solitary confinement coupled with a spare diet for a period not exceeding thirty days. Marcus said that in most countries solitary con-finement is regarded as an inhumane form of punishment (Marcus, 1988: 457–8).

Ishmael Ebrahim, being tried in the Supreme Court in 1988 for treason, said of his solitary confinement that he was put in a cell which had no visible ceiling and through which little air entered. For four days he was subjected to sharp and piercing noises that were at times continuous throughout the night, at other times intermittent. After a break of nine days, the treatment resumed for another seven nights. 'It was like living in a "hell"' (*Critical Health*, 1989: 40–1).

Deaths in detention

At least sixty-nine people have died in detention in South Africa since 1963. Deaths in detention ceased for a period after the death of Ahmed Timol in 1971, who died four days after he was detained, after a fall from the tenth-floor window at police headquarters at John Vorster Square. His detention, and events relating to his death, led to a country-wide protest against the Terrorism Act 83 of 1967 under which he was detained, and the extensive powers of the police.

The post-mortem revealed abrasions on his body. Detailed medical evidence was led by the state pathologist and the pathologist for the family, who stated that the bruises found on his body were inflicted between three and twenty-four hours before his death. However, the magistrate announced in his findings that no one was responsible for his death, and that Mr Timol had committed suicide rather than betray the political organization to which he belonged. He recommended that future detainees be examined by the district surgeon as soon as possible after their arrest.

A sharp increase in deaths in detention occurred in 1976 and 1977, probably associated with the many detentions following the Soweto riots, but deaths decreased sharply after the death of Steve Biko in 1977. Since then, 1986 was the year in which most deaths occurred.

An examination of deaths in detention shows that there are certain centres where deaths are more likely to occur. This, taken in conjunction with the sudden cessation of deaths after times of public outcry and scrutiny, suggests strongly that those in charge of detainees may have a large degree of responsibility for those deaths.

Suicide has been the most common form of death, especially in the case of deaths that have occurred within forty-eight hours of detention. Detainees have been found hanging in their cells, or else death has occurred through strangulation, and detainees allegedly jumping from windows or down a stairwell. There are many who believe that the high incidence of suicide verdicts — mostly suicide by hanging — may be attributed in part to strangulation techniques of torture being used during interrogation, and sometimes taken too far.

Other causes given for deaths in detention have been:

☐ Injuries sustained to the head or body.

☐ 'Natural causes', which include 'slipping in a shower', 'slipping on soap', 'falling down stairs', and hitting the head against a desk while fainting.

☐ Shot while attempting to escape.

In March 1989, an inquest into the death of Simon Marule was concluded. He was a twenty-year-old who died in 1986 in hospital with kidney failure soon after being transferred from prison. Two former detainees told the court how their cell mate was refused proper medication and left in pain, despite repeated requests for medical attention. At issue in the inquest were three points: allegations of the assault of Marule by the police at the police station prior to his admission to prison; the fact that no urine tests were conducted, which would have diagnosed his disease; and allegations that manifest symptoms of his disease had been ignored. However, the inquest concluded that no one could be held responsible, and that he had not died because of inadequate medical treatment (Human Rights Commission, 1989b).

Conditions in detention

It is sometimes difficult to categorize an aspect of detention as 'torture', rather than a condition which is a non-malicious, existing fact of life for many detainees. This exercise is made much harder by the fact that conditions of treatment and physical conditions vary greatly from one prison to another, and between prisons and police stations, where detainees are sometimes held. However, the regulations under which detainees are held are draconian. From June 1985 to June 1987, the prison authorities used methods such as solitary confinement and reduced diet to deal with those who contravened detention regulations, and these methods clearly fall into the description of torture. There is no doubt that the system of detention without trial is both punitive and violent in the manner in which it is used in this country (Marcus, 1988: 457).

Detainees commonly complain about the cell itself: the cell is small, it may have only cold water, it may have no drinking water available at all. The detainee may have no control over the lights at all, which are sometimes kept on for twenty-four hours a day (the better for the detainee to be observed through the peephole) (Foster *et al.*, 1987).

Standards of hygiene are another usual cause of complaint. Filthy blankets, soiled by excrement or vomit, are frequently cited by ex-detainees. Ablution facilities may be less than adequate. Women have complained about total lack of sanitary towels, or an insufficient supply during menstruation (CIIR, 1988: 17).

Food is the third major area of complaint. It appears to differ widely from one prison to another (CIIR, 1988: 17–18).

There are other conditions prevailing in the day-to-day life of detainees which also contribute to the general discomfort, hardship, and uncertainty of their lives in detention. Exercise is not always regular; it is not always permitted to receive writing, reading, and studying material; and parcels of food and clothing are received at the discretion of the authorities (*Human Rights Update*, 1988, (1)2: 15–16).

Medical care of detainees

The role of doctors will be discussed later in this chapter. The cases of Steve Biko, who died in detention with the complicity of the district surgeon, and that of Simon Marule, who died in detention from medical neglect according to his cell mates, illustrate that the medical treatment of detainees is sometimes uncaring, if not downright unsympathetic. Generally, detainees complain about a lack of trust, a lack of regular opportunities to see a doctor, and offhand treatment when they do get to see one (*Critical Health*, 1989).

The use of teargas

Teargas has been used on detainees in prisons. The Minister of Justice has given figures for the occasions on which it was used between 10 February 1987 and 31 January 1988 (*Hansard*, 1 March 1988, cols. 154–6). On seven occasions it was sprayed by hand with aerosol spray cans, and on two occasions tearsmoke cartridges were used. In a study conducted by Professor Peter Folb, Professor of Pharmacology at the University of Cape Town, and Mr Jo Talmud, a pharmacist, which was published in the *South African Medical Journal*, they say of the teargas used in South Africa that it should never be used 'indoors or in places from which those who have been exposed to it cannot readily escape'. Outdoors it is relatively safe, but asthmatics and chronic bronchitis sufferers are at risk (*The Star*, 11 October 1989).

> We were making our beds and tidying up, but they said we were slow and they sprayed teargas into the cell. And then later they sprayed water which made the blankets and mats wet. When they sprayed the teargas, they locked us in a closed cell. Some of us fainted and some of us vomited (Quotation from the statement of a fourteen-year old, 'The Last Affidavits', 1987: 33–4).

In the years 1985 to 1989, when the number of detentions was at its height, a huge amount of evidence was collected on the nature of detention and on the treatment of detainees during their imprisonment. Disclaimers by the authorities of any maltreatment ring hollow in the light of so much corroborating evidence in different studies, mostly collected from the personal experiences of ex-detainees. Physical and psychological abuse of detainees is systematic, and radical steps must be taken to stop these practices.

THE INDIVIDUAL AND SOCIAL EFFECTS OF DETENTION

Detention, and its probable sequel, restriction, have a devastating effect on the family, community, and society at large. The effects and after-effects of detention and restriction are covered in the following pages. They are considered in the stages of detention, release from detention, and being under restriction.

Effects of detention

The process of detention is an extremely dehumanizing one in which the detainee becomes powerless, and his/her life no longer predictable.

Once incarcerated, the detainee is removed from society, from his/her family, organizations, friends, comrades, and colleagues, and is totally dependent on a system which perceives him/her as an enemy, with which he/she cannot enter negotiations, and which is apparently not accountable, except to itself. The anxiety that the detainee experiences at having no control, is exacerbated by the fear of possible torture, or even death. The legislation under which he/she is held allows for indefinite detention, and the government, since June 1986, has success-fully plugged all the loopholes within its legislation concerning detention itself and also concerning what may be legally reported on the subject.

A detainee has very few rights. This is emphasized in the conditions governing both emergency detainees and Internal Security Act detainees. They have no rights to visits by legal representatives or family members; to physical contact with others; to religious visits by their own priest; to medical visits by their own doctors; or to study rights.

It is no surprise that detainees often suffer from acute psychological problems whilst being held, which can be generally grouped into either depression or anxiety.

A general sense of impotence and low self-esteem are often ex-perienced by the detainee, especially as a result of interrogation when the individual can be physically and verbally abused. It is often the case that a detainee introjects the interrogator's abusive and negative view of himself/herself, resulting in self-destructive attitudes and behaviour within the detainee. This invasion of the person produces feelings of protest, anger, and fear, but these emotions cannot be expressed without the detainee 'losing control' and 'showing weakness'. The identity of the detainee becomes fragmented as his/her perception of himself/herself and the reality of the outside world begin to break (Spitz, 1989). Such a sense of powerlessness and lowered self-esteem are fundamental components of depression, and if untreated can lead to suicidal tendencies.

The absence of normal communication and its replacement with interrogation and other psychological and sometimes physical violations (for instance, female detainees have alleged that the police have used body searches and vaginal examinations for no other reason than that of harassment and humiliation), may result in the detainee being unable to communicate normally with other people.

Besides conditions experienced directly by the detainee, added factors which compound the stress experienced in detention are fears and worries about the welfare and safety of family and friends, especially if the detainee is a breadwinner or faces dismissal from employment due to detention. Although there are some funds which assist the dependants of detainees, the money is never enough, and there are frequent problems in gaining access to them. Thus, when a breadwinner is held, all sorts of financial catastrophes may follow, such as the rent may not be paid, threatening eviction; hire purchase payments may be impossible, resulting in repossession; and there may not be enough money for food and clothing. Because he/she may feel responsible for his/her family's suffering, the detainee experiences a loss of morale, made worse if there were unresolved tensions between family and detainee at the time of detention.

Schoolchildren who are detained also experience severe setbacks to their educational careers. The interruption of studies, within an education system which is vastly inferior to its white counterpart, further jeopardizes the education potential of the child and his or her future role in society.

The emotional and psychological effects of detention are lessened or heightened in respect of whether a detainee is held with others or in solitary confinement (which is often the case with Internal Security Act detainees, especially section 29 detainees, who are held for the purpose of interrogation).

Professor C. Vorster notes:

> If confinement is kept up, the person loses contact with reality; s/he becomes totally disorientated and s/he exhibits symptoms you find in a person with psychosis — imbalance of the mind — such as high levels of anxiety, panic and delusions. S/he hallucinates, hears voices. Everything is distorted in terms of distance and height (*Critical Health*, 1989: 40).

Post-detention

The paralysing effects of detention are frequently experienced after release. The often-stressed individual is released into a stressed and stressful society. For the political activist this can be deeply frustrating, since the societal conditions that he/she was working against prior to his/her detention will not have improved, and may even have worsened.

The common after-effects of detention, in what is termed post-traumatic stress disorder (PTSD), are as follows: lack of concentration; flashbacks; a sense of acute alienation from family, friends, and society; bad dreams; insomnia; moodswings; depression; a sense of powerlessness; demotivation; low self-esteem; distrust; physical aches and pains; low libido or impotency; eating problems; and a sense of guilt at having left others behind in prison (DPSC: 1986a).

A released detainee might have all of these problems, or a combination of them to a lesser or greater degree.

After-effects, especially that of alienation, can be exacerbated if the detainee's family is unpoliticized and do not support, encourage, or understand the detainee, and perhaps resent him or her for putting such a strain, emotionally or financially, on the family. However, even if a family fully supports the detainee individually and politically, the sense of alienation experienced by many detainees cannot be overcome immediately.

It is often the case that detention *has* permanently changed the individual. In some cases youths detained in their late teens were only released in their twenties. In detention the detainee may be in an environment where new structures, such as cell groups and study groups, have been established. New relationships, increased political and personal maturity, treatment meted out whilst in detention, and the realities of surviving without established familiar family support roles and routines have meant that individuals can no longer relate, or need to relate, to support structures within the family.

This can be especially difficult for young people and their families. For many, a sense of independence and autonomy develops during detention, usually as a means of survival, and individuals cannot and do not want to revert to roles of the past. Also for many, both youth and adult, there is the sense that those who have not experienced detention, which in some cases included severe physical and psychological abuse, cannot possibly understand the released detainee. For some there is also the desire to protect their families from the knowledge of what they experienced whilst detained. This can lead the family to mirror the isolation and impotency experienced by the released detainee.

Changes also occur within the family; roles within the family often alter, subtly or dramatically, whilst a member is in detention. This is especially true if the detainee is a mother or father. Other members take over the roles usually played by the detainee, for example, that of 'head of the family', nurturer of small children, or breadwinner, and do not wish to relinquish these once the detainee is released. When the detainee returns, he or she is in effect a stranger, especially if there are small children in the family and the detention has been lengthy.

Release from detention can be an extremely stressful time for both the released detainee and the family, where happy family reunions develop into extremely stressful living conditions, especially if the released detainee is suffering from manifestations of PTSD and both the family and the released detainee are having to adapt.

Addressing the problem of PTSD can be exacerbated if the individual or his/her family and friends believe that the manifestations of PTSD reflect weakness of character, or if they believe that the individual should 'pull himself/herself together' within a defined period of time. This need to 'get better quickly' and thereby return to maximum effectiveness obviously increases the pressure placed on the individual and his/her family.

Counselling is available to help released detainees cope, but problems are often experienced when individuals are 'on the run', or do not have enough time because of other commitments. The treatment of released detainees entered a new dimension with the implementation of restrictions, which have been described as an 'insidious but powerful form of human destruction' (*New Nation*, 29 September, 1989).

Effect of restrictions

In the latter part of 1988 and in 1989, after hunger strikes, many detainees were released with restrictions. This has not only increased the after-effects experienced by released detainees and severely hampered their treatment, but has also introduced new hardships and dynamics, both physical and emotional.

Restrictions served on detainees as conditions for their release usually entail house arrest for between ten and twenty hours per day, prohibit participation in the activities of certain organizations or establishments, prevent attendance at meetings where the government is criticized, limit the restrictee to a specified magisterial district, prevent the restrictee from being in the company of more than a specified number of people, and require the restrictee to report to a police station once or twice a day.

With restrictions, the detainee cannot regard the detention as a past experience which he/she can start coming to terms with, because with restrictions the experiences have not been terminated, although the scenario might have altered. Restrictions have made recovery from detention even more difficult, as the individual is dealing with the after-effects of detention together with the present effects of restrictions.

In effect, the restrictee now becomes his or her own jailer, carrying the responsibility emotionally and financially of adhering to his or her restriction order, contravention of which renders him/her liable to a maximum sentence of ten years imprisonment or a R20 000 fine. Inter-action with the police continues as restrictees usually report at least once a day to a police station. This contact echoes the power relationships experienced in detention, and is perpetuated through restrictions dis-playing the restrictee's impotency, and lack of control and freedom. The restrictee can only visualize a future punctuated by reportings. Restric-tees have allegedly been harassed by the police in police stations, either by being kept a long time or by being insulted by members of the police.

Just as the detainee was isolated in his/her cell, the restrictee becomes isolated outside the cell, as social networks suffer and everyday events, such as visiting family or friends, being present at political meetings, attending church, and attending marriages and christenings, become subject to the permission of the state, and lead to a reliance on lawyers for ordinary matters. For many restrictees, burying their dead and attend-ing funerals are something permitted only by the authority of the state. Every movement is a legal matter where the restrictee is dependent on the 'goodwill' of the state and the tenacity and vigour of his or her friends to remain in contact.

Most restrictees come from financially pressurized families whose economic welfare has most likely already been profoundly affected by the detention of one of its members. Added to the family budget comes the cost of transport money to and from the police stations in order to report. This is an additional burden to an already over-stretched family budget. Jobs are lost through detentions, and to get them back is made harder by restriction orders. Being restricted to a particular magisterial district severely limits job opportunities in an already bleak job market. Similar impediments affect education. Continuing education is no longer just a matter of attending school, but must be fitted in with reporting to a police station. Some students and lecturers have been prohibited from entering educational establishments, and as a result are unemployable or cannot continue with their studies. Continuing with studies, often a luxury when money is scarce, is further disrupted when the restrictee is attempting to cope with the impaired concentration and motivation often experienced by those on release, in a home which is overcrowded and does not allow for the peace and quiet necessary for studying. The Education and Training Act 90 of 1979, as amended in 1989, means that individuals involved in political activities may be refused entry to schools by the state, or expelled from them.

This bleak situation only serves to continue to undermine the individual's already weakened self-esteem and lack of confidence as a result of detention itself.

In some cases families have been cut off from one another as restrictions dictate that the restrictee cannot live in the same area as his or her family. In such a setting it is to be expected that relationships, especially those within the family, already damaged through the separation of detention, will break down completely or suffer irreparable damage.

The fact that a restrictee's life and movements are extremely predictable render him or her greatly vulnerable to attack by 'unknown persons' or vigilante groups, a phenomenon which has greatly increased of late. There have already been at least two assassinations of restrictees in 1989, whilst others have been the target of assassination attempts. Attacks on anti-apartheid activists have involved the petrol-bombing of homes, which means that it is not only the restrictee who is in danger but also his/her family. Some restrictees have ceased to comply with their restriction orders as they believe that if they do, their lives, and that of their families, are endangered.

Society

Besides family and educational obligations and responsibilities, detainees often experience great concern regarding their organizations. The consequences of the removal of community leaders are dramatic. The most articulate representatives of the people are no longer available to express and guide community aspirations, and their restraining influence on the more militant members can no longer be exerted. When businesspersons in Port Elizabeth wanted to negotiate with genuine township leaders in the crippling consumer boycott of 1986/7, they had no one to talk to, as all the important community leaders were in detention. The same dire consequences pertain when trade union leaders are removed from their membership. The potential for wildcat strikes and irresolvable disputes is magnified, as the responsible negotiators languish in prison.

The violence of detention when detainees are tortured or assaulted is obvious, but what is more subtle is the severity for the individuals, families, and society as a whole.

What cannot be seen at this stage, but which presents frightening probable scenarios for the future, are the consequences of such wanton waste and abuse of human potential. This is especially true with regard to the children and youth who have experienced the violence of detention, restriction, and township life.

The latent derivation is a generation of adults who are psychologically scarred and crippled, estranged from society and family, and who are incapable of hope or trust. The bitterness, resentment, and anger resulting from detentions and restrictions that cannot be expressed or dealt with today will be expressed as uncontrollable aggression in the future.

Apartheid has created a society of dramatically contrasting experiences, one that is divided and distrustful. For the majority of white South Africans, the detention of thousands of fellow South Africans, many of whom are children, has been met with indifference or a ready willingness to believe that it is necessary for the maintenance of law and order, and that those detained are 'radicals' and 'revolutionaries'.

PREVENTION, AND CURE

The adage 'Prevention is better than cure' was never more true than in the case of violence in detention. However, until the state of emergency is lifted, normal political process is established, and detention without trial is no longer allowed under any legislation, we must look for ways in which the safety and health of detainees can be effectively safeguarded.

The main options are in the following areas:

☐ International pressure on the government, internal pressure, and widespread publicity.

☐ Legal safeguards aimed at reducing the vulnerability of detainees.

☐ Medical safeguards to stop any complicity by the medical profession in abuse of detainees, and in support of a medical code of ethics.

The release of detainees with the imposition of restrictions circumscribing their lives is not an answer. Psychological and social problems persist, and there is the constant threat and real danger of attack or assassination from right-wing and vigilante groups.

Exposure of the system

There is no doubt that the efforts made to draw international attention to the issue of detention without trial and to abuses in detention have had some controlling effect on the way people are treated in detention, and also on the extent to which detention without trial is used. The dramatic fall in the numbers of children detained is an example of the state responding to international pressure, which followed a concerted campaign to publicize the issue abroad. As the Nationalist government tries to open the negotiation process, this type of campaign is likely to become more effective. An end to detention without trial is already on the pre-negotiation agenda of the ANC and the government.

Monitoring groups are functioning in many parts of the country, often under extreme harassment, and it is essential for the protection of detainees that they continue their work. The secrecy surrounding who is in detention, where they are being held, and their states of health, protects their adversaries and makes detainees more vulnerable. It is an offence under the Public Safety Act 3 of 1953 to publish the 'circumstances of, or treatment in detention of a person, who is or was detained under regulation 3 of the Security Emergency Regulations' (*Human Rights Update*, 1988, 1(2): 19).

A phenomenon of the latter part of 1988 and 1989 was that detainees began to take their own initiatives in securing their release, and found ways in which to apply pressure for their release from inside prison. The effects of escapes from detention and hunger strikes by detainees have been to substantially reduce the number of people held under the Emergency Regulations, and have also drawn attention to the plight of those held indefinitely without trial. These actions came at a time when, through severe control of the media, the issue of repression in South Africa had been largely forgotten by the world at large.

Intervention by the courts

Over the years the courts have seen a constant stream of applications for interdicts restraining the police from assaulting detainees in their custody. In 1985 the Detainee's Parents Support Committee (DPSC) recorded seventeen court actions involving eighty-three detainees (DPSC, 1986b: 4). In 1986, the DPSC recorded fifteen court actions involving seventy-five detainees (DPSC, 1987b: 3). With a much lower detention rate in 1988, the Human Rights Commission recorded ten applications involving eleven detainees (Human Rights Commission, 1989c: 6).

These applications are not always successful. There is the case of Peter Mokaba, President of the South African Youth Congress, who was allegedly held at the Potgietersrust police station where he was kept in leg irons and handcuffs for long periods, and chained to a chair for days on end. He was not given water during this time and was not allowed to go to the toilet, wash himself, or sleep. He said that he was assaulted on his head and body with 'rubber batons, sticks, fists and open hands'. In replying affidavits, the police denied assaulting or injuring Mokaba except during his arrest, when 'necessary force' had been used to arrest him and he had been hit on the head twice with a revolver and had been butted three times in his side with an R1 rifle. He had allegedly passed on information about his assault to his mother who had a chance meeting with him at the Pietersburg police headquarters.

The application was dismissed with costs. It had been brought by Mokaba's sister, who the judge said had not succeeded in making out a *prima facie* case that her version of what had happened was correct, and that he was persuaded that the police version of events — which was direct rather than hearsay evidence — was correct. She had allegedly heard of the assault from Mokaba's mother who had been detained herself three days after her meeting with her son (*Human Rights Update*, 1988, 1(3): 36).

The Mokaba case illustrates the difficulties detainees have with taking applications to court, and with getting evidence accepted by the court. Section 29 detainees have no access to lawyers and therefore no means of bringing their own applications. Detainees under the Emergency Regulations have only discretionary access to lawyers.

In 1985 the disquiet about the treatment of detainees grew with an increasing number of reports of abuse, and the numbers of detainees growing alarmingly. The Minister of Law and Order continued to deny allegations against the police, dismissing them as propaganda and attempts to discredit the police. However, in one very important application, the court upheld allegations of assault which indeed showed that assault was systematic, at least in one area of the country. This was the case of an application brought by district surgeon Dr Wendy Orr and forty-three other applicants in the Port Elizabeth Supreme Court (*Orr v Minister of Law and Order*, 1985). The interdict restrained the police from ever assaulting detainees in Port Elizabeth and Uitenhage. The intervention of the district surgeon in this case made the application possible. It is the duty of all outside parties to take such responsible action where they are witness to abuse, or have evidence of it.

The role of the doctor

International medical bodies have laid down codes of practice for doctors, following the complicity of doctors in the atrocities of the Second World War. The World Medical Association has adopted the Tokyo Declaration which states that a doctor should in no way, in any situation, condone the use of torture. In the context of detention without trial, the district surgeon is required to visit and treat detainees. With the number of alleged assaults in detention, it seems that these doctors may either not be performing their obligatory duties, or that in doing so they are remaining silent and breaking international codes of medical ethics. In order to stop assaults in detention, the district surgeons must be made aware of their compulsory duty to speak out in terms of the Hippocratic Oath and of the Tokyo Declaration, which has been endorsed by the Medical Association of South Africa (MASA) (*Critical Health*, 1988: 42–3).

Professor S. A. Strauss, Professor of Law at the University of South Africa, has stated:

> The mere fact that a man becomes a prisoner ... is not regarded as divesting him of the right to receive adequate health care ... On the contrary, the modern view is that a special duty is cast upon police and prison authorities and upon medical officers, because in consequence of the deprivation of his liberty, the prisoner no longer has any access to medical practitioners and health care facilities (*Critical Health*, 1988: 38).

It is also imperative that doctors who speak out are supported by MASA because, from past experience, they are not likely to get sympathetic hearings from the institutions they are criticizing. Dr Orr was immediately taken off her prison duties and was ostracized following her exposure of assault of detainees (*Critical Health*, 1988: 43). Dr Paul Davis, who examined detainees on their release and noted that they had been assaulted, was subpoenaed in terms of section 205 of the Criminal Procedures Act to provide the names of the detainees (*The Citizen*, 9 February 1989). To have supplied the names would have been contrary to the principle of the inviolability of the doctor-patient relationship, and would have placed Dr Davis in an extremely difficult position.

Recommendations

In September 1982, the DPSC issued a memorandum on torture in detention. In it the following recommendations were made for the minimum rights of a detainee:

☐ access to a lawyer;

☐ access to relatives; and

☐ access to a doctor of choice.

In addition it recommended that there should be:

☐ An enforceable code setting out standards of interrogation.

☐ An effective and independent machinery for enforcing and policing the treatment of detainees.

☐ Clinical and personal independence of the district surgeon from the security police (DPSC, 1982).

As yet, there is no specific provision for any of these rights.

The study by Foster *et al.* (1987) made very much more detailed recommendations. Seventeen points were made with respect to the rights of detainees in prison, including the abolition of solitary confinement; the limitations and control of police and prison personnel, especially as regards interrogation and the methods used, and the advocating of compulsory videotaping of all interrogation sessions; and the provision for public monitoring of the situation, including full annual statistical reports to Parliament. The study also recommended that the courts be given more power, including the right to demand the appearance of the detainee in person before the court, and to order the release of any detainee; that confessions of detainees should be accepted by the court only if the state can prove that all safeguards have been complied with, and that psychological coercion has not been used; and that professional bodies, such as medical, mental health, legal, educational, and religious bodies appoint permanent committees to fight abuses of detainees on many different fronts (Foster *et al.*, 1987: 176–80).

This very briefly summarizes some of the measures proposed by the study. There have been no moves by the state to rigorously implement any of them — 'privileges' are granted to detainees, not rights.

In 1983, Amnesty International adopted its Twelve-point Program as part of its Campaign for the Abolition of Torture. Most of the points are covered by the Foster *et al.* (1987) study, but in addition they encourage governmental action in the following ways:

☐ The highest authorities of every country should demonstrate their total opposition to torture. They should make clear to all law enforcement personnel that torture will not be tolerated under any circumstances.

☐ Governments should use all available channels to intercede with governments accused of torture. Inter-governmental mechanisms should be established and used to investigate reports of torture urgently and to take effective action against it.

☐ All governments should ratify international instruments containing safeguards and remedies against torture, including the International Covenant on Civil and Political Rights and its Optional Protocol which provides for individual complaints.

Thus, well-considered proposals have been drawn up by different well-respected bodies, but the task in South Africa is to get the state to adopt them. Professionals such as medical, legal, and social workers are well-placed to make a firm stand on the issues.

REFERENCES

Bell, A. N. & Mackie, R. D. A. (eds.) (1982) 'Detention and Security Legislation in South Africa', proceedings of a conference, University of Natal.

Benatar, S. R. (1988) 'Ethical Responsibilities of Health Professionals in Caring for Detainees and Prisoners', *South African Medical Journal*, 74(9), 453–6.

Benatar, S. R. (1987) 'The Changing Doctor/Patient Relationship and the New Medical Ethics', *South African Journal for Continuing Medical Education*, 5 April, 27–33.

Browde, S. (1987) 'The Treatment of Detainees', text of unpublished paper delivered at NAMDA National Conference, April 1987.

Catholic Institute for International Relations (CIIR) (1988) *Cries of Freedom: Women and Detention in South Africa*, London: CIIR.

Coleman, M. & Webster, D. (1985) 'Repression and Detention in South Africa' In *South African Review*, 3, Johannesburg: Ravan Press & South African Research Services (SARS).

Contact Group of the Medical Schools of the Universities of Cape Town, Natal, and the Witwatersrand (1981), 'Recommendations Relating to the Health of Detainees', unpublished memorandum.

Cooke, H. (1986) *The War Against Children*, New York: Lawyers' Committee for Human Rights.

Critical Health, (1989) 'Detentions and Hunger Strikes', 26.

DACOM (undated), 'Coping in Crisis: A Self-Help Manual', Pietermaritzburg: DACOM.

DPSC (Detainees' Parents Support Committee) (1988) 'Review of 1987', Johannesburg: DPSC.

DPSC (1987a) Monthly Reports (March 1984–November 1987), Johannesburg: DPSC.

DPSC (1987b) Special Reports on the State of Emergency (July 1985–November 1987), Johannesburg: DPSC.

DPSC (1987c) 'Press Package on Torture and Detention', Johannesburg: DPSC.

DPSC (1987d) 'The DPSC Review of Detentions in 1986', Johannesburg: DPSC.

DPSC (1986a) 'Abantwana Bazabalaza: A Memorandum on Children under Repression in South Africa', Johannesburg: DPSC.

DPSC (1986b) 'Review of 1985', Johannesburg: DPSC.

DPSC (1982) 'Memorandum on Security Police Abuses of Political Detainees', Johannesburg: DPSC.

HRC (Human Rights Commission) (1989a) 'Bannings and Restrictions of Persons', Johannesburg: HRC.

HRC (1989b) 'Deaths in Detention', Johannesburg: HRC.

HRC (1989c) 'Days of Defiance: A Special Report on Repression', Johannesburg: HRC.

HRC (1989d — several) 'Hunger Strike Update', Johannesburg: HRC.

HRC (1989e — several) 'HRC Briefing', Johannesburg: HRC.

HRC (1988a) 'Detentions', *Work in Progress*, 1988, 32–5 and 56–7.

HRC (1988b) 'Detention Without Trial', Johannesburg: HRC.

HRC (1988c) 'A Free Choice? Memorandum on Repression and the Municipal Election', Johannesburg: HRC.

HRC (1988d) 'Report on Human Rights in South Africa', Johannesburg: HRC.

Human Rights Commission, South African Council of Churches and Southern African Catholic Bishops' Conference (1989) 'Human Rights and Repression in South Africa: The Apartheid Machine Grinds On', Johannesburg: HRC.

CALS (Centre for Applied Legal Studies) (1988–89) *Human Rights Update* 1(4) and 2(3), Johannesburg: HRC & CALS.

CALS (1988) *Human Rights Update*, 1(1–3), Johannesburg: CALS.

Jenkins, T. (1987) 'Ethical Issues in the Medical Care of Prisoners and Detainees', *South African Journal of Continuing Medical Education*, 5 April, 40–9.

LEAP (Legal Education Action Project) 'Know Your Rights Behind Bars', LEAP, University of Cape Town.

Levin, J. (1988) 'Intervention in Detention', *South African Medical Journal*, 74(9), 460–3.

Levin, J. (1986) 'Torture Without Violence: Clinical and Ethical Issues for Mental Health Workers in the Treatment of Detainees, *South African Journal on Human Rights*, 1, 177.

Marcus, G. J. & Dugard, C. J. R. (1983) 'Any Hope for Detainees? The Aggett Inquest and the Rabie Report Compared', *Lawyers for Human Rights Bulletin*, 2.

Marcus, G. (1988) 'Liability for the Health of Detainees', *South African Medical Journal*, 74(5), 456–9.

Mathews, A. S. & Albino, R. (1966) 'The Permanence of the Temporary — An Examination of the 90 and 180 Day Detention Laws', *South African Law Journal*, 83, 16.

McCarthy, G. (1989) 'Obstacles to the Treatment of Detainees in South Africa', *The Lancet*, 13 May 1989.

McKenzie, D. (1982) 'Medical Treatment of Prisoners and Detainees', *South African Medical Journal*, 61, 688.

McQuoid-Mason, D. (1986) 'Detainees and the Duties of District Surgeons', *South African Journal on Human Rights*, 1, 49.

'Medical Care of Prisoners and Detainees', Report of the Ad Hoc Committee of MASA into the Medical Care of Prisoners, *South African Medical Journal*, 63 (supplement), 1–5.

Motala, S. (1987) *Behind Closed Doors*, Johannesburg: South African Institute of Race Relations.

Police Powers, Part 2: Arrest and Detention (1989), LEAP, University of Cape Town.

Police Powers, Part 6: Restrictions on People Under the State of Emergency (1989), LEAP, University of Cape Town.

Ransome, O. J. (1987) 'Children in Places of Detention: A Code for Their Handling', *South African Medical Journal*, 71 (supplement).

Riekert, J. (1985) 'The Silent Scream: Detention Without Trial, Solitary Confinement and Evidence in South African Security Law Trials', *South African Journal on Human Rights*, 1, 245.

Schultz, E. (1987) 'Medical Care of Detainees'. In *Emergency Law*, edited by N. Haysom & L. Margan, Johannesburg: CALS.

Sieghardt, P. (1985) 'Professions as the Conscience of Society', *Journal of Medical Ethics*, 11, 117–22.

Spitz, S. (1989) 'The Psychology of Torture', unpublished paper presented at a seminar of the Project for the Study of Violence, University of the Witwatersrand.

Strauss, S. A. (1984) 'The Legal Rights of Prisoners and Detainees to Medical Treatment'. In *Doctor, Patient and the Law: A Selection of Practical Issues*, Pretoria: J. L. van Schaik.

'The Last Affidavits' (1987) a collection of sworn statements by the late Molly Blackburn and Brian Bishop, Pretoria: South African Catholic Bishops Conference.

Van Es, A. & Van Gurp, M. (1987) 'Health Professionals and Human Rights in South Africa', a report for the Johannes Weir Foundation, Leiden.

Webster, D. (1987) 'Repression and the State of Emergency'. In *South African Review*, 4, Johannesburg: Ravan Press & SARS, 141–2.

Webster, D. & Friedman, M. (1989) 'Suppressing Apartheid's Opponents. Repression and the State of Emergency June 1987–March 1989', Johannesburg: SARS.

15 Violence and child detainees

Adèle Thomas

INTRODUCTION

From birth, black children of South Africa are exposed to a systematic process of violation. The social fabric, moulded by all-pervading apartheid laws and structures, creates and exposes children to an insidious, chronic level of humiliation and deprivation, and acts of both subtle and overt violence. Black children in South Africa are subjected to the active violence of township shootings, beatings, and detentions, as well as to the passive or structural violence of the environment which has been created and maintained by apartheid philosophy and legislation.

As a context for the discussion of violence inflicted upon children by detentions, the structural violence and, accordingly, the violation of the basic rights of black children in South Africa, needs brief consideration.

The 1959 United Nations Declaration of Children's Rights states that, *inter alia*, all children have a right to be given enough to eat, to have a decent place in which to live, to receive good medical care, to have free education, to be protected from all forms of neglect, and to be afforded special protection to enable them to develop in a normal and healthy way in freedom and dignity.

A Report of the United Nations Children's Fund (1987: 40–9) illustrates how most of these basic rights of black children in South Africa have been violated:

☐ One third of black children below the age of fourteen years are underweight and stunted for their age.

☐ Fifty per cent of all deaths in the black population occur to children under the age of five years, whilst among whites only 7 per cent of all deaths occur in children under this age.

☐   Black children are fifteen times more likely than their white counterparts to die before their fifth birthday.

Black children die of diseases largely caused by the poor socio-economic conditions under which they live. Lack of adequate nutrition and poor housing, major factors in weakening resistance to disease, clearly illustrate the structural violence to which black South African children are subjected.

Discrimination is also evident in the area of welfare. The South African government upholds the 'residual' approach to welfare, in terms of which the well-being of citizens is seen as primarily their own and their family's responsibility, with the government usually intervening as a last resort. The document 'Social Welfare Policy and Structures of the Republic of South Africa'[1] states as a specific policy objective the limiting of state financial support of welfare services 'to a minimum'. No child in South Africa, therefore, has any guarantee that welfare services will be available to him or her, either in times of trouble, or as a means of promoting his/her well-being or preventing the development of problems for him/her in the first place. Additionally, when welfare services come into play after a crisis situation has developed, the availability and quality of services for the child will largely depend upon his/her race. As an example, Table 15.1 details amounts allocated to welfare services in the 1986–7 and 1987–8 national budgets (South African Institute of Race Relations, 1988: 435).

Table 15.1: State welfare budget allocations

State department	1986/7 (R)	1987/8 (R)
Constitutional Development and Planning (Africans in white-designated areas)	373 990 000	not available*
House of Representatives ('coloured')	409 267 000	629 787 000
House of Delegates (Asian)	106 547 000	157 610 000
House of Assembly (white)	684 097 000	769 936 000

* From the financial year 1987–8 the Health and Welfare budget for Africans was administered at provincial level. Figures for this period were not available at the time of writing.

These budget allocations must be seen against the estimated population proportions as at the end of June 1987, namely, 69,4 per cent Africans, 10,6 per cent 'coloured', 3,1 per cent Asian, and 16,9 per cent white (South African Institute of Race Relations, 1988: 10).

Discrimination in social welfare services and the inadequate provision of grants and other resources exacerbate the poverty and illness which are widespread amongst black South African children.

Further structural violation of children's rights can be seen in the area of education. Gross inequalities of educational resources between black and white exist, and barriers preventing black students from reaching top grades, such as overcrowding of classrooms, poorly qualified teachers, and the lack of proper library and laboratory facilities, are commonplace. As an example, a recent report[2] reveals that in 1988, of 170 966 African matriculation candidates, only 57,4 per cent passed and only 28,7 per cent achieved matriculation exemption. In contrast, 97 per cent of white pupils passed their examinations.

Against this background, apartheid has, over the years, fostered hostility and conflict. South Africa is in many respects a developing country, subject to all the effects of underdevelopment as well as to those of rapid urbanization and social transition. When apartheid is combined with these problems (of which it is also one of the causes, although by no means the only one), a recipe for unprecedented social dislocation arises. This takes forms such as massive poverty, unemployment, homelessness, widespread crime, and family breakdown, to name but a few. This combination of factors has resulted in an increasing number of children being exposed on a daily basis to violence. In this sense, detention, the topic of this chapter, is not the first exposure of township children to a process of violation and brutalization. Both detention itself and the trauma associated with detention may be seen as part of a continuum of violence in the lives of black children that has started even before their birth.

AETIOLOGY

More than thirty years ago, the separatist philosophy underlying the South African government's policy of Christian National Education led to the imposition of the much resented Bantu Education System — one designed to ensure that the African people of South Africa were not educated for jobs beyond their perceived place in an apartheid regime.

In 1976, thousands of children in Soweto openly, but peacefully, protested against this educational system.[3] The voices of these children were heard throughout the country and, as a result, these protests soon spread to other parts of the land. In the end the children won that particular battle but, in the process, many were shot and killed in Soweto.

The 1976 protest ushered in a new beginning to the opposition to apartheid and structural violence — the birth of a generation of politicized and politically active youth. Schoolchildren now became the leaders in seeking an effective means of changing the structure in which they were trapped. What began as the protest of children against an inadequate and racist educational system, in subsequent years broadened to encompass a fight to effect political change that would result in the transformation of South African society.

The impetus from these children, together with the strengthening of the anti-apartheid movement over the following nine years and the introduction of the discriminatory tricameral parliamentary system[4] in September 1984, all led to increased unrest and eventually to the declaration of a partial state of emergency on 21 July 1985 in thirty-six magisterial districts in South Africa. Along with this state of emergency came an increase in detentions without trial, a long-standing and permanent feature of the South African legal system.

However, more than in previous times, these detentions now included significant numbers of children who, in the subsequent months and years, were to lose not only their freedom, but years of irrecoverable childhood.

INCIDENCE

The detention of children is not a new phenomenon arising out of the recent states of emergency in South Africa. Officially released figures[5] from 1977 reveal that the following numbers of children were detained in terms of the security legislation:[6]

- [ ] 1977 — 259 (including children as young as 10 years of age)
- [ ] 1978 — 252
- [ ] 1979 — 48
- [ ] 1980 — 127
- [ ] 1981 — 49

The numbers dropped to eight children in 1982, and nine children in 1984 (Black Sash, 1986: 13).

In 1985, with the imposition of the partial state of emergency, the numbers of detained children rose steeply. By the end of 1985, up to 8 000 people, including 2 016 officially acknowledged children under the age of sixteen years, had been detained in South Africa. This represented approximately 25 per cent of the detainee population (Chikane, 1986: 334; Webster, 1987: 152).

In November 1986, independent monitoring groups reported that there were an estimated 4 000 children in detention country-wide.[7] Whilst releasing a somewhat lower figure, official reports stated that as at

15 October 1986, 2 677 children, including 254 children aged fifteen years and under, were in detention.[8]

During 1987, large numbers of children were released from detention (*International Children's Rights Monitor*, 1987: 14). However, official statistics nevertheless stated that 1 338 children had been held in detention during 1987,[9] of whom 281 were under sixteen years of age in June 1987.[10]

In February 1988, the Minister of Law and Order stated in Parliament that there were 234 children in detention comprising: 5 fifteen-year-olds; 89 sixteen-year-olds; 140 seventeen-year-olds.[11]

Independent monitoring groups estimated the number of detained children to be at least 250 at this time.[12]

Any discussion regarding the incidence of detentions is fraught with problems surrounding the acquisition of statistics. Official statistics do not include those children detained for less than thirty days, those children detained under the Internal Security Act 74 of 1982, as amended, nor those children detained in the independent homelands.[13] To add to the confusion, state figures usually do not follow a standardized format and age groupings and time periods may fluctuate, making meaningful comparisons from time to time well-nigh impossible. Often, too, official figures are cited for children under sixteen years of age only. There has been a reluctance on the part of state officials to supply figures relating to the detention of all children up to the age of eighteen years.

Attempts by independent bodies to monitor the numbers of children in detention are frustrated by the various definitions under which a detainee may be held. Being detained, for example, for public violence could include both those held because of their alleged role in violence associated with political activities, or because of their alleged involvement in a fight at a soccer match.

A further problem faced by monitoring groups in the acquisition of statistical information is that a released detainee may go into hiding for fear of being re-detained, and so may not report his/her release to a monitoring organization. Furthermore, a child may be detained for a lengthy period during which time he/she grows older, rendering out of date certain statistical information which may have pertained to him/her.

Added to these problems, regulations governing the state of emergency effectively curb press reporting and restrict information to those wishing to ascertain the numbers of children in detention at any point in time.

It is suggested that these statistical shortcomings in gathering information contribute, in part, to the discrepancy in figures released by official state sources and independent monitoring bodies. However, it is important to note that whilst these discrepancies do exist, even the more conservative state-supplied figures confirm that thousands of children in South Africa have been held in detention.

Whilst it was estimated[14] that as at March 1989 there were still fifty-two children in detention country-wide, both the actual numbers of children in detention as well as the proportion of children who make up the detainee population dropped during 1987 and 1988. Webster (1987: 152) states that in 1985, 25 per cent of detainees were children, a figure which rose to 40 per cent between June 1986 and June 1987, the highest percentage recorded. Webster (1988) later states that the figure then fell to 36 per cent between June 1987 and December 1987, and to 24 per cent during February 1988 and April 1988.

LEGISLATION GOVERNING THE DETENTION OF CHILDREN

The Child Care Act 74 of 1983 defines a child as any person under the age of eighteen years, and seeks to prevent anyone responsible for the child from ill-treating or neglecting him/her. Both this Act and the Criminal Procedures Act 51 of 1977 aim to protect children with regard to keeping them in places other than their own homes, detaining them whilst they await trial, regulating their appearance and treatment in court, and determining the nature of the sentence imposed upon them. This legislation recognizes that children are physically and emotionally more vulnerable than adults, and that they need love and care and assistance in meeting their survival needs. Indeed, the normal legal system respects the vulnerability of the child, a factor universally recognized and formally acknowledged as warranting specific mention in some thirty of the 560 Articles of the Geneva Conventions and their Additional Protocols of 1977.[15]

Under normal circumstances, the law protects children, *inter alia*, in the following ways:

☐ The Child Care Act provides for children to be cared for in places of safety if they have manifested behavioural problems warranting observation, if they are awaiting court decisions regarding their future care, or if they have been charged with offences and are awaiting trial. Such places of safety operate entirely separately from the prison system and are established specifically for children.

☐ The Prisons Act 8 of 1959, as amended, specifically states that no child who is awaiting trial may be detained in a prison or a police cell unless there is no place of safety where he/she may be kept. If it cannot be avoided that the child is kept in a prison cell or a police station, he or she is protected by not being permitted to associate with any person over the age of twenty-one unless this association is deemed not to be harmful to him/her. Similarly, if a child is unavoidably sentenced to serve a term of imprisonment, every effort is made to segregate the child from older and more hardened prisoners.

☐ If it transpires that a child convicted of a criminal offence is, in effect, severely neglected or has parents who are unwilling or unable to care for his/her well-being, it can be ordered that the criminal trial be stopped and the child be brought before a children's court and be dealt with in terms of the Child Care Act.

☐ When a child is brought to court, his/her parents or guardians are informed that they must attend the proceedings.

☐ All court proceedings concerning children are held in camera and no information may be published which would reveal the identity of the child.

☐ If a child is convicted of a crime, every effort is made to keep the child out of prison, and it can be ordered that the child be placed under the supervision of a recognized welfare body, or be sent to a reform school, or to a place of safety.

Two legislative acts govern the state of emergency in South Africa — the Public Safety Act 3 of 1953, as amended (under which states of emergency are declared), and the Internal Security Act 74 of 1982, as amended. This legislation overrides the provisions of any other law or common law, and accordingly supersedes all legislation designed specifically to protect the rights and secure the well-being of children in the country.

The Public Safety Act, as amended, provides for the summary arrest and detention of people, including children, under the Emergency Regulations. The regulations of this Act restrict access to the detainee, except with the consent of, and subject to conditions laid down by, the Minister of Law and Order. Information relating to a detainee is also restricted, resulting in the detained person being at the mercy of the security forces to whom almost complete immunity is granted.

The Internal Security Act, as amended, confers wide powers upon the Minister of Law and Order and on the police. This Act, *inter alia*, provides for the preventive detention of anyone considered to be a threat to state security (section 28), the indefinite detention of a person for purposes of interrogation (section 29), the detention of potential state witnesses for up to six months or until the trial is completed (section 31), and the short-term detention (up to 14 days) of people deemed to be contributing to public disturbance, disorder, or riot.

Under the current state of emergency, 'detention' means removal and incarceration without recourse. It is an indefinite period of punishment, usually without the filing of any charge. A detained child is subjected to the same provisions as his or her adult counterpart. Accordingly, children may be detained for the purposes of 'interrogation' until the Commissioner of Police is satisfied that no useful purpose will be served by their further detention. After six months, a Board of Review will consider a child's continued detention. The child does not appear before the Board of Review, and neither are his or her parents nor lawyers allowed to appear before this Board. The Board may call for oral evidence or representation from the child, and the child may send written representation to the Board, but if the child is not informed of this right, or is too afraid, or cannot write, it is unlikely that he or she will do so.

Under normal circumstances, arrested persons must be brought before a court within forty-eight hours, or the first court day after a weekend. They are eligible for pre-trial bail, can only be held for a defined period of time, have the right to consult with an attorney, and can be visited whilst in prison. Detainees, including children, have none of these rights. Indeed, children detained under section 29 of the Internal Security Act, as amended, have no access to anyone — family, lawyers, doctors, or spiritual advisers of choice, unless special permission is granted for visits, which are then strictly limited and take place under close surveillance.

Some children detained for suspected political involvement are arrested for public violence under the Criminal Procedures Act 51 of 1977. Technically, these children have the right to legal representation, but many are unaware of this right and it is not mandatory for the police or for the court to inform them accordingly. Thus many go unrepresented.

When a child is detained and placed in a prison, he or she is placed in an environment which is not only unconducive to his/her emotional and physical well-being, but which is in fundamental conflict with his/her normal development. Prisons were never intended to cater for children. There are no games, toys, or children's books; no trees to climb, soccer to play, bicycles to ride; no radios with which to listen to the latest music. Sick children may not see their own doctor, but may be taken, without their mothers, to a strange and possibly unsympathetic district surgeon. Visits by parents are usually subject to long delays. Children in detention are very likely to suffer separation trauma given the frightening circumstances under which detention occurs and which exist during detention, and given that occasionally very young children are detained.

Once in detention, should children be careless or negligent, should they perhaps use improper language, sing, whistle, or make unnecessary noise, they may be disciplined. Such discipline may take the form of withdrawal of privileges, placement in solitary confinement, restriction of diet, or, in the case of boys, corporal punishment.

In June 1987, regulations were promulgated which improved the lot of people in detention. These regulations provide for compulsory medical examinations after arrest, segregation from 'ordinary' prisoners, the receiving and sending of censored letters, and a restriction on the keeping of emergency detainees in police cells for longer than fourteen days without the consent of the Commissioner of Police.

However, legislation governing the state of emergency affords the child no special protection either outside or within the prison. Indeed, this legislation actively promotes the detention of children apart from their families and allows them to be subject to disciplinary procedures which are unjustified as punishment for children.

ABUSE IN DETENTION

The reported instances of physical and mental abuse to which children have been subjected whilst in detention have been well documented (Jacobs & Hollingshead, 1985; Lawyers' Committee for Human Rights, 1986; Committee of Concern for Children, 1986; Black Sash, 1986; Straker *et al.*, 1988). It has also been noted that physical examinations of ex-detainees support their claims of abuse (McLachlan, 1986: 345–6; Van Es & Van Gurp, 1987: 37; Webster, 1987: 167).

Types of abuse and torture reported by children released from detention include the following:

☐ Food deprivation (Committee of Concern for Children, 1986) — it is important to note here that children who are detained frequently come from deprived circumstances, and may already be suffering from forms of malnutrition. Detention may exacerbate these problems and, accordingly, may result in infections, and a low level of health generally.

☐ Solitary confinement, beating, kicking, enforced standing for long periods, enforced physical exercise, sleep deprivation, being kept naked during interrogation, suspension from poles, and electric shocks (Manson, 1986: 68).

☐ Verbal insults, the continuous transmission of high-pitched noises, kicking with boots, banging of detainee's head on wall or floor, the use of teargas in confined room or vehicle, enforced standing in an unnatural position, the forced drinking of contaminated water, beating on the soles of feet with sticks, beating on the ears, near suffocation by a rubber or canvas hood, and cigarette burns (Van Es & Van Gurp, 1987: 38–9).

☐ Lack of intellectual stimulation.[16]

☐ False accusations, threatened violence to the detainee and his or her family, and misleading information (Manson, 1986: 68).

☐ Threats of death to family or relatives; untrue statements of betrayal by friends; continuous surveillance in cell by close circuit television monitoring; the withholding of information about place of detention or the charge or the expected duration; pressure to make or sign false statements; interrogation at gun-point; long periods of interrogation by changing teams of interrogators; the use of terror tactics such as threats of incarceration in a dark cell; the forced looking at and touching of a corpse; fake execution; and fake necklacing[17] (Van Es & Van Gurp, 1987: 37–8).

A recently reported study[18] of 131 detainees details the physical and emotional abuse to which detained children were subjected. Forty per cent of the sample were children, and 4,7 per cent of them were between the ages of ten and fourteen years:

☐ 34 per cent had been detained in solitary confinement.

☐ 72 per cent evidenced physical abuse.

☐ 25 per cent had experienced attempted suffocation.

☐ 14 per cent had received electric shocks.

☐ Almost 22 per cent had lost consciousness as a result of their torture.

A further aspect of emotional abuse, namely the effects on children of separation from their normal environment and family, needs to be highlighted here. The right of a child to live with his or her mother and father should be enshrined in the nation's constitution and assured by law (Reynolds, 1986: 396). Under the present state of emergency in South Africa, in addition to children being physically separated from their parents, parents are often not told the whereabouts of their children, resulting in extreme anxiety on both sides. The current legislation governing the state of emergency in South Africa enforces and prolongs the separation of child from parent.

At least five children have also been known to have died in detention.[19]

Whilst thus far the detention of older children has been considered, mention needs to be made of children born in detention. One report notes that five children are known to have been born to detained mothers (Human Rights Commission, 1988), whilst another[20] states that during 1986, 2 280 black children under three years of age accompanied their mothers to prison. A child born to a mother in detention is severely disadvantaged. He or she has no regular access to the stimulation that normally occurs in a free environment. In addition, the mother's anxiety about being in detention may interfere with the bonding process with the child, a factor which may have serious detrimental affects upon the child's future development.

ABUSE IN THE WIDER ENVIRONMENT

Although the abuse of children in the wider environment has been presented in some detail in earlier chapters, the present discussion of the abuse of children in detention would be incomplete without relating it to a consideration of the abuse of children which is occurring in the general environments of the urban townships, where the apartheid system has engendered hostility and conflict. It is in these townships that, on a daily basis, children, not all radical or politically conscious, are exposed to violence. However, the ambient violence eventually involves all as active participants. Chikane (1986: 343) states that 'they find themselves either confronting the system or running away from teargas and bullets'.

Straker *et al.* (1988: 7–8) cite the case of an adolescent who, in approximately six weeks, was exposed to several incidents of trauma, most of which were serious enough to be termed catastrophic within the definition advanced by DSM III.[21] They were:

☐ being present at the murder of a man, a father figure to the adolescent;

☐ having his life threatened by being in a house which was petrol-bombed;

☐ being exiled from his community;

☐ taking refuge in a centre which was invaded by armed police; and

☐ being beaten by security police.

Chikane (1986: 342–3) has aptly summarized the violent world of the township child in the following way:

> It is a world made up of teargas, bullets, whippings, detention and death on the streets. It is an experience of military operations and night raids, of roadblocks and body searches. It is a world where parents and friends get carried away in the night to be interrogated. It is a world where people simply disappear, where parents are assassinated and homes are petrol-bombed.

By November 1985, it was reported that approximately 200 children had died in political township violence (United Nations Children's Fund, 1987), and a further 703 children had been injured in such violence during 1985 (Black Sash, 1986: 1). An analysis of some of these deaths revealed that forty-four of the children had been shot, seventeen had burned to death, one had been stabbed, and six had died of 'unknown causes'. Nineteen of the children were under ten years of age (Lawyers' Committee for Human Rights, 1986: 42). In March 1987, official state figures revealed that ninety-two juveniles had been shot to death by the police during 1986 (*International Children's Rights Monitor*, 1987: 12). A later report[22] states that during the period 1984–6, 312 children had been killed by police gunfire or police vehicles or whilst in police custody and that a further 1 000 had been wounded during this period.

EFFECTS OF DETENTION AND TOWNSHIP VIOLENCE

The effects of detention *per se* on children have been comprehensively documented (Manson, 1986; Van Es & Van Gurp, 1987; Straker *et al.*, 1988). It has been noted that the psychological effects of detention on a child approximate the DSM III category of post-traumatic stress disorder (PTSD) (Manson, 1986: 68). The onset of this disorder may be acute, appearing within six months after detention and having a duration of less than six months, or it may be delayed, that is with onset of symptoms at least six months after the trauma. The typical syndrome consists of depression, psychic numbing, feelings of helplessness, anxiety, fear, instability, agitation, low self-esteem, paranoia, confusion, inflexibility, and suicidal feelings. The child may also experience sleep disturbances, hyper-vigilance, loss of concentration, loss of memory, and psychosomatic disorders. Subsequent to detention, he or she may engage in aggressive or anti-social behaviour, or withdraw completely from human contact and interaction as a form of defence.

In conclusion, when considering the effects of detention and ambient township violence on children, mention must be made of the loss of education, the loss of hope, and the loss of childhood innocence.

Detained children lose years of education. Detention may stretch from weeks to years, during which period no schooling is afforded the child. After release, many children, for fear of being re-detained, spend much of their time on the run, again preventing the acquisition of any formal education. Those who do attempt to re-enter schools are frequently turned away by school authorities who fear that such children may be troublemakers.

As stressful as detention is, children released from detention go back into township situations which are equally stressful, traumatic, and threatening. In a real sense many of these children not only have to contend with what they have suffered, but must also be prepared to confront what they have to go through to effect change in the South African system. A recent report[23] notes the deepening sense of despair and resignation which is evidenced by children coming out of detention. It is suggested that this despair arises from having had something within themselves systematically destroyed — they have been robbed of their childhood and, hence, of their innocence.

In the process of exposing children to violence, both within detention and in the townships, it is understandable that adaptive behaviour necessarily occurs and that values begin to change. Township children are now learning a different set of survival techniques. In the words of Chikane (1986: 343):

> … their songs tell of the world as they perceive it, a violent world, a war situation. They move in groups in the townships: a commander in charge, his 'armed forces' around him. Their ammunition is stones, sticks and probably petrol bombs. They have different values.

Figures 15.1 and 15.2 are pictures, freely drawn by two children at the Othandweni Family Care Centre[24] in Soweto. They illustrate how 'normal' life in Soweto can be perceived by children.

When children are subjected to humiliation and brutalization, when they witness aggression to their family and community, and when they have little hope for their own futures, violence can quite often be a way of relieving this stress. In South Africa, we have now witnessed the occurrence of children themselves effecting acts of brutalization on informers or political opponents. Whilst these acts in themselves are horrific, the long-term consequences of such acts on the children who

Figure 15.1

Figure 15.2

perpetrate them are of deep concern. The full costs of this tragic loss of innocence and psychic damage will only be seen in the years to come.

Effects of violence and detention upon the family

Whilst attention both in South Africa and internationally has focused upon the effects of violence and detentions on children, lesser acknowledgement has been given to the effects which this has had upon family life, the most important of the primary environments within which a child grows.

Home life for a township child is punctuated with troops patrolling the streets, with periodic school boycotts, with friends and family in hiding or missing, or in some cases with suffering from physical disability as victims of violence. In some cases parents have been killed in front of their children. The effects of this situation are manifold. The fear of loss is always present — loss of life or limb, loss of property, loss of control over one's life, loss of loved ones. Family life is disrupted on all levels — socially, economically, and physically.

The detention of a child often has severe financial implications for the family. Parents may lose their jobs due to days and weeks spent trying to locate their detained child. In this process, high transport and legal costs may be incurred. After the child is released and returned to his/her family, they may be confronted with medical expenses for treatment of physical and psychological injuries which he/she may have sustained during detention.

A further problem is caused when a child is removed and placed in detention away from the routine of parental discipline. When the child has been exposed to a violent and harsh world, when he or she has been tortured and has had to grow up in a moment, an almost irreversible process begins to occur — that of the loss of respect for parental authority. Children may blame their parents for the present oppression and may perceive them as willing participants therein. Accordingly, the anger of children against the system may spill over into anger against the older generation. Responding to cues of brutalization, children may become reluctant to obey parental instruction, resulting in feelings of impotence, inadequacy, and guilt on the part of parents, and their consequent translation of this into a total abandonment of their parental roles.

Families are often divided because of actual or perceived political polarization between children and parents. This is particularly true if the latter are perceived to be actively involved in supporting the 'system', for example, by working as government employees. The constant friction between parents and children may result in children developing a distorted view of parent-child relationships. This, in turn, has negative implications for the role-modelling of relationships for future generations. An additional problem which often may occur for families in which a child has been detained is that of isolation of both the child and the family from other families in the community. Neighbours may fear that any association with the detained child or his/her family may result in their also being subjected to interrogation and detention.

In summary, it is suggested that the detention of children leads to vast disorganization in family roles, and family life in general. It has left many families with feelings of powerlessness, insecurity, and vulnerability. In addition to this, because families comprise the larger community, the detention of children has necessarily effected a broader structural change. When a community is traumatized through repression, when children are brutalized, when the overwhelming community feelings are fear and hostility, the gap between being a victim and being a perpetrator of violence may diminish or disappear. It is therefore understandable that in recent years, large-scale community violence has been witnessed, to a considerable extent initiated and maintained by youth who have themselves been schooled in violence by the environment in which they live.

THE DETENTION OF CHILDREN — A FORM OF CHILD ABUSE

The present legal system of South Africa not only fails to protect children from abuse, but provides a legal framework for abuse by promoting their detention apart from their families, and by allowing them to be subjected to various forms of physical and emotional distress whilst in prison.

Having considered the abuse of children in detention, and the effects of such detention upon children and their families, it is suggested that should such acts be perpetrated by any custodian of a child under normal child-care legislation, this would be regarded as child abuse. In addition, the exposure of children to violence on a daily basis through ambient township turmoil also constitutes a form of abuse and leads to the breakdown of family and community life. This violence which the township child experiences is a direct result of the apartheid system. Whereas traditionally the causes of child abuse have been sought in intra-personal or interpersonal problems in parents or within the family, today in South Africa we are faced with a different phenomenon — the abuse of children by the state through the process of detentions, and the institutionalization of child abuse through the system of apartheid.

CURATIVE INTERVENTIONS

When considering strategies of intervention in the areas of detention and ambient township violence, a distinction must be made between long-term and short-term strategies. Long-term strategies to combat the effects of detentions and violence necessarily involve fundamental political change. All those concerned with the welfare of South Africa's children have to strive to effect such political change towards the emergence of a non-racial, democratic, unified, and harmonious country. Short-term strategies are those which are feasible within existing political constraints but which, at the same time, support the goals underlying the long-term strategies.

It is the author's belief that in the short-term, within the present political structures in South Africa, action can be taken that will not only make a significant difference to the lives of children, but which will also fundamentally promote the building of a new structure in the country. In this process the input of non-governmental bodies is of crucial importance, and details of a proposed model programme in this regard will be discussed later.

As a point of departure, two suggestions regarding some general short-term strategies are now proposed:

1. It has been argued that the system of apartheid, and more specifically the state of emergency and the detention of children, constitute forms of child abuse in South Africa. However, at the same time it must be acknowledged that not all the children abused and maltreated under the present circumstances are necessarily innocent of misdeeds. Stones are thrown, arson is committed, people are murdered in township violence. What is being condemned here is the manner in which children allegedly guilty of such acts are handled. The state's attitude is that if children wish to throw stones or burn houses, they must face the consequences. No reasonable person would dispute that a form of action to prevent such acts must be taken and, to this end, legal provision has already been made. A child involved in a criminal act can be charged under the normal Criminal Procedures Act and be brought to trial within forty-eight hours. Procedures for dealing with juvenile delinquents are also contained within the Child Care Act.

    However, in South Africa these laws are not used. Rather, the state has chosen to detain children without trial, and to condone varying forms of abuse to children before, during, and after detention. The state has not only failed to protect its children, but has enacted legislation which, in fact, promotes the destruction of family and community life.

It is strongly advocated that the provisions of the Child Care Act 74 of 1983 and the Criminal Procedures Act 51 of 1977 apply in all cases of police or court action involving children. In this way the legal protection of the rights and interests of such children will be ensured at all times. Along with this recommendation is the concomitant one that back-up resources to the implementation of the provisions of the Child Care Act be expanded. Currently such resources, such as places of safety, are in short supply, and urgent attention should be focused upon allocating welfare expenditure to establish them.

2. Thus far in South Africa, no single strong independent body has systematically espoused the rights of the detained child. Rather, these efforts have been fragmented and uncoordinated, leading to mediocre results.

It is proposed that an Advocacy Board be established for the purpose of focusing specific and continued attention on the problems facing children in South Africa, for strengthening the work of existing organizations, and for assisting in the representation of the needs and interests of both detained children and those involved in township turmoil. It is suggested that this Board comprise progressive leaders in the field of child care, both in practice and in academia, representatives from the legal and medical professions, and leaders from those groups skilled in rendering rehabilitative services to children released from detention and their families. Issues which could immediately be addressed by this Board could include the establishment of the following:

☐ A system to ensure that at all times the child is treated in accordance with the provisions of the Child Care Act or the Criminal Procedures Act. This is particularly important if the child is found guilty of an offence. Such a system would also ensure regular access to the child by social workers of registered child-care and family-care agencies.

☐ A control system to ensure that once a child has been arrested, he or she obtains a fair and speedy trial leading either to a sentence or to his or her release.

☐ A system to ensure that the child's parents are fully informed should he or she be arrested for an offence, and that regular and frequent visiting rights are afforded the parents.

☐ A system to ensure the continued education of these children whilst awaiting trial and after their release.

☐ A system to ensure that the necessary therapeutic assistance is given to the child and his or her family during and after release.

In 1986, the South African Paediatric Association prepared a code for handling children in places of detention for the Medical Association of South Africa (1987). This code deals with, *inter alia*, the trial and sentencing of children, the physical environment of places of detention, and medical and psychological rehabilitation facilities. Whilst the formulation of such a code was perhaps the first breakthrough in an attempt to secure some rights for detained children, it could, too, have served the purpose of distracting attention away from the primary goal of advocating a fair and just system in which children are not incarcerated away from their families. The goal must be to abolish detention of all children in South Africa, as such detention cannot be made acceptable by improving conditions within the prison.

When considering the strategies previously alluded to, the author has chosen to present a model of a programme designed specifically to assist children who have been detained, or caught up in township violence. It is hoped that discussion of this programme, implemented by the Johannesburg Child Welfare Society, will provide the stimulus necessary for the consideration of similar projects elsewhere in South Africa.

The response of the Johannesburg Child Welfare Society to the detention of children

Introduction

It may be assumed that any organization rendering service in the field of child care will be confronted by the plight of children during this time of unrest, by the abuse brought to bear upon children by their detention and subsequent treatment whilst in detention, and by the consequent problems which they might face after their release. It must also be assumed that the reasons for the existence of child-care organizations is to assist children in need, irrespective of their political persuasions, and to mediate on their behalf should this be warranted. It may therefore be assumed that all child-care organizations would recognize the role which they have to play as regards the protection of children who may be subjected to abuse caused by detentions or township violence.

Sadly, in South Africa, this has not been the case. Many child-care organizations have chosen not to render service in this area, seeing it as belonging to the political domain and, in the process, losing sight of the child who may be caught up in this cycle of abuse.

The Johannesburg Child Welfare Society is the largest locally-based welfare organization in South Africa. Assistance is rendered to the children and families of Johannesburg and greater Johannesburg, which includes the two townships of Soweto and Alexandra.[25] In 1989 the population of Soweto was estimated[26] to be 1 800 000,[27] and that of Alexandra approximately 100 000.[28]

During 1985 reports were forthcoming of large numbers of children who were detained in and around Johannesburg, but primarily in Soweto and Alexandra. As at November 1986, 415 children had been reported as being detained in the Johannesburg area since the state of emergency was declared in 1985. Of these children, 237 or 57 per cent were aged sixteen years or less, and 63 or 15 per cent were fourteen years of age or under.

Another report in February 1987[30] indicated that approximately 25 per cent of all child detainees in South Africa came from Soweto, the actual figure being estimated by monitoring groups to be 684 children under the age of seventeen years.[31]

The Johannesburg Child Welfare Society recognized the problems related to the detention of children and, as part of its mission, responded to this need.

In January 1987 a crisis unit was established. Two social workers were employed to work exclusively on this project in the Johannesburg-Soweto-Alexandra area. The target groups for their intervention were the children in detention, those released from detention, and the families of both groups.

Problems associated with the project

In working towards the achievement of its mission in protecting children and promoting their rights, the Johannesburg Child Welfare Society has been amongst those groups in South Africa which have publicly denounced apartheid, detention without trial, and specifically the detention of children. However, one of the first problems encountered when embarking upon this project was pressure on the social workers by the children to declare a personal political position. This pressure has also been noted by Straker *et al.* (1988: 6) in their work with township children. Such demands are understandable, since the apartheid system as a whole, and certainly the unrest situation with the accompanying rise of vigilantes[32] in the townships, has created much suspicion about welfare organizations and their personnel. The main task initially was for the social workers to establish trust and credibility with the children, a task which took time, patience, and much commitment on the part of staff involved in this project.

A second problem encountered at the outset of this project was that of confronting the chaotic network of services which had mushroomed in response to community need. Fears of restrictions and bannings understandably resulted in 'low profile' work being undertaken by a variety of concerned groups. The price, however, which has to be paid when such informal networking occurs is a lack of standardized record-keeping, sometimes scant or often no record-keeping, unnecessary duplication of services, and clumsy referral or feedback systems. Added to these problems, it was found that services were often underutilized due to the lack of awareness on the part of the children about their existence, or to the fear of approaching such services due to a perceived stigma attached to the seeking of help for problems experienced as a result of detention. In this project it has been found that most released children initially seek out the legally-orientated support organizations, and that it is these organizations which refer ex-detainees to medical, psychological, or psychiatric services. Such a pattern has also been noted by others involved in this field (Manson, 1986: 70).

The third problem encountered by the staff involved in this project was that of gaining access to, and becoming part of the network of organizations rendering service in this area. Traditionally, child-care organizations in South Africa, the Johannesburg Child Welfare Society being one such organization, render services to abused, abandoned, and neglected children, as well as undertaking preventive services in the community. The Johannesburg Child Welfare Society was the first child-care organization to become formally committed to assisting children and their families in the unrest situation. Natural suspicion had to be allayed by the furnishing of assurances that the project was not state-funded, and the channels of communication, systems of reporting, referral, and feedback between the Johannesburg Child Welfare Society and other relevant organizations had to be carefully negotiated.

When conceptualizing this project, a major area of work activity identified was that of direct work with the children whilst they were in detention. The fourth major problem encountered was that of gaining access to these children. In spite of legal negotiations with the Security Branch of the South African Police, permission was refused for the social workers to have direct access to children whilst in detention.

The final major problem encountered in this project was one which is germane to all services of this nature operating in South Africa. Counselling of ex-detainees in South Africa differs from counselling as practised by teams in Denmark, Canada, Holland, France, and Switzerland working with victims of persecution and torture from other countries, where such ex-detainee refugees are assured a safe environment (Manson, 1986: 68). In South Africa the ex-detainee usually returns to his/her home with no assurance of safety. This lack of refuge usually results in fear on the part of the child and an under-utilization of supportive services due to his/her preoccupation with ensuring his/her safety. Van Es and Van Gurp (1987: 44) found that psychological counselling was usually a short process, because ex-detainees could never be certain of attending sessions due to geographical or security reasons, or because they might be re-detained.

The project in practice

The denial to social workers of access to detained children effectively precluded them from rendering direct assistance to these children. However, the Johannesburg Child Welfare Society, along with other concerned groups, was instrumental in ensuring that attorneys were allocated to the children to bring as much pressure to bear upon the authorities to either release them, or to bring them to trial in a court of law. It was also hypothesized that the active interest in a detained child by an attorney may decrease the incidence of abuse to him/her whilst in prison.

The focus of work in this project has thus been with children released from detention, and the families of both these children and the children still in detention. Between January 1987 and April 1989, 222 children previously released from detention and 105 families have been assisted in the project. All children have been between the ages of eleven and eighteen years, with the majority (56 per cent) being under the age of sixteen years.

In the project, social work intervention with children released from detention, the majority of whom are experiencing one or more symptoms of post-traumatic stress, is directed towards assisting them in relieving the trauma associated with detention. The child is given the opportunity to re-experience and deal with the traumatic event in an emotionally supportive setting. Intervention aims to help the child alleviate feelings of guilt, fear, and humiliation, and to regain a sense of adequacy and self-esteem.

It has been found that intervention is commonly not conducted on a long-term basis. Many children attend only the first counselling session.

This has necessitated the use of a crisis intervention approach, whereby as much as possible is achieved in the initial contact.

Rendering a holistic service to the child has also required the social workers to facilitate the referral of such children for medical treatment, as well as to promote their re-admission to schools for the purposes of continuing their education.

Due to feelings of isolation commonly experienced by these children, group work was considered to be a constructive medium through which to assist them. It soon emerged that such group meetings have two main functions. The first function, which evolved from the immediate needs of the children, is one of providing information and education. The children express concern about understanding the legal implications of the state of emergency, the various sections in law under which a person can be detained, the implications of these sections, and the rights of people when in detention. It has been found that only after these immediate informational needs are met can the second function of the group be fulfilled. This function is to provide a supportive environment in which the resolution of problems of members is facilitated by the mutual sharing and assistance provided by each group member. Common experiences in detention are shared, emotional support is given to, and taken by group members from one another, and the stress experienced by the children as a result of detention is placed within the context of the situation in which it occurred.

Because the detention of a child affects the entire family system, within the ambit of this project problems experienced by the families of detained and released children necessarily have had to be addressed.

Family counselling and intervention with families in groups have been introduced, and through these media intra-familial dynamics resulting from the detention of one or more family members are dealt with. Fears regarding detention are explored and families are prepared for, and assisted with the re-integration of the child into the family upon his/her release from detention. To assist in this process, the psychological and behavioural effects of detention are discussed with the family, and families are made aware of possible problems which may arise after the return of the child.

In addition to the psychological help, families involved in this project are also assisted in practical ways.

Upon the detention of a child, the family may not be informed of his/her whereabouts. This was illustrated in a case in Soweto where none of the relatives of a group of 350 detained school children were informed by the authorities of the detention of their children, nor of their whereabouts (Committee of Concern for Children, 1986). Similarly, the Johannesburg Child Welfare Society waited over two weeks for a reply to a telex concerning the location of twenty-two children held in detention (Committee of Concern for Children, 1986). A major function of the social workers attached to this project is to assist parents and relatives in locating their children.

Until recently, visiting rights had to be applied for by parents for each individual visit to a detained child. Whilst this situation has now improved somewhat, the social workers assist the often unsophisticated parents in making these applications and, if necessary, physically help them to undertake such visits.

Further roles of the social workers are to link parents of detained children to attorneys who may assist them in representation for the release of the children, as well as to provide information on the Emergency Regulations and their attendant legal implications.

As at the end of May, 1988, there were twenty-five known cases of Sowetan children in detention, and 121 detained children country-wide.[33] At the end of June 1988, fifteen children were known by staff in the project to be detained in the Johannesburg-Soweto area, and in March 1989, fifty-two children were estimated to be in detention country-wide.[34] These figures bear out the previously noted phenomenon of a significant decrease in the number of detained children. It is suggested that public objection, advocacy for the children by concerned groups, and the constant maintenance of pressure on the authorities by projects such as the one described in this chapter have, in combination, engineered this trend.

Whilst work involved in alleviating the immediate crisis of detention of these children and their families formed the major focus of intervention during 1987 and 1988, it was soon realized that equal attention had to be paid to re-integrating the children into their community. It has been noted by staff in the project that children released from detention struggle primarily with the following problems:

☐ difficulty in tackling ordinary life tasks, and social relationships;

☐ poor self-esteem;

☐ poor scholastic performance;

☐ social isolation within the community; and

☐ breakdown in family relationships.

In order to address itself to these problems more effectively during the coming year the programme is to be expanded from the case work, group work, and family intervention approaches to include a diversified range of services to the community as a whole. Whilst specific individual and group counselling to children released from detention and their families will still be an integral part of the programme, it is intended that the additional services offered to the community will serve as a means of integrating children released from detention and their families more fully into the community from which they have often been isolated. Such extended services will include a strong educational component, comprising library facilities, day care and after-school care, homework supervision, and school holiday programmes, in an endeavour to create an environment conducive to study and the enhancement of educational performance. Indoor and outdoor recreational facilities, programmes aimed at the negotiation of life tasks by means of youth leadership and life-skills techniques, as well as programmes which focus upon strengthening the family unit, will be available.

In summary, it is suggested that curative interventions aimed at assisting detained children must include both long-term and short-term strategies. Fundamental political change must occur in the country, the essence of which is the abolition of apartheid. In addition non-governmental bodies should, in an organized and credible manner, be advocating the rights of children who, under the present regime, are repressed by detentions and institutionalized violence. A simultaneous challenge to those groups concerned with the well-being of children is that of rehabilitating children who are victims of abusive laws and practices, and restoring to them a sense of their intrinsic worth and dignity.

CONCLUSION

> There are few countries in the world, at any time in history ... where so much historical weight has been placed upon such young shoulders (United Nations Children's Fund, 1987: 40).

Ever since the Soweto uprising in 1976, black children have been in the front line of the struggle for reform — at the 'cutting edge of the country's history' (United Nations Children's Fund, 1987: 40). They have thrust themselves into a position where they can no longer be ignored. But the price they have paid and continue to pay is great. Children, brutalized by physical and institutionalized violence have often, as a means of survival, resorted to violence themselves. In this process they are in danger of losing all sense of right and wrong and of learning to resolve their own future difficulties — whether social, domestic, or political — with forms of violence similar to those to which they have been exposed during childhood.

But what of the outlook for the future? When children have been abused through violence, when human potential has been squandered, when life is regarded as cheap and dispensable, it can be expected that this damage will reverberate throughout the country for years to come. There is nothing more important in South Africa today than to find ways in which the freedom and wholeness of all her children can be ensured, and through this process, the healing and renewal of hearts and minds can be achieved.

NOTES

1   Department of National Health and Population Development, April 1988.

2   *The Star*, 3 January 1989.

3   The triggering factor in these protests was the enforced teaching of subjects in the Afrikaans language which, to the children, represented the language of the oppressor.

4   In terms of the national constitution, the franchise was extended to 'coloureds' and Asians, with separate parliaments provided for each of these two groups and the white population group respectively. African people remain voteless at central government level.

5   Human Rights Commission, 1988, Fact Paper 1.

6   In terms of this chapter, unless otherwise specified, a child is a person under eighteen years of age as defined in the Child Care Act 74 of 1983.

7   *The Star*, 27 November 1986; *The Guardian*, 7 December 1986.

8   *The Weekly Mail*, 13 March 1987.

9   *The Star*, 17 February 1988.

10   *The Citizen*, 3 June 1987.

11   *Hansard* (A)2q, 16 February 1988, col. 6.

12   *The Star*, 4 February 1988.

13   Those territories formerly part of South Africa and now regarded as self-governing.

14   'In Touch'. Newsletter of the Concerned Social Workers, March 1989.

15 'ICRC and Children in Situation of Armed Conflict', Geneva: undated report of the International Committee of the Red Cross.

16 'Free South Africa's Children: A Symposium on Children in Detention', *Human Rights Quarterly*, 10(1), 1–108.

17 'Necklacing' is a method of execution in which a motor-vehicle tyre is draped round the neck, doused with petrol, and set alight.

18 'Free South Africa's Children: A Symposium on Children in Detention', *Human Rights Quarterly*, 10(1), 74.

19 'Free South Africa's Children: A Symposium on Children in Detention', *Human Rights Quarterly*, 10(1).

20 'Apartheid's Violence Against Children', General Conference Working Paper A1, International Conference on Children, Repression and the Law in Apartheid South Africa, Harare, 24–7 September 1987, 8.

21 The *Diagnostic and Statistical Manual* of the American Psychological Association, revised edition, 1987.

22 'Apartheid's Violence Against Children', General Conference Working Paper A1, International Conference on Children, Repression and the Law in Apartheid South Africa, Harare, 24–7 September 1987, 3.

23 'Free South Africa's Children: A Symposium on Children in Detention', *Human Rights Quarterly*, 10(1), 77.

24 The Othandweni Family Care Centre is a registered residential children's home which functions under the auspices of the Johannesburg Child Welfare Society.

25 Alexandra is an urban township for African people to the north-east of Johannesburg.

26 Figures cited are estimates as the many illegal and thus undeclared residents in the townships are not accounted for in official census figures.

27 Annual report of the Urban Foundation for the year ended March 1988.

28 Personal communication from the Alexandra Town Council.

29 *The Star*, 27 November 1986; *The Guardian*, 7 December 1986.

30 *The Weekly Mail*, 27 February 1987.

31 *The Star*, 16 & 19 February 1987.

32 Vigilantes are self-appointed groups of people who ostensibly seek to maintain law in the townships, often through violent means.

33 Personal communication from Black Sash, Johannesburg.

34 'In Touch', Newsletter of the Concerned Social Workers, March 1989.

REFERENCES

Black Sash (1986) 'Memorandum on the Suffering of Children in South Africa'.
Chikane F. (1986) 'Children in Turmoil: The Effects of Unrest on Township Children'. In *Growing Up in a Divided Society: The Contexts of Childhood in South Africa*, edited by S. Burman and P. Reynolds, Johannesburg: Ravan Press, 333–44.
Committee of Concern (1986) Memorandum submitted to the Minister of Law and Order during personal representation by members of the Committee of Concern for Children, Concerned Women (Cape Town), Union of Jewish Women, National Council of the Catholic Women's League, Women for Peace, African Scholar's Fund, Black Sash, Johannesburg Child Welfare Society, Lawyers for Human Rights and the National Council of Women.
Human Rights Commission (1988) *Human Rights Update*, July–September, 1(4).
International Children's Rights Monitor (1987) 'South Africa: Apartheid's Children', 4(2), 12–14.
Jacobs, M. & Hollingshead, J. (1985) 'Memorandum on Children under Repression', Cape Town.
Lawyers' Committee for Human Rights (1986) 'The War against Children: South Africa's Youngest Victims', New York: Lawyers' Committee for Human Rights.
Manson, S. (1986) 'Detention Rehabilitation', *Apartheid and Mental Health*, Johannesburg: Organization for Appropriate Social Services in South Africa, 67–73.
McLachlan, F. (1986) 'Children in Prison'. In *Growing Up in a Divided Society: The Contexts of Childhood in South Africa*, edited by S. Burman and P. Reynolds, Johannesburg: Ravan Press, 345–59.
Medical Association of South Africa (1987) 'Children in Places of Detention: A Code for their Handling', *South African Medical Journal*, Supplement, 20 June.
Reynolds, P. (1986) 'Afterword'. In *Growing Up in a Divided Society: The Contexts of Childhood in South Africa*, edited by S. Burman & P. Reynolds, Johannesburg: Ravan Press, 393–8.
South African Institute of Race Relations (1988) *Survey of Race Relations, 1987–8*, Johannesburg: SAIRR.
Straker, G. & the Sanctuaries Counselling Team (1988) 'Apartheid and Child Abuse', *Psychology in Society*, 9, 3–13.
United Nations Children's Fund (1987) 'Children on the Front Line: The Impact of Apartheid, Destabilisation and Warfare on Children in Southern and South Africa', New York: United Nations Children's Fund.

Van Es, A. & Van Gurp, M. (1987) 'Health Professionals and Human Rights in South Africa', report of a Mission on Health and Human Rights to the Republic of South Africa on behalf of the Johannes Weir Foundation, the Dutch Foundation for Health and Human Rights, Leiden.

Webster, D. (1988) 'Children in Detention', report presented at the Commission of Inquiry into the Detention of Children, University of the Witwatersrand.

Webster, D. (1987) 'Repression and the State of Emergency', *South African Review*, 4, 141–72.

Part 5

Towards the reduction
of violence

16 Towards the reduction of violence

B. W. McKendrick and W. C. Hoffmann

In the first chapter of this book, the writers attempted to outline a broad theoretical foundation for the understanding of violence, while the fourteen chapters that have followed it have explored in detail aspects of violence in societal, domestic, and institutional contexts.

The contents of this book will perhaps serve to promote awareness of violence in South Africa through an analysis of its possible causes, incidence, and consequences. However, at the same time they illustrate the complexity of the phenomenon. The causes of violence are multi-dimensional; its incidence is sometimes public, but often hidden; and its consequences have ramifications far beyond the immediate perpetrators and victims. Violence breeds upon itself, and its insidious influence reaches out into every corner of present society, and also into the future, for today's violence is the seed from which tomorrow's violence will grow.

SOME KEY CHARACTERISTICS OF VIOLENCE RELEVANT TO ITS REDUCTION

Despite the complexity of violence in its many manifestations, the authors suggested in Chapter 1 that all violent attempts to resolve conflict have certain deleterious consequences in common, as well as shared dynamics and characteristics. It is these latter aspects which merit major attention when the reduction of violence is considered, for halting or ameliorating violence requires that its causal dynamics be addressed. The authors suggest in this chapter that four of these can be singled out as being central to the reduction of violence: much violence in society is unrecognized as such; violence is almost always socially learned behaviour; violence produces counter-violence; and personal experience of violence is seminal to its repetition.

Much violence in society is unrecognized

Failure to recognize violence results from two main circumstances: the prevalence of violence in society, which desensitizes people to its prescence, and the secrecy which surrounds some settings in which violence occurs, such as the privacy of the home, and the legally-imposed secrecy shrouding some activities of the state.

In respect of the growth of violence in society, South Africa is caught up in a cycle of violence, repressive and revolutionary, political and civil, social and domestic, so that attempts to resolve conflict by violence have become typical, rather than isolated aberrations.

The everyday occurrence of visible violence has inured many South Africans to it, so that they tolerate it as an ordinary, normal, and legitimate solution to conflict. This desensitization has permitted attitudes and values to develop which sanction violence. Hence, for many, daily news reports of widespread civil and political violence, detentions, and murders are accepted as unremarkable, rather than cause for horror and outrage.

The permeation of society by violence has led to personal behaviours where violence is used as a first-line response to conflict, and also to a mental outlook which positively reinforces or excuses the use of violence. Increased use of interpersonal violence in the context of a violent society is well substantiated by empirical research — violence in society is correlated with personal violence such as wife and child abuse, and rape. Similarly, societal violence can be associated with personal latitude towards violent behaviour, such as viewing rape as 'not serious' or as being 'invited' by the victim; regarding violence in sport as being evidence of 'manliness'; perceiving corporal punishment in schools as a means of 'building character'; and defending as 'necessary' acts of coercion such as the detention in prisons of young children suspected of political activity.

A second circumstance which promotes the non-recognition of violence is secrecy, either secrecy as a product of family privacy, or secrecy as a deliberate, legally-sanctioned state policy.

Privacy of the home or family is a shield behind which domestic violence can flourish. Most child abuse and elder abuse, and almost all wife abuse, takes place in the home, perpetrated by a relative of the victim. Once it occurs, other personal or intra-familial dynamics come into play to reinforce secrecy. Thus, for example, in incest the victim is silenced by a fear of reprisal, and a fear that disclosure will result in the family's disintegration; while in abuse of the elderly, victims are often afraid to speak out for fear of being left destitute and totally without care. The notion of privacy of the home can extend also to children's residential homes, where children are placed under court order. A remarkable feature of such homes, discussed in detail by Giles in Chapter 13, is that inspecting authorities gather their information from staff, not children, and that allegations of abuse are investigated internally, not by impartial outsiders.

State-imposed secrecy is ostensibly justified by security considerations, and the activities of many institutions of society are thus veiled from public scrutiny. Protected institutions include the military, police, and the prisons service. Often, however, the shroud of secrecy acts to the disadvantage of the people who are the object of the state's attention, as is well illustrated in Chapters 14 and 15, which document the physical and emotional abuse of children and adults detained in terms of security and emergency legislation.

Non-recognition of violence and the possibility of violence, whether it arises from living in a violent society, family secrecy, or state policy, means that violence is allowed to thrive undetected, and sometimes unsuspected. If the aim is to reduce violence, the appropriate response is to expose the possibilities of violence or violence itself, and to educate people about their negative and damaging consequences. When violence is invisible, it will never be addressed; when people are made aware of it, its reduction becomes a possibility.

Violent behaviour is almost always socially learned behaviour

People learn to be violent. They learn by themselves being victims of violence, and by witnessing violent behaviours and attitudes that are unpunished, or positively sanctioned. This learning takes place against the background of a society in which the state itself models violent behaviour to its citizens, and where racist and sexist ideologies underlie the law of the land and the organization of society.

The state exemplifies violence to South Africans through legally-sanctioned violence, repressive violence, and the use of violence that is beyond the law.

Legally-sanctioned violence embraces instances where the state, within the criminal and associated law, employs violence as a means of coercion or punishment. Coercive legal violence is illustrated by legal police killings, such as those that sometimes occur in the control of riotous crowds. Legal violence as a punishment refers to sentences of whipping or the death penalty being handed down to persons found guilty of prescribed kinds of anti-social, criminal behaviour. In instances such as the latter, the state provides an exemplar to citizens of what Sloth-Nielsen in Chapter 3 calls 'a policy and practice that negates bodily integrity and the sanctity of life'. *Repressive violence* refers to the legally-sanctioned activities undertaken by the state to maintain the socially unjust policy of white privilege, or apartheid, in South Africa, and includes also violent state actions in terms of security and emergency legislation. *Illegal violence* concerns activities outside of the law under-taken by the state or its agents, with or without high-level approval, to damage opponents of the present government. Among such activities, listed by Cock in Chapter 2, are 'death squads', torture in detention, and arson and armed attacks against anti-apartheid organizations and their premises.

Through its policies and laws, the state demonstrates that in South Africa all people are not equal. Indeed, in terms of the law and the organization of society, some people are regarded as of more worth than others, especially white people and males.

In this societal context of authoritarian violence, racism, and sexism, social learning occurs. Put simply, social learning is learning which takes place through a person's life experience, either as a result of first-hand personal involvement, or through exposure to attitudes and behaviours, directly or via the media. People are most impressionable when they are children, and it is at this life stage that the most fundamental social learning takes place. Hence, the settings of the home and the school are of cardinal importance.

A major theme running through this book is that people learn, usually as children, to use violence as a means of resolving conflict and imposing their will. Winship, Holdstock, and Straker each point out in their respective chapters that children consciously and unconsciously learn violent behaviour because they are exposed to it at home or school, and the chapters of Vogelman, and Segel and Labe show that there is a relationship between early exposure to the submissive role of women, and subsequent acts of rape and wife abuse. Moreover, other authors consistently demonstrate a relationship between being a victim of abuse, and subsequently becoming a perpetrator of similar abuse.

Since human conduct, including violent behaviour, is socially con-structed, strategies for the reduction of violence must be aimed at the

nature of society and the amendment of negative socialization experiences to which many of its members — particularly its younger members
— are subjected. .

Violence provokes counter-violence

One totally consistent product of both historical and contemporary
sociological research is that violence, once unleashed, provokes
counter-violence. This finding holds true at all levels, from that of nations
down to that of individual citizens. In South Africa, too, this relationship
can be demonstrated from the macro to the micro level.

At the level of the country as a whole, the Nationalist government has
militarized the South African state. As Cock shows in Chapter 2, the
power of the military has grown and the ideology of militarization has
established the military as a key social institution. Recent reforms of
President De Klerk notwithstanding, the military and the police are the
most important forces in maintaining apartheid advantage and disadvantage. The response to state repression has been revolutionary
violence, which its perpetrators believe to be both justified and legitimate
as the only remaining response to the violence of the state.

Within the South African society, where violence is sanctioned in
different ways by the state and by its opponents, sub-groups adopt tactics
of force to pursue their interests and goals. So, for example, comrades
and vigilantes violently oppose each other in many townships, and
unprecedented violence and bloodshed have ravaged parts of Natal,
Kwa-Zulu, and the Transvaal as United Democratic Front/ANC and
Inkatha supporters vie to achieve domination. Each bloody incident
ascribed to one party is the stimulus for increased atrocity by the other,
so that again the cycle of violence and counter-violence is established.

Even at the personal level, the cycle of violence and counter-violence
is easily apparent. A topical example is given by Thomas in Chapter 15,
in relation to the children of black townships. Thomas suggests that:

> The violence which the township child experiences is a direct result
> of the apartheid system. Whereas traditionally the causes of abuse
> have been sought in intra-personal or interpersonal problems in
> parents or within the family, today in South Africa we face a
> different phenomenon — the abuse of children by the state
> through the process of detentions and the institutionalization of
> child abuse through the system of apartheid.

Thomas argues that when township children are subjected to humiliation and brutalization, when they witness violence to their families and

communities, and when they have little hope for their own futures, 'violence can quite often be a way of relieving this stress'.

This cycle of violence and counter-violence can only be interrupted at the first stage of 'violence': if the stimulus of initial violence is removed, the response of counter-violence will not arise. For those concerned with the reduction of violence, the message in respect of the present South African society is clear. Widespread political violence will not cease until the present socio-political order is replaced by one with which all can identify, so that force will not be needed to maintain it. This socio-political order is likely to be an egalitarian democracy.

Violence spreads and perpetuates itself

In addition to the phenomenon whereby violence grows through the stimulation of counter-violence, it also perpetuates itself in other ways. Principal amongst these is the inter-generational cycle of violent abuse, where the child, once abused, later becomes the abuser. In this way, violence breeds violence.

The underlying dynamic is that people tend to repeat behaviours to which they have been exposed. Hence, if as children force has been used to 'control' them, or to coerce them to the will of another, they learn this behaviour and are likely to use it when they become adults.

The empirical evidence supporting this conclusion is strong, since the conclusion has been confirmed in almost every abuse situation: child abusers and persons convicted of violent crimes including rape, were beaten or otherwise abused as children. In Chapter 9, Segel and Labe authenticate this in respect of wife abuse; in Chapters 6 and 8, Winship and Sandler and Sepel affirm it in respect of child abuse; and Holdstock in Chapter 12 provides convincing evidence that corporal punishment in schools not only encourages the victims to themselves adopt similar practices as parents, but that it also makes them more vulnerable to other forms of abuse:

> The violation of body space and the invasion of children's privacy which occurs during corporal punishment conveys to them that adults have special authority over their bodies, including the right to inflict pain. Apart from depriving children of the right to the dignity of their bodies, it disempowers them and prepares the ground for them to become victims, as in many instances of child abuse.

The fact that being victim to one form of violence makes a child vulnerable to another, and also that violence is spread inter-generationally, has special implications for any attempts to reduce it: violent acts, and hence the repercussions which they cause, need to be curbed; persons at risk of perpetrating violent abuse, or being victims of it, require identification, and appropriate interventive or protective actions need to be taken; and intervention is also required to heal the victims of violence so that their experience does not lead them to become perpetrators in turn.

TARGET AREAS IN THE REDUCTION OF VIOLENCE

A useful framework for the analysis of the target areas which need to be influenced in order to reduce violence is that of categories of prevention — primary, secondary, and tertiary. Primary prevention comprises measures which may promote or enhance non-violent means of conflict resolution, or prevent violence from occurring. Secondary prevention is concerned with the early identification of violence, and measures to 'nip it in the bud' so as to prevent its growth and spread. Tertiary prevention involves rehabilitation of both the victims and the perpetrators of violence. While the accent in any consideration of the reduction of violence must be on primary prevention, and thereafter on secondary, tertiary prevention also has an important place: as noted earlier, in order to break the cycle of violence, victims need to be healed, or they may subsequently become perpetrators.

Primary prevention

Four principal target areas invite priority attention in the primary prevention of violence. First is the diminution of structural violence, since violence that is built in to the organization of society affects all aspects of people's lives; second is the removal of secrecy barriers which protect some of the institutions of society from public scrutiny; third is education, both of the general public and key groups within it; while fourth is the reorientation of human welfare and allied organizations towards primary prevention.

The reduction of structural violence

A recurring concept throughout this book is that South Africa is a country epitomized by structural violence, in the shape of authoritarianism, racism, sexism, and legal violence. Accompanying this notion has been another, namely that structural circumstances affect the attitudes, values,

and behaviours of social institutions, communities, groups, and individuals. Hence, a critical consideration is to reduce structural violence.

Structural violence in the form of *racism* lies at the heart of the South
African socio-political system. The ideology of apartheid, concretized in
legal statute, has institutionalized racial advantage and disadvantage in
South Africa. Because this is deeply offensive to the majority of the
population, and also because it has led to great material disparity, the
system has required the use of force to maintain it, and has drawn
counter-violence in efforts to weaken and destroy it.

No unjust political order can be maintained indefinitely by violent
coercion, and apartheid is no exception. At the time of writing, 'talks
about talks' to replace apartheid with a 'democratic' system are being
mooted. Nevertheless, many interpretations of 'democracy' are revealed
in contemporary debate, with some of these falling far short of what will
be required to satisfy most South Africans. Any workable political model
must be one that will win the respect of all the people of the country, or
at least a substantial majority of them. Without this, the new system will,
like apartheid, have to be maintained by force, and its stability will be
threatened by counter-violence. Only one political dispensation seems
a possibility if structural political and racial violence is to be abolished.
This is an egalitarian democracy, where all adults are equally
enfranchised, and where all have equality in and before the law.

Structural violence is also apparent in *sexism*, both in the law and in
the organization of society. In recent years the South African Law
Commission has made a series of recommendations, which Parliament
has accepted and enacted, that have removed many of the legal disparities between men and women. However, some legal inequalities
remain, principally in the legislation governing some marriages. Even
more to the point, there is no legislation that forbids discrimination on
the basis of gender. These circumstances reinforce attitudes, values, and
behaviours in society which maintain women as inferior to men.

The absence of egalitarianism in the roles of men and women is at the
very root of women abuse in all its forms, including rape and wife abuse.
Action to remedy this is required at two levels. The first is to remove
gender inequalities from all aspects of the nation's law, and to make
discrimination on the grounds of gender illegal. The second is to recognize that women are at times particularly vulnerable to violence, because
they are generally physically less strong than men, and because their
biological and social mothering role can make them dependent. Thus,
reform of the criminal justice system is indicated to genuinely protect

battered and sexually abused women, so that they may obtain sufficient protection and recourse.

In addition to racism and sexism, structural violence is evinced in the *use of legal violence* by the state, the greater part of this without any just or humanitarian foundation. Three aspects of legal violence are ripe for abolition: corporal and capital punishment; repressive legislation that deprives people of their freedom without a criminal charge and trial in court; and corporal punishment in schools.

Corporal and capital punishment has no established deterrent effect, and, as is discussed in a subsequent section, can be replaced by other more humane punishments. *Repressive legislation*, which permits restrictions to be placed on citizens' freedom, is found in most nations in the shape of an act which enables a state of emergency to be imposed. Nevertheless, in South Africa, unique features taint the use of such legislation: this country has in addition 'security' legislation, which, used by itself or in tandem with emergency legislation, permits extraordinarily coercive control over the lives of people not charged with criminal offences; and furthermore, such legislation is used to enforce an unjust social order. *Corporal punishment in schools* is an anachronism that is not only brutal, but counter-productive, for it inhibits both the acquisition of inner discipline and educational learning.

All of the laws which permit the state and state-sanctioned violence discussed above merit repeal, other than a law which permits a state of emergency to be declared in situations of genuine national danger or calamity, and which requires the declaration and regulations made under it to be subject to the most stringent requirements of democratic approval.

If the state is to discourage the use of violence in society, it must model non-violent ways of conflict resolution to its citizens, based upon justice, lack of prejudice, and the ideals of civilized humanity. In the present stage of negotiation for transition in South African society, which hopefully will be the precursor to a more just and less violent social order, demonstration of non-violent behavioural and transactional patterns by political and social leaders could serve to model non-violent modes of conflict resolution to all South Africans.

The promotion of public accountability

The peculiar secrecy that surrounds the functioning of many state organizations invites the abuse of power. Legislation which hides from the public gaze the activities of soldiers, the police, and prison officers, places at risk the well-being of members of society.

The effects of lack of accountability are well illustrated by the accounts in this book of the many instances of physical and emotional abuse to which child and adult security detainees have been subjected. Recent 'reforms' announced by President De Klerk, whereby detainees will have access to their medical and legal advisers, are an improvement, but an anodyne. Any person deprived of his or her liberty, and who is in the total control of others, is acutely vulnerable to abuse. In such situations, anticipatory measures are required to protect the vulnerable, and the most effective of these is provision for open public scrutiny.

Education

That societal and personal violence thrives in South Africa is due in no small measure to its not being recognized.

Legal reform, accountability, and publicity are but part of any strategy to reduce violence. The other major part is education, in two forms. The first is education for living, so that people are prepared with the understanding and skills to manage conflict and stress on an interpersonal level through non-violent means, while the second is the education of key agents of society so that they recognize violence for the harmful, damaging behaviour that it is, and respond to it appropriately.

It is of note that the two major social roles which most people occupy in the course of their lives — marriage partner and parent — are roles for which they receive no formal preparation. In the absence of formal education, people rely on three major inputs to guide them in their role performance. These are their personal life experience, especially their experience in their family of origin, peer group example and pressure, and the media. Hence, the authoritarianism, racism, and sexism to which they were exposed in childhood can become the guides for their own adult lives, and the abuses to which many of them were subjected can be repeated.

A strong case can be advanced for the inclusion of education for living in the curricula of all schools, so that — as Winship puts it in Chapter 7 — the curriculum provides a balance between subject education and education for living. This would enable scholars to be prepared for their future marital and parental roles and responsibilities, and also equip them to deal with the dangers that face them as children. For example, part of education for living could be sex education, and learning about how to avoid or deal with situations of sexual abuse. Paradoxically, however, provincial education authorities have thus far been unwilling to permit significant education for living programmes within state

schools, since they regard this form of education as a parental preroga-
tive.

In addition to the content of their curricula, schools can make a major
contribution to the reduction of violence in other ways. Principal among
these is for school systems and teachers to exemplify non-violent modes
of resolving intra-personal and interpersonal conflict. The heart of this,
suggested by Holdstock in Chapter 12, is through the development of
open communication, shared reasoning and responsibility, and positive
reinforcement of non-violent behaviour.

While the education of the general public is the most important aspect
of education as a tool to lessen violence, there are sub-groups within the
population that have a critical role in the reduction of violence. Members
of these sub-groups need educational input about the nature of violence
and how they may participate in diminishing it. To use some examples
from chapters of this book, these sub-groups range from the police,
prison officers, and child-care workers, all of whom often have total
control over others, to persons who have the power to regulate violence,
such as the parliamentarians who make the laws of the land, or the senior
office-bearers of sporting bodies who formulate the rules of the game.

Reorientation of helping services to primary prevention

A salient characteristic of social helping institutions in South Africa is that
they are preoccupied with tertiary prevention, providing rehabilitation
and therapy after the damage has occurred. This focus has developed as
the consequence of many influences, amongst them the visibility and
obvious urgent plight of some victims, large numbers of people already
in acute or chronic need, a tendency in the public to support endeavours
to aid people who are already in a serious situation, and state funding
and subsidization policies.

However, in the same way that an awareness has developed in the
health field that, in the interests of the best and most humane use of
available resources, the emphasis of health care must move from
hospital-based therapy to primary health care, so too is it logical that
social services should increasingly stress the promotion of healthy living
and the prevention of social problems.

A major message contained in this book is that in many instances of
domestic and institutional violence, groups of people at risk of being
victims of violence can be identified, and hence protective and preventive measures are feasible. One of the fullest illustrations of this is given
by Eckley, when he deals with elder abuse in Chapter 11. Existing
knowledge enables a profile to be drawn of the old people who are most

vulnerable to violence from their care-givers, and Eckley sketches a series of practical responses that are designed to support care-givers and relieve the stress upon them, hence reducing the risk of the old person being abused. The same reasoning can be applied to other groups susceptible to violence. In all instances, however, the difficulty in implementing preventive procedures, even when vulnerability to violence is recognized, is a lack of resources — money and people — to implement programmes within a human welfare dispensation that is currently focused upon tertiary intervention. Preventive programmes will be costly, but they can be justified both by humanitarian considerations and their potential to reduce the demand on expensive therapeutic and rehabilitative interventions.

Hoary as the adage is, prevention *is* better than cure, and in no instance is this more true than in the prevention of violence. Violence is a cancer in society, and its harmful effects transcend by far its immediate victims and perpetrators; once initiated, violence breeds more violence, both inter-generationally, and through counter-violence; and targets for action to prevent the incidence of violence can be identified. Moreover, within the easy reach of a determined society are rational, practical strategies to prevent violence.

Secondary prevention

The emphasis in secondary prevention is upon the early identification of violence when it occurs, and the provision of a speedy and appropriate response to it. The undergirding philosophy is that timeous intervention has the possibility of preventing the violence from becoming chronic and/or breaking the violence cycle. Five main areas are suggested for attention: alternative sentencing to reduce the use of legal violence; the use of existing humane laws; the promotion of early identification of abuse; timeous responses to break the cycle of violence; and impartial investigation of allegations of violence.

Alternative sentencing to reduce the use of legal violence

In South Africa, in the style of the Old Testament, violent crime invites violent retribution. Persons convicted of murder, some rapes, and other specified offences usually connected with violence, may be sentenced to death. Since this form of punishment is not known to have a deterrent effect, and because it sets an example of violence that is corrosive to society, there is no valid argument for its retention. Persons convicted of serious offences can be punished and contained by prolonged incarceration.

A similar logic can be applied to legal corporal punishment, which can be handed down as a sentence for certain criminal acts, some of which involve violence as a component. Again there is no evidence that whipping *per se* has any special deterrent effect, and again it involves the state in modelling violence. Furthermore, there is evidence to indicate that the violence of whipping is associated with subsequent violent behaviour by victims. Hence a weighty case can be made for the abolition of the legal corporal punishment of offenders, and its replacement with non-violent punishment.

While it is true that as a result of apartheid inequality there are reduced sentencing options available for younger black offenders, the criminal law contains a greatly under-used provision for the non-violent punishment of offenders of all races, namely community service orders. This form of sentence could well be used in place of corporal punishment with double beneficial effect: the state could thereby demonstrate a preference for non-violent punishment, and offenders — including violent offenders — would be introduced to constructive community-building activities.

The use of existing humane laws

A flagrant example of the abuse of children by the state is the detention of children, including children suspected of having committed violent acts, in terms of security and emergency legislation. This has led to serious criticism of the state, such as that levelled by Thomas in Chapter 15:

> The present legal system in South Africa not only fails to protect children from abuse, but provides a legal framework for abuse by promoting their detention apart from their families, and allowing them to be exposed to various forms of physical and emotional abuse while in prison.

Ironically, legislation exists in South Africa (the Child Care Act 74 of 1983, and the Criminal Procedures Act 51 of 1977) by which children accused of criminal offences, including violent offences, may be handled in a humane way with full recognition of their vulnerability as children. With legislation such as this at the disposal of the state, there can be no valid excuse for the use of other, inhumane legislation to deal with children allegedly involved in political acts.

Promotion of early identification of abuse

The occurrence of child abuse, particularly sexual and physical abuse, is currently receiving widespread public attention, and existing legislation requires medical and allied professionals to report all instances of abuse which come to their notice. Yet it is probably only a small minority of abused children who are detected through contact with a doctor or other medical professional, since the majority are not likely to be presented for medical attention.

Another way must be found to identify abused children at the earliest possible stage of abuse, and the most obvious means for this is through schools. All children in South Africa are required to attend school between prescribed ages, and the school thus presents itself as an institution of society ideally suited to secondary prevention.

The hegemony of the teaching profession in South African school systems acts against the inclusion in the school team of other professionals who are particularly equipped to detect and respond to the abuse of children. Most notably in the white education system, education authorities have for many years resisted the intrusion into their 'turf' of school social workers. Social workers are distinctively prepared to identify and respond helpfully to children who manifest the outward behaviours of abuse, and their absence from school systems is perhaps the single largest gap in society's attempt to halt the incidence of child abuse at the earliest possible time.

Timeous responses to break the cycle of violence

For many reasons, discussed in earlier chapters of this book, secrecy prevents the early discovery of domestic abuse — of children, wives, and the elderly. Existing human welfare services have thus only recently, and in respect of only one type of abuse, moved to create accessible avenues for victims to report the abuse at an early stage.

This exception is child abuse. As a consequence of private sector and state initiative, telephone 'hotlines' and similar accessible means have been created for victims and others to report suspected abuse, and for their immediate linkage with sources of intervention.

Child abuse has become visible; other forms of interpersonal abuse have not. Comparable readily available and receptive reporting and assistance systems are needed for rape, wife abuse, elder abuse, and other forms of interpersonal violence. Without the provision of easily accessible means whereby victims can reach out for help, society colludes with the perpetrators of domestic violence and reinforces the personal and family circumstances that keep abuse a 'family secret'.

Impartial investigation of allegations of violence

It has been argued in this book that people who are forced to be part of institutions (such as, for example, schools, children's homes, and prisons) are uniquely vulnerable to abuse.

This vulnerability means that when allegations of abuse occur, they should be taken most seriously and investigated by persons who do not have any vested interest in covering-up or hiding the abuse. Hence, in South Africa, where public and private institutions are unusually protected from public scrutiny, allegations of abuse demand investigation by neutral outsiders. The means of doing this in children's homes are explored in full by Giles in Chapter 13, and apply to all institutions of which people are compelled to be part. This includes prisons and other places of detention, the military, where through conscription many are present under compulsion, and the school system.

If a society wishes to be as free of violence as possible, it must ensure that those who are especially vulnerable to violence, such as those within institutions, have access to even-handed and neutral recourse in the event of violence taking place. The provision of such recourse will require purposeful change to existing legislation.

Tertiary prevention

A claim made in preceding sections of this chapter is that in South Africa, human welfare services neglect primary and secondary prevention in favour of tertiary prevention. While this claim has substance, it does not mean that tertiary prevention services are adequate.

South Africa is a developing country, and its human welfare services do not approach those of most developed northern hemisphere countries in either availability or accessibility. Moreover, the policy and practice of apartheid has skewed human welfare resources in favour of whites, and away from people of colour, especially Africans.

Hence, whites enjoy the greatest range of human welfare resources, and services of the highest quality, while the converse applies to Africans. As the bulk of the white population is urbanized, most resource organizations are found in cities and towns. Although a steadily increasing proportion of the African population has also become urbanized, services to assist them are sparse in urban areas: until the 1980s, government policy was to regard Africans as 'temporary sojourners' in cities and towns. Thus, many helping resources, such as, for example, residential homes for African children, were discouraged in urban areas. Despite this, however, there is a paucity of organized human welfare services for Africans in rural areas, too.

A further feature of the therapeutic and rehabilitative services available in South Africa is that, with the exception of child physical and sexual abuse, there are few resources specifically directed towards the victims of violence, and virtually no specialized ones for perpetrators. Indeed, a perusal of the directory of services for the victims of violence in the Appendix shows surprisingly few resources for some, such as abused women, where only three shelters exist in the whole country.

It seems that non-recognition of violence — or, where it is recognized, lack of awareness of its seriousness — may be one of the root causes of this situation. This observation is supported by the fact that when child sexual and physical abuse was brought to the attention of the public during the 1980s, there was rapid response by the state and the private sector, resulting in the introduction of a range of appropriate services. It is perhaps time for the media to create awareness of the existence of other victims of violence besides abused children.

In addition to a lack of awareness, another less benign factor is at work in the poor provision of services to the victims of violence, particularly political violence: fear. Welfare organizations, generally under white control and often dependent upon state subsidies to meet their expenses, have for the most part been fearful to respond to the needs of detainees and ex-detainees. Perhaps one of the most chilling statements in this book is Thomas' observation in Chapter 15 that 'many welfare organizations have chosen not to render services to detained children and their families, as they see this as belonging in the political domain'.

This statement, which is substantiated by the slim list of resources for detainees and their families in the directory that follows, is a horrifying example of how the violence of an apartheid society has tainted all people — even the people who control welfare organizations which are devoted to the well-being of children and families have developed distorted perceptions of human need.

If violence and its consequences are to be addressed in South Africa, one component must be formal services to treat and rehabilitate the victims and perpetrators of violence. Without these services, existing interpersonal violence will become chronic, and violence will also spread inter-generationally. The task of creating adequate resources will require the extension of existing services in both scope and accessibility, and it will also require the creation of new resources for the victims and perpetrators of those forms of interpersonal violence that are presently overlooked.

It is certain that actions to reduce violence at the primary, secondary, and tertiary level will involve considerable cost. It is equally certain that because of their scope, state leadership — both moral and financial — will be required. As South Africans enter a decade in which they hope to design a 'new South Africa', one of the many issues that they will have to consider is the importance of having a society that is as free of political violence as possible. Hopefully, a future democratic political dispensation will reduce structural violence, and hence also counter-violence and intergroup and interpersonal violence, but the effects of generations of aggression and force are likely to be felt for many years to come.

Some of the foundations of a civilized democracy are equality in and before the law, respect for the rights and dignity of every person, and protection of the defenceless. Violence, expressed in many forms but always through force and coercion, seriously undermines these foundations. If the aspiration is for a democratic society, then an inescapable part of the task is to promote non-violent means of conflict resolution and stress reduction, from the level of the state to that of the individual citizen.

Appendix
Resources for victims of violence

Organized resources exist to assist people and families who have been victims of violence, particularly in the main population centres of the country. The directory which follows indicates the main sources of assistance in respect of child abuse, child and adult detainees, persons who face corporal or capital punishment, elder abuse, and victims of rape and/or wife abuse.

CHILD ABUSE

Four main forms of assistance are available when child abuse is suspected:

1. Telephone services
(a) Toll-free child emergency services

A 24-hour professional service providing information and counselling to children who have been abused (telephone 0100-833).

(b) Regional Childline services

Voluntary services manned by trained counsellors to receive calls from abused children or concerned adults, and provide advice on where to get help.

Cape Town (Life Line):	(021) 461-111
(Safe Line):	(021) 233-333
Durban:	(031) 309-2525 or (031) 309-2444
Johannesburg:	(011) 484-3044
Port Elizabeth:	(041) 563-232
Verulam:	(0322) 330-490

2. Child welfare societies

There are 175 local child welfare societies throughout the Republic which provide services to abused children and their families. Telephone numbers of local societies appear in telephone directories under 'Child welfare' and/or 'Kindersorg'. Information about the nearest local society can also be obtained from the South African National Council on Child and Family Welfare (PO Box 30990, Braamfontein 2017). Telephone (011) 339-5741.

3. Major provincial hospitals

All major provincial hospitals have departments of Paediatrics and Social Work, through which facilities for the investigation and treatment of child abuse are offered.

4. South African Police Child Protection Units

Child Protection Units are manned by specially-trained members of the Criminal Investigation Department to deal with all criminal matters in relation to children. Their contact telephone numbers are:

Bloemfontein:	(051) 303-351
Cape Town:	(021) 453-697
Durban:	(031) 231-101/2
East London:	(0431) 438-497
East Rand:	(011) 873-3630
Johannesburg:	(011) 477-1390
Kimberley:	(0531) 811-163
Kroonstad:	(01411) 26-711
Krugersdorp:	(011) 665-3300
Mossel Bay:	(04441) 3-666
Nelspruit:	(01311) 52-711
Pietermaritzburg:	(0331) 427-680
Pietersburg:	(01521) 911-731
Port Elizabeth:	(041) 547-916
Port Shepstone:	(0391) 22-524
Potgietersrust:	(01541) 2171
Pretoria:	(012) 325-1800
Richards Bay:	(0351) 52-155
Stilfontein:	(018) 44-330
Vereeniging:	(016) 222-881
Walvis Bay:	(0642) 2281 ext. 51

CHILD AND ADULT DETAINEES

The following are organizations and contact individuals in respect of services to child and adult detainees and their families:

Durban: DCC (Attention: Barbara), PO Box 3932, Durban 4000.

Grahamstown: Legal Resources Centre (Attention: S. Steward), 116 High Street, Grahamstown 6140.

Heidelberg: Thusong Advice Centre, 3a Kismet Street, First Floor, Indian Shopping Complex, Heidelberg 2400.

Johannesburg: Detainees Aid Centre, 209 Darragh House, 13 Wanderers Street, Johannesburg 2001, telephone (011) 232-741/2; Johannesburg Child Welfare Society, PO Box 2539, Johannesburg 2000, telephone (011) 331-0171.

Kimberley: NEHAWU, PO Box 181, Kimberley 0531.

Kroonstad: Bizzah Makhate, 41 Seeisoville, Kroonstad 9500.

Mdantsane: Phatheka Mthintsicana, 24 NU 13, Mdantsane 5219.

Nelspruit: Y. Vawda, P O Box 2875, Nelspruit 1200.

Pietermaritzburg: Dacom Detainees Advice Centre, PO Box 2338, Pietermaritzburg 3200.

Port Elizabeth: Kate Turner, PO Box 2767, North End, Port Elizabeth 6056.

Potchefstroom: Poor Fund Committee, Shop No. 10, Ikageng Shopping Centre, cnr Curlewis and Ross Streets, Potchefstroom 2520.

Salt River: Relief Centre on Top, Community House, 41 Salt River Road, Salt River 7925.

Soweto: NICRO, Roodepoort Road, Soweto, telephone (011) 29-5236.

CORPORAL AND CAPITAL PUNISHMENT
Corporal punishment

The National Institute for Crime Prevention and the Rehabilitation of Offenders (NICRO) offers counselling and assistance services at its local offices to persons who have suffered trauma as a result of whipping. Branches of the Institute are listed in local telephone directories under 'NICRO' and 'NIMRO'. Information about local services can be obtained from the Institute's head office (PO Box 10005, Caledon Square 7905). Telephone (021) 461-7253.

Capital punishment

(a) Legal services

Legal Aid Bureau: all major centres have a branch of the Legal Aid Bureau, which will arrange *pro deo* legal representation for persons charged with crimes that carry a possible death penalty. Legal Aid Bureaus are listed in the local telephone directories.

Lawyers for Human Rights aim to provide persons sentenced to death with full access to all legal remedies. The organization can be contacted at 713 Van Erkom Building, Pretoria Street, Pretoria 0001, telephone (012) 212-135.

(b) Support and counselling services

Voluntary organizations exist in some local centres to campaign for the abolition of the death penalty and to counsel persons condemned to death and their families. Up-to-date contact information concerning local organizations is obtainable from The Society for the Abolition of the Death Penalty, PO Box 80, Plumstead 7800.

ELDER ABUSE

The following local organizations offer services to combat elder abuse and to intervene in its occurrence:

Port Elizabeth: Algoa Bay Council for the Aged, PO Box 513, Port Elizabeth 6000, telephone (041) 559-171.

Boksburg: Boksburg Council for the Aged, PO Box 1002, Boksburg 1460, telephone (011) 522-510.

Cape Town area: Cape Peninsula Organization for the Aged, PO Box 83, Howard Place 7450, telephone (021) 537-475; Christelike Maatskaplike Raad, 10 Boston Street, Bellville 7530, telephone (021) 941-064.

Durban area: The Association for the Aged, 80 Aliwal Street, Durban 4001, telephone (031) 323-721; Highway Aged Co-ordinating Council, 211 Medical Centre, Pinetown 3600; Durban Association for the Indian Aged, PO Box 4671, Durban 4000, telephone (031) 316-634.

East London: East London Senior Citizens Association, PO Box 11138, Southernwood 5213, telephone (0431) 21-416.

Johannesburg: Johannesburg Association for the Aged, PO Box 31850, Braamfontein 2017, telephone (011) 725-5330.

Kempton Park: Kempton Park Council for the Aged, PO Box 1433, Kempton Park, telephone (011) 972-4220.

Krugersdorp: Krugersdorp Council for the Aged, PO Box 825, Krugersdorp 1740, telephone (011) 660-1315.

Pietermaritzburg: Pietermaritzburg Association for the Aged, 6 Lotus Road, Northdale 3201, telephone (0331) 75-535.

Pretoria: Pretoria Council for the Aged, PO Box 1574, Pretoria 0001, telephone (012) 286-045.

Soweto: Soweto Care of the Aged, PO Box 512, Meadowlands 1852, telephone (011) 930-3620.

RAPE AND WIFE ABUSE

1. Support, information, and counselling services

Cape Town: Cape Town Rape Crisis, 12 Nuttle Road, Observatory 7925 (includes residential shelter facilities), telephone (021) 479-762.

Johannesburg: People Opposing Women Abuse (POWA), PO Box 93416, Yeoville 2196 (includes residential shelter facilities), telephone (011) 642-4345; Frieda Hartley Shelter, Regent Street, Bellvue 2196 (residential shelter facility only), telephone (011) 648-6006.

Pietermaritzburg: Pietermaritzburg Rape Crisis (paging service), telephone (0331) 56-279.

2. Legal protection

Peace Orders: available from magistrates' courts, in terms of the regulations of the Criminal Procedure Act 51 of 1977.

Supreme Court Interdicts: available only from the Supreme Court. Applicants should first approach an attorney, or, if in financial need, their local Legal Aid Bureau.

Index